W9-CWY-774

London Borough of Hammersmith and Fulham

FULHAM LIBRARY
598 FULHAM ROAD, SW6 5NX
(736 1127/8)

Please return this book to the Library from which it was borrowed
on or before the last date stamped. Fines will be charged on overdue
books at the rate currently determined by the Borough Council.

19. NOV. 1983			
Limehouse 26.8.88 +2			
	WITHDRAWN		
	FROM STOCK		

X1

270.4 CHE

FL:82 - 16929

Renewal may be made by post, telephone
or personal call, quoting details immediately
above and the last date stamped.

The Papacy and England
12th–14th Centuries

C.R.Cheney

The Papacy and England
12th-14th Centuries

Historical and legal studies

VARIORUM REPRINTS
London 1982

British Library CIP data

Cheney, Christopher R.
The papacy and England, 12th-14th centuries:
historical and legal studies. — (Collected studies
series; CS154)
1. Church and state
2. Papacy — History — to 1309
3. England — Church history — Medieval period, 1066-
1485
I. Title
262'.13'0902   BX1263

ISBN 0-86078-099-6

Copyright © 1982 by   Variorum Reprints

Published in Great Britain by   Variorum Reprints
                                         20 Pembridge Mews London W11 3EQ

Printed in Great Britain by   Galliard (Printers) Ltd
                                       Great Yarmouth Norfolk

VARIORUM REPRINT CS154

CONTENTS

Preface   i–ii

This volume contains a total of 346 pages

PREFACE

This collection reflects three aspects of my study over a long period of the records of Church government and of Anglo-papal relations. One group of lectures and essays (VIII-XV) relates to episodes in Pope Innocent III's dealings with John, king of England. These had obvious political significance, but also produced results of unforeseen kinds on the English Church and society in general. The last of the group, on Magna Carta and the Church, explains why I include the preceding papers on Magna Carta in a volume devoted to ecclesiastical history. Three papers (I, II, XVI) have grown out of a long-sustained concern in the diplomatic of the papal and episcopal chanceries. A third group (III-VII) shows the response which my wife and I have made to the stimulus Stephan Kuttner and the Institute of Medieval Canon Law have provided to all medievalists who are interested in the extraordinary growth of Roman canon law from Alexander III to Innocent III and in the textual formation of decretal-collections in that period.

The volume reproduces papers written in the space of thirty years, with some fresh annotation. Where, to my knowledge, I have been proved wrong in particular interpretations or erred in matters of fact, I have corrected the text or added a note at the end of the article. I have also added references to some later literature, selecting in particular books and articles which give bibliographical guidance. Apart from these corrections and additional notes, the essays are reproduced as they were first printed.

I am grateful to Mrs Eileen Turner and Variorum for admitting this book to the series of Collected Studies. I also acknowledge with thanks the permission freely granted by the publishers and editors of the original papers, to whom copyright belongs and who are indicated in the Table of Contents, for the present reproduction.

C. R. CHENEY

Cambridge
August, 1981

L. B. H. & F.
PUBLIC LIBRARIES

I

THE STUDY OF THE
MEDIEVAL PAPAL CHANCERY

WHEN the University of Glasgow did me the
honour of inviting me to give a lecture on the John
Edwards Foundation, I was told that his benefaction
to the University had the object of promoting
studies in palaeography and diplomatic. These are
subjects which lend themselves best to minute
discussion between half a dozen specialists seated
round a table ; they are less well suited to formal
lecturing before a large audience. But it seemed to
me that the medieval papal chancery provides a
topic which might at once come within the terms of
reference set down by the benefactor and serve to
show how palaeography and diplomatic can interest
and instruct the historian. For if its study depends
in a large measure on the critical assessment of
particular documents, the results of such study
illuminate the whole history of papal government
and of most other governments of medieval
Christendom. There is only one book written in
English on the papal chancery : Reginald Lane
Poole's Birkbeck Lectures on the history of the
papal chancery down to the time of Innocent III.
I want to consider some features of the work which
has been going on since he published them in 1915.
The main difficulty in attempting a survey of the
sort I contemplate is the continuous and multi-

6

farious labour in this field. A thirteenth-century poem about the Roman curia says:

> Ut multe cernuntur apes in vallibus Ethne
> Sic ope multorum curia fulta viget.[1]

I have fifty minutes to discuss the activities for fifty years of swarms of scholars, mostly German, Austrian, French, and Italian, all as busy as bees. I can hardly fail to be either obscure or superficial; I am certain to be incomplete.[2]

To begin, consider the elements of the subject: the *papacy*, in relation to *palaeography* and *diplomatic*. The papacy, regarded as a governmental institution, has the longest continuous history of any government in Europe. Its authority has been based on, and buttressed by, tradition. And from the fourth century onwards that tradition has been handed down in writings: official pronouncements of Roman pontiffs. The drafting, diffusion, and preservation of papal letters which record the popes'

[1] Quoted by R. L. Poole, *Lectures on the History of the Papal Chancery down to the time of Innocent III* (Cambridge, 1915), p. 163. The poet, Master Henry of Würzburg, wrote *c.* 1261–4.

[2] The bibliographical references in the notes are merely illustrative of recent work and are usually confined to recent articles and monographs which may direct the reader to older (sometimes more important) works. The following abbreviations are used: *AUF=Archiv für Urkundenforschung, BÉC=Bibliothèque de l'École des Chartes, BIHR=Bulletin of the Institute of Historical Research, BISI=Bulletino dell'Istituto storico Italiano per il Medio Evo e Archivio Muratoriano, BJRL=Bulletin of the John Rylands Library, EHR=English Historical Review, MHP=Miscellanea Historiae Pontificiae, MIöG=Mitteilungen des Instituts für österreichische Geschichtsforschung, QFIAB=Quellen und Forschungen aus italienischen Archiven und Bibliotheken, RHE=Revue de l'Histoire Ecclésiastique, RHM=Römische historische Mitteilungen, ST=Studi e Testi.*

7

judgments, assert their rights, and report the submission of others to their will, have been a major
factor in establishing papal authority. So the pope's
secretariat has always been immensely influential.
In the Middle Ages this was the chancery, with
draftsmen, scribes, archivists, and so on. Because
they were highly organized and highly conservative,
they developed characteristic habits of handwriting
which we must appreciate if we are going to understand the history of the chancery: that is where
palaeography enters into these studies.[1] But the
formalism of the clerks did not stop at inventing
calligraphic forms. The whole stylistic form of
documents, the method of their production and
registration, were subjected to the sort of rules
which all government departments must devise
when business develops from the exceptional to the
normal. The very size of the papacy's empire—
which embraced the entire Latin Church—required
the observance of rules. If fraud was to be avoided,
people in distant provinces had to know what a
papal privilege or letter looked like; and nowadays
the historian has to know what office-rules prevailed
if he is to understand the surviving documents.
This is where *diplomatic* comes in. For diplomatic,
according to the definition of Dom Jean Mabillon,

---

[1] Paul Rabikauskas, *Die römische Kuriale in der päpstlichen Kanzlei* (*MHP* vol. xx no. 59, 1958). For later periods see H. Bresslau, *Handbuch der Urkundenlehre* (2nd ed. 1912–31) ii. 531–6 and works there cited; also R. von Heckel, ' Eine Kanzleianweisung über die schriftmässige Ausstattung der Papsturkunden aus dem xiii Jh. in Durantis Speculum Judiciale ', *Festschrift für Georg Leidinger* (Munich, 1930) pp. 109–18.

is the establishment of ' certain and accurate terms and rules by which authentic instruments can be distinguished from spurious, and certain and genuine ones from uncertain and suspect ones.'[1] This definition must be supplemented by that of Monsieur Tessier. For him the object of diplomatic is ' knowledge of the rules which have, through the ages, governed the elaboration and drafting of instruments, considered as historical sources.'[2]

When Poole published his lectures on the papal chancery, in 1915, he declared that ' nothing at all dealing with it has ever been published in English ' ;[3] yet as a teacher at Oxford he had long been in the habit of beginning his course in diplomatic with papal documents.[4] In this field there was already available a wealth of material to draw upon. Without going back so far as Mabillon and the seventeenth century, one must recall the great advances in publication and criticism of texts effected during the nineteenth century. Long before Poole himself started transcribing bulls in 1880, while an assistant

[1] *De Re diplomatica* (Paris, 1681) p. 1.
[2] *BÉC* xci (1930) 260. See also the remarks on definitions by M. Tessier's successor at the École des Chartes, R. H. Bautier, ibid. cxix (1961) 213-4.
[3] *Lectures*, p. vi.
[4] Notes on his lectures in Michaelmas Term 1897, made, and given to me, by the late Rose Graham, show the plan he adopted. Succeeding Readers in Diplomatic at Oxford followed his example. Writing in 1901 on the teaching of palaeography and diplomatic, Poole observed: ' a convenient arrangement is to begin with Papal documents, which have the advantage of simplicity in their structure and at the same time of developing the greatest possible regularity of form and diction.' *Essays on the Teaching of History*, by F. W. Maitland and others (Cambridge, 1901) p. 29.

9

in the British Museum, Philipp Jaffé and August Potthast had provided basic calendars of papal letters from the earliest times to 1304. Augustin Theiner, prefect of the Vatican Archives from 1855 to 1870, had published no less than twenty-nine volumes of documents from papal records, among them a large folio of capital importance for British history: *Vetera monumenta Hibernorum et Scotorum historiam illustrantia . . . a.d. 1216–1547* (Rome, 1864). Meanwhile the École des Chartes and the Monumenta Germaniae Historica gave training in critical method to many French and German scholars. Then, on 1 January, 1881, Pope Leo XIII opened the 'Archivio Segreto' to all scholars, and so provided stimulus to national institutes of research in Rome, notably the French, Austrian, Prussian, Belgian.[1] Even the British government paid W. H. Bliss to extract entries relating to Great Britain and Ireland from the papal registers.[2] Bliss

[1] The most useful general guide to the archives is that of K. A. Fink, *Das Vatikanische Archiv: Einführung in die Bestände und ihre Erforschung* (2nd edition, Rome, 1951), to be supplemented by three volumes of *Sussidi per la Consultazione dell'Archivio Vaticano*, published in *ST* vols. 45, 55, 134 (1926–47). Students in Great Britain will also find particularly useful D. E. R. Watt, 'Sources for Scottish History of the Fourteenth Century in the Archives of the Vatican', *Scottish Historical Review*, xxxii (1953) 101–22 and Leslie Macfarlane, 'The Vatican Archives, with special reference to Sources for British Medieval History', *Archives*, iv (1959) 29–44, 84–101 (and separately). Some idea of the work of scholars of all nations in the Vatican Archives may be gained from the two volumes already published of the valuable *Bibliografia dell'Archivio Vaticano* (Vatican, 1962–3), prepared under the direction of Giulio Battelli. Cf. below, p. 15, note 1.

[2] Bliss omitted from his calendar many letters which ought to have been included. For this and other defects of the *Calendar*

and Charles Johnson and J. A. Twemlow had produced eleven volumes by 1915. Members of religious Orders, Benedictine, Dominican, Jesuit, played their part, too, in the generation whose achievements Poole's book records.

So, if I begin my brief survey of studies in the papal chancery with the year 1915, it is not because there was then a new revelation or a sudden leap forwards. The best people to work in this field during the next fifty years were far from being dwarfs themselves, but they stood on the shoulders of giants, Delisle, Von Sickel, Bresslau, and others. None the less, the achievements of the last half-century are impressive.

An essential condition of progress in palaeography and diplomatic is that as many related documents as possible shall be accumulated and compared; and we only understand office procedure and the working of the official mind when we see it repeated many times. Since the medieval popes corresponded with all the world, from Prester John to the kings of Connaught, their correspondence has to be retrieved in every country of the West. The challenge has been taken up by scholars, with gallantry if not always with sufficient forethought or united action. In the last fifty years our documentary sources have been greatly enlarged, and it is of this that I shall speak next.

One naturally thinks first of the printing of papal

see Watt, loc. cit. pp. 104–10, 112–14, and *Selected Letters of Pope Innocent III concerning England*, ed. C. R. Cheney and W. H. Semple (Nelson's Medieval Texts, 1953) p. xxxiii n. 2.

letters. The most notable architect of a scheme of comprehensive publication was Paul Fridolin Kehr, a pupil of Theodor von Sickel.[1] Kehr died in his eighty-fourth year in 1944. He set on foot preliminary exploration of archives in various parts of Europe in 1897. Slightly younger than Poole, he had been at work long enough in 1915 for Poole to recognize his obligations to him.

In 1924 Kehr wrote: ' Once I had a vision. I saw in my mind's eye a row of thirty volumes in which was assembled and sifted the whole documentary material of the papacy for the whole of the West for four or five centuries, with all the more important archive deposits arranged according to the same critical point of view and prepared for investigation, ranging from Drontheim to Carthage, from Dublin to Cracow, from Coimbra to Constantinople. Will this dream ever come true? '[2] A Protestant himself, Kehr had conveyed to his Catholic friend in the Ambrosian library at Milan, Achille Ratti, the importance of his vision. And in 1922 Ratti became Pope Pius XI. Rome was able to open

[1] On Kehr's work see Walther Holtzmann's memoir in *Deutsches Archiv*, viii (1950) 26–58 and his paper ' Paolo Kehr e le Ricerche archivistiche per l'*Italia Pontificia* ', *Miscellanea Archivistica Angelo Mercati* (*ST* vol. 165, 1952) pp. 43–9. See also P. F. Kehr, ' Ueber die Sammlung und Herausgabe der älteren Papsturkunden bis Innocenz III (1198) ', *Sitzungsberichte der preussischen Akademie der Wissenschaften*, Phil.-hist. Kl. x (Berlin, 1934) 83–92.
[2] *Deutsche Literaturzeitung*, xlv (1924) 1133, in the course of reviewing his project on the appearance of *Germania Pontificia*, vol. ii part 1. Kehr, wrote Holtzmann, believed that ' one could only approach an understanding of things on the basis of the most exact knowledge of all the assembled material.' *Deutsches Archiv*, viii. 57.

doors which would otherwise have been barred: to the muniment-rooms of Spanish churches, for instance. Moreover, papal support permitted the setting up in 1931 of a trust fund, the 'Pius-Stiftung für Papsturkunden und mittelalterliche Geschichtsforschung', in Switzerland, to guarantee the financial basis of this long-term work in an uncertain world. The result has been, if not the whole realization of Kehr's vision, a survey of most of the archives of Western Europe and the bringing to light of thousands of papal letters before the year 1198 in the series of *Papsturkunden*.

These volumes of papal documents have been produced country by country, province by province, containing reports on the local sources and printing the texts of papal letters not listed in the Jaffé-Loewenfeld *Regesta*.[1] The second stage is represented by the ten volumes of *Italia pontificia*, of which Walther Holtzmann was editing the latest until his death in November 1963. This work arranges its material in the order of the institutions it concerns, provides full bibliographical apparatus, and calendars with historical notes every papal letter from the archives of these institutions, whether or not it was listed in Jaffé-Loewenfeld. *Italia pontificia* is complete.[2] Whether *Germania pontificia*

---

[1] In its second edition (Leipzig, 1885–8) by S. Loewenfeld, F. Kaltenbrunner, and P. Ewald: usually known as 'Jaffé-Loewenfeld', or 'J.L.'.

[2] Volume X being in the press, 1965. See also 'Nachträge zu den Papsturkunden Italiens X', *Nachrichten d. Akad. der Wissenschaften in Göttingen*, Ph.-hist. Kl. 1962, pp. 205–47 (Göttingen, 1963).

13

can soon be extended beyond the third volume
(published in 1935) and whether comparable volumes for other countries will see the light in our
day remains doubtful. Perhaps we shall have to be
content with the first stage: the volumes of *Papsturkunden* supplemental to Jaffé-Loewenfeld. These
volumes suffer from the disadvantages of other
temporary structures which endure. Because they
were provisional, the people who planned them
neglected certain services which would be regarded
as indispensable in permanent work. *Papsturkunden*
is ill-indexed, its annotation is insufficient, the texts
are clipped. Nevertheless, it is of the very greatest
value for students of diplomatic and of ecclesiastical
history. All honour to those who spent long years
in its preparation.

Out of Kehr's first project grew another. During
the last quarter of the twelfth century canon
lawyers were collecting letters of the popes concerned with legal questions.[1] Some letters were
collected in the provinces from the copies of the
recipients; others were assembled in the Roman
curia from copies kept there.[2] Many decretal

---

[1] The process is illustrated and discussed in two recent English
publications: *Papal Decretals relating to the Diocese of Lincoln
in the Twelfth Century* (Lincoln Record Soc. vol. 47, 1954) and
Charles Duggan, *Twelfth-century Decretal Collections and their
Importance in English History* (London, 1963). See also W.
Holtzmann, ' Kanonistische Ergänzungen zur Italia Pontificia ',
QFIAB xxxvii (1958) 55–102, xxxviii (1959) 67–157, and
separately.

[2] See W. Holtzmann, ' Die Register Papst Alexanders III in
den Händen der Kanonisten ', *QFIAB* xxx (1940–1) 13–87 and
' La Collectio Seguntina et les Décrétales de Clément III et de
Célestin III ', *RHE* l (1955) 400–53; A. Vetulani, ' L'origine

letters of the twelfth century survived only in these lawyers' collections. They throw light on the development of legal doctrine and legal draftsmanship in the curia and on the record-keeping of the chancery. Holtzmann saw that if they were properly edited they could yield much other historical information. But the texts are usually corrupt, especially as regards the spelling of proper names, which did not interest the lawyers. How badly editing is needed I can illustrate by a decretal letter of Alexander III which occurs in the *Corpus Iuris Canonici* under an address to the abbot of Neuclen. Other texts read Nevolo, Novo Loco, Noneno, Noblos, Neblosa, and so on. It is only when we get back to the earliest decretal collections, from which the others were copied, that the name takes shape as Neubothe or Novebotle = Newbattle, Midlothian, a Cistercian abbey at that time engaged in litigation with Holyrood Abbey.[1] The proper editing of these decretals was one of Holtzmann's main preoccupations in recent years: he has bequeathed his material for an edition to the Institute for Research and Study in Medieval Canon Law at Yale.

Kehr's scheme was to stop in 1198. The reason was that from this year, the first year of Innocent

des Collections primitives des Décrétales à la Fin du xiie siècle ', *Congrès de Droit canonique médiéval* . . . *1958* (Bibliothèque de la *RHE*, fasc. 33, 1959) pp. 64–72; C. R. Cheney, ' Decretals of Innocent III in Paris, B.N. ms. Lat. 3922A ', *Traditio*, xi (1955) 151–62 and ' Three Decretal Collections before Compilatio IV ', ibid. xv (1959) 464–84, especially pp. 471–2.

[1] J.L. 14023. The earliest forms appear in *Collectio Wigorniensis* and *Collectio Belverensis*, for which see Duggan, op. cit.

III's pontificate, there is a more or less continuous series of papal registers of correspondence preserved in the Vatican Archives. Dr. Giulio Battelli estimates that these registers contain a quarter of a million letters for the years 1198–1417.[1] Having regard to the enormous increase in survivals from this period a scheme as ambitious as Kehr's could not be contemplated. Yet some effort seemed desirable. Scholars who are interested in questions of diplomatic cannot be satisfied with the registers : they want to see all the marks of chancery procedure which are only visible on the original letters.[2] And historians in general want more than the registers because it has become evident that the quarter million letters enregistered represent perhaps no more than a tenth of those originally despatched. The *Registrum* of the bishopric of Glasgow preserves the copies of thirty-six letters of thirteenth-century popes concerning Glasgow : only one of these is found in the papal registers.

So a scheme was put forward, about twelve years ago, by Franco Bartoloni, less ambitious than Kehr's, but still of great magnitude. A census, or *Censimento*—a brief calendar on cards—was to be made, to include all papal letters in existence for the years

---

[1] G. Battelli, ‘ Le ricerche storiche nell'Archivio Vaticano ’, *Relazioni* of the Tenth International Congress of Hist. Sciences (Rome, 1955) i. 451–77, at p. 457.

[2] See, for example, the useful material assembled by Dr. Peter Herde, in his important *Beiträge zum päpstlichen Kanzlei- und Urkundenwesen im 13 Jahrhundert* (Münchener Hist. Studien. Abteilung Geschichtl. Hilfswissenschaft, Bd. 1. Kallmünz-Opf, 1961) pp. 45–9, 177–80, 198–228.

from 1198 to 1417.[1] Bartoloni's premature death soon afterwards jeopardized the scheme; but at least some scholars are working towards a complete description of *original* bulls in Italy, Austria, Switzerland, and France.[2] It is to be hoped that they will cast their net more widely and recruit workers in other fields.

If this, like Kehr's vision, is something to dream of for the future, there has elsewhere been plenty of solid accomplishment in the matter of publication. I mean the advance made in publishing, in one form or another, *in extenso* or in calendar, the Vatican registers. The work was under way before Poole's time and still not all the registers of the fourteenth century are published. But much has been done. I cannot indicate all the editions of enregistered letters.[3] The French School of Rome alone has

[1] See Franco Bartoloni, ' Per un Censimento dei Documenti pontifici da Innocenzo III a Martino V (escluso) ', *Relazioni, Communicazioni ed Atti*, Convegno internazionale di Studi per le Fonti del Medioevo Europeo, Roma, 14–18 aprile 1953, ii. 7–40, with 6 tables and 9 plates.

[2] See Leo Santifaller, ' Der " Censimento " der spätmittelalterlichen Papsturkunden ', *MIöG* lxxii (1964) 122–34, and Anton Largiadèr, *Die Papsturkunden des Staatsarchivs Zürich von Innozenz III bis Martin V: ein Beitrag zum Censimentum Helveticum* (Zürich, 1963).

[3] A useful bibliography was produced by L. Santifaller for the Austrian Academy in 1958: *Neuere Editionen mittelalterlicher Königs- und Papsturkunden: eine Uebersicht*, Oesterreichische Akad. der Wissenschaften: Mitteilungen der Wiener Diplomata-Abteilung der Monumenta Germaniae Historica, VI (Vienna, 1958) pp. 40–56. Under this head must be noted a new and critical edition of the surviving registers of Innocent III, sponsored by the Austrian Academy and the Institute of Austrian Historical Research, now proceeding under the direction of Leo Santifaller. See his announcement in *MIöG* lxv (1957) 237–41, followed by

17

filled more than 20,000 large quarto pages of print with texts and summaries. In the last generation, too, serious study has begun on a new form of papal correspondence, the *Brevia*, which succeeded early in the fifteenth century to the secret letters of the fourteenth, missives sealed with wax, not with the leaden *bulla*.[1]

I have spoken so far of letters; but these are not the only documentary remains. As the whole field of papal archives is explored, other types of evidence emerge. The financial records of the Apostolic Camera reflect light on the procedure and the personnel of the chancery.[2] Formularies and

important 'Studien und Vorarbeiten' in *MIöG* lxv (1957) and lxviii (1960) and in *RHM* i (1956–7) and after, by H. Feigl, O. Hageneder, and A. Haidacher. Volume I of *Die Register Innocenz' III*, containing *1 Pontifikatsjahr, 1198/99. Texte*, and edited by O. Hageneder and A. Haidacher, has appeared in 1965 (Publikationen der Abteilung für hist. Studien des österreichischen Kulturinstituts in Rom. Abt. II Reihe I, bearing the imprint 1964).

Santifaller's bibliography also lists regional collections, not based exclusively on the Vatican Archives. Since it was published there have appeared the work of Largiadèr (above, n. 2) and M. P. Sheehy, *Pontificia Hibernica: medieval Papal Chancery Documents concerning Ireland, 640–1261* (Dublin, 1962).

[1] See especially K. A. Fink, 'Die ältesten Breven und Brevenregister', *QFIAB* xxv (1933–4) 292–307 and 'Die politische Korrespondenz Martins V nach dem Brevenregistern', ibid. xxvi (1935–6) 172–244, and 'Zu den Brevia Lateranensia', ibid. xxxii (1942) 260–366; Gottfried Lang, *Studien zu den Brevenregistern und Brevenkonzepten des xv Jahrhunderts aus dem Vatikanischen Archiv* (Publikationen des ehemaligen Oesterreichischen hist. Instituts in Rom, Bd. iv, 1938); C. M. de Witte, 'Notes sur les plus anciens Registres de Brefs', *Bulletin de l'Institut Historique Belge de Rome*, xxxi (1958) 153–68.

[2] It should be noted that registers of cameral business came to be included in the Vatican series along with chancery registers proper. See M. Giusti, 'I Registri Vaticani e le loro Provenienze originarie', *Miscellanea Archivistica Angelo Mercati (ST* vol. 165, 1952) pp. 383–459.

chancery ordinances make their contribution. Documentary additions which are not very bulky may often be more significant for the study of the chancery than whole volumes of the registers of bulls.

In particular, we know much more now of the way in which petitions (*supplicationes*) reached the pope and were dealt with by the chancery. This partly comes from hard work on the enormous series of registers of petitions, which begin in 1342. In this regard I content myself with citing the two admirable volumes of Scottish supplications to Rome, 1418 to 1428, calendared by E. R. Lindsay and Mrs. Annie Dunlop; and Mrs. Dunlop continues the good work.[1] But both for this and for an earlier age historians now draw on another source which tells more about the actual procedure of the chancery. Very occasionally actual petitions are found. Sixty years ago nobody had so much as seen one original petition earlier than 1472. Then a Russian scholar found an original of the year 1384 in St. Petersburg, and soon afterwards Dom Berlière lighted on no less than twenty-six from the years 1362 to 1378. These, like almost all, if not all, later discoveries, were retrieved from the binding of a manuscript. They must have passed as waste paper to a bookbinder at Avignon, and been used by him as packing for the spine of a book. Other petitions, going back to John XXII, from

---

[1] *Calendar of Scottish Supplications to Rome*, vol. i (1418–22) ed. E. R. Lindsay and Annie I. Cameron, vol. ii (1423–28) ed. Annie I. Dunlop (Scottish History Soc. publications, 3rd series, xxiii, xlviii, 1934, 1956).

the binding of a book in the Bibliothèque Nationale at Paris, were published by Émile Van Moë in 1931. Still more continue to turn up, over the length and breadth of Europe, now that scholars are alert to notice what these small, dirty bits of paper, on which various hands have been at work, amount to.[1]

When a petition was approved, and had a date set upon it, the next stage was to prepare a minute, or *nota*, for a letter. Not many years ago Mr. Barraclough identified some fifty scraps of paper, taken years before from a binding in Gonville and Caius College, Cambridge, as the remnants of original minutes of letters of the years 1316 and 1317—draft provisions to benefices, drawn up in favour of poor clerks.[2]

The progress marked by publication in print is matched by advance in facilities for photographing documents. When Poole wrote, fifty years ago, he was hampered by having to rely on a relatively small corpus of facsimiles of papal privileges; for comparatively few original bulls were to be found in Great Britain. Nowadays, at the cost of a few hundred pounds, any library in the world can have

---

[1] G. Battelli, ' Una supplica originale per *fiat* di Urbano V ', *Studi di Palaeografia e Diplomatica in onore di Vincenzo Federici* (Florence, 1944) pp. 277–92; F. Bartoloni, ' Suppliche Pontificie dei secoli xiii e xiv ', *BISI* lxvii (1955) 1–188; G. Tessier, ' Du nouveau sur les Suppliques ', *BÉC* cxiv (1956) 186–92; P. Gasnault, ' Suppliques en matière de Justice au xive siècle ', *BÉC* cxv (1957) 42–57, which has a convenient bibliography.

[2] G. Barraclough, ' Minutes of Papal Letters, 1316–17 ', *Miscellanea Archivistica Angelo Mercati* (*ST* vol. 165, 1952) pp. 109–27, with two plates. Mr. Barraclough gives (note 4) a bibliography of earlier discoveries of minutes.

a microfilm copy of all the Vatican registers of the thirteenth century; and when, a few years ago, I wanted to compare the signatures of cardinals on solemn papal privileges of the twelfth century, I was able, through the kindness of a colleague, to examine many scores of unpublished photographs of original documents in Austrian archives. For palaeographical and diplomatic work ready access to photographs is essential. The building up of a microfilm collection should be the concern of every university History Department.

The available material has increased. How has it been used? To what extent has it given new meaning to our studies? Naturally the advances made have not been confined to exploiting newly-edited documents; they have involved looking at familiar material with new eyes and asking new questions. So I am led on, from the more purely editorial work, to the critical work in diplomatic, of the last fifty years. What has this meant for the student of the papal chancery and for the historian of the medieval Church? Our knowledge of papal government has gained in breadth and depth.

The chancery being what it was—the pope's secretariat—questions turn on such matters as how letters were drafted, penned, and despatched, what records were kept, and who were the people who did the work.[1] Instructions about the framing of

[1] An excellent view of the problems and of ways of approach may be seen in Dr. Herde's *Beiträge* on the thirteenth-century chancery. On matters of despatch see Yves Renouard, ' Comment les Papes d'Avignon expédiaient leur courrier ', *Revue Historique*, clxxx (1937) 1–29. On personnel see lists of chancellors and

papal letters may be found in chancery ordinances
and in guide-books for chancery clerks; these help
to elucidate the legal principles which underly the
phraseology.[1] A style of writing may reflect the
demands of government. It has been suggested
that the peculiar curial script was abandoned by the
chancery in the eleventh century, in favour of the
generally legible caroline minuscule, because the
papacy was beginning to exercise 'true governmental functions throughout the Church.'[2] I have
already spoken of the petitions presented to the
pope. These lay behind all papal letters which
granted indulgences, provisions, and other favours,
or which instructed judges in lawsuits. When we
have an original petition in this form, we see upon
it the pope's autograph *fiat*, with or without quali-
fication, and we see the order from the vice-chan-
cellor or referendary for the making of the ensuing
instrument. And so we learn more about the

notaries in H. Bresslau, *Handbuch der Urkundenlehre* (2nd ed.,
1912–31 and index, 1960). More recently L. Santifaller published
*Saggio di un Elencho dei Funzionari, Impiegati e Scrittori della
Cancellaria Pontificia dall'inizio all'anno 1199*, 2 vols., 1940
(*BISI* lv-lvi). Herde, *Beiträge*, gives valuable lists of officials for
the time of Innocent IV and of proctors for Bavarian petitioners
at Rome 1198–1303.

[1] G. Barraclough, 'The Chancery Ordinance of Nicholas III.
A study of the Sources', *QFIAB* xxv (1933–4) 192–250; R. von
Heckel, 'Studien über die Kanzleiordnung Innozenz' III',
Historische Jahrbuch, lvii (1937) 258–89; P. Herde, 'Marinus
von Eboli, *Super revocatoriis* und *De confirmationibus*: zwei
Abhandlungen des Vizekanzlers Innocenz' IV über das päpstliche
Urkundenwesen', *QFIAB* xlii-xliii (1964) 119–264, and separately.

[2] Walter Ullmann, in *Journal of Ecclesiastical History*, x (1959)
233, and see his *Growth of Papal Government in the Middle Ages*
(1955) p. 328.

passage of business through the curia and about
the people concerned. During the latter part of the
fourteenth century one finds petitions which have
been ante-dated, in order that a candidate for
provision might get the advantage over a rival.[1]
Awareness of such diplomatic fictions as this is
obviously essential if one is to understand the
intricacies of papal government and the operations
of the *plenitudo potestatis*. Something may also be
learnt by comparing petitions presented to the pope
with copies of petitions as they left the petitioner.
There are differences of form.[2] This fact and the
existence of formularies for petitions teach us that
petitions were normally re-cast in the curia by
professional hands, before being presented to the
pope.[3] Further, if we compare petitions and

[1] For the practice of ante-dating see Bresslau, *Handbuch*, ii.
111–15, 475–7, and more briefly, D. E. R. Watt, *Scottish Hist.
Review*, xxxii (1953) 104–5.

[2] Cf. P. Herde, ' Ranshofer Urkundenstudien: (1) Eine Petition
an Papst Klemens IV ', *Zeitschrift für bayerische Landesgeschichte*,
xxiv (1961) 185–99.

[3] R. von Heckel, ' Das Aufkommen der ständigen Prokuratoren
an der päpstlichen Kurie im 13 Jh.', *Miscellanea Francesco Ehrle*,
ii (*ST* vol. 38, 1924) 290–321. Von Heckel printed in *AUF* i
(1908) 500 sqq. the ' Libellus de formis petitionum secundum
cursum Romane curie ' of Guala Bichieri, *c.* 1226. G. Barraclough printed ' Formulare für Suppliken aus der ersten Hälfte
des 13 Jh.' in *Archiv für kath. Kirchenrecht*, cxv (1935) 435–56,
and in his *Public Notaries and the Papal Curia* (Papers of the
British School at Rome, 1934) calendared a ' Formularium notario-
rum curie ' from the early years of the fourteenth century.
Petitioners paid curial officials to re-draft petitions (Bresslau,
Handbuch, ii. 6 n. 1). In 1302 the abbot elect of St. Albans paid
at the curia ' pro tribus litteris supplicatoriis ' (*Gesta Abbatum mon.
S. Albani* (Rolls Series) ii. 57). See further, Herbert Chitty and
E. F. Jacob, ' Some Winchester College Muniments ', *EHR* xlix
(1934) 1–13.

ensuing letters we see how far the chancery was influenced by a phraseology supplied from outside. The interest of this is not confined to formal matters. A case in point is that of papal bulls which seem to erect new universities, by giving schools the status of *studia generalia*. A recent essay on the bull of John XXII for the university of Cambridge, 9 June, 1318, points out that the confirmatory character of the enactment clause can only be accurately interpreted by reference to the petition lying behind it.[1] And Dr. Battelli observes that a petition sometimes provides more details than were carried over into the ensuing bull or brief.

All clerks who work in offices find it convenient to have models of letters which can be used again and again. The papal chancery was no exception. It used formularies to frame its letters. The *Liber Diurnus Romanorum Pontificum* has long been famous as the oldest of these. Its original core goes back to Pope Gregory the Great, if not further. Since Poole wrote about it, much ink has been spilt on the *Liber;* but its construction remains something of a mystery.[2] Poole supposed that it

[1] A. B. Cobban, 'Edward II, John XXII and the University of Cambridge ', *BJRL* xlvii (1964) 49–78, especially p. 73.

[2] A new edition of the principal texts was produced by Hans Foerster at Bern, 1958. For the older history of editions and discussions to 1929 see H. Leclercq, s.v. in *Dictionnaire d'Archéologie et de Liturgie*, ix (1929) 243–344. For later differences of opinion about the nature of the *Liber*, principally represented by Wilhelm Peitz's defence of a chancery origin and Santifaller's denial, see G. Battelli, *s.v.* in *Enciclopedia Cattolica*, vii (1951) 1262–7, and Foerster's comments on ' der jüngste Streit ' in *Liber Diurnus Romanorum Pontificum*, pp. 29–36.

24

was the formulary of the chancery until after the days of Gregory VII. It is now established that if ever it had been an effective formulary it had ceased to fulfil that function long before the Hildebrandine age. But in those days it still interested the curia as a sort of canonistic source-book. The reduction in the rôle of the *Liber Diurnus* by modern scholars does not, of course, alter the fact that the chancery needed collections of formulas. If early formularies do not survive, that is simply a salutary reminder of how much material has been lost. But formularies do survive from the thirteenth century onwards, and receive much attention in modern times.[1]

Diplomatic study has wide implications here, for the recurrent formula may provide a clue to papal policy or papal doctrine. In a well-known lecture Poole showed how the dating clauses of bulls of the eighth and ninth centuries illustrate the withdrawal

---

[1] L. von Rockinger, *Briefsteller und Formelbücher des elften bis vierzehnten Jh.* (Quellen zur bayerischen und deutschen Geschichte, ix, 1863–64). For the formulary attributed to Marino of Eboli and calendared by Fritz Schillmann under that name in 1929 (Bibliothek des preuss. Hist. Instituts in Rom, Bd. xvi) see references in Herde, loc. cit., p. 21 n. 1, above. See also Barraclough, *Public Notaries*; P. Herde, ' Der Zeugenzwang in den päpstlichen Delegationsreskripten des Mittelalters', *Traditio*, xviii (1962) 255–88; the same, ' Papal Formularies for Letters of Justice (xiii-xiv cent.) ', in *Proceedings*, Second International Congress of Medieval Canon Law, Boston, 1963 (1965); Georges Tessier, ' Note sur un manuel à l'usage d'un officier de la Cour pontificale (xiiie siècle) ', *Études d'Histoire du Droit canonique*, dédiées à Gabriel Le Bras (Paris, 1965) i. 357–71 (which describes the volume formerly belonging to Paul Durrieu, mentioned by R. Fawtier in *Registres de Boniface VIII*, Introduction (1939) pp. xviii–xix).

of the popes from the Byzantine to the Frankish sphere of influence,[1] and Dr. Ullmann has connected the adoption of the term 'sacrum palatium Lateranense' in the ninth century with the pope's acceptance of the Donation of Constantine.[2] Ullmann, too, points to the formula found in the *Liber Diurnus* by which the pope of the early Middle Ages forbade his successors to modify his privilege: this was subsequently dropped; moreover, a new clause appears in papal privileges, to safeguard the 'iustitia' of the holy Roman church. Both changes, says Ullmann, signified 'the pope's legal and jurisdictional freedom from any cramping restrictions imposed by a predecessor.'[3] Again, the history of the clauses of protection in papal privileges for monasteries illustrates, as nothing else can, how monastic exemption evolved.

A clerk's most useful formulary is the one which is closest to current practice. No formulary remains up to date for long, and none can be comprehensive. So the clerk supplements his use of formularies by taking as models the enregistered copies or drafts of recent letters.[4] Realization of this fact brings us

---

[1] 'Imperial Influences on the Forms of papal Documents', *Proceedings of the British Academy*, viii (1917), reprinted in his *Studies in Chronology and History* (Oxford, 1934). The point had already been made by continental scholars: see E. Mühlbacher, *MIöG* Ergänzungsband, iv (1893) 501.

[2] *Growth of Papal Government*, pp. 326–7; and see C. R. Ligota, 'Petrus, Petra, Ecclesia Lateranensis', unpublished doctoral thesis, Cambridge, 1956.

[3] *Growth of Papal Government*, p. 293.

[4] The earliest bulls for canonization of saints issued by Innocent III's chancery (1199–1203) follow the same pattern, and there is cross-reference in the papal register from the later to the earlier

to one of the thorniest problems: what were the arrangements at Rome and Avignon for keeping records?

That the Roman see kept registers of its letters from very early days has never been doubted. But when one has said that one has said practically all that is commonly agreed. Were these registers comprehensive? If not, what was the basis of selection? Are the surviving registers original? If not, are they copies made for the use of the chancery or for some other purposes of the curia, and are they complete copies? If original, were they taken from letters already prepared for despatch or taken from drafts?

Discussion has turned on the earliest so-called original register, Reg. Vat. 2, that of Pope Gregory VII, which is one of the principal source books for the conflict over investitures and the Hildebrandine reforms. In the last twenty years old doubts about its nature have been revived. If Leo Santifaller is right, there lay behind Reg. Vat. 2 another more comprehensive register, perhaps written on papyrus.[1] Raffaelo Morghen has recently revived the

---

(Migne, *Patrologia Latina*, ccxv. 59 and *Selected Letters of Innocent III*, ed. Cheney and Semple, pp. xxiv, 27 n. 5). Cf. Fawtier, *Les Registres de Boniface VIII: Introduction* (1939) pp. civ-cv.

[1] L. Santifaller, *Beiträge zur Geschichte der Beschreibstoffe im Mittelalter* (*MIöG* Ergänzungsband, xvi, Heft I, 1953) pp. 94–113, where (p. 94 n. 7) there is a bibliography of recent writings, to which add Borino's arguments in *Studi Gregoriani*, ed. G. B. Borino, v (1956) 391–402, vi (1959–61) 363–90. See also the following notes. Poole had expressed doubts in 1915 about the then prevalent doctrine that Reg. Vat. 2 was the ' original ' chancery register (*Lectures*, p. 127 n. 2).

opinion expressed by Jaffé a century ago that the existing register is an extract from a lost chancery register, extracted for political purposes at a critical juncture under Gregory VII's personal direction; and he adds some plausible arguments.[1]

Similar debate, based on more ample material, has raged over the registers of Innocent III. Here the conclusion of Father Friedrich Kempf, S.J., that the annual registers are 'original' and contemporary, has been generally—though not universally—accepted.[2] His work on the special register 'super negotio imperii' makes interesting deductions from the handwriting, dating undated letters, and tracing the stages when the papal curia first decided that the disputed election in the Empire demanded a special record, and when the tortuous policy of the pope called for a temporary halt in registration.[3] Ingenious discussion of this sort

[1] R. Morghen, 'Ricerche sulla Formazione del Registro di Gregorio VII', *BISI* lxxiii (1961) 1–40, citing other recent literature.

[2] F. Kempf, *Die Register Innocenz III. Eine paläographisch-diplomatische Untersuchung (MHP* vol. ix no. 18, 1945). Friedrich Bock expressed dissent in 'Studien zu den Original-registern Innocenz' III (Reg. Vat. 4–7A)', *Archivalische Zeitschrift*, li (1955) 329–63, and 'Gregorio VII e Innocenzo III. Per un confronto dei Registri Vaticani 2 e 4–7A', *Studi Gregoriani*, v (1956) 243–79. Bock was severely criticized by W. Holtzmann in *Deutsches Archiv*, xii (1956) 231–2 and by O. Hageneder in *MIöG* lxv (1957) esp. 308–30. Kempf replied to him in 'Zu den Originalregistern Innocenz' III: eine kritische Auseinandersetzung mit Friedrich Bock', *QFIAB* xxxvi (1956) 86–137.

[3] Kempf, *Die Register*, and his edition of *Regestum Innocentii III papae super negotio Romani imperii (MHP* vol. xii no. 21, 1947). Cf. my review in *EHR* lxiv (1949) 365–8, and Helene Tillmann, *Papst Innocenz III* (Bonner Historische Forschungen, Bd. 3, 1954) p. 94 n. 39, p. 122 n. 161.

sometimes seems to venture too far into the hypothetical. Arguments depend sometimes on over-confident assertions about handwriting, and there still remains a wide area where dogmatism is not justified.[1] On the other hand, a recent reconstruction of lost parts of the register ' super negotio imperii' rests on solid foundations. It had long been conjectured that this register did not end, as it now does, in the year 1209, but it was difficult to be more precise. Dr. Anton Haidacher has now found a thirteenth-century register of tribute of the Roman curia (Vatican Archives, Indice 254) which provides the evidence : the register continued at least until 1211 and contained not less than 107 letters additional to the 194 which survive.[2]

These discussions about registers have a byeproduct : the recognition that the curia must have kept, along with the annual registers of letters, a multitude of other records. When Poole wrote, it was assumed that the papal letters obtained by the Venerable Bede from Rome were copied out of the

---

[1] On ' Schriftvergleich ' Kempf says: ' ich halte ihn für eine der exaktesten Methoden der Geschichtswissenschaft ' (*QFIAB* xxxvi (1956) 107). Cf. O. Hageneder's reservations about subjective judgments on script, *MIöG* lxv. 305, 322.

[2] ' Beiträge zur Kenntnis der verlorenen Registerbände Innozenz' III ', *RHM* 4 Heft (1960/61) 37–62, esp. pp. 51–8, 61–2. Dr. Haidacher's work also throws more light on the lost annual registers of Innocent III, on which see also Helmuth Feigl, in *MIöG* lxv (1957) 242–5. Other recent work on lost registers includes G. Battelli, ' " Membra disiecta " di Registri pontifici dei sec. xiii e xiv ', and Edith Pásztor, ' Ricostruzione parziale di un registro pontificio deperdito del sec. xiii [Innoc. IV an. 7] ', in *Mélanges Eugène Tisserant*, iv. 1–34, v. 199–207 (*ST* vols. 234–5, 1964).

registers; nowadays one is less sure.[1] Coming down to the thirteenth century, Friedrich Bock has drawn a picture of a chancery cluttered up with drafts and copies ; and surviving decretal collections confirm the impression that the canonists at the curia had more than the letters in the existing registers at their disposal.[2]

What I have said sufficiently demonstrates, I hope, how the study of palaeography and diplomatic improves our understanding of the medieval papacy. But the value of this study does not stop there. This for two reasons. In the first place, no medievalist can get away from the papacy, whether he is an ecclesiastical historian or not. The popes were involved in both other-worldly and worldly concerns. They were at once a universal and an Italian power, and so their activities crop up everywhere. Three random examples will illustrate

[1] W. Levison, in *Bede, his Life, Times, and Writings*, ed. A. Hamilton Thompson (Oxford, 1935) pp. 138–9. K. Silva-Tarouca, ' Die Quellen der Briefsammlungen Papst Leos des Grossen. Ein Beitrag zur Frage nach den Quellen der ältesten Papstbriefsammlungen ', in *Papsttum und Kaisertum. Festschrift Paul Kehr* (Munich, 1926) pp. 23–47.

[2] Bock, in *Archivalische Zeitschrift*, li (1955) 329–64. Cf. C. R. Cheney, in *Traditio*, xv (1959) 470–2, and C. R. and Mary G. Cheney, in *QFIAB* xli (1961) 32–4. There were also special registers of Innocent III besides the register on imperial business: see Feigl, *MIöG* lxv (1957) 244–7. For the state of things at the end of the thirteenth century see R. Fawtier in *Mélanges d'Archéologie et d'Histoire*, lii (1935) 244 sqq. and in *Registres de Boniface VIII: Introduction*, pp. ciii–cv. For the later Middle Ages see F. Bock, ' Päpstliche Sekretregister und Kammerregister. Ueberblick und Ergänzung früherer Studien zum Registerwesen des Spät-mittelalters ', *Archivalische Zeitschrift*, lix (1963) 30–58, and the literature on briefs (above p. 17 n. 1).

the varieties of papal influence outside the strict limits of church government as usually conceived. In 1156 a Scottish squire sought from Pope Adrian IV a bull of protection for his landed property. In 1219 the king of Man made himself tributary to Rome. In 1299 Pope Boniface VIII bestirred himself about Edward I's claims on Scotland. When such things could happen, giving rise to correspondence and diplomatic exchanges, it would have been strange if the secretariats of princes and prelates had not sometimes followed the lead of the papal chancery. To note and measure this is instructive. Every advance in the study of papal diplomatic should encourage comparative study with other chanceries.

In various regions the calligraphy of papal bulls left its mark on episcopal *acta*,[1] while a single peculiarity, like the papal ' tittle ' abbreviation, was borrowed by the French royal chancery under Louis VII, the English under Richard I, the Scottish under Alexander II. Again, the papal chancery evolved its own style of rhythmical prose during the twelfth century, the *cursus curie Romane*. In the next century a writer in Paris remarked on its use by the clerks of cardinals and bishops and by certain other courts.[2] John of Bologna, Italian secretary of Archbishop John Pecham of Canterbury, was moved about 1280 to write a dictaminal

---

[1] E.g. C. R. Cheney, *English Bishops' Chanceries 1100–1250* (Manchester, 1950) pp. 52–4. Resemblances between papal and episcopal documents in some continental bishoprics are much closer and more continuous.

[2] Rockinger, *Briefsteller und Formelbücher*, p. 501.

treatise based, as he says, on his experience in the Roman curia ; he says it is to teach inexpert English clerks how to frame official letters.[1] The *cursus* came into use in the English Privy Seal office in the fourteenth century; and long before this the diplomatic correspondence of kings of England had borrowed elegant preambles from papal models.[2] These were mere matters of form, albeit ones which may be useful evidence for a historian. More important, as Mr. Barraclough points out, the actual processes evolved in the papal chancery were sometimes copied. He shows how the English chancery in Henry III's reign adopted both methods and formulas of papal origin in granting letters expectative for benefices to royal clerks.[3] Moreover, Dr. Herde's recent work on the personnel of the papal chancery in this period confirms Barraclough's observations about the enrolment of curial officials in the ranks of the English king's clerks. Somewhat earlier, in 1212, we find Innocent III authorizing his *corrector litterarum apostolicarum* to enter the service of Simon de Montfort, earl of Leicester and vicomte of Béziers, and become the head of his chancery.[4] If we study the papal pro-

[1] Ibid. pp. 603–4.

[2] N. Denholm-Young, ' The cursus in England ', *Oxford Essays in Mediaeval History presented to H. E. Salter* (Oxford, 1934) pp. 68–103. The same, on Richard de Bury's *Liber epistolaris*, in *Transactions of the Royal Hist. Soc.* 4th series, xx (1937) 140–44 and in his edition of the *Liber epistolaris*, Roxburghe Club, 1950.

[3] G. Barraclough, ' The English Royal Chancery and the Papal Chancery in the reign of Henry III ', *MIöG* lxii (1954) 365–78, especially pp. 374–8.

[4] Migne, *Patrologia Latina*, ccxvi. 690 (Potthast 4589).

cedure of petitioning, we may well learn more about the system under other governments. After all, Bresslau pointed out long ago how a thirteenth-century king of Hungary, Bela IV (1235–72) displeased his nobles by insisting that 'however eminent they might be they might not initiate any business in his court nor speak directly to him unless they proferred petitions to the chancellors '. And King Bela, we are told, had reformed his chancery *ad instar Romane curie*.[1]

So much for the value of comparative study, with the reminder that in the matter of influences there was no rule of one-way traffic. My second reason for calling attention to advances in papal diplomatic is of an even more general nature. During the past fifty years the papal chancery has engaged the interest of a great many acute and learned scholars ; it has provided material in abundance on which one can sharpen one's critical faculties. The work done and the work being done is exemplary : not in the sense that it is all good, but because it confronts us with the problems which recur in the history of all administrations. The lessons learnt by students of the papal chancery, the warnings to be derived from some scholars' aberrations, can be applied elsewhere. The methods adopted by the Pius-Stiftung, the Austrian Institute, and the totality of workers in this field are worth careful study.

---

[1] Bresslau, *Handbuch der Urkundenlehre*, ii. 3; cf. ibid. i. 313 n. 5. See a written petition to Philip of Swabia (1207) edited by P. Zinsmaier, ' Suppliken des Klosters Tennenbach an Philipp von Schwaben ', *MIöG* liii (1939) 187–92.

33

To illustrate this by way of conclusion. When
Poole gave his survey of the papal chancery before
1216 in seven lectures and when Harry Bresslau,
in his massive *Handbuch der Urkundenlehre für
Deutschland und Italien*, treated of the papal chancery
from ancient times to the Renaissance, they very
properly permitted themselves some cautious
generalizations about areas which were as yet
incompletely charted. They noted the main con-
tours of the landscape, but they could not be
expected to observe all its structural features or the
unevennesses of the terrain at the sides of their
path. After more careful exploration, more studies
in depth, it seems that Poole and Bresslau were over-
impressed by the formalism of papal documents and
by the seeming rigidity of late medieval chancery
ordinances. Poole's book leaves the impression that
Innocent III's scribes never failed to produce
masterpieces of calligraphy, ' diplomatically without
fault'.[1] Bresslau, according to Dr. Herde, envisaged
the thirteenth-century chancery too much as a body
of bureaucratic officials in the modern sense, with
fixed functions, tied to prescribed rules of office-
work.[2] But intent study of documentary remains and
of personnel shows informality, unprofessionalism.

[1] E.g., *Lectures*, pp. 39, 94, 122.
[2] Herde, *Beiträge*, p. ix. Cf. Gasnault on the procedure for
petitions in the fourteenth century in *BÉC* cxv (1957) 50. Already
in 1939 Professor Fawtier, while speaking of ' le culte de la forme '
in the chancery of Boniface VIII, elsewhere observed: ' la chancellerie apostolique apparaît avec une organisation assez libre et
dans laquelle des initiatives individuelles, plus ou moins heureuses,
restent possibles et sont fréquentes.' (*Registres de Boniface VIII :
Introduction*, pp. xviii, lxvii).

The old rigid classification of papal letters proves
to be misleading. Registration may have proceeded
differently from pontificate to pontificate. There
were various ways of handling petitions, even if the
method adopted by certain suppliants at the court
of Avignon, who wrapped their petitions round
stones and threw them at the pope, was judged
inadmissible.[1] Reflection on these matters may be
salutary when we study other governments, to
discourage the making of unrealistic patterns. If
the papal chancery could be informal, inconsistent,
and inaccurate, what of less highly organized
chanceries? Or did the enormous scope of papal
business make the papal chancery less efficient,
though more impressive, than the royal chanceries
of the West?

One of the most crucial questions of diplomatic
—in a sense the basic diplomatic question—is that
of determining the context in which a given
historical document came into existence. Recent
studies of the papal chancery have been much
concerned with what I may call the characterization
of the document. We realize that some documents
were only composed for use in certain eventualities,
and never took effect;[2] that drafts lay about in the
papal offices—and might be copied—which would

---

[1] *Calendar of Entries in the Papal Registers: Petitions to the Pope (1342–1419)*, ed. W. H. Bliss (1896) pp. vii–viii.

[2] H. Tillmann, ' Ueber päpstliche Schreiben mit bedingter Gültigkeit im xii und xiii Jh.', *MIöG* xlv (1931) 191–200. Diplomacy everywhere required similar procedure; see for example the alternative forms provided by Edward III's government for the negotiators in Scotland, 1328 (E. L. G. Stones, ' An Addition to the " Rotuli Scotiae " ', *Scottish Hist. Rev.* xxix (1950) 27).

never go out with official sanction;[1] that decretals might be re-touched by the lawyers after their despatch;[2] that acts of general councils were revised before they were formally published.[3] Above all, the studies in the papal registers put us on our guard in all matters of registration in other chanceries. Was registration meant to be complete? Was it for the benefit of the administration or of its clients? Was there only one type of register? How did the clerk decide what date to set upon the enregistered copy? Historians have been prone to use English chancery enrolments without asking such questions as these. The questions cannot in fact be answered until much more labour has been spent in studying the handwriting of the rolls, in comparing enrolled texts with originals, and in various operations which are normal for students of the papal chancery.[4]

This leads me to emphasize a point made manifest by Kehr. If diplomatic commits the critic of texts to a study of the office which produced the texts, the office itself cannot be studied simply on the basis

---

[1] C. R. and Mary G. Cheney, ' A draft Decretal of Pope Innocent III on a case of Identity ', *QFIAB* xli (1961) 29–47, especially pp. 32–4.

[2] F. Kempf, *Die Register Innocenz III*, pp. 108–18.

[3] S. Kuttner, ' Die Konstitutionen des ersten allgemeinen Konzils von Lyon ', *Studia et Documenta Historiae et Iuris*, vi (1940) 70–131; the same, ' Conciliar Law in the Making ', *Miscellanea Pio Paschini*, ii (*Lateranum*, n.s. xv, 1949) 39–81; the same, ' The Date of the Constitution " Saepe " . . .', *Mélanges Eugène Tisserant*, iv (*ST* vol. 234, 1964) 427–52.

[4] Professor F. A. Cazel makes a welcome attempt to use such methods for establishing the date of an enrolled letter of King Henry III, *EHR* lxxix (1964) 690–1.

of its own internal accumulation of records. We learn about a chancery by handling its products, and they are dispersed. Just as Kehr concentrated on papal documents to be found in the archives of the recipients all over Europe, we shall best reconstruct the history of some other chanceries by looking outside them. Nor is the work just a task of accumulation. The products of chanceries must be examined with reference to the archive-deposits in which they are found. This is the only critical approach.[1] Hence the importance of the works of Dr. Florence Harmer and Messrs. Bishop and Chaplais on English writs. Mr. Bishop's *Scriptores regis* applies palaeographical criticism to the twelfth-century English royal chancery. Both in Scotland and England we now have the beginnings of *Regesta regum* comparable to Kehr's scheme. Professor Barrow's splendid volume on Malcolm IV is an example of the services which the projected eight volumes of royal acts may perform for Scottish diplomatists and historians.

Another lesson for us all emerges from the work I have been surveying. It is this. Whenever some one important class of record survives and is easily accessible, the historian tends to exaggerate its importance and to take it at its face-value. In England we have been so proud of our chancery rolls and our annual pipe rolls of the exchequer that we have left in a relatively neglected state the

----

[1] The point was stressed by M. Robert H. Bautier in his ' Leçon d'ouverture ' at the École des Chartes, 1961 (*BÉC* cxix (1961) 212–3).

scattered remains of the pre-enrolment age, the broken files of so-called 'Ancient correspondence', the masses of chancery warrants and miscellanea. Likewise, I suspect that it is because of England's unique series of episcopal registers that so little has been done in the past to collect episcopal *acta* and to illuminate those parts of diocesan administration of which we may learn from court-books and formularies. In all these cases we cannot draw a picture of the administrative office in just proportions unless we make the effort to collect the fragments and reconstitute scattered *fonds*.

We must also fasten vigilantly on all references to vanished records. Once upon a time there were other records, more numerous than the existing ones. To know that a series of records has been lost may depress the historian; but the mere knowledge of its former existence may be of the utmost value to him. It is, for example, pretty certain that registers of letters like those of Pope Innocent III were prepared in the days of his predecessors, though the continuous series of Vatican registers begins with this pope. In the same way, we cannot attribute any innovation in the English Exchequer to the year of the earliest surviving pipe roll, 1130; for it has long been recognized that the series of pipe rolls did not begin then.

The critical approach to records has not been invented by students of the papal chancery. Some of its greatest exponents moved on to papal diplomatic from the study of the Frankish and imperial chanceries. Dr. A. L. Brown's recent paper[1] on the authorization of letters under the Great Seal of England and his re-assembling of records of the Privy Seal office is as important a piece of diplomatic enquiry as the modern works on papal petitions ; it is independent work, similar in character. So I do not wish to imply that scholars in other fields have not moved independently in the same direction as students of the papal chancery, nor that they have failed to forge critical tools of their own. I only plead that every historian's path is full of pitfalls ; the most insidious dangers come not from dearth of documentary material but from misunderstanding of what exists and from ignorance of what existed. Serious studies in palaeography and diplomatic which have been devoted to interpreting a splendid range of records may help us all in our several pursuits.

[1] A. L. Brown, ' The authorization of letters under the Great Seal ', *BIHR* xxxvii (1964) 125–56. For work on the evidence for the Privy Seal and Signet offices to be derived from dispersed records, unofficial or semi-official copies of lost files, see M. Édouard Perroy's *Diplomatic Correspondence of Richard II* (Camden 3rd series, xlviii, Royal Hist. Soc., 1933) especially pp. xiv-xxvii, Prof. J. Otway-Ruthven, *The King's Secretary and the Signet Office in the fifteenth century* (Cambridge, 1939), and Miss M. D. Legge's edition of *Anglo-Norman Letters and Petitions from All Souls MS. 182* (Anglo-Norman Text Soc., vol. 3, 1941), especially pp. x-xi, xvi-xix.

ADDITIONAL NOTES

Important works on the papal chancery since 1966 are too numerous to list. Leonard E. Boyle,O.P., A Survey of the Vatican
Archives and of its medieval holdings (Pontifical Inst. of Mediaeval Studies, Toronto, 1972) pp.173-221,gives an extensive bibliography; for other works see below, Add. Note II p.1.Hermann
Diener surveyed the main registers in the Archives for the period 1378-1523 in QFIAB 51 (1972) pp.7-68. Brigide Schwarz studied the scribal organisation of the Curia,1198-mid fifteenth century, in Bibl. Dtschen Hist. Inst. in Rom 37 (1972) and the 'cor-
rectores litt. apostolicarum' in QFIAB 54 (1974) pp.122-91. In
the Kehr project (see pp.11-13 above) Germania pontificia has
come to life again with Provincia Maguntinensis pars IV (Göttingen,1978); Papsturkunden continues with important volumes on
Templer und Johanniter (R. Hiestand, 1972) and Nördliche Ile-
de-France und Vermandois (D.Lohrmann, 1976); and Kehr's
Reiseberichte zur Italia pontificia are edited in 5 vols. with a
sixth vol. of Indices by R. Volpini (Città del Vaticano,1977). A
general impression of main trends of recent study can be gained
from the proceedings of the Third International Congress of Diplomatic held at Rome in September-October 1971, as published
in Annali della Scuola Speciale per Archivisti e Bibliotecari dell'
Università di Roma, Anno XI (1971) and Anno XII (1972).

P.15, lines 14-16: The fraction - 'perhaps no more than a
tenth' - may be correct for the thirteenth century, but my colleague, Dr. P.N.L. Zutshi, observes that changes in the practice of registration under John XXII probably meant an increase in
the proportion after that time.

P.22, line 5: It should have been made clearer that during the
fourteenth century ante-dating was elevated to a system in the
granting of expectatives in forma pauperum: letters were dated
earlier for scholars according to their merit and influence. See,
beside references in n.1, A. Tihon,'Les expectatives in forma
pauperum' Bull. Inst. Hist. Belge de Rome 5 (1925),pp.51-118.

II

SOME FEATURES OF SURVIVING ORIGINAL
PAPAL LETTERS IN ENGLAND [1]

My title shows that this communication is concerned with
the *Censimento* planned by the regretted Franco Bartoloni, which
has made much progress in several parts of Europe. This Congress is a suitable occasion to bring to the notice of continental
students of diplomatic the material in England and Wales which
may take its place in a general *Censimento*.

Let me begin with four brief statements of fact. First,
there are far fewer original papal letters preserved in England
and Wales than in most of the continental countries of Europe.
The reason is obvious. The Church of England renounced papal
authority more than four hundred years ago and at the same
time suppressed most of its religious corporations. This led to

---

[1] Fuller references for papal letters of the thirteenth century cited
above by date only will be found in the list at the end of this paper.
The following abbreviations have been used in the footnotes and in the
list at the end: BERGER - *Les registres d'Innocent IV*, ed. É. BERGER, 4 vols.,
1884-1921. *BIHR - Bulletin of the Institute of Historical Research, University
of London*. CAPES - *Charters and Records of Hereford Cathedral*, ed. W. W.
CAPES (Cantilupe Soc., 1908). *EHR - English Historical Review*. HERDE -
P. HERDE, *Beiträge zum päpstlichen Kanzlei- und Urkundenwesen im 13
Jht.*, 2nd edition, Kallmünz, 1967. *Letters Innoc. III - Letters of Pope
Innocent III concerning England and Wales*, ed. C. R. and M. G. CHENEY,
Oxford, 1967. *MIöG - Mitteilungen des Instituts für österreichische Ge-
schichtsforschung*. MIQUEL ROSELL - *Regesta de letras pontificias del Ar-
chivo de la Corona de Aragón*, ed. F. J. MIQUEL ROSELL, Madrid, 1948.
Polychronion - L. SANTIFALLER, 'Ueber eine Urkunde Papst Innozenz' IV
für Capodistria-Koper', *Polychronion: Festschrift Franz Dölger* (1966), pp.
450-61. Pott - *Regesta pontificum Romanorum a. d. 1198-1304*, ed. AUG.
POTTHAST, 2 vols., Berlin, 1874-5. *P.R.O.* - Public Record Office, London.
PUE - Papsturkunden in England, ed. WALTHER HOLTZMANN, 3 vols., Göttingen, 1930-52. *PUS - Die Papsturkunden der Schweiz von Innozenz III bis
Martin V ohne Zürich*, ed. ANTON LARGIADÈR, 2 vols., Zürich, 1968-70. *PUZ -
Die Papsturkunden des Staatsarchivs Zürich von Innozenz III bis Martin V*,
ed. ANTON LARGIADÈR, Zürich, 1963. Rymer - *Foedera, conventiones, litte-
rae ...*, ed. T. RYMER, 3 vols., Record Commission, 1816-30. *SB - Schedario
Baumgarten*, ed. GIULIO BATTELLI, vols. i-ii, Città del Vaticano, 1965-1966.

a wholesale and deliberate destruction of papal documents in England at this early period.

Secondly, although we in England and Wales possess fewer original papal letters than other countries, there are more than most scholars suspect to exist. On a preliminary estimate, we have above 2100 originals, of which 1600 come within the scope of the *Censimento*: 1198-1417.

Thirdly, it is possible to discover information about most of these documents in printed lists and guides, and by far the greater number are recorded in printed *regesta* of a fair standard of accuracy. But these aids to research seem to be little known on the Continent, despite the lead given by Walther Holtzmann in his study of the earlier *Papsturkunden*[2]. Baumgarten's *Schedario*, it is true, includes descriptions of letters in the Public Record Office, London, and in the British Museum, and this has perhaps created the illusion that he exhausted English resources. But Professor Battelli has warned us against assuming that Baumgarten's explorations were thorough[3], and Dr Largiadèr has pointed out how far he was from exhausting the Swiss sources[4]. In England Baumgarten only described about one third of the bulls in the Public Record Office and the British Museum, and he looked nowhere else in England. One result of this is that of the original letters of Innocent III to be found in England and Wales he noted only ten out of fifty-three. Baumgarten did not have the advantage of the business-like list and index of 427 papal documents in the British Museum published by Dr. H. I. Bell in 1921[5], or of the list of about 1170 original papal letters in the Public Record Office published by His Majesty's Stationery Office in 1923[6]. It is unfortunate that neither of these indispensable tools for students found its way into Professor Santifaller's *Neuere Editionen mittelalterlicher Königs- und Papsturkunden* (Wien, 1958), or the *Repertorium Fontium Historiae Medii Aevi* (1962), or Professor Van Caene-

---

[2] *PUE* I. i. 56-57, 172-173.
[3] *SB* p. xlii.
[4] *PUS* i. xiii-xiv.
[5] 'A list of original papal bulls and briefs in the Department of MSS., British Museum', EHR xxxiv (1921), 393-419, 556-583.
[6] P.R.O. Lists and Indexes no. xlix: *List of Diplomatic Documents, Scottish Documents and Papal Bulls preserved in the P.R.O.* (London, 1923), pp. 219-324. A corrected reprint, New York: Kraus Reprint Corporation, 1963.

gem's *Kurze Quellenkunde* (1963), or into the elaborate bibliography of Professor Herde's *Beiträge*. There are also more recent lists of the much smaller miscellaneous collections of papal letters in the Bodleian Library and Lambeth Palace, by Professor Kathleen Major and Miss Jane Sayers respectively [7]. These attempt rather more than the earlier, bigger, lists in the way of diplomatic description.

My fourth observation is this: that although we are fairly well provided with lists, the diplomatic of these letters has not received much intensive study in England. The very fact that the material is so much less copious than in more favoured parts of continental Europe has made comparative study difficult. But I hope to persuade you that English material can make a significant contribution to the totality of work on papal chancery practice and on matters of papal government. Perhaps I may be permitted to repeat some words spoken in 1964: 'An essential condition of progress in palaeography and diplomatic is that as many related documents as possible shall be accumulated and compared; and we only understand office procedure and the working of the official mind when we see it repeated many times. Since the medieval popes corresponded with all the world, from Prester John to the King of Connaught, their correspondence has to be retrieved in every country of the West. The challenge has been taken up by scholars, with gallantry if not always with sufficient forethought or united action' [8].

After these preliminary remarks, let me say something about the distribution of the existing papal letters and about their addressees. I shall conclude with comments on the value of the material for the student of papal diplomatic within the chronological limits of the *Censimento*.

For this period England possesses about sixteen hundred original letters, of which no less than 1072 are in the Public Record Office and 166 are in the British Museum. When we have added to this ninety in the library of the archbishop of Canterbury at Lambeth and seventy-one in the archives of Durham

[7] KATHLEEN MAJOR, 'Original papal documents in the Bodleian Library', *Bodleian Library Record*, iii no. 33 (Dec. 1951) 242-256; JANE E. SAYERS, 'Original papal documents in the Lambeth Palace Library: a Catalogue', *BIHR Special Supplement*, no. 6, Nov. 1967.

[8] C. R. CHENEY, *The Study of the Medieval Papal Chancery* (Glasgow, 1966), p. 10.

4

Cathedral, we are left with a residue of about three hundred distributed between more than forty private and public collections. This dispersal is not surprising. At the Reformation in the sixteenth century there probably occurred an immediate and total destruction of the boxes of *papalia* in ecclesiastical muniments. The papal letters which remain entire are rarely the big privileges and letters of grace which had been stored as a group with special care; they are more often those which had been in other, local, sections of classified archives. A few medieval corporations survived the Tudor ecclesiastical revolution — the cathedrals, Westminster Abbey, the colleges of Oxford and Cambridge. They retained most of their archives. But except at Durham they have lost most of their papal privileges. Westminster Abbey is the richest, after Durham and Hereford, with twenty-three bulls; but these were not Westminster's main corpus of *papalia*, which numbered 209, from Paschal II to Boniface IX: all lost [9]. What remain mostly concern Luffield Priory and the London collegiate church of St Martin-le-Grand, of which Westminster had acquired the property to endow King Henry VII's chapel c. 1504. Hundreds of other monasteries suffered total dissolution. Their records either stayed in the possession of the Crown or passed through the hands of successive owners of the dispersed monastic lands. In either case, the papal letters were exposed to immense risks. There was no profit in retaining papal privileges which no longer served as title-deeds; on the other hand, their thick parchment was useful for binding books. Some of them were cut up to make covers for court-rolls and quires of accounts. I have counted forty-three such survivals in fourteen separate repositories, often badly defaced, and there must be many more [10]. Sir William Petre was a servant of King Henry VIII concerned with the suppression of many monasteries and enriched with many of their lands. His clerks cut up some of the monasteries' privileges to cover his estate-books and his descendants have preserved the fragments. Ironically enough, the one papal bull preserved intact in the

---

[9] See J. A. ROBINSON and M. R. JAMES, *The Manuscripts of Westminster Abbey* (Cambridge, 1909), pp. 94-95 and L. E. TANNER, 'The nature and use of Westminster Abbey muniments', *Trans. Royal Hist. Soc.*, 4th series xix (1936) 57.

[10] For example, *BIHR* xxi (1946) 39-40, xxxviii (1965) 192-200, *Letters Innoc. III*, no. 1089.

Petre muniments is the indult which Sir William acquired from Pope Paul IV in 1555, during the Marian Reaction, confirming his possession of the property of dissolved monasteries [11].

The Public Record Office has the lion's share of papal documents today because the royal government in the Middle Ages learnt to take good care of its records. A large proportion — three quarters or more — of the papal letters in the Office were received by the medieval kings and have remained in official custody ever since, until the nineteenth century either in the Chapter House at Westminster or in the Tower of London. But Baumgarten was wrong in supposing that this represents almost all the papal letters sent to the king [12]. We have medieval inventories of them and can measure the losses since these were composed: 68 out of the first 81 listed in Stapeldon's inventory of 1323 are in the Public Record Office now [13]. Others escaped from public custody since the Middle Ages and ended up in the British Museum, or the Bodleian Library, or (in one case) in the binding of a volume in the library of Peterhouse, Cambridge [14]. But the public records also include papal letters which did not come directly from the Curia to the king, but which have accumulated as the result of escheat and confiscation and litigation, either at the time of the Reformation or before or since: for example, twenty-five from the Order of the Temple, fifty-two from Cardinal Wolsey [15]. The monastic documents seized in the reign of Henry VIII mostly went into the Augmentation Office of the Exchequer [16]. This accounts for the series of no less than fifty-three papal letters from the archives

---

[11] F. G. EMMISON, *Guide to the Essex Record Office* (1969), pp. 102, 106, 126, 206.

[12] *Römische Quartalschrift*, xxvi (1913) 99*.

[13] See particularly, *The Antient Kalendars and Inventories' of the Treasury of His Majesty's Exchequer*, ed. F. PALGRAVE (3 vols., Record Commission, 1836) i. 1-155: Bishop Stapeldon's inventory, a. d. 1323.

[14] A substantial group of important letters concerning the king is in B.M. mss. Cotton Cleop. E. i and ii, Cotton ch. vi. 6, Lansdowne ch. 558, of which several can be identified in Bishop Stapeldon's inventory of 1323 (nos. 72, 73, 75, 157). Numerous later briefs (Leo X - Clement VII) from the public records are in mss. Cotton Vitell. B. ii - Vitell. B. xi. Other strays are in Bodleian ch. Staffs. 54 (30 April 1250, cf. P.R.O., S.C. 7/20/20 of the same date) and in Cambridge, Peterhouse ms. 38, a letter of 29 March 1291 (cf. Pott. 23633 and Stapeldon no. 77).

[15] Nine more letters for the Templars are in Lambeth Palace Library. Briefs for Cardinal Wolsey in the B.M. mss. Cotton Vitell. B series probably strayed from the public records.

[16] *Lists and Indexes* no. xlix, pp. [vii-viii]; *PUE* I. i. 3-63.

of Holy Trinity Priory, Aldgate[17]. So this relatively small London house of Austin canons makes a much better showing than most of the great Benedictine abbeys of medieval England. Originals from St. Augustine's, Canterbury or St. Albans or Bury St. Edmunds are of the greatest rarity. Even the cathedral priories of Canterbury and Norwich have little to show. True, the archbishop of Canterbury's archives at Lambeth Palace do contain a respectable number of papal originals — eighty-three for the period under review — but only seven of them (nos. 19, 28, 32, 33, 41, 53, 75) were Canterbury muniments in the Middle Ages; the rest come from various religious Orders and houses, and many, if not all, of them arrived at Lambeth between 1535 and 1537[18].

Apart from the few institutions (like the Public Record Office) which might be expected to preserve or inherit papal letters in the natural course of events, many repositories — the largest being the British Museum — contain *papalia* today which have been bought and sold. Most English collections of *papalia* are fortuitous. Their present location shows no obvious connection with their original provenance. If Englishmen were at one time great destroyers of papal letters, for the last four centuries they have been great collectors. Many letters in England now come from continental owners in the past. Originals from the abbey of St. Bertin at St. Omer have percolated into the British Museum, the John Rylands Library at Manchester, and Liverpool Cathedral (and further, to Columbia University Library, New York); another was sold at Sotheby's by auction on 14 June 1971 (lot 1436) and bought by a bookseller for £ 45. The British Museum has eleven papal bulls for the Norman Cistercian abbey of Foucarmont, and also harbours a mandate (9 August 1245) to the provost and dean of Lautenbach, in the diocese of Basel, concerning the abbey of Maursmünster (Marmoutier), near Saverne. The Public Record Office has a letter of 15 May 1281

---

[17] These belong to the period of the *Censimento*. There are also four outside this period, 1137, 1147, 1160, 1418. For the peculiar circumstances of this priory's dissolution in 1532 see E. JEFFRIES DAVIS in *Trans. Royal Hist. Soc.*, 4th series viii (1925) 127-50.

[18] Miss Sayers has discussed the circumstances in which they came to Lambeth ('Original papal documents', pp. 2-4). The largest number from any one archive is the twelve from Bury St. Edmunds. A thirteenth-century inventory of Bury charters enumerates 119 *papalia* (B.M. ms. Harl. 638 fos. 118 sqq.; cf. ms. Harl. 1005 fo. 228).

in favour of a nunnery at Coblenz. At Matlock in Derbyshire is a letter of provision of Gregory XIII (1572) for an Italian clerk in the neighbourhood of Lucca, and in the County Record Office at Hertford is a letter of Urban VIII (1628) to the clergy of the city and diocese of Valencia. I need insist no more on the random dispersion of this material, and come to consider the use of the papal documents in England for diplomatic study.

From Delisle and Diekamp in the nineteenth century to those of the younger generation today who work in this field — Professor Herde, Monsieur Barbiche, Dr. Stelzer, and others — a select band of scholars has toiled to discern the procedural pattern of the medieval papal chancery in the physical features of its products, in the methods of writing and sealing and despatch, in the annotations both on the face and the dorse of the documents. These enquiries will be most fruitful if they are conducted by scholars who can assemble a large body of material relating to a limited period and locality and link it to the work of other students of other regions. We need to pool resources from all parts of Europe. We are studying the working of papal government. In the thirteenth and fourteenth centuries that great machine was partly activated by curial officials at the centre; but much of its activity depended on initiative and stimulus injected from the various provinces of the Western Church. Local princes and prelates had their particular needs and desires. They sent their proctors to the Curia, or employed curial officials and hangers-on as proctors. Each locality or religious Order may have had its own way of going to work in the Curia and its preferred agents.

For the present, I have concentrated on the mid thirteenth century and have examined most of the original letters of Pope Innocent IV to England and Wales, which amount to about 208. So my remarks will mainly concern the time of Innocent IV. In studying the products of his chancery I am, of course, no pioneer. Berger and Diekamp were before me; more recently and more thoroughly, Professor Herde has been at work, while much evidence has been assembled by Professor Santifaller and his school and by Dr. Largiadèr. Indeed, much of my own study on the English material simply confirms the findings of these scholars which have been based on more copious continental evidence. But in the present state of knowledge such confirmation may be useful. Moreover, it may be that the particular circumstances of Anglo-papal relations during Innocent IV's pontificate and the peculiar nature of the English sources will throw light on certain features which are not perfectly clear elsewhere. In this connexion it is to be noted that for this pontificate the *Schedario* of Baumgarten is particularly meagre. It includes only sixteen of the 208 original letters (including *SB* 121, mistakenly attributed to Innocent III). A re-examination of the sixteen reveals a good many points at which Baumgarten failed to read the chancery marks correctly or else failed to see them.

England is relatively poor in privileges, and many of those which remain are sadly mutilated[19]. It presents a notable contrast to Switzerland in having hardly any letters for the Mendicant Orders, whereas Professor Largiadèr lists nearly seventy letters for the Friars Minor and Preachers. On the other hand, England is fairly rich in documents with a political or semi-political and fiscal flavour. A high proportion of the letters of Innocent IV for England concern the Crown; about eighty out of 208 are directed to the king or impetrated by his agents. This might aid a study of the format chosen in the papal chancery for its letters addressed to royalty. There seems to be wide variety, which perhaps accords with the varying nature of the business. It should encourage comparison with French and Spanish archives; for those at Paris and Madrid must be very numerous and Miquel Rosell lists fifty-seven in the Archives of the Crown of Aragon. Letters close are rarer than at some other periods. Of a total 167 letters close in the Public Record Office for the years 1198-1417 only one comes from Innocent IV (17 November 1254)[20]. The English evidence for other pontificates suggests that the choice of the form was not always consistent or predetermined. A letter of Gregory IX about payment of the annual tribute from England and Ireland, 9 July 1236, was probably intended for closure, for it is endorsed sideways with the address ('Illustri Regi Anglie') in the hand of the face and in the usual position for a folded letter close: but it

---

[19] A fine privilege of Innocent IV (27 April 1246) for the church of Hereford survives, measuring 565 (+ *plica* 40) x 570 mm.
[20] Cf. HERDE, p. 73. Stapeldon's inventory of 1323 noted 57 letters close. Miquel Rosell lists six of Innocent IV at Barcelona.

was in fact sent open and no scribe's signature is visible on the *plica* [21]. Apart from the royal letters, the English collections contain thirty letters of Innocent IV for the Cistercian Order or particular Cistercian houses. There is no other large group.

The handwriting of the letters and the scribal marks are naturally of the sort with which scholars are acquainted in all parts of Europe where papal authority extended. The English examples, like the rest, show slight irregularity of form in *litterae communes*, rules for spacing of dates are occasionally neglected, a few mistaken spellings creep in; but in general they show a high standard of neatness and consistency. The economy in the use of parchment which characterises the products of earlier pontificates, in all but solemn privileges, was to disappear in the second half of the century, but in Innocent IV's time it was still maintained. A mandate of 23 October 1252 measures no more than 104 (+ *plica* 16) × 145 mm.[22] By contrast, the conciliar decree for a crusade, issued in the form of letters patent on or after 17 July 1245, occupies a sheet 578 (+ *plica* 24) × 644 mm. Even when the proportions of these letters are generous, the margins on either side are narrow.

When we come to examine the chancery marks on originals, we have to reckon with many obstacles to an exact appraisal. Many of the documents are in poor condition, at least at the extremities, so that the notes added in the upper corners of letters are often obliterated or torn away, or the *plica* has been cut off. While it is common knowledge that the officials of the chancery often erased notes after the completion of the letter and its correction, one cannot always distinguish damage done to the surface of the parchment by contemporary erasure from the damage resulting from later vicissitudes. Moreover, ink-stains which appear at first sight to indicate either an erased marginal note or a palimpsest may prove on more careful inspection to be nothing more than the 'off-set' of a parchment lying folded in damp conditions. The endorsements and the writings on the *plica* suffer from being written on the hair-side of the parchment and the pen has not always been able to form clear

---

[21] Cf. Diekamp in *MIöG* iv. 606. Similar letters about the tribute survive from later in the century and were sent open.

[22] Cf. 27 April 1244: 116 (+ *plica* 15) x 130 mm.; 1 March 1251: 108 (+ *plica* 16) x 130 mm.

letters in travelling over the uneven surface. Every document, therefore, needs the closest possible scrutiny and, even so, the reader must sometimes admit defeat. In my *iter anglicanum* it has not so far been possible to examine all the letters under the ultra-violet lamp. Later on, more details may come to light and misreadings may be corrected.

During Innocent IV's time the elaboration of chancery marks does not seem to have gone very far. They seem to increase towards the end of his pontificate, and are more systematic under Alexander IV. As regards the signature of the *scriptor*, few if any letters still go out without it, though in half a dozen English letters there seems to be no trace of it. It is almost always to be found on the right-hand side of the *plica*. The only scribe of Innocent IV who writes his name consistently on the left of letters to England is *magister Antonius*[23]. The seventy different signatures on letters to England include fifteen which are not recognizable in earlier printed lists. They also provide earlier dates than hitherto observed for the activities of certain *scriptores*: for example, John of Benevento (12 and 20 February 1244)[24], Adegerius of Parma (15 September 1245), John of Parma (20 July and 10 October 1248), Philip of Florence (29 October 1243), Simon of Vercelli (5 February 1244). Script-comparison seems to establish that *Sym. Ver.* is not the same person as the man who signs as *Sy. v.* (9 August and 5 April 1245 respectively)[25]. Some signatures leave room for disagreement: *AG* and *JG* can easily be mistaken for *AC* and *JC*. Is the scribe of 6 October 1246 whose signature I read as *Sce* Professor Herde's *Ste* of 14 November 1247 and Professor Santifaller's *Sce* of 11 April 1248?[26] If so, which of us is reading the signature correctly?

I do not find a single scribe engaged exclusively in one sort of business or for one client. Duplicates are seldom by the same hand. The largest number of letters from one hand is seven, to the credit of *Jac̄ p̄*, between 1245 and 1254, with two

---

[23] 10 March 1246 and 15 Feb. 1248. Cf. *SB* 1333-1334, 1341, 1349, all of the year 1243, all in the Archives Nationales, Paris. HERDE, pp. 29-30 remarks of this scriptor 'er zeichnet auf der *Plica* rechts [*sic*] mit *ant'*. A very narrow *O* appears on the left of a letter of 15 Sept. 1245.

[24] He signs as Jo. bñ. (HERDE, p. 54 cf. 38 (1245-1253) and perhaps 'Jo. b. (?)' is the same (*Polychronion*, p. 456 (9 Feb. 1244)).

[25] Cf. HERDE, p. 44 n. 399.

[26] Ibid., p. 55; *Polychronion*, p. 456.

more letters (duplicates) of 13 May 1255[27]. *Jo. bñ* (John of Benevento) is responsible for six in the time of Innocent IV, and for another of 15 May 1255. The signature *l. p.*, which Dr. Largiadèr found in Switzerland on thirty-one of the thirty-six letters to the Dominicans, and on no others, occurs on two letters in the Public Record Office: one for Philip Basset, a baron in the king's service, the other for King Henry III[28].

Apart from the *scriptor's* mark on the *plica* a majority of the letters still show no other chancery mark on the face. Marks of uncertain significance are visible in the top right-hand corner of at least thirty-four letters. Diekamp explained them as marks of correction, but his hypothesis has not found favour in more recent times. The variety of the marks which occur in this position is such that a larger accumulation of details is needed before any explanation can be given with complete confidence[29]. It may therefore be useful to state in brief the English evidence for the pontificate of Innocent IV. Sometimes the evidence is simply that a letter or two have been erased. *a* and *as* occur, sometimes clearly legible, sometimes erased. Other letters or groups of letters are generally cancelled with two parallel diagonal strokes from the top right: //. They include *B, Bar, ca, fm̃, Guas* (not *Guar*, as *SB* 1975), *ha, Jo, Joh, Ra, Ro, Rof, Rup* (or *Dup*). Under one cancelled *Jo* (13 May 1252) and one cancelled *Ro* (18 December 1249) are three dots forming a triangle. The same sign appears under *fm̃* (23 March 1251); in this case *fm̃* is written twice, the second below the first, in different ink. This duplication of *fm̃* is the nearest parallel in the English Innocentian documents to the sequence of abridged names which Baumgarten and Herde noted in some later letters. But letters of Gregory IX provide two remarkable notes in this position. One is a mandate of 10 September 1230 addressed to the prior of Dunstable and others, to enquire into the rights of the archbishop of Canterbury in the election of bishops of Rochester. The scribe's signature is on the right of the *plica*. The endorsement *Cant'*, in the middle near to the top, suggests that the

---

[27] Cf. HERDE, pp. 37, 54, 264, Miquel Rosell (9 Jan. 1245), BERGER, i. p. lxviii, *Polychronion*, p. 457 (1251-1253).
[28] 12 June 1246, 1 Oct. 1250. Cf. HERDE, p. 54 (1245-1250); *Polychronion*, p. 457 (6 May 1252), and *Der Schlern*, xl (1966), 93 (27 March 1256).
[29] *MIöG* iv. 523; HERDE, pp. 193-4, 288-9 (where the marks are called 'Expeditionsvermerke').

letter was impetrated for the archbishop. On the face, in the top right-hand corner, written in four lines, are four names, all lightly deleted horizontally: *ad Thom(am)*, *Philpp*, *(et) ali(us) Phil(ippus)*, *Petrus*. Another mandate (20 February 1238) orders the prior of Holy Trinity, Aldgate, and the dean and chancellor of St. Paul's, London, to settle a case on the complaint of St. Martin's-le-Grand, London, against the abbot and convent of Walden and others. In the top right-hand corner are three lines with three abridged names, of which the reading is doubtful; only the first of them is deleted. If these are not the initials of correctors, it is observable that many of the texts so marked bear other evidence of correction in their text. Thus, the Hereford letter of 23 March 1251 cited above shows that the words 'super ipsis' have been squeezed into a small space over an erasure, and words have been deleted and roughly erased from the middle of the top margin.

There are a few notes for the preparation of duplicates: *fiat similis* (11 October 1250) and *fiat consimilis* (18 October 1252) in the middle of the top margin, and *fiant due de curia statim* (12 October 1245)[30] and *fiant due* (5 November 1252) on the left of the plica. A small figure *i* in the middle of the *plica* seems to indicate the preparation of duplicates: this is borne out by letters of 19 October and 5 November 1252 and probably by one of 22 May 1253. On the other hand, two pairs of surviving letters, 16 April 1250 and 30 January 1252, bear no visible sign of being marked for duplication. Tax-marks appear hardly at all: a letter of 30 April 1250 has a note *pro script* ... (?) under the *plica* on the left. When the dorse bears a note of registration, a letter *R* (with a stroke through the second descender) sometimes appears on the face, to the right of the initial *I* of *Innocentius*. I have remarked seven examples of this; on the other hand it is absent from seven other letters which have the note of registration on the dorse[31].

Turning to the dorse, we find the large note of registration in the form of earlier days. One example, already remarked

---

[30] There are single oblique strokes through the *e* of *due* and the *C* of *Curia*.
[31] Present: 25 April 1244, 6 April 1251, 1 Sept. 1252, 5 Nov. 1252, 13 March 1253, 5 Sept. 1253, 9 Sept. 1254. Absent: 23 June 1249, 11 July 1249, 27 Oct. 1249, two of 11 Oct. 1250. The last two bear other notes on the left of the top margin.

by Baumgarten [32], deserves mention. It is a letter of 23 June of the sixth year (1249) on behalf of the Order of Sempringham. It has the usual large *R*, with *script'* in the loop, followed by 'Nota quod hec littera posita est in registro septimi anni in xxv° capitulo'. The Vatican register for the seventh year of Innocent IV is missing.

Of all chancery endorsements the commonest is that usually described as the proctorial mark [33]. It is almost always set in the middle of the upper part of the dorse and the parchment has often been pumiced to receive it. If we are to call it a proctorial mark, we must recognize that we use the word 'proctorial' loosely. It is not necessarily the name or epithet of a proctor. It may indicate a principal who is himself in the Curia or a mere messenger. It may be used where a letter goes out on the initiative of the pope [34]. It may only name the ultimate recipient, e.g. *Rex*, on the assumption that the responsible official of the chancery will know the person to whom he is authorized to release a letter for the king of England. As we know already from continental sources, the Cistercians and Templars maintained permanent proctors of their own, known to curial officials. So a large capital letter T on the dorse sufficed to tell the officials to whom to deliver an indult to the Templars, and the word *Cistercium* sufficed for the Order of Cîteaux [35].

With this proviso I come to proctorial marks on letters to England. (Baumgarten did not note these marks on his cards for the English material). If the Cistercians used their own brethren to impetrate letters, they may have been monks who were resident in the Curia. Certainly, individual English houses of other Orders, such as Holy Trinity, Aldgate, or Whitby, and private persons in England tended to employ clerks who knew their way around the Curia. Eunufrius de S. Angelo, who had clients in Austria, Silesia, and west Germany, also received let-

---

[32] *Römische Quartalschrift*, xxviii (1914), 127*.

[33] I shall not discuss the small, often indistinct, signs which are visible on the top left-hand dorse of 34 out of 208 English Innocentian originals. The most common are *a*, *I*, *J*, and *y*.

[34] *Paulus* on an exhortation to King Henry III to hasten his journey to the Holy Land, 3 Dec. 1250. Paulus was employed at least once by Holy Trinity, Aldgate, 1 Oct. 1253 (and ? 29 July 1250). Cf. DIEKAMP, *MIöG* iv. 604 and BERGER, i. p. lxxiv.

[35] The additional notes *frater E* and *frater h* occur six and four times respectively on letters for Cistercian houses, in Feb. and March 1244. Cf. BERGER, i. p. lxxii, *SB* i. p. xxxi, and HERDE, p. 53 n. 447.

ters for Holy Trinity, Aldgate (30 March 1251) and St. Paul's,
London (December 1261)[36]. We know from other sources that
these churches sent their own members to the Curia to start
the process of impetration of letters; but they seem to have got
professional proctors to carry the business through. An agent
who does not seem to have been noticed in continental records
but whose name scarcely suggests an Englishman is *Perotus* or
Perrotus. It appears on the dorse of four letters, 1250-53: one
in favour of the Order of Sempringham (11 August 1250), one in
favour of the nuns of Flamstead (11 September 1253), one which
confirms the immunity of non-collegiate secular churches from
procuration fees at the archbishop of Canterbury's visitations (27
May 1252), and one which announces the pope's intention of
reducing the burden of his provisions on the Church of England
(22 May 1253). Perotus, then, did not act for a single client; but
more one cannot say. Papal chaplains who were provided to
English benefices may have collected their letters themselves
and their names are endorsed on the letters: Master Martin,
clerk of the Camera (15 June 1238), Master John of Asti (15
January 1246 and 27 June 1248), Master Berardus of Naples
(23 July and 26 September 1250, 18 February 1253). Likewise
Italians who got English benefices for their sons or nephews
might appear in person: in this category are Odo Brankaleonis
(11 December 1237) and James de Ponte (21 May 1253).

Like the endorsement *asperges me*[37], we have unidentifiable
epithets endorsed on letters to England: *Sagitta Ionathe* (28 January and 18 December 1249, 3 November 1253, 23 January
1254, 28 August 1255), *capud Leonis* (23 August 1256), *Nazarenus*
(1 February 1240), and *proles regia fracta* (9 August 1245). It is
safe to assume that these indicate persons well known in the
Curia. They appear on the dorse of letters for ecclesiastical
corporations and individuals. I should dearly like to know the
significance of *sobrietas*, which appears in the usual place for a
proctorial mark on a magnificent engrossment of the conciliar
decree for a crusade, 'Afflicti corde', of July 1245. If *paupertas*
indicated the Minorites, what did *sobrietas* signify?

---

[36] Cf. *Polychronion*, p. 461 (1253), HERDE, p. 137 (1255), W. STELZER in
Römische Hist. Mitteilungen, 11 Heft, 1969, pp. 214-215 (1257-65).

[37] For which see Diekamp, *MIöG* iv. 606; *PUZ* pp. 58-61; *PUS* i. 369;
STELZER, 'Beiträge zur Gesch. der Kurienprokuratoren im 13 Jht.', *Archivum
Historiae Pontificiae* viii (1970), 117.

Only four of the Innocentian letters to England so far examined witness to the activity of the *auditor litterarum contradictarum*[38]. The earliest, 15 September 1245, grants the chapter of Hereford Cathedral that the common revenue may be distributed among residentiary canons only. The proctorial endorsement shows that Roffredus de Ferentino was the chapter's agent in the Curia[39]. Below his name is the note: 'Magister Ricardus thesaurarius herrefordensis. Huguicio Petrileonis domini pape capellanus contra quod non fiat sibi preiudicium'[40]. Two other letters (23 March 1251), impetrated by James Fesulanus for the chapter of Hereford, bear notes of contradiction. One of them, a mandate, provides for the making of a *caucio*, and orders: 'Redd(atur) bullata sub pena ex(communicatio)nis domino auditori'. Our last example is dated 23 October 1252 and instructs the prior of St. Mary of Southwark to hear and decide a case on the complaint of the dean and chapter of St. Martin's-le-Grand, London, against the abbot and monastery of St. John, Colchester, Michael dictus Tour, and other clerks and laymen of the dioceses of London and Winchester. In the centre of the dorse is written: 'Jocius de London' inpetrat. Willelmus de Hereford contra pro Hugone rectore de Godechestere. Fiat caucio cum tenore mandati . . . Petrus de Vercellis pro abbate et conventu de Waltham'. On the *plica* is the scribe's signature, *lā. m.*, identified by Professor Herde as Lancerius Mediolanensis. In the top right-hand corner of the face is *Jo*, cancelled thus: //. In the top left-hand corner of the dorse is *y*, and in the top

---

[38] For the procedure see JANE E. SAYERS, 'Canterbury proctors at the Court of *Audientia litterarum contradictarum*', *Traditio*, xxii (1966), 311-345 and her *Papal Judges Delegate in the Province of Canterbury 1198-1254* (Oxford, 1971), pp. 57-58. Cf. HERDE, p. 216 n. 338, who cites an endorsement on an original concerning a *caucio* dated 6 March 1255. Further examples of slightly later date are discussed by WINFRIED STELZER, 'Aus der päpstlichen Kanzlei des 13 Jhts.', *Röm. Hist. Mitteilungen*, 11 Heft, pp. 210-221 and 'Ueber Vermerke der beiden Audientiae auf Papsturkunden in der zweiten Hälfte des 13 Jhts.', *MIöG* lxxviii (1970) 308-322.

[39] He was employed by them to impetrate at least four more letters (26 Oct., 15 Nov. (*bis*) 1245, 27 April 1246, and perhaps 3 March 1251). Between 1247 and 1254 he acted as proctor for the archbishop of York, and in Aug. 1275 was still on leave of absence from his Yorkshire benefice while in the service of the archbishop and others in the Roman Curia. For his involvement in forgery at the Curia (1253-54) see HERDE, *Beiträge*, p. 85.

[40] A mandate dated 19 Oct. 1245, arising from the complaint of Huguicio, a non-resident canon, against this rule, was enregistered immediately after the letter (Berger, 1672).

middle a quatrefoil with a cross on each side and below it; the same device in the top middle occurs on another letter for St. Martin's-le-Grand (15 February 1248).

These features expose no peculiarities in the English evidence: they were observed in continental documents long ago by Diekamp [41]. It may be more interesting to look at some of the marks on letters obtained for the king of England.To begin with two letters from the first year of Gregory IX, both dated 28 February 1228: they both show a large *VV* on the dorse, and this may indicate a curial agent. But one of them has the name *Alex'* written below *VV*. This letter is addressed to two English bishops and the archdeacon of Salop in the diocese of Coventry. On the face of this letter, in a very small hand at the middle of the top margin, are the words 'Reddantur Covitre'. The recipient, then, was the third of the addressees. He was Master Alexander of Swerford, archdeacon of Salop, a king's clerk of great celebrity. He handled this affair for Henry III in the Curia, and he was there later in the same year on the king's business [42].

Later in Gregory IX's pontificate some letters addressed to the king are simply endorsed *Rex, Rex Anglie, Illustri regi Angl'*. Some have no name at all; but in 1239-40 two which are in favour of the king are endorsed with *Novilla* (21 October 1239 and 8 February 1240) and one has the name *Ros* (12 January 1240): these both suggest Englishmen. With Innocent IV endorsement of letters for royalty is more regular. At first, *Rex* is enough — the addressee rather than his agent. But on 22 July 1244 a highly distinguished agent of King Henry III appears: the pope replies to a royal request brought by Master Henry de Secusia, provost of Antibes, papal chaplain, and on the dorse of the letter, in the usual position, is *Magister H.* This was Master Henry of Susa, later famous as the Cardinal Hostiensis, who was on the point of leaving King Henry III's service after being for eight years his legal adviser and proctor. As Noël Didier showed, he had played a dubious rôle in the affair of the bishopric of Winchester during these years. He was now ensuring his future

---

[41] *MIöG* iv. 605-607.
[42] *Close Rolls of Henry III 1227-1231* (HMSO 1902), p. 141; and in Jan. 1231, ibid., p. 467. Cf. A. B. EMDEN, *Biographical Register of the University of Oxford to a. d. 1500* (Oxford, 1957-59), iii. 1832.

by closer attachment to the Curia. Matthew Paris wrote that, like the raven which did not return to Noah's ark, Henry never came back to England, appropriating money with which the king had intended to bribe the pope and cardinals [43].

The next originals of letters impetrated for the king of England are a group of nine (including three duplicates) of April and July 1245, all endorsed with the name *Tayo*. This must be the Peter de Tayo for whom Master Lawrence de Sancto Martino obtained a grant of ten marks from the crown on 15 December 1245 [44].

Master Peter was replaced by one *Reginaldus*, who makes five appearances on proctorial marks between September 1245 and June 1249. He must be the Master Reginald of London who was rector of Chartham (in the patronage of the archbishop of Canterbury) in 1238 and who on 23 July 1240 witnessed an act of Archbishop Edmund, in company with *magistri* in the archbishop's service [45]. In 1243, Master Reginald of London, being then rector of Orpington (another living in the archbishop's gift) was employed by Berardus de Setia, papal *scriptor*, as his proctor in lawsuits in England connected with Berardus's pensions and benefices [46]. He may or may not be the Reginald of London (not described as master), clerk, who received a dispensation to proceed to orders, though illegitimate, on 7 December 1246 [47]. He can be more certainly identified with the Reginald, clerk of London, whom the pope licensed, on 6 July 1247, to receive two benefices with cure; the pope did this out of consideration for the king of England, of whom Reginald was a servant [48]. Further papal letters throw a little more light on the man. On 19 December 1247 executors were instructed to make provision for Master Reginald, king's proctor and chaplain of the bishop of Porto, in some English church; and a second mandate of 28 April 1248, evidently concerned with the same man, calls him

[43] N. DIDIER, 'Henri de Suse en Angleterre (1236?-1244)', *Studi in onore di Vincenzo Arangio-Ruiz* (Napoli, 1952), ii. 333-351. Cf. MATTHEW PARIS, *Chronica Majora*, ed. H. R. LUARD (Rolls Series), iv. 286.

[44] *Calendar of Liberate Rolls 1245-1251* (HMSO 1937) p. 15.

[45] *Cartulary of the Priory of St Gregory, Canterbury*, ed. A. M. WOOD-COCK (Royal Hist. Soc., Camden 3rd series vol. lxxxviii, 1956) pp. 155, 157, nos. 215, 218.

[46] *Annales Monastici*, ed. H. R. LUARD (Rolls Series) i. 129.

[47] BERGER, 2808.

[48] BERGER, 3053.

Reginald of London, clerk and king's proctor [49]. These letters suggest that Reginald was an Englishman who had been in the service of Archbishop Edmund, had entered the service of the cardinal legate Otto in England after the archbishop's death in November 1240, and returned with him to the Curia in 1241 where Innocent IV later created Otto bishop of Porto. From at least the year 1246 the king's agent, Lawrence de Sancto Martino (later bishop of Rochester) commissioned Reginald to act as proctor on the king's business. The English chancery rolls already recorded on 13 September 1246 that Master Lawrence had deputed Reginald of London 'ad audienciam in curia Romana pro nobis [sc. rege] custodiendam' [50]; on 18 May 1247 and 29 April 1248 money was assigned to him as the king's proctor in the Curia [51]; and on 28 April 1248 the king notified the pope that he appointed Master Reginald of London, clerk, as his proctor in the pope's court [52].

After Reginald's disappearance from the scene in 1249, all the letters impetrated for King Henry III from Pope Innocent IV which survive in original are endorsed with the names of known English *nuncii* and proctors. Roger Lovel, king's clerk, answers for ten, Robert Anketil for eighteen, John Chishull for two.

Whether in any given case the endorsement indicates the official proctor *ad impetrandum* or simply the recipient of the sealed engrossment for delivery does not always appear. Occasionally the name appears in the body of the letter as that of the king's agent. Henry of Susa has provided one example of this already. A letter of 27 September 1252 to King Henry, which bears the mark and name of '+ Anketil' in the usual 'proctorial' position on the dorse, is said to be in response to a request brought by 'Robertus Anketil clericus et nuncius tuus'. Another letter to king (11 April 1250) with the same endorsement has a further note emanating from the English chancery: 'Talis littera verbo ad verbum missum est archiepiscopo Dublinensi, Midensi, et aliis in Hibernia per Hugonem de Bradel' de Windes-

---

[49] BERGER, 3497, 4496.
[50] P.R.O., C 62/22 m. 3, whence calendared in *Cal. Liberate Rolls 1245-1251*, p. 79.
[51] Ibid. pp. 122, 175, paid each time through the agency of Lawrence de Sancto Martino.
[52] *Calendar of Patent Rolls 1247-1258* (HMSO 1908) p. 13, where the *Regin'* of the original roll is read in error as *Roger*.

hor' die martis ante ascensionem. Item alia eisdem tunc per eundem de decima proventuum ecclesiasticorum colligenda per biennium ante passagium, quam Robertus Anketil impetravit'. On the other hand, the pope addressed an order to the bishops of Ely and Carlisle on 8 April 1245 at the request of the king's *nuncius*, Master Lawrence de Sancto Martino, and this bears the 'proctorial' mark on the dorse, *Tayo*, like others of that year. I suppose him to be a clerk whom the king's *nuncius* encountered in the Curia and employed as proctor, as he later employed Master Reginald of London. Another letter (5 September 1253) shows the name of a royal agent or *nuncius*, Roger Lovel, in the usual proctorial position; but a partly illegible note below the registration mark shows that the letter was impetrated 'per magistrum N[icholaum de] plindoñ . . .'[53]. This was Nicholas de Plumton, or Plympton, who received sixty marks for expenses when going to the Curia on 29 May 1253, impetrated letters of 23 May 1254, prepared in duplicate, about the crusading tax (as we know from a royal letter close), and was active in the Curia between 1250 and 1256[54].

Endorsements may give information about the delivery of letters. A letter of 18 October 1252 instructs the bishops of London and Chichester not to allow the king of England to be molested in regard to lands, rights, and goods, while on crusade. It bears on its dorse the sign +, in a circle, which we associate with Robert Anketil, though his name is not visible; beneath it is the note: 'Conservatoria domini Regis Anglie deponenda penes dominum Octobonum' (the pope's nephew, Ottobuono Fieschi, cardinal deacon of St. Adrian, legate in England from 1265 to 1268, and pope as Adrian V in 1276). This letter was enregistered, but the surviving original does not show it, possibly because the registration-mark was endorsed on a duplicate. On the face, top left-hand corner, is 'fiat consimilis' and in the top centre 'R(ecipe) [quivis *del.*] Adeg' [*inserted*] y'. The scribe was Adegerius of Parma[55].

---

[53] Endorsed: 'scriptum in Registro clxv capitulo anno xi°'. The name of Lovel, first written in the usual form of the endorsement *R. Luuel* has been changed in a different ink to read *R. Louiell'*.

[54] *Cal. Liberate Rolls 1251-1260* (HMSO 1960) p. 130, cf. ibid. *1267-1272* (1964) p. 262; *Close Rolls 1253-1254* (HMSO 1930) p. 77; and see the index to *Cal. Patent Rolls 1247-1258*.

[55] For Adegerius see HERDE, p. 28. He also wrote duplicate texts of a letter of 19 Oct. 1252, both of which bear the name of Anketil and have

With these letters — between 1245 and 1254 — we seem to reach a new stage in the working of Anglo-papal relations. Henry III has a constantly increasing amount of business at the Curia, and the Curia for most of these years is within closer range at Lyon. So the king's government finds it both desirable and feasible to entrust much of its business to Englishmen. It maintains English *nuncii* and proctors in the Curia for extended periods. The endorsements on originals supply some indications of this. But I would emphasize that we know more about these individuals than can be learnt from the backs of papal letters. This leads me on to a final general proposition: we shall use the originals in our *Censimento* to best advantage if we use them in conjunction with other evidence. We must begin by relating them to all other papal letters which exist in copy — perhaps twenty times as many as the originals. And that is not enough. Local records, and correspondence between the provinces and the Curia other than papal letters, can elucidate these letters and explain obscurities in chancery procedure. Evidence of these sorts enable us to improve the *Censimento* and use its evidence with more confidence. Frankly, I am sceptical about using originals alone to answer any question of diplomatic. I am sceptical because of the irregular survival of originals and of the small proportion of the chancery's total output which they represent. Moreover, in very many cases the originals are in such a poor state of preservation that chancery-marks are invisible or can only be guessed. Guesses can mislead. Whether they come *instinctu divino* or *instinctu diaboli* is not always easy to determine. The lists of *scriptores* so far published are not only incomplete; they include ghosts, the offspring of misreading. Monsieur Barbiche has eliminated a large number of Fawtier's supposed *scriptores* of Boniface VIII [56]. I am prepared to wager that there are ghosts in all scholars' lists, my own included. We need to control the list of scribes by careful attention to the handwriting of texts. As for the proctorial

---

no registration-mark. A letter by his hand for Durham Cathedral Priory is as early as 15 Sept. 1245; on the left-hand side of its *plica* is written: 'Recipe qui vis' and in the usual position of the proctorial endorsement is the word *Taurus*.

[56] BERNARD BARBICHE, 'Les « Scriptores » de la chancellerie apostolique sous le pontificat de Boniface VIII (1295-1303)', *Bibliothèque de l'École des Chartes* cxxviii (1970) 115-187.

marks on letters, we must look elsewhere for corroborative evidence.

In England we are fairly well supplied with corroborative evidence. For the whole of the thirteenth and fourteenth centuries the chancery and exchequer enrolments are a copious source of information about royal *nuncii* and proctors. Besides these, the Public Record Office has a great series of 'Ancient Correspondence' — a class created in the nineteenth century — now admirably listed and indexed[57]. Much of it is printed, in Rymer's *Foedera* in the seventeenth century, in Shirley's *Royal Letters* in the nineteenth, or, best of all, in Dr. Pierre Chaplais's *English Diplomatic Documents 1100-1272* (H.M.S.O., 1964). Master Henry of Susa, Roger Lovel, Robert Anketil, and others, whose activities in the Curia I have mentioned, appear in these records constantly, with facts about them which enable us to estimate their status and reconstruct their careers. Sometimes we have the instructions they received for the impetrating of letters, sometimes their reports from the Curia about the success of their endeavours. The diligent student of original papal letters must piece together all this information.

English bishops' registers and miscellaneous ecclesiastical muniments provide material to illuminate the *Censimento* on more strictly ecclesiastical business. For instance, Archbishop John Pecham's register contains instructions for proctors *ad causas* in the Curia. At Westminster Abbey are preserved account-rolls which show how a great Benedictine house conducted its business at Rome. At Winchester College there is material preparatory to the issue of papal letters for Bishop William of Wykeham[58], and at Magdalen College, Oxford, similar material

---

[57] Note that while the recently revised *List of Ancient Correspondence of the Chancery and the Exchequer* (P.R.O. Lists and Indexes no. xv, revised edition, New York 1968) is of great value, even more can be learnt from the subsequent *Index to Ancient Correspondence of the Chancery and the Exchequer* (P.R.O. Supplementary Lists and Indexes, 2 vols., New York, 1969), for this gives an index, not only of the calendar, but of the original documents. For a full survey of the medieval resources of the Public Record Office see *Guide to the Contents of the P.R.O.*, vol. i (HMSO 1963), and for an admirable view of some of the principal categories, PIERRE CHAPLAIS, *English Royal Documents: King John to Henry VI 1199-1461* (Oxford 1971). See also Dr Chaplais's essay 'English diplomatic documents to the end of Edward III's reign' in *The Study of Medieval Records: Essays in Honour of Kathleen Major*, ed. D. A. BULLOUGH and R. L. STOREY (Oxford, 1971) pp. 22-56.

[58] HENRY CHITTY and E. F. JACOB, 'Some Winchester College muniments', *EHR* xlix (1934) 1-13.

from the time of a later bishop of Winchester, William Wayne-flete[59]. I conclude that if the science of diplomatic involves the study of administrative methods, those of us who wish to understand the material in the *Censimento* must be prepared to explore other sources as well.

POST SCRIPTA

Note to p. 13.

Miss Jane Sayers has discussed 'Proctors representing British interests at the papal court, 1198-1415' in a paper, published since my paper was written, in *Proceedings of the 3rd International Congress of Canon Law, Strasbourg, 1968* (Mon. Iuris Canonici, Series C, Subsidia vol. 4, Città del Vaticano, 1971), pp. 143-63. The identification of 'Tayo' made above on p. 17 seems preferable to that made by Miss Sayers, pp. 144-5.

Add to p. 15 note 38.

Another example, unfortunately illegible for the greater part, is of 28 January 1249 and introduces the names *Fesul'*, *Magister Guillelmus de Dunelmo*, and *W. Gueremua*.

---

[59] *Calendar of Charters and Documents relating to Selborne and its Priory*, ed. W. D. MACRAY (Hampshire Record Soc. 1891) i. 134-144 (a. d. 1468). Cf. Hist. MSS. Commission *Fourth Report* (HMSO 1874) 463a (a. d. 1473), 463b (a. d. 1410-21 and expenses of litigation in 1256 for which see also SAYERS, *Papal Judges Delegate*, p. 267).

THIRTEENTH-CENTURY PAPAL LETTERS IN ENGLAND INDICATED ABOVE ONLY BY DATE

1215	24 Aug.	B.M. ms. Cotton Cleop. E. i fo. 155. Pott. 4990. Rymer, I. i. 135. *Letters Innoc. III*, no. 1018. Stapeldon's inventory no. 75.
1228	28 Feb.	P.R.O., SC 7/15/35. Pott. 8136. Rymer, I. i. 189.
»	»	P.R.O., SC 7/15/17 (and dupl. SC 7/15/16). Pott. 8135. *SB* 911. Rymer, I. i. 189.
1230	10 Sept.	Lambeth, Papal documents 28.
1236	9 July	P.R.O., SC 7/15/2. Pott. 10201. *SB* 1200 (wrong reference). Rymer, I. i. 233 (*s. a.* 1237). Cf. Stapeldon's inventory no. 119.
1237	11 Dec.	P.R.O., SC 7/15/7. *SB* 1233.
1238	20 Feb.	Westminster Abbey, Muniments 13174.
	15 June	P.R.O., SC 7/15/24.
1239	21 Oct.	P.R.O., SC 7/15/12. Pott. 10800. *SB* 1285. Rymer, I. i. 239.
1240	12 Jan.	P.R.O., SC 7/15/3. Pott. 10840. *SB* 1288. Rymer, I. i. 238 (*s. a.* 1239).
	1 Feb.	P.R.O., SC 7/15/27.
	8 Feb.	P.R.O., SC 7/15/18. Pott. 10844. Rymer, I. i. 238 (*s. a.* 1239).
1243	29 Oct.	P.R.O., SC 7/20/14. Pott. 11168. Rymer, I. i. 250 (*s. a.* 1242).
1244	5 Feb.	B.M. Add. ch. 17849.
	12 Feb.	B.M. Harl. ch. 111 A. 13.
	20 Feb.	National Library of Wales, Aberystwyth, Penrice and Margam deeds 141.
	25 April	P.R.O., SC 7/20/4. Pott. 11351. Rymer, I. i. 252 (*s. a.* 1243). Berger 641.
	27 April	Windsor, St. George's Chapel Archives, Papal documents 1. Hist. MSS. Commission, *Reports on Various Collections*, vii. 16.
1244	22 July	P.R.O., SC 7/20/3. Pott. 11437. Rymer, I. i. 256.
1245	5 April	B.M., Harl. ch. 83 A. 23.
	7 April	P.R.O., SC 7/20/13 (dupl. 7/20/17). Pott. 11622. Rymer, I. i. 255 (*s. a.* 1244).
	8 April	P.R.O., SC 7/20/19. Pott. 11623. Rymer, I. i. 255 (*s. a.* 1244).
	17 July	B.M. ms. Cotton Cleop. E. i fos. 197v-198r. Pott. 11733. Matthew Paris, *Chron. Majora* (Rolls Series), iv. 445-455. Berger 1367. Stapeldon's inventory no. 157.
after	17 July	P.R.O., SC 7/20/45. *SB* 1641. Rymer, I. i. 279 (*s. a.* 1252).
	21 July	P.R.O., SC 7/21/3. Pott. 11737. Rymer, I. i. 261.
»	»	P.R.O., SC 7/21/7 (dupl. 7/21/15). Pott. 11739. Rymer, I. i. 261.
»	»	P.R.O., SC 7/21/11 (dupl. 7/21/18). Pott. 11738. Rymer, I. i. 261.
	27 July	P.R.O., SC 7/22/33. Rymer, I. i. 261.
	9 Aug.	B.M., Add. ch. 13540. *SB* 1595.
	15 Sept.	Durham, D. & C. Muniments 3. 1. Pap. 16.

	15 Sept.	Hereford, D & C. Archives, 2515. Capes, p. 80. Berger 1671.
	12 Oct.	P.R.O., SC 7/21/2. Pott. 11950. Rymer, I. i. 263.
	26 Oct.	Hereford, D & C. Archives, 2516. Capes, pp. 80-81.
	15 Nov.	Hereford, D. & C. Archives, 2517. Capes, p. 81.
	» »	Hereford, D. & C. Archives, 2518. Capes, pp. 81-82.
1246	15 Jan.	P.R.O., SC 7/20/44.
	10 March	P.R.O., SC 7/19/25.
	27 April	Hereford, D. & C. Archives, 1853. Capes, pp. 78-80.
	12 June	P.R.O., SC 7/21/14. Pott. 12153. Rymer, I. i. 260 (misdated).
	6 Oct.	P.R.O., SC 7/21/10. Pott. 12288. Rymer, I. i. 266.
1248	15 Feb.	Westminster Abbey, Muniments 13185.
	27 June	P.R.O., SC 7/19/29.
1248	20 July	P.R.O., SC 7/20/18.
	10 Oct.	Lambeth Palace, Papal documents 45.
1249	28 Jan.	Duhram, D. & C. Muniments 3. 1. Pap. 22.
	23 June	B.M., Stowe ch. 572. *SB* 1905.
	11 July	P.R.O., SC 7/20/39.
	27 Oct.	P.R.O., SC 7/21/32. Pott. 13849. *SB* 1922. Rymer, I. i. 270.
	18 Dec.	P.R.O., SC 7/22/28. Pott. 13885. Rymer, I. i. 271.
1250	11 April	P.R.O., SC 7/20/41. Pott. 13950. Rymer, I. i. 272.
	16 April	Hereford, D. & C. Archives, 1330. Capes, pp. 85-86.
	» »	Hereford, D. & C. Archives, 1331 (dupl. of 1330).
	30 April	Oxford, Bodleian Libr., ms. ch. Staffs. 54. Major, 'Original papal documents', no. 10.
	» »	P.R.O., SC 7/22/30. Pott. 13965. Rymer, I. i. 274.
	23 July	Winchester College, Muniments 2119 (Andover 1a). *Reg. Henry Woodlock* (Canterbury and York Soc.), ii. 1023.
	» »	Winchester College, Muniments 2120 (Andover 1d). *Reg. Henry Woodlock*, ii. 1024.
	29 July	P.R.O., SC 7/19/20.
	11 Aug.	B.M., Stowe ch. 573. *SB* 1969.
	26 Sept.	Winchester College, Muniments 2121 (Andover 1b). *Reg. Henry Woodlock*, ii. 1025.
	1 Oct.	P.R.O., SC 7/20/2. Pott. 14077. Rymer, I. i. 275.
	11 Oct.	P.R.O., SC 7/21/19. Pott. 14086. *SB* 1976. Rymer, I. i. 275. Berger 4887.
	» »	P.R.O., SC 7/19/24. Pott. 14085. *SB* 1975. Rymer, I. i. 276. Berger 4888.
	3 Dec.	P.R.O., SC 7/19/21.
1251	1 March	P.R.O., SC 7/64/48.
	3 March	Hereford, D. & C. Archives, 2520. Capes, pp. 89-90.
	23 March	Hereford, D. & C. Archives, 2521. Capes, pp. 92-93.
	» »	Hereford, D. & C. Archives, 2522.
	6 April	P.R.O., SC 7/20/11. Pott. 14291. Rymer, I. i. 277. Berger 5211.
1252	30 Jan.	Hereford, D. & C. Archives, 2523. Capes, p. 93.
	» »	Hereford, D. & C. Archives, 2524 (dupl. of 2523).
	13 May	P.R.O., SC 7/35/5.
	27 May	B.M., Harl. ch. 111 A. 19.
	1 Sept.	P.R.O., SC 7/20/30. Pott. 14704. *SB* 2096. Rymer, I. i. 285. Berger 5946.
	27 Sept.	P.R.O., SC 7/20/23. Pott. 14721. Rymer, I. i. 285.
	18 Oct.	P.R.O., SC 7/20/33. Pott. 14751. Rymer, I. i. 287. Berger 6039.
	19 Oct.	P.R.O., SC 7/20/28 (and dupl. 7/20/25). Pott. 14753. Rymer, I. i. 287.

	23 Oct.	Westminster Abbey, Muniments 13169.
	5 Nov.	P.R.O., SC 7/20/34 (and dupl. 7/20/24). Pott. 14764. *SB* 2104. Rymer, I. i. 287. Berger 6072.
1253	18 Feb.	Winchester College, Muniments 2122 (Andover 1c). *Reg. Henry Woodlock*, ii. 1026.
	13 March	P.R.O., SC 7/20/40. Pott. 14910. *SB* 2124. Rymer, I. i. 280 (*s. a.* 1252). Berger 6400.
	21 May	P.R.O., SC 7/19/26. Berger 6748.
	22 May	P.R.O., SC 7/21/22. Pott. 14983. Rymer, I. i. 281 (*s. a.* 1252). Berger 6556.
	5 Sept.	P.R.O., SC 7/21/23. Pott. 15118. *SB* 2174. Rymer, I. i. 293. Berger 6985.
	11 Sept.	Hertfordshire County Record Office, 19687.
	1 Oct.	P.R.O., SC 7/19/30.
	3 Nov.	Hereford, D. & C. Archives, 1856. Cf. Potthast 15163.
1254	23 Jan.	Hereford, D. & C. Archives, 2525. Capes, p. 104.
	20 May	B.M. ms. Cotton Cleop. E. i fo. 194v. Cf. Stapeldon's inventory no. 72.
	23 May	P.R.O., SC 7/22/25. Pott. 15383. Rymer, I. i. 303.
	9 Sept.	P.R.O., SC 7/19/27. Pott. 15512. SB 2253. Rymer, I. i. 307. Berger 8034.
	17 Nov.	P.R.O., SC 7/20/1. Pott. 15558. *SB* 2263. Rymer, I. i. 312.
1255	13 May	P.R.O., SC 7/1/19.
	» »	P.R.O., SC 7/1/24 (dupl. of 7/1/19).
	15 May	Hereford, D. & C. Archives, 2833. Capes, pp. 106-7.
	28 Aug.	Hereford, D. & C. Archives, 2526.
1256	23 Aug.	P.R.O., SC 7/1/25. Cf. Pott. 16530. Rymer, I. i. 345.
1261	Dec.	Lambeth Palace, Papal documents 63. *Docts. illustrating the hist. of St. Paul's Cathedral* (Camden Soc., New series xxvi (1880), 9-10)).
1264	24 March	B.M. ms. Cotton Cleop. E. i fo. 221v. Pott. 18839. Rymer, I. i. 438. Cf. Stapeldon's inventory no. 73.

ADDITIONAL NOTES

P.1, line 5: A major contribution is made to the Censimento by Bernard Barbiche, Les actes pontificaux originaux des Archives Nationales de Paris, tomes I-II (1198-1304), Città del Vaticano:Biblioteca Apostolica Vaticana (1975, 1978) which inaugurates an Index actorum Romanorum pontificum under the auspices of the Commission Internationale de Diplomatique. P.N.R. Zutshi has prepared a detailed study and calendar of 'Original papal letters to England, 1305-1417', unpublished, Cambridge, Univ. Libr., Ph.D. thesis, 1981. Jane E. Sayers has in hand a more comprehensive collection, calendaring all papal letters, existing either in original or in copy, addressed to recipients in England and Wales, 1216-1303 (see Journal of Soc. of Archivists vol.6 no.2 (Oct.1978)pp.92-4).

P.8, line 10 from foot: For earlier letters close in England see below, VIII pp.234-7, and Add.Note. Barbiche lists 141 original letters close in the Archives Nationales for the period 1204-1409, of which two-thirds come from 1305-34 (Les actes I pp.lxxvii-lxxxv).

P.13 n.33: In the 14th century a mark in this osition seems to indicate a notary (Zutshi, op.cit. vol.i p.71 n.27).

III

AN ANNOTATOR OF DURHAM CATHEDRAL MS C. III. 3, AND UNPUBLISHED DECRETALS OF INNOCENT III.

SUMMARY: Durham MS. C. III. 3 contains *Compilatio Prima* and Gilbert's collection of decretals, with a collection in 190 chapters (*Dunelm. IV*) drawn mainly from other collections of the time of Innocent III. *Dunelm. IV* was probably completed by 1205; although its compiler did not rely mainly on local sources, he included some decretals from recipients' copies in the north of England, and he was possibly connected with the church of Durham. — Throughout the MS. are marginal additions: legal glosses, *quaestiones*, and 84 decretals, mostly of Innocent III. The principal annotator was an Englishman, who wrote at different times between 1205 and 1215. — The annotator had a canonistic library at his disposal, had access direct or indirect to the papal registers (now lost) of 3 and 4 Innocent III, and picked up letters locally. His notes suggest an interest in teaching, and he cites Hug., Silvester, Alanus, etc. — Appendix I analyses the decretal additions. Appendix II prints two hitherto unknown texts: Reg. Innocent III lib. 3 ep. 5 concerns tithe in the kingdom of Cyprus; lib. 3 ep. 26 to the king of France about his marriage to Ingeborg provides the full context for short extracts preserved by Bernard and found in *Extra* [C. R. Ch.].

SUMMARIUM: Codex ms. Durham C. III. 3 continet I *Comp. ant.* et collectionem decretalium Gilberti una cum quadam collectione quae vocatur *Dunelmensis IV* et 190 capitulis conflatur quaeque praecipue desumpta sunt ex aliis collectionibus tempore Innocentii III compositis. *Collectio Dunelmensis IV* probabiliter absoluta est a. 1205; quamvis compilator non dependeat praecipue a fontibus qui ad illa loca spectant, nihilominus aliquas decretales desumpsit ex quibusdam exemplaribus in partibus Britanniae septentrionalis receptis; compilator ipse cum Ecclesia Dunelmensi nexum habuisse videtur. — In toto Codice manu scripto additiones marginales leguntur, quae sunt glossae legales, *quaestiones*, 84 decretales quae maxima ex parte Innocentium III auctorem habent. Praecipuus glossator vir erat natione Anglicus qui notas apponit variis intervallis inter aa. 1205 et 1215. Qui bibliotheca operum iuris canonici usus est et facultate gaudebat inspiciendi directe vel indirecte Registra anni tertii et quarti Innocentii, quae hodie deperdita sunt; insuper collegit litteras in locis, ubi commorabatur. — Notae demonstrant eum cupidum docendi fuisse; glossator noster citat Huguccionem, Silvestrum, Alanum aliosque. — In Appendice I additiones decretalium analysi subiiciuntur; in Appendice II autem binae litterae decretales, quae hucusque ignotae erant, eduntur: Reg. Innocentii III, lib. 3, ep. 5 de decimis in regno Cypri solvendis; lib. 3, ep. 26 ad regem Francorum de matrimonio eius cum Ingeburga, quarum integer textus complet breves partes, quas Bernardus conservavit et Liber *X* exhibet.

40

In a paper published in 1955 on *Collectio Seguntina* Walther Holtzmann described in passing the manuscript which contains the subject-
matter of this paper (1). The manuscript had previously been noted
by Professor Kuttner in *Repertorium der Kanonistik*, and by Professor
Ullmann in *A Scottish charter and its place in medieval canon law* (2).
Holtzmann wrote:

Ce ms. n'est rien d'autre qu'une vaste compilation. On y lit d'abord (fos.
1-73v) une Comp. I (3); puis (fos. 75-121) une collection de Gilbert, dans laquelle le scribe a integré la plupart des chapitres que le ms. de Weingarten-
Fulda ne donne qu'en appendice; dans les marges on a ajouté plus tard de
nombreuses décrétales, surtout d'Innocent III. Vient ensuite (fos. 123-158)
la *Dun(elmensis) IV*, qui est un conglomérat d'éléments très différents. Elle
comprend 190 décrétales (en appendice une série d'additions surtout des lettres d'Innocent III). Le compilateur a fait son choix dans diverses collections.
Jusqu'au ch. 67, il semble que sa base soit un Régnier de Pomposa; en tout

---

* I gratefully acknowledge the permission of the Dean and Chapter of Durham to use
and publish from their ms. and also thank the Director of the Institute of Medieval Canon
Law for the loan of a microfilm copy.

The following abbreviations have been used: D = Durham Cathedral ms. C. III. 3.
DUGGAN = C. DUGGAN, *Twelfth-century Decretal Collections and their importance in English
history* (London, 1963). JL = *Regesta Pontificum Romanorum*, ed. P. JAFFÉ, S. LOEWENFELD,
etc. (Berlin, 1885-8). Kan. Erg. = W. HOLTZMANN, *Kanonistische Ergänzungen zur Italia
Pontificia*, Sonderdruck aus *Quellen u. Forschungen aus ital. Archiven u. Bibliotheken*, 27-8
Tübingen, 1959). POTT. = *Regesta Pontificum Romanorum*, ed. A. POTTHAST (Leipzig, 1874-5).
Reg. = *Regest. Innocentii PP. III*, ed. MIGNE, *Pat. lat.* 214-7 (Paris, 1858). *Repertorium* =
= S. KUTTNER, *Repertorium der Kanonistik*, 1140-1234 (*Studi e Testi*, 71, Rome, 1937). TH. =
= A. THEINER, *Vetera monumenta Slavorum meridionalium historiam illustrantia* (Rome, 1863)
pp. 47-70. ZRG = *Zeitschrift der Savigny-Stiftung für Rechtsgeschichte, Kan. Abteilung.*

Decretal collections are cited according to *sigla* used by KUTTNER, HOLTZMANN, and
DUGGAN, *loc. citt.* In particular, the following editions and analyses have been used: *ACL*,
ed. J. D. MANSI, *Concilia, 22. Alan.* and *Gilb.*, ed. R. VON HECKEL, *ZRG* 29 (1940). *Bern.*,
ed. H. SINGER, *Die Dekretalensammlung des Bernardus Compostellanus antiquus* in: *SB der
Wiener Akad., phil.-hist. Kl.* 171, i. 1914. *1, 2, 3,* and *4 Comp.*, ed. ANTONIO AGOSTIN, *Antiquae collectiones decretalium* (Ilerda, 1676) and E. FRIEDBERG, *Quinque compilationes antiquae*
(Leipzig, 1882). *Hal.*, analysed F. HEYER, *ZRG* 4 (1914) 590-2. *Luc.*, ed. J. D. MANSI, *S. Baluzii Miscellanea* (Lucca, 1762) 3, 367-91. *Rainer.*, ed. MIGNE, *Pat. lat.* 216, 1173-1272. *Roff.*
ed. DUGGAN. *Rot. III*, ed. CHENEY, *Traditio* 11 (1955) 149-62. *Sangerm.*, ed. H. SINGER,
Neue Beiträge in: *SB der Wiener Akad., phil.-hist. Kl.* 171, i. 1913. *Tanner.*, ed. W. HOLTZ-
MANN, *Die Sammlung Tanner* in: *Festschrift zur Feier des 200 jähr. Bestehens der Akad. d. Wiss.
in Göttingen, phil.-hist. Kl.* 1951, pp. 83-145. *Wig.* ed. H. E. LOHMANN, *ZRG* 22 (1933) 36-187.
X, ed. E. FRIEDBERG, *Corpus Iuris Canonici*, 2 (Leipzig, 1881).

(1) *La Collectio Seguntina et les décrétales de Clément III et de Célestin III* in: *Revue d'hist.
ecclésiastique*, 50 (1955) 400-53.

(2) *The Juridical Review* (Dec. 1949), 225-41.

(3) Ending, as KUTTNER noted (*Repertorium*, pp. 300-1) with JL 14179.

cas, cette première partie, composée presque exclusivement de décrétales d'Innocent III, contient plusieurs grandes séries qui se retrouvent telles quelles dans la collection de Régnier. Les ch. 68-138 proviennent d'une collection voisine de la collection Tanner ou de la *Sangermanensis;* les ch. 139-150 sont des décrétales d'Innocent III, et enfin les ch. 151-190 (4), soit la dernière partie, sont extraits d'une collection « primitive » contenant des décrétales de Clément III et de Célestin III. Les 18 lettres de ces papes conservées par la *Dun. IV* ne nous aideront guère pour la reconstitution du texte primitif, mais le ms., dans son ensemble bigarré, est un témoin caractéristique des efforts constants déployés pour tenir à jour le manuel de droit canonique qu'était la *Comp. I* (5).

Some day a scholar will have to amplify Holtzmann's description and analyse completely the various parts of this fascinating manuscript (6). It demands a codicological study, besides details of the contents. In particular, *Dunelmensis IV* should be calendared and its structure exposed (7). The object of the present paper is much more modest. It is simply to call attention to some of the annotations which make the book especially remarkable.

Although no attempt will be made here to deal comprehensively with *Dunelm. IV*, a few words about it are called for, if only to put the later additions to the manuscript in their right setting. *Dunelm. IV* at first sight gives the impression of a piece of local English or Scottish work. Ullmann emphasized its local character when he noted how a Scottish private charter had been introduced to elucidate a related decretal concerning Melrose Abbey (8). This decretal, like the accompanying charter, must surely have been taken directly or indirectly from a recipient's copy and not from the copy in Reg. Vat. 5. Two other decretals point the same way: to the bishop of Durham (fo. 124r*b*) and to the abbots of Roche and Welbeck (fo. 154v*a*); they have not been found elsewhere (9). On the other hand, if we confine ourselves to the Innocentian decretals, *Dunelm. IV* does not contain a disproportionate number of letters addressed to

---

(4) In a letter to me on 11 Feb. 1957 HOLTZMANN described the section ch. 151-182 as " extracts from a primitive collection of the type of Lucensis-Seguntina ". Cf. *Kan. Erg.* p. 10.

(5) *Revue*, pp. 405-6.

(6) A complete microfilm is in the library of the Institute of Medieval Canon Law.

(7) Professor ULLMANN proposed this in 1949 (*loc. cit.* p. 232 n. 19).

(8) *Loc. cit.*

(9) Printed in *Letters of Pope Innocent III concerning England and Wales*, ed. C. R. and MARY G. CHENEY (Oxford, 1967) nos. 535, 777. No. 535 is the mandate referred to in POTTHAST 2149 (*Reg. 7, 15*).

42

the British Isles: eleven out of seventy-seven. In other words, the original compiler of the collection did not rely mainly on local sources but, having access to local muniments, he made use of them from time to time. This does not disprove the English provenance of the manuscript which, indeed, is highly probable; but it suggests that the compiler (very possibly connected with the church of Durham) had various canonistic sources to draw on, besides those documents which the hazards of local litigation brought to hand. In this eclectic activity he did but work like the other compilers of Innocent III's time who gathered supplements to earlier collections. Starting with a basic collection such as *Gilbert*, they might pillage another collection for decretals which did not appear in their basic one. They might also draw directly on curial sources (registers or drafts), and on isolated letters in recipients' copies. As Kuttner shows, the Vercelli ms. of *Gilbert* and *Alan* contains a collection of Innocentian decretals to supply all the chapters of *Comp. III* which were to be found neither in *Gilbert* and *Alan* nor in the marginal additions to the text of *Alan;* while the Salzburg manuscript contains a shorter supplement extracted on the same principle from *Bernard* (10). The four supplements to *Francofurtana* in Paris, B. N. ms. Lat. 3922A show accumulations from a greater variety of sources, which probably included both the Curia and Norman recipient-copies (11), and similar characteristics are exhibited by the group of three short collections, *Pragensis*, *Palatina I*, and *Abrincensis II*, put together between *Comp. III* and *Comp. IV* (12).

Some years ago Ullmann tentatively suggested that *Dunelm. IV* " may well present Alan's compilation in a preparatory state " (13); but this is hardly confirmed by a closer scrutiny. The two collections have in common a few letters unknown elsewhere and a few peculiar readings (14), but neither can be derived from the other (15). The

---

(10) *The collection of Alanus: a concordance of its two recensions* in: Rivista di Storia del Diritto, 26 (1953) 37-8.

(11) W. HOLTZMANN, *Das Ende des Bischofs Heinrich II. von Chur* in: Zeitschrift für schweizerische Geschichte, 29 (1949) 152 n. 18 and C. R. CHENEY, *Decretals of Innocent III in Paris, B. N. ms. lat. 3922A* in: Traditio, 11 (1955) 149-62.

(12) CHENEY, *Three decretal collections before Comp. IV* in: Traditio, 15 (1959) 464-83.

(13) *Loc. cit.*, p. 232.

(14) *Dunelm. IV* fo. 130v (nos. 41 and 43) = *Alan.* app. 79 and 5, 2, 10. *Dunelm. IV* fo. 131 rb (no. 48) = *Alan.* app. 42 in reading " Cantuariensi " where the other collections read correctly " Antivarensi ".

(15) *Dunelm. IV* foll. 130va, 131ra, 132ra (nos. 43, 45, 50) omit the addresses found in

disparity of contents is too marked to treat either of these two collections as the product of the other. At the same time it may be noted that, besides the link with *Rainer* which Holtzmann found in the first section of *Dunelm. IV*, the early Innocentian material in some details resembles sixteen chapters of *Rotomagensis III* (16). For example, Potthast 67 appears in both *Rot. III* 2 (cf. p. 155) and *Dunelm. IV* fol. 124vb (no. 10) as " decano Astoriensi ", where *Alan* and *Bernard* agree with the Register in reading " Astoricensi ". Pott. 88 comes under the title " De constitutionibus " in *Rot. III* 3 (cf. p. 155), *Dunelm. IV* fol. 123ra (no. 1), *Comp. III*, and *Extra*, whereas in *Alan* it comes under the title " De confirmatione utili vel inutili ", and in *Rainer* and *Bernard* under " De rescriptis et eorum interpretatione ". But only a complete analysis and penetrating comparison could disclose the true pedigree of *Dunelm. IV*. We are concerned with the additional matter.

The three principal contents of the volume, *Comp. I, Gilbert*, and *Dunelm. IV*, left plenty of room for additions. The collections had been written in fairly small, neat bookhand, two columns to a page, and occupied less than a quarter of the whole area. After the fashion of the time in such works, the page had been prepared and ruled with annotation in view. Blank space was left for one set of notes in the inner margin and two parallel sets in the outer margin, with more blank space at top and bottom. Whole folios remained to be filled between *Comp. I* and *Gilbert* and between *Gilbert* and *Dunelm. IV*, while the end of *Dunelm. IV* on fol. 158r is followed by six more leaves for miscellanea. The annotation of the collections, though irregular in incidence, is copious, and all the extra folios have been filled. All of it seems to be in English handwriting of very early in the thirteenth century. The whole presents a disorderly appearance and, at first sight, a variety of script. But on closer examination the bulk of the notes seem to be one man's work, filling his margins at intervals over the years, sometimes writing carefully, sometimes lapsing into slovenliness (17).

Alan. 1, 7, 2, and app. 53 and 79. HOLTZMANN rejected the suggested relationship between *Dunelm. IV* and *Alan.* in *Tanner.* p. 97 n. 30 and *Rev. d'hist. eccl.* 50 p. 405 n. 3.

(16) *Traditio*, 11, 153-8.

(17) Certain features of the bookhand suggest that the collections themselves may possibly be the work of the principal annotator; but a closer analysis would be necessary to establish this. As it is I am most grateful to Mr. T. A. M. Bishop for his valuable expert advice upon the hands of the annotators.

44

What can be learnt about date and provenance? The original collection of Gilbert was perhaps compiled by the end of the year 1202, and the appendix (here incorporated in the text) contains no later decretal. *Dunelm. IV* contains no letter which can be certainly or probably dated after 1204 (18). The handwriting of the notes is compatible with the view that the principal annotator began his work in or soon after 1205. The papal letters which he copied include, along with many earlier ones, four of 1205, eleven of 1206, four of 1207, and three of 1208 (19). The inference that he collected his letters within a few years of their issue is confirmed by certain additions to the manuscript by other hands. It was another scribe who, at the end of Gilbert, copied four papal letters of 1213-15 concerning ecclesiastical elections in England. Yet another hand put seven extracts from the Fourth Lateran canons at appropriate points in the margins of *Comp. I.* Finally, at the foot of fol. 14r we find a mandate of Honorius III to the dean and penitentiary of York and a canon of Ripon. This is copied in full, save for a few words, and is dated 17 November 1220: it is the latest dateable document in the book.

The appearance of these additions leads us to infer that the original annotator was active (at least so far as his copying of decretals extended) between 1205 and 1215. This would appear to be at least compatible with other marginalia to *Comp. I* and *Gilbert* which cite canonistic opinion. Here are references to " *Mr. W.* ", " *B.* ", " *Hug*", " *Silvester* ", " *Alanus* ", " *Bazan* ", " *Vincentius* " (20). To determine where the annotator worked must be left to experts. If he was an Englishman, as seems probable, then it must be remembered that the years 1208-1213, during a time of general interdict, were not particularly favourable to the study of the canon law in England, and little if any legal teaching took place in Oxford during the years 1209-14. Nor was there in England, during these years, so much business as usual for ecclesiastical courts. On the other hand, an uncertain number of English clerics and scholars spent the years of the interdict abroad, until their recall in 1213. If this book was the property of an English clerk in Paris or Bologna it might be easier to explain a rather odd palaeographical feature. This annotator constantly uses arabic numerals. It looks like a fashion picked up

---

(18) " Pastoralis officii " (Pott. 2350) is the latest, on fol. 153ra.

(19) The latest with a date is no. 34, of 22 Nov. 1208.

(20) Cf. *Repertorium*, pp. 325-7, 355, etc.

in southern lands: certainly arabic numerals are very rare in England in this period (21).

Whoever possessed the book was a diligent worker. Along with many legal glosses and questions, he added to his three collections 84 decretals, from Alexander III to Innocent III, besides verbatim extracts from the *Corpus Iuris Civilis* and a canon from Gratian (22). Only five times did he make the mistake of copying decretals already in the book (23). He added thirteen of his decretals at appropriate places in the margins of *Comp. I*, and at the end of it added one section of the long letter of Celestine III, " Prudentiam tuam " (no. 22 below). Thirty more letters are distributed in the margins of *Gilbert*, fourteen in the margins of *Dunelm. IV*. Where this collection ends on fol. 158ra two more decretals are added in, apparently, two other book-hands (nos. 70, 71). Then, at the top of the second column, the principal annotator copies no. 72 in the free and easy charter-hand which has already appeared often in margins. But he has several styles of writing, and resolves to be neat. His small, clear, regular hand fills with decretals the remainder of this page and the two columns of the next. Then, in the first column of fol. 159r, beginning to copy no. 82, the writer breaks off after five lines, in the middle of the column, leaving the rest of the page blank for the completion of this very lengthy letter. But no. 82 was never completed. Instead, three letters are inserted (probably at a later time) in column 2, in even more compressed writing. Foll. 159v-160va contain eleven more letters by the same scribe, seemingly written at one time. With the exception of nos. 72 and 95 (no. 95 was already in *Comp. I*) all these letters forming an appendix to *Dunelm. IV* are of Innocent III from 1198 to 1206 (24). Nos. 83 and 87 repeat texts which were already in *Dunelm. IV*.

We have seen that it is hard to determine how *Dunelm. IV* was composed and impossible to suppose that all its contents were drawn from one source. When we survey the annotator's work, we face an even more confused problem. For while nos. 76-82 and 86-96

---

(21) Cf. G. F. HILL, in : *Archaeologia* 62 (1910) 139, 171, 172.

(22) On fol. 1or the text of C. 3 q. 4 c 2 is copied in the top margin.

(23) Nos. 20, 46, 83, 87, 95.

(24) The preponderance of Innocentian letters in this section raises the question whether the accepted ascription of no. 72 to Lucius III is justified. It does not seem to be found in any twelfth-century collection.

46

have the appearance of being copied at one time (25), there is no reason to suppose that the 63 marginal additions were all made at the same time : indeed, the variety of script (even though all by the same hand) makes this most improbable. And if continuous composition is ruled out, the probability is increased that the annotator drew his material from various sources.

The analysis shows that twenty of the added letters are pre-Innocentian, sixty-four are of Innocent III (26). Twelve of the pre-Innocentian were still sufficiently regarded in the early thirteenth century to find their way into *Alan* (*c.* 1206), and except for nos. 3 and 22 the rest are in *Sangermanensis* (*c.* 1198). All told, thirty-three letters re-appear in *Alan*, and several of them reveal close relationship. Nos. 31 and 32 are adjacent in *Alan*, and no. 32 is only known from these two sources; no. 40, likewise, is only known from these two sources. Nos. 60, 64, and 65 occur in the same sequence in *Alan*, with the same addresses. In no. 60 the address differs from those given in the register and in the other collections; in no. 64 (not found in any other collection) the address departs from the enregistered copy; no. 65 agrees with *Alan* against *Alcobacensis II* and others, where it is ascribed to Celestine III. No. 74 is in the form which appears in *Rot. III* and *Alan* in contrast to the text in *Bernard* and elsewhere (27). But despite the thirty-three letters common to *D* and *Alan* (including nos. 39, 40, 87 of his appendix), it is not possible that one collector borrowed all from the other. The discrepancies are too numerous. For example, only a small part of no. 90 is found in *Alan*, whereas no. 82 is only a fragment of the decretal as *Alan* has it. Finally, no. 70 omits the opening words of *Alan's* text but includes more of the original after the words " et infra ".

The other collection which most conspicuously invites comparison is *Bernard*'s, produced in 1208. Forty-three of the Durham annotations reappear in *Bernard*. But here again instances in which *D* contains more of an original letter than *Bernard* are fairly numerous (see especially no. 89). Neither here nor elsewhere does it seem possible to establish a certain relationship with any known collection.

---

(25) The incomplete text of no. 81 was apparently corrected and lengthened, to contain the last words of the version found in *Alan.*, after the entry of nos. 83-85 on col. 2 of fol. 159r.

(26) The number of 96 in the analysis below is made up with five letters and seven extracts from the Fourth Lateran canons by later hands.

(27) See *Traditio*, 11, 156.

One may note Holtzmann's guarded remarks about some earlier collections: " On garde l'impression d'une certaine parenté... Je ne crois pas cependant que l'on puisse en déduire avec certitude un lien quelconque de filiation: trop d'intermédiaires restent inconnus " (28).

Turning to other possible sources: there is some internal evidence that among the annotations at the end of the book are extracts either from the papal registers or else from some collection like *Rot. III* which shows direct dependence on the registers. Nos. 86-92 form a group which can be associated with the registers of the second and third years of Innocent III. Nos. 87-92 agree with the lost register of the third year as recorded in the *Rubricellae*. No casual selection from other sources and no systematic classification could have produced this group in this order. No other collection has been found to contain all of these seven letters: only one is found in *Rainer*, two are in *Rot. III*, two in *Alan* (one of them abridged), three and parts of two more in *Bernard*. One of the seven texts (no. 88) is otherwise entirely unknown, one (no. 89) is not found complete elsewhere. Nos. 73 and 74 suggest the same origin. They both appear in *Alan*, but widely separated from each other. In *Rot. III*, on the other hand, where they are consecutive, they form part of a series of extracts from the lost papal register of the fourth year. Besides these significant collocations, it is worth noting that nos. 69 and 88 are otherwise only recorded in the registers.

No. 56 is common to the Durham marginalia and to the appendix to *Tanner*. An imperfect text of no. 71 is found in another supplement to *Tanner* (ms. Tanner 8 p. 591) which Holtzmann did not publish. Finally the principal annotator preserves three texts of which no other trace survives (nos. 62, 63, 94). All were addressed to England. They immediately pose the question of local acquisitions from recipients' copies. In no. 71 we have a letter to England only otherwise found in the English Tanner ms.; the papal register did not contain it, and our collection preserves the full dating clause. No. 93, addressed to Durham on the subject of conversion *ad arctiorem ordinem*, could have been taken from the papal register, as it was taken by *Bernard;* but this letter, too, was probably copied into *D* from the original, or from a local Cistercian copy such as the one entered into a *Rabanus Maurus* from Kirkstead Abbey (29). Additional colour

(28) *Rev. d'hist. eccl.* 50, 405. See further his sceptical pronouncement in *Kan. Erg.* p. 14.

(29) Kirkstead, co. Nottingham. The ms. is Cambridge, Univ. Libr. Ff. 4.1 fol. 131r.

48

is given to this conjecture by the fact that the next letter (no. 94) in *D* was also sent to England, later in the same year, addressed to the cardinal legate John of Ferentino, about a provision to a Yorkshire church in the patronage of St. Mary's Abbey, York. The legate visited St. Mary's Abbey in August 1206 (30).

In connexion with these English additions by the original annotator, it is relevant to notice the papal letters copied by other hands on foll. 14r and 122v. These were all addressed to England. No. 7, a letter of Honorius III (1220), concerns a lawsuit in the diocese of York. Nos. 52-4 concern the activities of Nicholas de Romanis, cardinal bishop of *Tusculum*, legate in England in 1213-14; their reappearance (with no. 55) in an early thirteenth-century muniment book of Durham Cathedral Priory is significant. The chapter of Durham was involved with the legate in trying to choose a bishop. It had every reason to possess copies of these letters, two of which are unregistered and otherwise unknown. Doubtless they represent the recipient-tradition. They were copied into *D* not long after the event. Although that does not prove that *D* was compiled at Durham or that the original annotations were made there, it shows pretty clearly that the book was there at latest in the next generation.

All this suggests that the collector who made the additions to *Comp. I*, *Gilbert*, and *Dunelm. IV* was an English north-country scholar. His basic texts included one compiled in England. He had at his disposal a canonistic library, he had access to the papal registers directly or at second hand, and he was able to pick up letters of canonistic interest, such as no. 93, which circulated separately in England and Scotland. His very extensive notes in many parts of the book show how he used the decretals, perhaps for teaching. There are notes and comments (" Nota quod ", " Videtur quod "), questions (" Queritur an "), propositions (" Ponamus quod "), and appeals to authority (" Magister dicit "). In many places sprawling pencilled notes (by the same man) have been partially erased to make room for notes in ink. The citations of civil law are numerous, and whole pages are devoted to the assembling and classifying of references. For the book as a whole was a working book, used by a lawyer who may well have been both teacher and practitioner. It must be emphasized that he was no mere collector: the decretals with which we are concerned form a relatively small part of the total annotation.

---

(30) See *Eng. Hist. Rev.* 46 (1931) 443-52 and 76 (1961) 658.

Perhaps a through scrutiny of this complicated material would enable us to locate the man, even name him. But this is beyond the scope of the present study and the competence of the writer. To conclude, a brief comment is called for on the hitherto unpublished texts which the anonymous annotator has preserved for us.

All of these six letters came from Innocent III and four of them were addressed to England. Nos. 63, 71, 94 can be placed respectively in the years 1199, 1201, and 1206. In view of the general pattern of the annotations no. 62 may probably be dated before the end of 1208. These four letters take their place in a collection of *Letters of Pope Innocent III concerning England and Wales*, edited by C. R. and Mary G. Cheney, as nos. 125, 348, 719, 817B. The other two letters, nos. 88 and 89, are printed below. They can be identified with letters of February-March 1200, listed in the *Rubricellae* of the lost papal register of Innocent's third year.

Letter 88 appears to be entirely unknown except for its summary in the *Rubricellae*. Here it occurs as the fifth item in Theiner's edition, addressed " Tripolitano et Anteradensi episcopis: quod regem Cipri moneant et compellant solvere decimas ecclesiasticis personis, alioquin ipsum excommunicent et regnum Cipri supponant ecclesiastico interdicto ". It may therefore be dated late in February 1200. The text requires little commentary. Cyprus, conquered by King Richard I of England, had passed in 1192 to the titular king of Jerusalem, and was ruled by King Aimery from 1194 to 1205. The Latin lords who settled there, stepping into the shoes of their Greek predecessors, levied the same tax of one third of the produce of the land from their tenants of the classes of *parici* and *perperiarii* (31). It was the tithe due from this source of wealth that King Aimery and his Latin subjects were now withholding, despite earlier recognition that tithe was due to the Latin churches. Celestine III had approved and confirmed the imposition of tithe by the Latin hierarchy in Cyprus in a bull of 20 February 1196 (32). Even if the canonists of Innocent III's time did not regard this as a matter of sufficient importance to justify the inclusion of this letter in their collections, the topic it touched was a live issue for the ecclesiastical administrator. Canon 54 of the Fourth Lateran Council provided that tithe

---

(31) George (F.) Hill, *A history of Cyprus*, 2 (Cambridge, 1948) 9.
(32) Migne, *PL*, 206, 1147-8. Tithe had been paid to the Greek churches (Hill, *op. cit.* 2, 46-47).

50

should be paid to the Church on rents and taxes derived from untithed land.

Letter 89 to the king of France provides for the first time the whole context for two extracts contained in *Bernard, Comp. III*, and *Extra*, of which other traces are left in the *Gesta Innocentii PP. III*. It occurs in *D* in a series of letters of which the other five can be identified with letters in the same sequence in the (lost) papal register; and this enables us to identify it with the letter addressed to the king of France on the subject of his treatment of Queen Ingeborg, recorded in the *Rubricellae* of the register, as letter 26 of the third year: " Regi Francie, quod adultera reiecta legitimam revocet, suo ac sui regni statui salubriter providendo " (33). This identification links it in the register with a surviving letter to the archbishop of Rouen dated 11 March 1200 (34); so that Potthast's assignment of the extracts to the summer may be rejected, and his entry under no. 1074 combined with his entry under no. 983.

The marital relations of Philip Augustus and Ingeborg had already caused concern to Pope Celestine III in 1195 and after. His protests at the divorce obtained by Philip from French bishops had neither reconciled the couple nor kept the king away from Agnes of Meran. The author of the *Gesta* rightly says that the old pope had let things drift: " Quanto idem papa ferventior circa hoc apparuit in principio, tanto tepidior est inventus in fine " (c. 50). In January 1198 the young new pope approached the problem with the clear determination to be — here as elsewhere — a new broom. One of his earliest letters (no. 4 in the register) instructed the bishop of Paris on the subject. But here, as in other matters, Innocent found more formidable opposition than he had bargained for. The case was only settled to his partial satisfaction in 1213. It is unnecessary to recount in detail the events which led to the letter of March 1200 (35). After wholly ineffective letters to the king during 1198 (POTT. 199, 362), in the following year the papal legate in France, Cardinal Peter of Capua, was instructed to lay all the French king's lands under interdict unless the king took back his wife within a month.

---

(33) POTT. 983. I use for convenience the numeration of *Theiner*'s edition, though this is faulty.

(34) POTT. 969, TH. 3, 25.

(35) See particularly R. DAVIDSOHN, *Philipp II August von Frankreich und Ingeborg* (Stuttgart, 1888) and A. CARTELLIERI, *Philipp II August* (Leipzig, 1899-1922), vols. 3 and 4.

Rather than pronounce the interdict in the heart of the king's dominions, Peter judged it discreet to convey the pope's instructions to
the French prelates in a council at Dijon, in the county of Burgundy,
which took place in December 1199. On 13 January 1200 interdict
was pronounced in France (though not enforced by all the bishops).
It was a signal for retaliatory measures by Philip and for further exchanges between king and pope which led to the sending of the legate
Octavian in July. He lifted the interdict in September. Our letter
89 belongs to an early stage in these proceedings. It records the
pope's reception of the king's messengers, and his reply to their complaints about the laying of the interdict. The letter was used by
Bernard and Peter of Benevento to elucidate the powers of legates
and the limitations on the right of appeal. But the author of the
Gesta used more of it for his narrative of the dispute, and at times
he is found to have paraphrased its sentences (36). He emphasized
the distinction which Innocent makes here about the two courses
open to Philip — to submit either to the *ius dictatum* or to the *ius
dictandum* — which found no place in the canonists' extracts. The
letter as a whole helps to illuminate the course of events and adds
one more to the fairly numerous examples of Innocent's style of
writing to peccant monarchs. Not a few of the tropes are found in
other letters of Ingeborg's case, before as well as after this time,
even in letters of Celestine III. The tone, the biblical quotations,
the medical metaphors, will also be found in letters to other princes.

APPENDIX I

1. *Pars consilii sub illo titulo: De modo recusandi iudicem.* Cum speciali
prohibicione... procedendum. *D* fol. iv. 4 *Conc. Lat.* c. 48 pars i. 4 *Comp.*
2, 12, 5. *X* 2, 28, 61. Not in the hand of the original annotator. The rubric
is that of 4 *CL*.

2. Celestinus [a] Wintoniensi [b] episcopo et abbati S. Albani. Quia Willelmus qui dicebatur... iudicaretur. *D* fol. 7 v. *JL* 14140. *ACL* 22, 9. *Cant.*
1, 55. *Roff.* 57. *Alan.* 1, 20, 3. 2 *Comp.* 2, 1, 4. *X* 2, 1, 11.

   [a] Celestinus *D*; Celestinus III *Alan.* 2 *Comp.*; Alexander *ACL Cant. Roff.*   [b] Wintoniensi *D Alan.* 2 *Comp.*; Wigorniensi *ACL*.

---

(36) MIGNE, *PL*, 214, xciii-ciii (ch. 48-57), especially ch. 51, 53.

3. Alexander 3 Forariensi [a] episcopo. Mirabile gerimus quod in excusacione... providere. *D* fol. 7v. JL - . *Frcf.*, printed in *Kan. Erg.* p. 56 no. 65, where *D* is collated, wrongly described as Dunelm. C. III. 7.

a Forariensi *D*; Ferrariensi *Frcf.*

4. *Consilium sub illo titulo: De restitucione spoliatorum.* Sepe contingit quod spoliatus... succurratur. *D* fol. 7v. 4 *Conc. Lat.* c. 39. 4 *Comp.* 2, 3, 3. *X* 2, 13, 18. In the hand of no. 1. The rubric is that of 4 *Comp.*

5. *Consilium sub illo titulo: De testimonio de auditu reprobato [a] in causa matrimonii.* Licet ex quadam... separare. *D* fol. 11v. 4 *Conc. Lat.* c. 52. 4 *Comp.* 2, 7, 6. *X* 2, 20, 47.

a reprobato *D*; reprobando 4 *CL*. In the hand of no. 1. The rubric is that of 4 *CL*.

6. *In Extra de pre(scriptionibus)* c. ult. [a] In. 3 archiepiscopo Pisano. Si diligenti animo... potestate. *D* fol. 13v. POTT. 2769. 6 May 1206. *Reg.* 9, 63. *Bern.* 1, 25, 5 and 2, 2, 4. 3 *Comp.* 2, 17, 7 and 2, 2, 4. *X* 2, 26, 17 and 2, 2, 12.

a Not the last chapter in this title of 3 *Comp.* or *X*. *D* has the full enregistered text except for " et infra " = " Super alio vero articulo... obiectum ".

7. Honorius e. s. s. d. dil. filiis decano S. Petri et penitentiario Eboracensi et magistro Ade de Richem(und) canonico de Rip(on) Eboracensis diocesis sal. et ap. ben. Cum causam que inter abbatem et monachos monasterii de Sall'... omittendis. Quod si non omnes etc. Dat' Laterani xv kal. Dec. pont. nostri anno v.

D fol. 14r. POTT. —. 17 Nov. 1220. Not in *Reg. Honorii III.*

In a different hand from the other annotators'. The mandate concerns the church of Tadcaster (co. York WR). For the judgment of the delegates see a deed by the defendant, Robert de Lelay (1224) in *The chartulary of the Cistercian abbey of St. Mary of Sallay in Craven*, ed. JOSEPH McNULTY (Yorks. Archaeol. Soc., Record Series vols. 87, 90, 1933-4) ii. 115. For an earlier mandate to other judges in the case, 23 Oct. 1218, see *ibid.* ii. 114.

8. In. 3 Eliensi et Rovestrensi [a] et magistro Benedicto [b]. Auditis et intellectis attestationibus... representent [c]. *D* fol. 14v. POTT. 2681. 3 Feb. 1206. *Reg.* 8, 205. *Chron. abbatiae de Evesham* (Rolls Series, 1863) pp. 191-3. Brit. Mus. ms. Harl. 3763 fol. 101r. *Alan.* 2, 14, 5. *Bern.* 2, 15, 5 and 1, 29, 3. 3 *Comp.* 2, 17, 5 and 1, 24, 2. *X* 2, 26, 15 and 1, 41, 3.

a Rovestn̄ *D*; Ronec episcopis *Alan.*; Roffensi episcopis *Reg. Chron*; *Bern.* 3 *Comp. X.* b Benedicto *D Alan. Bern.*; B. canonico Londoniensi *Reg. Chron*, om. et mag. B. 3 *Comp. X.* c om. Quod si forte noluerint... representent *Bern.* 3 *Comp. X.*

9. Lucius 3 Vigor [a] episcopo. Pars c. Ex literis [b]. Super eo vero [c] quod sententiam... retineri faciatis [d]. *D* fol. 15r. JL 15204. *Sangerm.* 5, 2, 11. Lyon, Bibl. de l'Univ. ms. 6 (after 2 *Comp.* 5, 9, 3). *Alan.* 2, 15, 4. 2 *Comp.* 2, 18, 4. *X* 5, 20, 2.

a Vigor *D*; Wigor *Sangerm. Alan.*; Wigorniensi 2 *Comp. X.*   b Pars c. Ex literis *D Alan.* 2 *Comp.*; Fraternitatis tue litteris susceptis et infra *Sangerm.*, om. *X.*   c vero *D*;

autem *Alan.* 2 *Comp. X.*   *d* ret. faciatis *D;* retineas *Sangerm.;* facias ret. *Alan.;* ret. facias diligenter 2 *Comp. X.*

10. *Pars consilii sub illo titulo: De modo recusandi iudicem.* Porro commonito ad appellationis... observantias speciales. *D* fol. 15v. 4 *Conc. Lat.* c. 48 pars ii. 4 *Comp.* 2, 12, 5. *X* 2, 28, 61. Cf. no. 1, in the same hand.

11. In. 3 universis episcopis per Tusciam constitutis. Quod olim in lege fuerat *a*... ulcisci. *D* fol. 22r. POTT. 1134. ? Aug. x Sept. 1200. TH. 3, 165. *Bern.* 3, 1, 4, printed by SINGER, pp. 71-3.

    a in lege fuerat *D;* fuit in lege *Bern.*

12. Innocencius 3 *a*. Cum decorem domus domini et infra *b*. Interdum ludi fiunt... zelatores *c*. *D* fol. 22v. POTT. 2967. 8 Jan. 1207. *Reg.* 9, 235. *Bern.* 3, 1, 7. 3 *Comp.* 3, 1, 4. *X* 3, 1, 12; 3, 3, 8; 1, 17, 15.

    a add Gnesnensi archiepiscopo et eius suffraganeis *Reg.*   *b* abridged as 3 *Comp. X.* *c* quod vos... zelatores *D. Reg.* 3 *Comp.; om. X.*

13. In. 3 Rosanensi archiepiscopo. Quod super hiis articulis et infra. Cum autem sacerdotes latini... facultatem. *D* fol. 23v. POTT. 919. 31 Dec. 1199. *Reg.* 2, 261. *Bern.* 3, 4, 1.

14. In. 3 Constantinopolitano patriarche. Inter quatuor animalia et infra. De clericis autem qui... detenti. *D* fol. 24v. POTT. 2860. 2 Aug. 1206. *Reg.* 9, 140. *Bern.* 1, 25, 6. 3 *Comp.* 3, 4, 2. *X* 3, 4, 10.

15. Innocencius 3 archiepiscopo Patracensi. Ex tue devocionis insinuacione recepimus et infra. In ecclesiis autem... possit agi facilius *a*. *D* fol. 24v. POTT. 3090. 19 Apr. 1207. *Reg.* 10, 51. 3 *Comp.* 3, 4, 3. *X* 3, 4, 11.

    a facilius agi possit 3 *Comp. X.*

16. Innocencius 3 archidiacono et cantori *a*. Cum iamdudum et infra. Verum quoniam... tollerari. *D* fol. 25r. POTT. 1071. ? May x June 1200. TH. 3, 106 (cf. POTT. 1186, *Reg.* 3, 41, TH. 3, 214). *Rot. III* 31. *Bern.* 3, 7, 5. 3 *Comp.* 3, 5, 5. *X* 3, 5, 18.

    a episcopo, archidiacono, et cantori Tornac' TH. etc.

17. In. 3 *a* archidiacono Senon'. Dilectus filius T. *b* canonicus Lingonensis... compescendo. *D* fol. 25v. POTT. 2754. 19 Apr. 1206. *Reg.* 9, 57. *Bern.* 3, 5, 6. 3 *Comp.* 3, 5, 6. *X* 3, 5, 19.

    a add archiepiscopo et *Reg.* etc.   *b* G. *corr. to* T. *D.*

18. *Consilium sub illo titulo: De matrimonio et de eius artacione.* Non debet reprehensibile iudicari... alligatam. *D* fol. 44r. 4 *Conc. Lat.* c. 50. 4 *Comp.* 4, 3, 3. *X* 4, 14, 8. In the hand of no. 1. The rubric does not correspond to 4 *CL* or 4 *Comp.*

19. *Consilium sub illo titulo: De pena contrahencium clamdestina coniugia.* Cum inhibicio copule... ulcionem. *D* fol. 47r. 4 *Conc. Lat.* c. 51. 4 *Comp.* 4, 2, 1. *X* 4, 3, 3. In the hand of no. 1. The rubric is that of 4 *CL.*

54

20. *De clericis qui relicto clericali habitu arma ferunt.* [a] In audiencia nostra talis... debent. *D* fol. 67v. JL 16574. 17 May 1190. *Hal.* 39. *Luc.* 28. *Segunt.* 23 (dated). *Rot. I* 25, 7. *Tanner.* app. 23. *Sangerm.* 2, 8, 2. *Abr. I* 2, 6, 1. *Gilb.* 5, 14, 11. 2 *Comp.* 5, 18, 14. *X* 5, 39, 25.

a No inscription *D;* Idem (Clemens III) preposito Focalriensi in eodem libro *Hal. Segunt.;* Idem preposito Folcalkariensi in libro iii reg. *Rot. I;* Clemens III preposito Falc. *Luc.;* Clemens preposito Folcariensi *Tanner.;* Idem ex registro Alexandri III *Sangerm.;* Idem (Celestinus) *Gilb.;* Celestinus III 2 *Comp.;* Idem (Clemens III) *X*.

21. *Consilium sub illo titulo: De pena excommunicationis iniuste.* Sub interminacione divini... castigetur. *D* fol. 71v. 4 *Conc. Lat.* c. 49. 4 *Comp.* 5, 15, 6. In the hand of no. 1. The rubric is that of 4 *CL*.

22. [a] Illam vero questionem quarto loco... medio tempore [b]. *D* fol. 74r. JL 17019. 17 June 1193. *ACL* app. in Lincoln Cathedral ms. 121 fo. 58v. *Cott.* fo. 286v. *Roff.* 151 (dated). *Pet.* 2, 81. *Crac.* 11. *Hal.* 2. *Segunt.* 107(d). *Luc.* 21. *Rot. I* 24, 2. *Tanner.* ap. 1.

a No inscription *D;* Item idem (Celestinus III) Rotomagum decano in eodem libro *Rot. I;* etc. *b D* breaks off incompletely here; *add* nihil immutari oportet. Canonica nihilominus... quamcitius abstinebit (abst. consultius *Pet. etc.*). *Pet., Luc.* etc.

D contains only one section of the letter " Prudentiam tuam "; it occurs at the beginning of a page otherwise filled with notes, following the end of 1 *Comp.* on fol. 73v. The whole letter is found in this position with other texts of 1 *Comp.* (Cf. *Repertorium*, p. 300. For references by glossators see *ibid.* pp. 324, 418 n. 3). See also C. DUGGAN, *Traditio*, 18 (1962) 461 n. 19.

23. Innoc. 3 Dolensi episcopo et Savigneo [a] et de Ardent' [b] abbatibus. Auditis et intellectis meritis... irritandam. *D* fol. 75v. POTT. 2472. 22 Apr. 1205. *Reg.* 8, 35. *Rot. III* 91 (with ending: "per apostolica... Dat' anno VIII"). *Bern.* 1, 8, 15. 3 *Comp.* 1, 6, 14. *X* 1, 6, 29.

a Savigneo *D;* Savign' *Rot. III* 3 *Comp.;* de Savigneio *Reg.;* Sagonensi *X*. *b* Ardent' *D;* Ardena *Reg. Rot. III;* Ardenna 3 *Comp. X*.

24. Idem (Innoc. III) Atrebatensi episcopo et abbati S. Bretini [a] Morinensis diocesis et S. de Vallibus [b]. Ad nostram presentiam accedentes dil. filius prepositus archidiaconi [c] et quidam alii... obstante et infra. Nos igitur... nostra cessare. *D* fol. 75v. POTT. 2481. 2 May 1205. *Reg.* 8, 45. *Bern.* 1, 8, 17. 4 *Comp.* 1, 3, 7, printed by FRIEDBERG, pp. 135-7.

a Bretini *D;* Bertini *Reg.* etc. *b add* canonico Laudunensi *Reg.* etc. *c* filius prep. archidiaconi *D;* filii prep. archidiaconus *Reg.* etc.

25. [a] Cum olim nobis de obitu... coactionem aliquam intulisse [b]. *D* fol. 76r. POTT. 949. Jan. x 21 Feb. 1200. *Reg.* 2, 277. *Bern.* 1, 8, 4. 3 *Comp.* 1, 6, 4. *X* 1, 6, 19.

a No inscription *D;* archidiacono et capitulo Capuano *Reg.* etc. *b* obitu... intulisse *D. Reg.;* obitu et infra *Bern.* 3 *Comp. X; add* Cum autem ex utriusque... committentes *Reg.* etc.

26. Alexander 3 Parisiensi episcopo et abbati S. Remigii et decano Meldensi [a]. Conquestus est nobis R... faciatis [b]. *D* fol. 78r. JL 14049. *Wig.* 7, 66. *Brug.* 31, 1. *Sangerm.* 6, 1, 3. *Abr. I* 6, 1, 1. *Alan.* 2, 5, 2. *2 Comp.* 2, 7, 2.

    a Parisiensi... Meldensi *D. Alan. 2 Comp.* (cf. *Sangerm.* 6, 1, 6); *om. Brug. Sangerm.;* Wigorn' et priori de Kinelde(wrde) *Wig.*   *b add.* permittatis turbari *Wig. Brug.*

27. Celestinus 3 [a]. Accepta conquestione canonicorum [b] quod... procedas. *D* fol. 83v. JL 14108. *Alan.* 1, 3, 7. *2 Comp.* 1, 2, 2. *X* 2, 28, 35.

    a Celestinus 3 *D;* Alex. III Tarraconensi archiepiscopo *Alan.* etc.   *b add* Pampilonensium *Alan.* etc.

28. In. 3 [a] Rotomagensi archiepiscopo et eius suffraganeis [b]. Ad reprimendam maliciam perversorum... omittas. *D* fol. 84r. POTT. 250. 1 June 1198. *Reg.* 1, 228. *Alan.* 1, 15, 3. *Bern.* 1, 23, 2. *3 Comp.* 1, 20, 2. *X* 1, 31, 8.

    a add in registro *Alan.*   *b om.* et eius suff. *3 Comp.*

29. In. 3 [a] episcopo S. Andree, abbati de Beroch, T. priori, R. archidiacono, et magistro L. officiali. Cum dil. filius abbas et cano(ni)ci etc. et infra. Ad quartum autem... prevalere [b]. *D* fol. 88r. POTT. 3053. 20 March 1207. *Reg.* 10, 31. *Rot. III* 55. *3 Comp.* 2, 5, 4. *X* 2, 12, 6.

    a In. 3... officiali *D, add* S. Andree *3 Comp.;* ...episcopo et H. abbati de Aberbruhot, Th. priori, Radulpho archidiacono, et mag. Laurentio officiali S. Andree *Reg.;* Idem episcopo S. Andree et collegis suis *Rot. III;* Idem episcopo et officiali S. Andree *X.*   *b Rot. III* gives the whole letter.

30. Alex. tercius Cestrensi episcopo [a]. Cum [b] dubia semper... revocetur. *D* fol. 88v. JL - . *Wig.* 7, 23. *Claustr.* 222. *Brug.* 48, 2. *Sangerm.* 10, 65.

    a Cestrensi episcopo *D;* Eboracensi archiepiscopo *Wig. Brug. Sangerm., add* pro archidiacono de Cestre *Wig.*   *b* Cum *D. Wig. Brug. Sangerm.;* Dum *Claustr.*

31. In. 3 Brinensi [a] episcopo. Pars c. Licet [b]. Postulasti [c] preterea utrum ... compellendus. *D* fol. 89r. POTT. 2656. ? 13 Jan. 1206. *Reg.* 8, 189. *Alan.* 2, 8, 3. *Bern.* 2, 3, 3. *3 Comp.* 2, 3, 3. *X* 2, 6, 3.

    a Brinensi *D;* Brixiensi *Reg.* etc.   *b* Pars c. Licet *D. Alan.;* Tue fraternitatis devotio... distinguendum *Reg.;* Tue frat. devotio et infra *Bern.* 3 *Comp. X.*   *c* Postulasti... fraternitati *D;* Consuluisti... fraternitati *Reg.* 3 *Comp.;* Consultationi *X.*

32. In. 3. Pars c. Ex parte tue. Super eo vero [a] quod... omittas. *D* fol. 89r. POTT. - . *Alan.* 2, 8, 2, printed by VON HECKEL, pp. 247-8.

    a vero *D;* autem *Alan. D* reads " quesivisti " for " quesisti scilicet " *Alan.*, " parcium " corr.to " partem " for *Alan* " qua parcium ", " petite et " for " petite vel ", " valiat " for " possit ", " absentabit " for " absentaverit ".

33. In. 3 archidiacono [a] Parisiensi et magistro R. de Corson [b] canonico [c]. Post cessionem dil. filii et infra. Cum igitur super hoc... admittendum. *D* fol.

56

90r. POTT. 2887. 2 Oct. 1206. *Reg.* 9, 164. *Bern.* 2, 10, 1. 3 *Comp.* 2, 11, 1. *X* 2, 19, 7.

a add and del. sancti au *D.*   *b* R. de Corson *D*; R. de Corzon *Reg.*; R. de Curcon *Bern.* 3 *Comp.*   *c add* Noviomensi Parisius commoranti *Reg. Bern.* 3 *Comp.*; *om.* et mag ... canonico *X.*

34. In. 3 episcopo Baiocensi. Cum in iure et infra. Preterea quesivisti cum... mandatur. *D* fol. 90r. POTT. 3538. 22 Nov. 1208. *Reg.* 11, 176. 3 *Comp.* 1, 18, 10. *X* 1, 29, 31.

35. Lucius tertius [a]. Precipimus ut N. ecclesiam restitui... amoveri [b]. *D* fol. 90v. JL 13825. *ACL* 22, 8. *Wig.* 4, 36. *Cant.* 1, 57. *Roff.* 54. *Sangerm.* 6, 1, 9. *Abr. I* 6, 1, 4.

a Lucius tertius *D;* Idem (Alex. III) Cantuariensi archiepiscopo et Wigorniensi episcopo *ACL* etc.   *b ACL* omits "Si quis vero... amoveri ", found in Sangerm. and all other texts and printed by SINGER, pp. 246-7.

36. Innocentius 3 priori de Bolet' [a] et J. rectori ecclesie de Thorell' [b] Ex tenore literarum... admittendi. *D* fol. 91v. POTT. 2030. 24 Nov. 1203. *Reg.* 6, 177. *Rot. III* 78. *Alan.* 2, 11, 3. *Bern.* 2, 11, 9. 3 *Comp.* 2, 12, 8. *X* 2, 20, 35.

a Bolet' *D;* Boeltum *Reg.* (other variants not noted here).   *b* Thorell' (or Thorill') *D;* Comillis *Reg.*

37. Celestinus 3 abbati [a] S. Facundi. Contingit interdum ut... fiat. *D* fol. 91v. JL 17625. *Alan.* app. 45. 2 *Comp.* 2, 14, 3. *X* 2, 22, 5.

a add et conventui *Alan.*

38. In. 3 abbati et conventui S. Petri Cugull' [a]. Cum olim essemus et infra. Te igitur cum testibus... extitisse. *D* fol. 91v. POTT. 720. 31 May 1199. *Reg.* 2, 79 (and 286). *Alan.* 2, 12, 2. *Bern.* 5, 17, 2. 3 *Comp.* 5, 16, 2. *X* 5, 33, 12.

a Cugull' *D;* Eugubini *Reg.* etc.

39. In. 3 [a]. Pars c. Super consultacione. Nos quidem consulere... absolvet. *D* fol. 92r. JL - . *Alan.* app. 80 and 2, 13, 8, printed by SINGER, *Bernardus,* p. 116. *Rot. I* fo. 162vb.

a Innocentius III *D. Alan. Rot. I,* probably in error; see no. 40.

40. Innoc. 3 [a]. Super consultacione etc. et infra. Quod vero in fine... celebrandum. *D* fol. 93r. JL - . *Alan,* app. 108 and 4, 11, 3, printed by VON HECKEL, p. 286. *Rot. I* fo. 151vb.

a Innocentius III *D. Alan* (4, 11, 3); Alexander III *Alan.* app. Cf. no. 39. The decretal was disowned by Innocent III: see SINGER, *Bernardus,* pp. 29-36, 114-7, *Traditio* 15, 480-3 and 17, 538 n. 7.

41. Vigorniensi episcopo. Ex parte tua fuit propositum... securum. *D* fol. 94r. POTT. 1664. 22 Apr. 1202. *Reg.* 5, 23. *Rot. III* 50. *Alan.* 2, 16, 9. *Bern.* 2, 18, 7. 3 *Comp.* 2, 19, 5. *X* 2, 28, 47.

42. *a* Cum super controversia etc. et infra. Mandamus quatinus si... civiles. *D* fol. 94r. POTT. 1091. ? June x July 1200. TH. 3, 131. *Bern.* 2, 17, 8. 3 *Comp.* 2, 18, 7. *X* 2, 27, 17.

a No inscription *D;* Episcopo Astoricensi et S. Ysodori ac de Carraceto abbatibus TH.; Idem (Innoc. III) Ast. ep., S. Isidori Legionensi et de Cantazeto abbatibus 3 *Comp.*

43. In. 3 Rofenen' *a* et Londoniensi episcopis *b*. Bone memorie O. de Camera... compellatis. *D* foll. 94v-95r. POTT. 2609. 21 Nov. 1205. *Reg.* 8, 154. *Abr. I* app. 1. *Bern.* 2, 18, 11. 3 *Comp.* 2, 19, 9. *X* 2, 28, 51.

a Rofenen' *D;* Rofensi *Reg.* etc.   *b add* et priori S. Albani Londoniensis diocesis *Reg.*

44. In. 3 decano Cataburgensi *a*. Cum dilecte in Christo filie abbatissa... resignato. *D* foll. 96r-95v. POTT. 2813. 17 June 1206. *Reg.* 9, 108. *Bern.* 2, 19, 1. 3 *Comp.* 2, 20, 1. *X* 2, 30, 4.

a dec. Cataburgensi *D;* de Helwatheshusen et de Herwatheshusen abbatibus et decano Padebrunensi *Reg.*

45. In. 3 Lundensi *a* archiepiscopo. Tue discrecionis prudenciam et infra. Ad illud preterea... peragendam. *D* fol. 96v. POTT. 1752. 8 Nov. 1202. *Reg.* 5, 101. *Rot. III* 52a. *Alan.* 5, 21, 15. *Bern.* 3, 1, 6. 3 *Comp.* 3, 1, 3. *X* 5, 37, 6.

a Lundensi *D Rot. III;* om. *Alan.;* Lugdunensi *Reg.;* Lundon' 3 *Comp. X.*

46. Alex. 3 Eboracensi archiepiscopo. Relatum est auribus... ordinentur. *D* fol. 97v. JL 14350. *ACL* 47, 7. *Wig.* 5, 13. *Claustr.* 333. *Bamb.* 42, 37. *Brug.* 47, 13. *Lips.* 47, 39. *Cass.* 51, 36. *Cpd.* 42, 37. *Sangerm.* 7, 109. *Tanner,* 6, 4, 3. 1 *Comp.* 2, 20, 39. *X* 3, 8, 3.

47. Innocentius 3 abbati et conventui Premonstr(at)ensi. Edoceri *a* per literas tuas postulasti *b*... discreta. *D* fol. 97v. POTT. 3305. 27 Feb. 1208. *Reg.* 11, 3. 3 *Comp.* 1, 2, 11. *X* 1, 3, 21.

a add a nobis *Reg.* etc.   *b* lit. tuas postulasti *D;* vestras lit. postulastis *Reg.;* postulastis (*om.* per vestras lit.) 3 *Comp. X.*

48. *a* Pars c. Laudabilem etc. ut infra. Rursus ut dicis quidam simpliciter *b*... continebat *c*. *D* fol. 105r. JL 17649. 21 Jan. x 12 March 1193. *Rot. I* fo. 149v. *Segunt.* 91d. *Luc.* 74. *Alan.* 4, 4, 1. 2 *Comp.* 4, 4, 2. *X* 4, 6, 6.

a No inscription *D;* Celestinus III *Luc.* etc.; Idem (Celestinus) Aconintano episcopo in libro primo reg. *Rot. I;* Idem (Cel.) Acon. episcopo in eodem libro *Segunt.*   *b* ut dicis quidam *D;* quidam ut dicis *Rot. I Segunt. Luc.;* quidam ut dicit *Alan.* 2 *Comp.;* quidam *X.*   *c* continebat *D;* continet *Segunt. Luc.;* contineret *Rot. I Alan.* 2 *Comp.;* continere videtur *X.*

The whole decretal is in *Rot. I, Segunt.,* and *Luc.* (printed p. 380). The seven other parts are in *Gilb.* (cf. VON HECKEL, pp. 206-7). In *D* this section is added at the foot of the page of *Gilb.* which contains the title "De voto et voti redemptione".

49. Innocentius III. Cum dilecti filii *a* etc. et infra. Inquiratis super premissis ... terminata. *D* fol. 112v. POTT. - . *Alan.* 5, 1, 8. 4 *Comp.* 5, 1, 1. *X* 5, 1, 20.

a dil. filii *D. Alan.;* dilectus filius 4 *Comp. X.*

58

50. In. 3 abbati S. Columbe Cenonis *a*. Ex parte tua fuit... videtur. *D* fol. 117r. POTT. 2708. 10 March 1206. *Reg.* 9, 17. *Bern.* 3, 24, 4. 3 *Comp.* 3, 23, 3. *X* 3, 30, 27.

a Senonensis *Reg.* etc.

51. In. 3 *a*. Pars cap. Officii. Postremo quesisti... solvemus *b*. *D* fol. 117v. POTT. 3660. *Reg.* 11, 262. *Alan.* app. 12 and 5, 21, 3. Montecassino ms. 46 p. 538 (addition to *Gilb.*, see *Repertorium*, p. 313). 3 *Comp.* 5, 21, 15. *X* 5, 39, 42.

a add Cynthio S. Laurentii in Lucina presbitero card. ap. sedis legato *Reg.* etc. *b om.* Ex hoc tamen articulo... solvemus 3 *Comp. X.*

52. *De electionibus episcoporum et abbatum.*
Innocencius etc. N. dei gracia Tusculano episcopo etc. Cum non possit... compescas. Dat' Laterani ii kal. Nov. p. n. a. XVI. *D* fol. 122va. POTT. 4840. 31 Oct. 1213. *Reg.* 16, 138, and other texts, whence printed in *Selected letters of Pope Innocent III concerning England,* ed. C. R. CHENEY and W. H. SEMPLE (Nelson's Medieval Texts, 1953) p. 166. Other texts include Durham, Dean and Chapter Muniments, Cartuarium vetus fol. 164v.

53. *De modo eligendi.*
Innocencius etc. N. Tuscalano (!) episcopo etc. Cum honeste principum... presentari. Dat' Lat' etc. *D* fol. 122va. POTT. - . ? late Oct. 1213. Durham, Dean and Chapter Muniments, Cartuarium vetus fol. 164v. Divided into two parts, both with address to Stephen, archbishop of Canterbury: Cambridge, Univ. Libr. ms. Ff. 5, 46 fo. xv. Printed in *Letters of Pope Innocent III concerning England and Wales,* ed. C. R. and MARY G. CHENEY (Oxford, 1967) no. 939.

54. *Increpacio pape ad Tusculanum.*
Innocencius etc. Tusculano etc. Illius testimonium invocamus... reputemur. *D* fol. 122vb. POTT. - . ? Feb. x Apr. 1214. Durham, Dean and Chapter Muniments, Cartuarium vetus fol. 165r. Printed in *Letters of Pope Innocent III* no. 968.

55. *Privilegium Innocencii de libera electione.*
Innocencius episcopus etc. ven. fratribus et dil. filiis universis ecclesiarum prelatis per Angliam constitutis etc. Dignis laudibus attollimus magnificenciam... infirmitatem. *D* fol. 122vb (first three lines of letter only). POTT. 4963. 30 March 1215. Original, London, P. R. O., S. C. 7, 19, 7, printed T. RYMER, *Foedera* (1816-30) I. i. 127 and *Selected letters of Pope Innocent III* p. 198. Many copies survive, including one in Durham, Cartuarium vetus, fol. 165v (cf. nos. 52-54).

56. *a* Sedes apostolica etc. et infra. Questioni autem qua queritur... competat. *D* fol. 124r. POTT. - . *Tanner.* app. 11, printed by HOLTZMANN, p. 144.

a No inscription *D;* Innocentius Senonensi archiepiscopo *Tanner.* The address was perhaps suggested by that of *Tanner* app. 12 (POTT. 2062), which has the same incipit " Sedes apostolica ". But *Tanner*. app. 12 (= *Reg.* 6, 190) is complete, and this cannot be a part of it.

57. Innocencius 3. Idem Henrico *a* S. Hillarii canonico Pictav'. Super literis que... interponat. *D* fol. 124r. POTT. 3519. 18 Oct. 1208. *Reg.* 11, 161. 3 *Comp.* 1, 2, 10. *X* 1, 3, 20.

a Henrico *D;* Magistro Aimero *Reg.;* Aymoni 3 *Comp.*

58. *a* Proposuit nobis dil. filius W... differatis. *D* fol. 132r. JL -. *Wig.* 4, 9. *Claustr.* 150. *ACL* 49, 11. *Sangerm.* 7, 48. *Abr. I* 7, 3, 2.

a No inscription *D;* Dunelmensi episcopo et fratribus de (*om.* de *ACL*) de Revesbi *Wig.* *ACL;* Idem (Lucius III) *Sangerm.*

59. *a* Veniens ad ap. sedis clemenciam *b* W... assignes. *D* fol. 132r. JL -. *Wig.* 4, 12. *Claustr.* 153. *Sangerm.* 7, 51, printed by SINGER, p. 297. *Abr. I* 7, 3, 4.

a No inscription *D;* Idem (Lucius III) Eboracensi archiepiscopo *Sangerm. Abr. I;* Ebor. archiepiscopo *Wig.*   *b* ap. sed. cle. *D. Sangerm. Abr. I;* nos *Wig.*

60. In. 3 Machanensi *a* episcopo. Accedens ad ap. sedem... persone. *D* fol. 141va. POTT. 1066. ? May x June 1200. TH. 3, 92. *Rot. III* 30. *Alan.* 2, 6, 3. *Bern.* 5, 11, 1. 3 *Comp.* 5, 9, 1. *X* 3, 5, 24 and 5, 17, 7.

a Machanensi *D;* Machoniensi *Alan.;* Cracoviensi TH.; Crachoniensi *Rot. III;* Glaconiensi 3 *Comp.;* Zamorensi (*or* Saronensi) *X.*

61. In. 3 abbati Trium Fontium *a*. Ex parte abbatisse... accedant. *D* fol. 143v. POTT. 1803. 10 Jan. 1203. *Reg.* 5, 137. *Alan.* 5, 16, 3. *Bern.* 5, 17, 3. 3 *Comp.* 5, 16, 3. *X* 5, 33, 13.

a abbati Trium Fontium *D;* electo Cathalaunensi et abbati Trium Fontium *Reg.* etc.

62. In. 3 abbati de Wltahm (!) et decano S. Pauli et priori S. Trinitatis Lond'. Prior et conventus de Meretun... procedatis. *D* fol. 144r. POTT. -. Printed in *Letters of Pope Innocent III concerning England and Wales* no. 817B.

63. In. 3. Ex conquestione dil. filiorum nostrorum prioris et monachorum de Dover... imponatis. *D* fol. 146v. POTT. -. ? Jan. 1198 x May 1199. Printed in *Letters of Pope Innocent III* no. 125.

64. In. 3 Herbipolensi episcopo *a*. Officium nobis credite... omittas. *D* fol. 147v. POTT. 875. 24 Nov. 1199. *Reg.* 2, 216. *Alan.* 2, 13, 5.

a Herbipolensi episcopo *D. Alan.;* Archiepiscopo Maguntino episcopo Sabinensi *Reg.*

65. In. 3*a* episcopo et canonicis sancti V *b*. Ex tenore literarum... reservetur. *D* fol. 147v. JL 17641. Bamberg ms. Can. 20 fo. 62v. Salzburg, St. Peter's Archabbey a. ix. 18 (see *Kan. Erg.* no. 48 and p. 168). *Rot. I* 24, 8

60

(fo. 162v*b*). *Luc.* 22. *Monac.* 38. *Alcob. II* 22. *Alan.* 2, 13, 6. Printed *Kan. Erg.* no. 48 pp. 41-42.

a In. 3 *D. Alan.;* Celestinus III *Rot. I Luc.;* Idem (Cel. III) *Alcob. II Bamberg Salzburg.* *b* episcopo et canonicis sancti V *D. Alan.;* priori et can. S. Venantii *Bamberg;* priori... Valn' *Salzburg;* priori... Vernacii *Rot. I;* priori... Ranerii *Luc.;* priori... Venecii *Alcob. II.*

66. Alex. III Marco *a* cardinali. Super eo vero... dissolvi. *D* fol. 148v. JL 14161. *Pet.* 1, 27. *Brug.* 53, 11. *Sangerm.* 9, 73. *Abr. I* 8, 13, 2. *Alan.* 2, 11, 2. 2 *Comp.* 2, 12, 2. *X* 2, 20, 22. See also *Kan. Erg.* no. 2 p. 20.

a Marco *D. Alan.* 2 *Comp.;* L(aboranti) S. Marie in porticu (card.) apostolice sedis legato *Brug.;* Marito in porticu *Pet.;* Martico in portico *Sangerm.;* Marco porticii *Abr. I;* Mattheo *X.*

67. In. 3 Abricensi (!) et de Lucen' et de Monte Morall' *a* abbatibus Abricensis diocesis. Ex insinuatione dil. filii prioris... terminetis. *D* fol. 151r. Pott. 2412. 10 Feb. 1205. *Reg.* 7, 216. *Bern.* 2, 18, 10. 3 *Comp.* 2, 19, 8. *X* 2, 28, 50. See also Singer, *Neue Beiträge,* p. 391.

a Abricensi... Morall' *D;* ... Abrincensi episcopo et... de Montemorello et de Lucerna *Reg.,* other variants not noted here.

68. *De rescriptis.*

In. 3 *a*. Plerumque contingit quod... habetur *b*. *D* fol. 151v. Pott. 3671. *Reg.* 11, 275. 3 *Comp.* 1, 2, 13. *X* 1, 3, 23.

a No address in *Reg,* where this forms part of the canonical collection added to book 11 (cf. *Traditio,* 15, 471-2); Idem (Innoc. III) 3 *Comp. X.* *b* habetur *D;* habeatur *Reg.* etc.

69. Innocencius 3 episcopo Parisiensi *a*. Vestra prudencia nos... sepissime altercacione discucietur et infra. Super quo vobis... puniatis. *D* fol. 156v. Pott. 3043. 11 March 1207. *Reg.* 10, 15. Cf. *Letters of Pope Innocent III concerning England and Wales* no. 638.

a Episcopo Parisiensi *D;* Episcopo et... decano Parisiensi *Reg.*

70. *a* Fraternitatis *b* tue per... civili *c*. *D* fol. 158ra. Pott. 440. 23 Nov. 1198. *Reg.* 1, 432. *Rot. III* 19. *Alan.* 5, 14, 3. *Bern.* 3, 2, 1. 3 *Comp.* 5, 15, 1. *X* 5, 32, 2.

a No inscription *D;* Huberto Cantuariensi archiepiscopo *Reg.;* Idem (Innoc. III *X*) Cant' archiepiscopo *Rot. III* 3 *Comp. X;* Innoc. III in registro Cant' archiepiscopo *Alan.* *b* fraternitatis *D;* fraternitati *Reg.* etc. *c* fraternitatis (= Migne, line 263) ... civili (line 285) *D;* Cum ex iniuncto nobis apostolatus officio... civili (line 285). Clericos preterea qui... expiari (line 370 followed by date) *Reg.;* parts as follows: Cum ex iniuncto et infra. Cum autem que premisimus (line 251) ... civili (line 285) et infra. Quia iustum est (line 307) ... me credunt etc. (line 366) *Rot. III;* Cum ex iniuncto nobis officio etc. ut infra. Infra *XXX* dies (line 266) ... innovare (line 296) *Alan.;* Cum ex iniuncto nobis et infra. Cum autem que premisimus (line 251)... expiari (line 370) *Bern.;* Cum ex iniuncto et infra. Districta (*om.* dudum) tibi (line 9) ... cessares (line 13) et infra. Cum autem que (line 251) ... civili (line 285) et infra. Super eo quoque (line 333) ... expiari (line 370) 3 *Comp.;* Cum ex iniuncto et infra. Fraternitati tue mandamus quatinus quicquid edificatum est in ecclesia de Lameth post operis nuntiationem (line 263) ... irritandum (line 284) et infra. Super eo quoque (line 333) ... expiari (line 370) *X.*

An annotator of Durham Cathedral MS. C. III. 3   61

71. Innocencius episcopus etc. dil. filiis archidiacono, S. Ridell' clerico, et magistro Rened' *a* de Sausenton canonico Lincoln' *b* sal. et ap. benedictionem *c*. Dilecto filio magistro *d* W. clerico... reputari. Nullis literis etc. *e* Quod si non omnes etc. *e* Dat' Anagnie xvii kal. Sept. p. n. a. quarto *f*. D fol. 158ra. Pott. - . 16 Aug. 1201. Bodleian ms. Tanner 8 p. 591. Printed *Letters of Pope Innocent III concerning England and Wales* no. 348.

   a *recte* Benedicto D.   b ? *recte* London' D.   c Innoc. ... benedictionem D; Innoc. III ms. Tanner.   d magistro D; om. ms. Tanner.   e etc. D; om. ms. Tanner.   f Dat' ... quarto D; om. ms. Tanner.

72. Innocencius III *a*. R. de Columbellis *b* super ecclesia... et vacuum habetur *c*. D fol. 158rb. JL 15210. *Alan.* 1, 3, 8. *2 Comp.* 1, 2, 6. *Rainer.* app. 7 (cf. *Repertorium*, p. 310).

   a Innocencius III D; Lucius III *Alan.* 2 Comp.; Innoc. III Lucius III *Rainer.*   b R. de Columb'is D; R. de Columpnellis *Alan.*; Rotbertus de Columbellis 2 Comp.; A. de Columbellis *Rainer.*   c et vac. habetur D; habeatur et vacuum *Alan.* 2 Comp. *Rainer.*

73. *Error condicionis matrimonium solvit.*
In. 3 Racesburgensi *a* episcopo. Ad nostram noveris... concedas potestatem *b*. D fol. 158rb. Pott. 1356. ? April x May 1201. Th. 4, 45. *Rot. III* 37. *Alan.* 4, 5, 1. *Bern.* 4, 7, 1. 3 *Comp.* 4, 7, 1. X 4, 9. 4.

   a Racesburgensi D; Razeburgensi Th. 3 Comp. X; Racesburgenensi *Rot. III;* Zaresburgensi (archiepiscopo) Bern.; om. *Alan.*   b potestatem D; facultatem *Rot. III Alan. Bern.* 3 Comp.

74. *In obbediencia (!) prestanda prelatis prescriptio locum non habet.*
In. 3 priori et capitulo S. Torquati *a*. Cum non liceat... ratam habemus *b*. D fol. 158rb. Pott. 1360. ? April x May 1201. Th. 4, 50. *Rot. III* 38. *Alan.* 2, 14, 4.

   a In. 3 ... Torquati D. *Rot. III;* Innoc. III in registro priori et capitulo sancti A. *Alan.*; priori et capitulo S. Torcari TH.   b habemus D; habebimus et faciemus autore domino inviolabiliter observari *Rot. III Alan.* Alan's text was wrongly connected by Von Heckel with Pott. 800; see *Traditio*, 11 (1955) 156.

75. *Non debent subiecti obbedire (!) ei qui maiori non obbedit.*
Idem Coll' *a* archiepiscopo. Mediator dei et... exhibere. D fol. 158rb. Pott. 1864. 22 March 1203. *Reg.* 6, 24-25. *Alan.* 1, 14, 2 (abridged).

   a Coll' D; Colocensi Reg.; Collocenensi *Alan.*

76. *De restitutione.*
Idem abbati et conventui S. Silvestri. Ecclesia S. Marie... habere. D fol. 158va. Pott. 879. 27 Nov. 1199. *Reg.* 2, 239. *Bern.* 2, 9, 1 (abridged). 3 *Comp.* 2, 2, 5 and 2, 6, 1. X 1, 2, 10 and 2, 16, 3-4.

77. *Revocari debet quod post legitimam appellacionem vel earum aliquam *a* fiunt (!).*
b Significavit nobis dil. filius I. magister... audiatis etc. *c* D fol. 159ra. Pott.

2208. 14 May 1204. *Reg.* 7, 68. *Bern.* 2, 18, 8 (abridged). 3 *Comp.* 2, 19, 6.
X 2, 28, 48.

a add fit, *expunged D.* *b* No inscription *D;* .. episcopo, decano, et.. precentori Herefordensibus *Reg.* etc. *c* etc. *D;* diligenter app. remota... altero etc. *Reg.;* diligenter app. remota... proponenda 3 *Comp.;* *X* ends at: factum partes etc.

78. Simplici assercioni non creditur. *a* Literas etc. A mulierem renitentem et invitam in monasterium truderunt etc. ne unquam consensit quod probavit et aufugit cum potuit. Canonici et moniales e contra dicebant quod consenserat, suam tamen assercionem simplicem sacramento confirmare negantes *b*. Nos attendentes... credendum *c*. *D* fol. 159ra. POTT. 2228. 31 May 1204. *Reg.* 7, 85. *Rot. III* 84. *Bern.* 1, 28, 3. 3 *Comp.* 2, 11, 3.

a No inscription *D;* Priori de Essebi et magistro H. de Gillevillis (Gilevilla *Bern.*) canonico Lincolniensi et magistro A. de Wilna (Villa *Bern.*) rectori ecclesie de Bareswrth Lincolniensis diocesis *Reg. Bern.* 3 *Comp.;* Idem priori de Essebi et magistro H. de Vilevilla canonico Lincoliensis diocesis *Rot. III.* *b* Literas... negantes (only a digest of the text) *D;* Literas vestras accepimus... questionem *Reg. Rot. III Bern.* 3 *Comp.* *c add* Nos igitur attendentes... discretioni vestre per... procedatis *Reg.* etc.; *add* Nullis literis etc. quod si non omnes duo vestrum etc. Dat' Laterani ii kal. Jun. *Reg.*

79. *Fructus debent computari in sortem.*
a Cum contra nobilem *b*. *D* fol. 159ra. POTT. 3869. 1198 x 1209. 3 *Comp.* 3, 17, 3. *X* 3, 21, 6.

a No inscription *D;* L. de Montefortino 3 *Comp.;* R. *X.* *b* nobilem *D;* nob. virum *G.* Deentem civem... corporalem 3 *Comp.;* G. civem... corporalem *X.* *D* contains no more than the incipit.

80. *Usque ad annum delegatus potest excercere iurisdictionem.*
a Querenti quid per... invenitur. *D* fol. 159ra. POTT. 3865. 1198 x 1209. Lambeth ms. 105 fo. 218. *Alcob. II* 40. *Alan.* 1, 13, 1. *Bern.* 5, 24, 4 and 1, 21, 7. 3 *Comp.* 5, 23, 4 and 1, 18, 5. *X* 5, 40, 20 and 1, 29, 26.

a No inscription *D;* Innoc. III *Alan.;* eidem (archiep. Cant.) Lambeth ms.; Idem priori S. Fridiani Lucani *Alcob. II* 3 *Comp. X;* Idem Prenestino episcopo *Bern.*

81. *Ostendenda est terra super qua quis convenitur.*
a Significantibus etc. ipsi *b* T. et R... et causam audiatis, alioquin remittatis eos ad priores iudices *c*. *D* fol. 159ra. POTT. 3868. *Alan.* 2, 2, 1. *Bern.* 2, 18, 9. 3 *Comp.* 2, 19, 7. *X* 2, 28, 49 and 2, 3, 2.

a No inscription *D;* Innoc. III magistro G. archidiacono et W. Normanno et G. de Crethes (*om.* de Crethes *Alan*) canonicis Suessionibus (Suedinensibus *Alan.*) *Alan.* 3 *Comp. X.* *b om.* etc. ipsi *Alan.* etc. *c* et causam audiatis... iudices *D* (later addition in same hand), *Alan;* attemptatum aud. causam et ap. re. fine debito terminetis 3 *Comp.;* attentatum etc. *X.*

82. *Que in capitulo aguntur non facile possunt probari nisi per canonicos a*.
b Veniens ad apostolicam... proponere *c*. *D* fol. 159ra. POTT. 2270. 12 July 1204. *Reg.* 7, 117. *Alan.* 1, 18, 1. *Bern.* 2, 11, 13. 3 *Comp.* 2, 12, 11. *X* 2, 20, 38.

a D's rubric is taken from the last sentence of the letter, omitted below. *b* No inscrip-

An annotator of Durham Cathedral MS. C. III. 3   63

tion *D. Reg.;* Idem de Novem Fontium (Novo Fontin. 3 *Comp.;* Novo Fonte *X*) et Case Dei abbatibus in Claromontensi diocesi constitutis *Bern.* 3 *Comp. X.;* Innoc. III in registro Eliensi Episcopo. Pars cap. Pastoralis officii *Alan.*   *c D* breaks off, leaving a quarter column and a whole column to complete the letter. For the variants of the other texts see VON HECKEL, *Gilbertus-Alanus,* p. 241.

83. Innoc. 3*ᵃ* Cantuariensi archiepiscopo. Quod super his sedem ap. et infra *ᵇ*. Quesivisti preterea quid... expressum. *D* fol. 159r*b*. POTT. 1137. ? Aug. x Oct. 1200. TH. 3, 160. *Rainer.* 39, 7. *Dunelm. IV* no. 30 (fo. 128v). *Alan.* 3, 18, 7. *Bern.* 2, 12, 2. 3 *Comp.* 2, 13, 2. *X* 2, 22, 7.

a add in registro *Alan.*   *b* Quod super... infra *D* etc.; *om. Alan.*

84. Innocentius 3 Cenadiensi episcopo et abbati de Ciscor' *ᵃ*. Cum in iuventute... commendantes *ᵇ*. *D* fol. 159r*b*. POTT. 2837. 7 July 1206. *Reg.* 9, 113. *Bern.* 2, 13, 2. 3 *Comp.* 2, 14, 2. *X* 2, 23, 15.

a Ciscor' *D;* Cikedor' *Reg.;* Ciquedor' 3 *Comp.*   *b* Space left in *D*, perhaps for completion of letter: " Quia vero pater... veritatem " (cf. *Bern.* 5, 18, 5. 3 *Comp.* 5, 17, 3. *X* 5, 34, 12)·

85. Innocentius 3 Metensi archidiacono. Tua nuper a nobis devotio *ᵃ*... respondendum. *D* fol. 159r*b*. POTT. 1447. July x Aug. 1201. TH. 4, 128. *Rot. III* 44a. *Bern.* 3, 9, 2. 3 *Comp.* 3, 7, 2.

a nuper a nobis devotio *D. Rot. III Bern.;* nuper devotio (*or* nobis nuper devotio) 3 *Comp. D*'s text corresponds to 3 *Comp.,* not to the fuller version of *Rot. III.*

86. *Episcopales translationes non possunt fieri absque pape assensu.* Innocencius Bambergensi episcopo et magistro Prepositino scolastico Maguntinensi. Licet in tantum etc. Hoc autem... transire. *D* fol. 159va. POTT. 942. 26 Jan. 1200. *Reg.* 2, 278. *Rot. III* 54. *Bern.* 1, 7, 4 (further abridged). 3 *Comp.* 1, 5, 4. *X* 1, 7, 4.

87. Idem Toletano archiepiscopo et abbati S. Leucadie. Accedens ad presentiam... fatigari. *D* fol. 159va. POTT. 952. 22 x 29 Feb. 1200. TH. 3, 3. *Rainer.* 33, 1. *Dunelm. IV* 32 (fo. 129 r*b*). *Alan.* app. 98.

88. Idem Tripolitano et Anteteredensi *ᵃ* episcopo (!). Accedens ad presentiam... patiatur. *D* fol. 159va. POTT. 956. Feb. x March 1200. TH. 3, 5. Printed below.

a Anteteredensi *D;* Anteradensi TH.

89. Idem illustri regi Francorum. Novit ille qui... adimpleres. *D* fol. 159rva. POTT. 1074. ? March 1200. TH. 3, 26. Fragments in *Bern.* 1, 22, 6 and 2, 18, 3. 3 *Comp.* 1, 19, 5 and 2, 19, 1. *X* 1, 30, 7 and 2, 28, 43. Printed in full below.

90. *ᵃ* Si terrarum principes... miraris (!) *ᵇ*. *D* fol. 160ra. POTT. 1005. ? 21 Apr. 1200. TH. 3, 31. *Alan.* 1, 16, 5 (abridged). *Bern.* 1, 25, 1, printed by SINGER p. 51.

a No inscription *D;* Episcopo Castellanensi TH.; Innoc. III in registro *Alan.;* Idem Castellano episcopo *Bern.*   *b* miraris *D;* merearis *Alan. Bern.*

64

91. [a] Accedens et infra. Cum igitur nobis... possessione gauderet [b]. *D* fol. 160r*a*. Pott. 1001. 5 Apr. 1200. Th. 3, 51. *Urkunden... der Republik Venedig*, ed. G. L. F. Tafel and G. M. Thomas (*Font. rer. austr. dipl. Abt.* II, xii, 1856) 282. *Rot. III* 28. *Bern.* 2, 3, 2. 3 *Comp.* 2, 3, 2. *X* 2, 6, 2.

a No inscription *D;* Ierosolimitano patriarche et archiepiscopo Cesariensi *Urkunden,* etc. *b* gauderet *D;* letetur *Urkunden,* etc. Only *Urkunden* has the complete text, which continues "Ideoque fraternitati vestre... " to the date.

92. [a] Cum [b] ex literis... resedit [c]. *D* fol. 160r*a*. Pott. 1013. ? Apr. 1200. Th. 3, 67. *Bern.* 1, 29, 5. 3 *Comp.* 1, 24, 4. *X* 1, 41, 5.

a No inscription *D;* Episcopo et capitulo Oscensibus Th. etc. *b* Cum *D;* Tum *Bern.* 3 *Comp. X.* *c add* Ut an data... circumventus *Bern.* 3 *Comp.;* Ut an data... procedemus *X.*

93. *De regularibus transeuntibus ad religionem.* [a] Licet quibusdam monachis... alienus. *D* fol. 160r*b*. Pott. 2763. 29 Apr. 1206. *Reg.* 9, 62. Cambridge, Univ. Libr. ms. Ff. 4, 1 fo. 130r (with date). *Bern.* 3, 25, 4. 3 *Comp.* 3, 24, 4. *X* 3, 31, 18.

a No inscription *D;* .. priori et conventui Dunelmensibus *Reg.* Cambridge ms.

94. Innocentius I. cardinali. Licet de plenitudine... detentore. *D* fol. 160v*a*. Pott. - . Feb. x Oct. 1206. Printed in *Letters of Pope Innocent III concerning England and Wales* no. 719.

95. Alexander abbati et monachis S. Andree. Si de terra... surripiendas. *D* fol. 160v*a*. JL 13739. *ACL* 38, 4. *Belv.* 4, 9. *Wig.* 2, 17. *Cant.* 1, 62. *Roff.* 50. *Fontan.* 2, 29. *Claustr.* 105. *Sangerm.* 6, 7, 16. *Tanner.* 5, 6, 10. 1 *Comp.* 5, 28, 9. *X* 5, 33, 6.

96. *Qui duas commissiones ad diversos impetravit utroque debet carere.* Innocentius 3 [a] R. [b] cantori et R. priori de Monte Leprosorum et I. de Sagio canonico Rotomagensibus [c]. Ex tenore literarum... utriusque. *D* fol. 160v*a*. Pott. 1966. 12 July 1203. *Reg.* 6, 120. *Rot. I* fo. 159v*a*. *Alan.* 1, 3, 9. *Bern.* 1, 4, 6. 3 *Comp.* 1, 2, 5. *X* 1, 3, 16.

a add in registro *Alan.* *b om.* R. *Rot. I.* *c om.* et I. de Sagio can. Rot. *Alan.*

APPENDIX II

88.

Idem Tripolitano et Antaradensi episcopis [a].

Accedens ad presenciam nostram venerabilis frater noster Paphensis episcopus tam pro ecclesia sua quam pro aliis in Cipri insula constitutis oblata

a Anteteredensi episcopo *D*.

nobis peticione monstravit quod cum ipso principio constitucionis earum de voluntate karissimi in Christo filii A. illustris regis Ierusalem et Cipri et Latinorum in eadem *b* insula commorancium fuerit ordinatum ut decime ipsis ecclesiis ab eodem rege et Latinis omnibus ibidem existentibus de universis de quibus homo Latinus et Christianus decimas dare tenetur sine diminucione qualibet solvantur *c*, tam ipse rex quam quidam alii eiusdem regni, volentes sicut non convenit retro respicere et quod promiserunt domino cum integritate persolvere irracionabiliter retinere, tercias de fructibus et laboribus Grecorum quas percipiunt, de quibus *d* decime solvi debent ecclesiis memoratis, pro certo precio maliciose vendentes, de bizanciis illis qui eis de fructibus et laboribus provenire noscuntur decimas ecclesiis tribuere contradicunt. Preterea cum de fetibus animalium sicut tam in scripto concessionis ipsius regis quam privilegio felicis memorie C. *e* pape predecessoris nostri continetur expressum, dare *f* decimas debeant, ipsi sicut dicitur fetus armentorum *g* et equitiorum (!) excludunt *h* et non nisi de minoribus animalibus decimas asserunt persolvendas. Vero nos, volentes quod serenitas regia in bone voluntatis proposito perseveret et suos faciat perdurare, per scripta nostra rogavimus regem ipsum et ei *j* in remissionem iniunximus *k* peccatorum ut ipse decimas ecclesiis sine diminucione persolvat, retentas hucusque resarciat, et faciat a Latinis aliis *l* cum integritate persolvi; nec inde *m* debitum suum per aliquam exemptionem vel pactum diminuat vel ab aliis diminui quantum in se fuerit patiatur *n*.

---

b eadam *D.*   *c* solventur *D.*   *d* de quibus repeated *D.*   *e* S. *D.*   *f* darent *D.*
g ? armentorum, part oblit. *D.*   *h* excludere *D.*   *j* eis *D.*   *k* iniunctissimus *D.*   *l* alii
D.   *m* adeo *D.*   *n* patitur *D.*

89.

Idem illustri regi Francorum.

Novit ille qui nichil ignorat personam tuam de corde puro et conscientia bona et fide non ficta diligimus et ad honorem et profectum ipsius ferventi animo aspiramus. Recognoscimus enim et fatemur quod reges *a* et regnum Francorum in devocione sedis apostolice pre ceteris *b* regnis et regibus *c* non solum prosperitatis tempore set etiam in adversitatis articulo firmius perstiterunt, et ideo, preter commune debitum quo cuntis (!) tenemur, asserimus et testamur nos et Rome ecclesiam tibi et regno tuo teneri specialiter ad graciam et favorem. Verum quanto personam regiam 'sinceriori caritate diligimus, tanto de hiis que ad salutem tuam pertinere noscuntur nos oportet sollicius cogitare, cum et propter debitum officii pastoralis coram districto iudice teneamur in novissimo discussionis examine de te reddere racionem. Intelligentes ergo pro certo, cum id quasi notorium nulla possit tergiversacione celari, quod sentencia illa divorcii, quin *d* immo illius ludibrii fabula (1), contra karissimam

---

a regis *D.*   *b* teceris *D.*   *c* corr. from regalibus *D.*   *d* quod *D.*

(1) Cf. *Gesta Innocentii*, ch. 53 (col. c) and *Reg.* 2, 197.

66

in Christo filiam nostram I. Francorum reginam illustrem, solam et indefensam et quid *e* ageretur penitus ignorantem ut pote lingue *f* Francorum ignaram, subito quasi cum impetu, iuris ordine non servato, fuit *g* promulgata, quam velud ipso iure nullam felicis memorie C. papa predecessor noster irritam nunciavit (2), ad quam non oportebat in iudicii forma procedere cum in mandatis non sit ordo iudiciarius observandus, intelligentes etiam nichilominus quod, post appellacionem ex abundanti ad sedem apostolicam interpositam quam ipsa regina sepe fuit per nuncios subsecuta, et post inhibicionem per literas et per nuncios a sede apostolica tibi factam ne interim quasi lite pendente aliam superduceres, (fo. 159v*b*) tu minus discreto usus consilio et predictam reginam a te illicite removere ac aliam illicite superducere procurasti, serenitatem vestram per literas nostras frequenter curavimus ammonere ut superinductam a consorcio tuo *h* removeres et reginam reciperes memoratam, faciens ei regalem honorificentiam exiberi (!), iuris tibi licentiam non negantes quominus facta restitutione legitima postmodum loco et tempore competentibus audiremus benigne si quid contra duceres *j* racionabiliter proponendum ; set cum fuisset a nobis diutius expectatum in nullo sumus exauditi. Ne vero contra mandatum divinum aput nos esset accepcio personarum, si aliter iudicaremus de divitibus et potentibus et aliter de pauperibus et abiectis et in manibus nostris esset iniqua mensura et statera *k* dolosa ut aliter istis et illis aliter metiretur, dilecto filio nostro P. sancte Marie in via lata diacono *l* cardinali tunc temporis legato apostolice sedis dedimus in mandatis ut, omni appellacione remota, nisi monitis nostris adquiesceres, in *m* totam terram tuam interdicti sententiam *n* promulgaret, ita quod preter baptisma parvulorum et penitencias moriencium nullus in ea presumeret divinum officium celebrare. Ipse vero mandati nostri fidelis et diligens executor, licet apud Divionum ex parte regia fuerit appellatum, idem cardinalis, non ut appellacioni deferret set differet ad tempus, ut alibi mandatum nostrum commodius adimpleret, tandem apud Viennam, quibusdam archiepiscopis et episcopis convocatis inter quos quidam de regno tuo fuere presentes, dictam sentenciam promulgavit, et mandavit eam per literas suas quibus eam tenorem literarum inseruit nostrarum inviolabiliter observari. Regalis autem sublimitas, quod dolentes referimus, contra eos qui tamquam obbediencie *o* filii sentenciam illam servare ceperunt in tantum excanduit quod eos rebus propriis spoliatos a sedibus suis compulit *p* exulare, non attendens quod in his que ad eius iurisdictionem pertinent temporalem apostolica sedes eam nullatenus impedivit *q* quo minus ei obbediatur (!) a subditis set pocius eam adiuvit quociens exspedire (!) cognovit; unde nec ipsa spiritualem *r* iurisdictionem apostolice sedis debuit impedire quo minus eam posset per sibi subditos excercere. Nuper (3) autem primo dilectos filios nostros Michaelem et Walterum *s* milites et postmodum

---

e quod *D.*   *f* linguam *D.*   *g* fuerit *D.*   *h* suo *D.*   *j* contradiceres *D.*   *k* statura *D.*   *l* a(post.) s(edis) for diacono *D.*   *m* etiam *D.*   *n* vel ad satisfactionem congruam interpolated *D.*   *o* obbedire *D.*   *p* compuluerit *D.*   *q* corr. from impediret *D.*   *r* corr. from specialem *D.*   *s* di. fi. nostri nichil Walterus *D.*

(2) JL 17241-3, and cf. *Gesta*, ch. 50 (col. xcv).

(3) The extract in *Bern.* 1, 22, 6, etc., begins here and extends to " suscepisset ".

dilectum filium magistrum F. decanum Aurelianensem cum literis tuis benigne recepimus et curavimus multipliciter honorare *t*, sicut per ipsos poterit plenius tue serenitati patere. Ipsi autem in nostra et fratrum nostrorum presencia constituti contra eundem cardinalem ex parte tua querimoniam intenderunt, videlicet quod, cum tibi esset certa racione suspectus, post appellacionem ad nos interpositam extra fines regni Francorum in terram tuam interdicti sentenciam promulgavit; qui eciam *u* in animam tuam promiserunt et obtulerunt iurare quod tu coram legatis et delegatis nostris super hoc negocio iuri stabis; et quod propter huiusmodi negocium *v* nec per nos nec per alios fueris ex parte nostra citatus ut iuri pareres, predictam petentes sentenciam recepta huiusmodi caucione iuratoria relaxari. Ceterum ad ea que contra cardinalem obiecerant et eis respondimus et tue magnificencie respondemus quod et si fines regni Francie exierat nondum tamen fuerat metas legationis sue egressus, cum non solum in regno Francorum set in Viennensi, Lugdunensi, Bisuntinensi provinciis iniunctam sibi a nobis legacionis sollicitudinem suscepisset. Preterea (4), dictam interdicti sentenciam ipse non edidit set pocius explicavit, nec fuit dictator ipsius set *x* verius executor. Unde cum secundum ius canonicum et legale ab executoribus non licet appellari (!) nisi forte modum excederent exequendo, et nos in literis super hoc directis ad ipsum appellacionis obstaculum curavimus inibere (!), huiusmodi appellacioni non fuerat deferendum. De suspicionis obiectu, licet eum merito tibi fuisse non credamus suspectum, non tamen et si fuisset propter appellacionem interpositam ab eo desistere debuisset *y* ad quod non proprio motu set nostro pocius precepto processit. Quod (5) autem nobis offers iuratoriam caucionem credimus distinguendum: utrum iuri dictato intelligas an dictando. Si iuri dictato, ut videlicet secundum ius quod dictavimus a consortio tuo superinductam removeas et reginam recipias antedictam, libenter recipiamus caucionem oblatam, immo sine caucione qualibet, si hoc feceris, pro regie dignitatis honore sentenciam relaxemus interdicti, dum modo prius episcopi et clerici destituti plenam fuissent restitucionem adepti. Si vero iuri dictando, videlicet ut secundum ius quod dictabimus affinitatis articulus decideretur, licet te *z* adeo ecclesie Romane credimus esse devotum quod sentenciam quam tulerit recipias et observes et ob hoc caucionem huiusmodi non petamus, ipsam tamen non denegamus recipere si eam sponte volueris exibere (!) ad cautelam, dummodo superinducta remota reginam prius recipias memoratam. Ad exequendum autem ius quod dictavimus non erat utique tibi facienda citacio set ammonicio premittenda. Cum iuxta canonicas et legittimas sancciones acusacione (!) non egeant manifesta, monemus celsitudinem tuam et exortamur (!) in domino quatinus deum habens pre oculis quid ad salutem, honorem, et famam tibi maius expediat intra te ipsum atenta (!) meditacione revolvas, pensesque sollicite quod nichil prodest *a* homini si mundum universum lucretur, anime vero sue detrimentum patiatur, et quod non feliciter regnat qui deo eciam observacione catholice disci-

---

t honerare *D.*   *u* et *D.*   *w* negociacionem *D.*   *x* se *D.*   *y* debuisse *D.*   *z* om. te *D.*
a prodes *D.*

(4) The extract in *Bern.* 2, 18, 3, etc., begins here and extends to " processit ".
(5) Cf. *Gesta Innocentii*, ch. 53 (col. xcix).

pline non servit, cum servire deo secundum sacre scripture testimonium sit regnare. Si enim ut debes sensualitatem subbicias (!) racioni, si diligenter inspicias et subtiliter discucias, veraciter [b] intelligas plenius nostre caritative [c] dilictionis (!) affectum, quia per hoc non nisi correccionem tuam querimus et salutem, officio medentis utentes, quod si forte morbus egrotantis amici unguento curari non potest ei a superiori medente (fo. 160ra) satagit subvenire. Speramus autem in domino et in potencia virtutis ipsius quod in proximo sencies opem apostolice medicene (!) ac, plene curatus tanto devocius nobis in accionibus graciarum assurges quanto nos plenius non palpasse fallaciter wlnus tuum set curasse fideliter recognosces [d]. Memor esto, fili, dictum prophete [e] dicentis, immo domini pocius per profetam: Popule [f] meus, qui beatum dicunt ipsi [g] te decipiunt. Nec patiaris personam regiam olei sacri liquore [h] perfusam peccatoris oleo impinguari, nec adquiescas peccatoribus te volentes lacerare. Consule, quesumus, conscientiam; consule quoque famam; et mandatis apostolicis humiliter adquiescas. Inspiret igitur menti tue is qui ubi wlt spirat, ut utilitatem preferres voluntati, quinimmo utilitatem in voluntatem convertas, ut et voluntas sit utilis et utilitas voluntaria, et id solum appetas et affectes quod utile tibi fuerit et salubre [i]. Hoc autem celsitudinem tuam nolumus ignorare, quoniam usque adeo in potencia divine virtutis confidimus et de iustitia et veritate speramus quod si vel tecum possemus esse presentes vel presentem te habere nobiscum, nullius rancoris scrupulus in pectore remaneret set plenius affectus nostros recognoscens, et monimenta nostra reciperes voluntarius et spontaneus adimpleres.

---

[b] vericaciter *D*.　　[c] c'tate *D*.　　[d] recognoscentes *D*.　　[e] prophetie *D*.　　[f] populus *D*.
[g] ipse *D*.　　[h] loquore *D*.　　[i] salubrue *D*.

ADDITIONAL NOTES

P.40: The ms. is described in W. Holtzmann, Studies in the collections of twelfth-century decretals, ed. C.R. and M.G. Cheney (Monumenta Iuris Canonici, series B vol.III, 1979) pp.300-18, in connection with the analysis of Collectio Dunelmensis II (formerly called Dunelm.IV, and so described above).

P.45, line 1: This overstates the rarity of arabic numerals in early 13th century English mss. Not only are they found in earlier scientific mss., but canonistic mss. sometimes use them by the end of the 12th c.: e.g., Collectio Petrihusensis (Peterhouse 114) writes 'Alex.3' and arabic numbers appear in glosses in Gonville & Caius Coll.676 (283); Walter Ullmann kindly drew my attention to the latter. Kuttner and Rathbone note BL Royal 2 D ix, an Anglo-Norman ms. with rubrics of the Bambergensis group, from Pershore (Traditio vii (1949-51) p.284 n.18). Kuttner had already observed (Repertorium der Kanonistik (Studi e Testi, 71, 1937) p.205 n.3) that 13th cent. juristic mss. written in France and England made use of arabic numerals in contrast to those written at Bologna. Even patristic mss. provide early examples. Neil Ker calls to my notice Edinburgh Nat. Libr.6121, late 12th cent., of Cistercian origin, in which the numbering of items in arabic 'could be contemporary'. See further, F. Steffens, Paléographie latine (Paris, 1910), pp.xxxix-xl.

IV

DECRETALS OF INNOCENT III IN PARIS, B.N. MS LAT. 3922A

The Paris manuscript, lat. 3922A of the Bibliothèque Nationale, contains an important group of legal works, written in the early part of the thirteenth century, some of which have in recent years interested historians of the canon law.[1] One section (fols. 118v-126v) has not, to my knowledge, been described fully in print. In 1951, Dr. Walther Holtzmann, who had examined it some years before, kindly brought it to my notice. The bearing of this section on the questions posed by other parts of the volume cannot be thoroughly appreciated until the volume has been examined *as a whole*: for this we must await the description by Mme. Rambaud, conservateur au Cabinet des Manuscrits, who is engaged in cataloguing the canonistic manuscripts of the Bibliothèque Nationale.[2] For the moment, an analysis of this section may have some value in throwing light on the methods of compilators and in discovering a few new or improved texts. The whole volume seems to emanate from the Anglo-Norman school and Rouen was probably its place of origin. The collection of decretals on fols. 148r-167v has therefore been suitably christened 'Rotomagensis.'[3] It may be convenient to style it 'Rotomagensis I'; then the collection on fols. 211r-227v, based upon Compilatio I, may be called 'Rotomagensis II,'[4] and the section with which this article is concerned becomes 'Rotomagensis III.'[5]

---

[1] The brief description of the MS (wrongly attributed to the fourteenth century) in *Catalogus codicum mss. Bibliothecae Regiae* 3 (Paris 1744) 528 is wholly inadequate. Portions are described by S. Kuttner, *Repertorium der Kanonistik (1140-1234)* (Studi e Testi 71; Città del Vaticano 1937) 295, 297, 313, by Walther Holtzmann, 'Über eine Ausgabe der päpstlichen Dekretalen des 12. Jahrhunderts,' *Nachrichten Akad. Göttingen* 1945.23-5 and 'Das Ende des Bischofs Heinrich II. von Chur,' *Zeitschrift für schweizerische Geschichte* 29 (1949) 151-2, and by Ch. Lefebvre, 'L'école canonique rouennaise de la fin du xiie siècle: la collection dite de Rouen et ses rapports avec les collections contemporaines,' *Revue historique de droit français et étranger* 4e série 30 (1953) 324-5 and 'Collectio Francofurtana,' DDC 5.878-83.

[2] I am obliged to Mme. Rambaud for expediting the supply of microfilms of this MS from the Bibliothèque Nationale.

[3] By Dr. Holtzmann. It had been named 'Parisiensis III' by Dr. Kuttner, *Repert.* 297, after its present location.

[4] Described as 'Parisiensis IV' by Kuttner, *Repert.* 313.

[5] Other decretal-collections will be referred to as follows: the Gregorian Decretals (described as X) and Compilationes III and IV (C.III and C.IV) in Friedberg's editions; Gilbert (Gilb.) and Alan (Al.) in the first, Weingarten (W) recension, as analyzed by R. von Heckel, 'Gilbertus-Alanus: Die Dekretalensammlungen des Gilbertus und Alanus nach den Weingartener Handschriften,' *Zeitschrift der Savigny-Stiftung für Rechtsgeschichte,* Kanon. Abt. 29 (1940) 116-357, and Alan in the second, Vercelli (A) recension, as analyzed by S. Kuttner, 'The Collection of Alanus: a Concordance of its Two Recensions,' *Rivista*

Copyright © 1955 by Fordham University Press

Rotom. III contains only nine folios, and of these folios 120^v, 121^r, 122^v are completely blank. Short as this section is, it contains a series of 95 letters of Pope Innocent III, of which the latest dated letter belongs to 25 May 1207. They are written in a very small French hand, two columns to the page, 70-75 lines to the column; the last two letters are in another hand, but both hands belong to the first decades of the thirteenth century. In the margins there are no glosses, but titles have been set alongside most of the letters: 'de consuetudine,' 'de constitutionibus,' 'de prebendis,' etc., corresponding to the *tituli* of decretal-collections.[6] These titles and the form in which the letters are presented (abridging protocols and omitting dates, occasionally shortening the text with an 'et infra'), show that the collection was made by a canonist.

It is well known that the pontificate of Innocent III saw prodigious legal activity in the court of Rome and, in consequence, attempts were made, both officially and unofficially, to select and collect the pope's decretals and rescripts.[7] The collections compiled by Rainer, Gilbert, Bernard, and Peter of Benevento were systematic in their arrangement. Rotom. III, by contrast, is unsystematic. It differs, however, from others placed by Dr. Kuttner in the 'unsystematic' category. In the first place, these collections often offer no more than a handful of Innocentian decretals;[8] and the more lengthy ones (with the exception of Gilb. appendix) contain decretals of earlier popes. Secondly, it is rare to find even small collections of the unsystematic type which contain much Innocentian material later than 1201: Gilb. appendix does not go beyond June 1202 and the latest letter in the appendix to Alan W is of 7 Aug. 1206.[9] Thirdly, these collections are not in datal order.[10] In contrast, Rotom. III is a long series covering ten years of Innocent III's

---

di storia del diritto italiano 26 (1953 [1955]) 37-53; Rainerius of Pomposa (Rain.) as printed in PL 216.1173-1272; Lucensis (Luc.) as printed in Mansi's edition of E. Baluze, *Miscellanea* 3 (Lucca 1762) 367-391; Abrincensis (Abrinc.) and Bernardus Compostellanus (Bern.) as analyzed by H. Singer in *Sb. Akad. Vienna* 171 (1913-14).

The annual registers of Innocent III (Reg.) are as printed in PL 214-5. Po. stands for *Regesta pontificum Romanorum*, ed. A. Potthast (2 vols. Berlin 1874-75).

[6] I have indicated in the notes which follow the concordance a few titles which do not correspond closely to those in the systematic collections.

[7] Cf. the remarks of Friedrich Heyer in *Zeitschrift der Savigny-Stiftung*, Kanon. Abt. 4 (1914) 593.

[8] E.g. Collectio Valentiennensis, Kuttner, *Repert.* 307.

[9] Heckel 144. The letter 'Pastoralis officii' of 19 Dec. 1204 to the bishop of Ely (Po. 2350) is a fairly frequent addition to collections of earlier material (cf. Kuttner, *Repert.* 300-11).

[10] Collectio Palatina (Kuttner, *Repert.* 308) offers a series of 15 letters in something approaching chronological order; all but the first (Po. 1806) range between 1 July 1209 and 18 Aug. 1212, and all but Po. 3872 and Po. 4006 are found in the registers.

pontificate and not straying outside; and it is a series which adheres very closely to chronological order, though with some transposition of groups.

The chronological sequence becomes the more significant when it is observed (1) that the dates of the letters hardly ever appear in these copies; (2) minor deviations from exact chronological order usually correspond to deviations in the papal registers; (3) where whole groups of letters are misplaced the grouping seems to be connected with the divisions of the annual registers. From the analysis which follows it will be seen that all the letters of identifiable provenance in the group 1-53 come from Reg. Vat. 4 (years 1 and 2) and Reg. Vat. 5 (years 3-5); in another group, 55-67, all those of identifiable provenance are found in Reg. Vat. 7A (for the tenth year); while letters 72-93 may all belong to the years 6-8 which are covered by Reg. Vat. 5 and Reg. Vat. 7.

A closer comparison of the texts with those in the registers reveals no form of error or abbreviation which could not be accounted for in a direct copy; likewise, comparison with the texts in the systematic collections do not point to the dependence of Rotom. III on them. In general, its copies are fairly free from error. Thus it is of some importance to find 19 letters from the lost registers of the third and fourth years, identifiable in the fourteenth-century calendar printed by Theiner. These may well be closer to the original registers than the texts of the known decretal-collections, or at least represent another line of descent from the registers; in one instance (no. 33b) it adds a section otherwise unknown to a letter in Reg. 3.[11] Four more letters (nos. 42, 46, 68, 70) appear from their position in Rotom. III to belong to the fourth year, though they cannot be identified in Theiner's calendar. Besides these, there are seven letters which have not been found in the registers. The unpublished letters, which are printed below, raise problems about the composition of Rotom. III and the completeness of the Innocentian registers in their existing form and as they are recorded in Theiner's calendar. The position in Rotom. III of no. 38 makes it virtually certain that (contrary to von Heckel's supposition) Alan was right in declaring it to be 'in registro'; this must affect our view of similar rubrics elsewhere in Alan, even if we cannot identify them with entries in the register at the present day.[12]

The collection includes only 95 letters, out of nearly 3000 enregistered by the papal chancery during these ten years, and compared with 382 letters used in Alan W and about 400 letters of this period incorporated in X. Only 70 of the 400 are found in Rotom. III, together with 25 others, of which 14 appear in other decretal-collections.[13]

---

[11] See notes to concordance, below.

[12] E.g., Al. W 2.4.3 (Heckel 163).

[13] Rotom. III contains ten letters from Reg. 1, or about one quarter of those found in decretal-collections.

The list of letters in Rotom. III shows at once that this is not the sort of collection which would have been extracted from the registers by a canonist who was gathering Innocentian material for the first time. His extracts must have been intended to supplement others. And here we must note Dr. Holtzmann's remarks on some other contents of MS latin 3922A. He observes that the core of the manuscript (apart from abridgements of Gratian and parts of the civil law) is a Collectio Francofurtana (fols. 173r-209v). Second comes Rotom. I (fols. 148r-167v), intended as a supplement to Francofurtana. Then comes Rotom. II (fols. 211r-227v), which is in effect an abridged Compilatio I with a few additions: only those decretals are given in full which are not to be found in the foregoing collections. Further, abridgements of Gilbert and Rainer follow (fols. 227v-242r), which likewise refrain from re-copying letters already at hand in the other collections.[14] Now Rotom. III fits into the scheme of the volume. It appears designed to exclude any decretal which occurs in these other collections. None of its letters is found among the Innocentian letters of Rotom. I or Rotom. II. Not one of the decretals in Gilb. reappears in Rotom. III. Two only of the letters are common to Rotom. III and Rainer: perhaps the collector had not, at this stage in his work, established the principle of selection.[15]

It is difficult to avoid the conclusion that these 95 letters (or at least the large majority of them) were extracted by the compiler of our manuscript from the papal registers, extracted with the deliberate intention of providing a supplement to his other collections. The object, maybe, was to bring together a large corpus of material in a new systematic decretal-collection; but this is mere supposition.

From the concordance which follows it will be seen that 58 of the letters in Rotom. III are wholly or in part in Alan, 74 in Bernard, and 70 in C. III. It must be remembered, however, that these are only a small proportion of the Innocentian decretals in these systematic collections. Moreover, although it is not rare to find Bernard and/or Alan abridging a letter in the same fashion as Rotom. III (e.g. nos. 4, 32), the systematic collections occasionally contain more than is found in Rotom. III (e.g., no 68 [cf. Alan], nos. 24, 35 [cf. Bernard]).

---

[14] Holtzmann, *Zeitschrift für schweiz. Gesch.* 29.152 n. 18.

[15] They are Rotom. III 3 and 6 (Rain. 15.4 and 20.3). I have not verified that these letters are in the text of Rain. in MS lat. 3922A.

CONCORDANCE OF ROTOM. III, REGISTERS, AND DECRETAL-COLLECTIONS

Rotomag-ensis III	Potthast Reg. pont.	Regist. of Innoc. III	Alan (W)	Alan (A)	Bernard	Compilatio III	X
1	517	1.63	App. 51	—	3.5.1	3.36.1	3.47.1
2	67	1.77	1.4.3	1.4.3	1.5.1	—	—
3	88	1.98	2.18.1	2.20.1	1.4.12	1.1.5	1.2.9
4	99	1.103	3.4.4	3.4.4	3.7.3	3.5.3	3.5.17
5	126	1.127	3.4.2	3.4.2	3.10.1	3.8.1	3.8.4
6	164	1.143	4.1.2	4.1.2	2.16.1	5.14.2	5.31.9
7	186	1.144	5.16.1	5.17.3	3.1.1	—	—
8	239	1.192	1.1.3	1.1.3	1.3.1	1.1.1	1.2.6
9	230	1.222	—	—	1.4.11	5.23.6	5.40.22
10	241	1.232	—	—	1.10.3	1.9.2	1.11.10
11	252	1.247	3.13.1	3.13.1	3.21.1	3.20.1	3.27.3
12	271	1.265	2.12.4	2.13.4	2.11.1	2.12.1	2.20.28
13	308	1.307	1.11.1	1.15.1	1.16.2	1.13.2	1.20.6
14 a	377	1.368			3.12.1a	3.10.1a	3.12.1
b			5.2.1	5.2.1	3.12.1b	3.10.1b	2.28.56
c					—	—	1.23.9
15	406	1.392	2.10.1	2.11.2	1.21.1	1.18.1	1.29.22[1]
16	420	1.414	3.4.5	3.4.5	3.7.4	3.5.4	—
17	422	1.416	3.10.2	3.10.2	3.15.2	—	—
18	424	1.422	1.4.4	1.4.4	1.5.2	1.3.1	1.4.2
19	440	1.432	5.14.3	5.14.4	3.2.1	5.15.1	5.32.2
20	584	1.540	—	—	5.13.4	—	—
21	591	1.549	5.12.5	5.13.7	—	—	—
22	597	1.556	—	—	2.14.4	2.15.3	—
23	604	1.571	1.4.1	1.4.1	1.5.3	1.3.2	1.4.3
24	657	2.30	1.6.3	1.6.3	1.8.1	1.6.1	1.6.16
25	750	2.104	5.2.3	5.2.2	5.16.3	5.14.1	5.3.36
26	820	2.172	5.2.2&4	5.2.3	5.3.5	5.2.5	5.3.33
27	852	2.190	1.6.12	1.8.13	1.8.3	1.6.3	1.6.18
28	1001	T.3.51[2]	—	—	2.3.2	2.3.2	2.6.2
29	1027	T.3.71	—	—	1.4.8	1.2.6	5.40.16
30 a	1066	T.3.92	2.6.3	2.7.3	5.11.1	5.9.1	3.5.24
b							5.17.7
31	1071	T.3.106	—	—	3.7.4	3.5.4	3.5.18
32 a	1110	T.3.139	—	—	1.29.1	1.24.1	1.41.2
b					2.1.2	2.1.2	2.1.12
33 a	1128	T.3.147	5.21.8a	5.22.12a	3.22.4	3.21.3	3.28.12
b			—	—	—	—	—
c			—	—	5.22.19	5.21.12	5.39.38
d			5.21.8b	5.22.12b	1.28.2	1.23.2	1.40.5
34 a	1056	T.3.151	1.14.1	1.18.2	1.22.2	1.19.2	1.30.4
b			—	—	5.14.2	—	—
c			—	—	1.10.4	1.9.3	1.11.11

[1] Also in Compilatio IV 1.11.3.

[2] T. = Theiner, i.e. the fourteenth-century calendar of the lost registers of the third and fourth years of Innocent III, printed by A. Theiner, *Vetera monumenta Slavorum meridionalium historiam illustrantia* (Rome 1863) 47-63.

Rotomag-ensis III	Potthast Reg. pont.	Regist. of Innoc. III	Alan (W)	Alan (A)	Bernard	Compilatio III	X
35	1338	T.4.19	—	—	2.11.3	2.12.3	2.20.30
36	1339	T.4.29	4.17.1	4.17.1	4.16.1	4.16.1	4.21.5
37	1356	T.4.45	4.5.1	4.5.1	4.7.1	4.7.1	4.9.4
38	1360	T.4.50	2.14.4	2.16.4	—	—	—
39	1402	T.4.75	App. 52	5.22.2	2.10.2	2.16.1	2.25.2
40	1401	T.4.79	1.5.3	1.5.3	1.8.16	1.6.15	1.6.30
41	1418	T.4.101	5.21.5	5.22.9	5.22.9	—	—
42	1180	T.4.174	—	—	—	2.7.2	2.14.6
43	1423	T.4.127	App. 54	2.1.5	1.21.3	1.18.3	1.29.24
44 a	} 1447	T.4.128	—	—	3.9.2	3.7.2	—
b			{ 3.8.2	3.8.2	3.13.2	3.11.2	3.10.8
c			2.16.8	2.18.11	—	—	—
45 a	} 1469	T.4.144	{ 1.3.10	1.3.10 }	3.27.5	3.26.5	3.34.9
b			3.18.5	3.18.5 }			
46	3867	T.4.235	2.11.8	2.12.8	2.11.5	2.12.4	2.20.31
47	1560	T.4.236	2.5.4	2.6.4	2.6.3	2.6.3	2.13.13
48	1620	5.1	5.21.13	5.23.8	5.22.10	5.21.6	5.39.33
49	1638	5.7	4.7.2	4.7.2	4.8.2	4.8.2	4.11.7
50	1664	5.23	2.16.9	2.18.12	2.18.7	2.19.5	2.28.47
51	1734	5.82	3.19.5	3.19.7	3.28.2	3.27.2	3.35.6
52 a	} 1752	5.101	5.21.15	5.23.10	{ 3.1.6	3.1.3	5.37.6
b					} 4.10.4	4.10.4	—
53	1771	5.113	1.8.1	1.10.1	1.10.1	—	—
54	942	2.278	—	—	1.7.4	1.5.4	1.7.4
55	3053	10.31	—	—	—	1.25.3	1.43.6
56	—	—	—	—	—	—	—
57	—	—	—	—	—	—	—
58	3105b	10.61b	—	—	—	5.10.5	5.19.15
59	3043	10.15	—	—	—	—	—
60	3061	10.29	—	—	—	2.20.3	{ 2.30.7
							} 2.1.15
61	3664	11.271	—	—	1.21.10	1.18.9	1.29.30
62	3110	10.66	—	—	5.22.4	5.23.8	5.40.24
63	3101	10.62	—	—	5.22.1	5.12.3	5.27.7
64	3105a	10.61a	—	—	5.4.2	—	—
65	3100	10.58	—	—	5.18.6	5.1.7	5.2.2
66	3077	10.45	—	—	—	3.18.6	3.24.9
67	3090	10.51	—	—	—	3.4.3	3.4.11
68	5035	—	App. 55	1.9.3	3.10.2	—	1.10.3[3]
69	1285	T.4.11	3.6.3	3.6.3	3.9.4	3.7.3	3.7.6
70	—	—	—	—	—	—	—
71	—	—	—	—	—	—	—
72	1836	6.2	4.10.1	4.10.1	—	—	—
73	1852	6.15	—	—	3.16.1	3.14.1	3.17.5
74	1877a	6.36a	1.6.2a	1.6.2a	2.17.10	2.18.9	2.27.19
75	1946	6.108	4.14.1	4.14.3	4.14.6	2.15.10	2.24.24

[3] Also in Compilatio IV 1.6.1.

Rotomag-ensis III	Potthast Reg. pont.	Regist. of Innoc. III	Alan (W)	Alan (A)	Bernard	Compilatio III	X
76	1957	6.110	5.11.3	5.12.6	3.18.1	3.17.1	3.21.4
77	1944	6.103	3.2.2	3.2.2	3.4.2	3.3.1	3.3.5
78	2030	6.177	2.11.3	2.12.3	2.11.9	2.12.8	2.20.35
79	2108	6.219	2.13.7	2.15.9	2.14.12	2.15.9	2.24.23
80	2115	6.224	2.11.7	2.12.7	2.11.10	—	—
81	2133	6.241	3.21.1	3.21.1	1.22.4	1.19.4	1.30.6
82	2038	6.183	App. 100	5.23.2	5.22.14	5.21.8	5.39.35
83	2209	7.66	3.16.3	3.16.3	3.25.7	3.24.7	3.31.20
84	2228	7.85	—	—	1.28.3	2.11.3	—
85	2242	7.96	2.18.2	2.20.2	2.19.2	2.20.2	2.30.5
86	2434	8.7	—	—	—	—	—
87	2467	8.31	—	—	5.22.12	5.23.7	5.40.23
88	—	—	—	—	—	—	—
89	—	—	—	—	—	—	—
90	—	—	—	—	—	—	—
91	2472	8.35	—	—	1.8.15	1.6.14	1.6.29
92	—	—	—	—	—	—	—
93	—	—	—	—	—	—	—
94	2079	6.202	3.8.3	3.8.3	—	—	2.12.7[4]
95	3012	9.265	—	—	5.17.7	5.16.6	5.33.16

NOTES TO THE CONCORDANCE

No. 1. Address reads 'Amacen' episcopo' (Reg. reads 'Armachano archiepiscopo'). The only letter in Rotom. III which is found in Luc. (107).

2. Address reads 'Astorien'' (Reg. reads 'Astoricen'').

3. Title 'de constitucionibus' = C. III, not Al. or Bern. Text abridged as in Al. and Bern. Rain. has the letter (15.4) but omits more of it.

5. Title 'de distribucione *ecclesiasticorum* bene*ficiorum*' not found in other collections.

6. Rain. has the letter (20.3).

8. Title as *5.*

9. Address (complete in C.III) abridged to 'abbati de Alcobacia.'

11. Address reads 'Teoloci' for 'Teodoci.'

14. Title, in a second hand, 'Ut beneficia ecclesiastica sine diminutione conferantur' = Bern., not Al. At the section 'Quia vero maiorum...' (fol. 119va) the same hand adds marginally: 'hucusque in dec' novis.' A corrector adds 'apud deum' marginally before 'acceptione personarum.' These words are in Reg. and are added marginally in Al. W (Heckel p. 291 note c). Rotom. III, like Al., includes the closing section: 'Quod cum probatum ... laboravit.'

16. Title as *5.*

---

[4] Also in Compilatio IV 1.12.1.

156

24. Address reads 'Mutrensi ... Werden'' (Reg. reads 'Mitrensi ... Verden'). In margin: 'R' lib' ii de apell'.'

One third of fol. 120rᵇ, fols. 120ᵛ, 121ʳ are blank. Between nos. *24* and *25* the copyist might have left space to copy several important decretals which occur in Reg. at this point (e.g., Reg. 2.37 and 38).

29. At the end of the text as in X continues: 'studeas diligenter quod propter hoc nostrum non cogimur reiterare mandatum et tu ad iniuncta tibi negotia exequenda efficacem videris sollicitudinem adhibere.'

31. Reads 'Sidunensi' for 'Sicluniensi.'

32. Address as in Theiner and Bern. Text abridged as in Bern. C. III changes address and includes more of the text.

33. This gives a more correct sequence than has been inferred from the other texts.

(b) 'De clericis autem qui super criminibus convicti vel confessi a diocesanis episcopis officio beneficioque secundum instituta canonica sunt privati, etsi utrumque receperint ab apostata et excommunicato, quia tamen id obesse debet potius quam prodesse, respondemus episcoporum sententias observandas.'

34. Address 'C. tituli sancti Laurentii...' etc. The position in Rotom. III permits us to correct Potthast's and von Heckel's identification of Po. 1056 and Reg. (Theiner) 3.89. This must be Reg. (Theiner) 3.151.

Most of fol. 122rᵇ and fol. 122ᵛ are blank (cf. note on no. *24*).

35. Begins without address: 'Constitutus in presentia nostra magister Robertus procurator dilecti filii magistri R. de Sancto Edmundo etc.': nothing more.

38. Address 'priori et capitulo Sancti Torquati.' Both address and text correspond closely to Al., who reads 'Innoc. III in registro, priori et capitulo Sancti A.' which von Heckel believed to be drawn from an unregistered variant version of Po. 800 (Reg. 2.150) addressed 'Vimanensi, de Costa et de S. Tornaco prioribus': he inferred that Al.'s source was not the register (p. 255). But the position of the text in Rotom. III shows it to have been Reg. 4.50 'priori et capitulo Sancti Torcari' (Po. 1360, Theiner p. 57). The text in Bern. (2.15.2), C. III (2.17.2) and X (2.26.12) is from Po. 800. The chief difference in the text is that Rotom. III and Al. read 'non obstante prescriptione que locum in tali casu nequit habere' in place of 'prescriptione temporis non obstante' of the earlier letter.

42. An otherwise unknown letter (see text below, p. 158). From its position it should belong to June–July 1201, but it is not in the calendar of the register of the fourth year.

46. The position in Rotom. III suggests that this belongs to the fourth year, but if so, in the absence of address, it is unidentifiable in the calendar of the register.

51. The abridgement 'Cum ad monasterium Sublacense personaliter venis-
semus cupientes etc. et infra in fine: Abbas vero cui...' contains more than
Reg. 5.82 as printed by Migne. But the full text is found in the original
register and was printed by Card. J. B. Pitra, *Analecta noviss. spicilegii Soles-
mensis altera continuatio* I (Rome 1885) 490.

54. This is the first case where Rotom. III departs from the order of Reg.

56 and *57* are otherwise unknown (see texts below, p. 159). They appear
among a group of ten letters from the tenth year, but are not themselves
found in the existing register (cf. Fr. Kempf, *Die Register Innocenz III*
[Misc. Historiae Pontificiae 18; Rome 1945] 43).

58 and *64* provide the only instance of Rotom. III separating two parts
of one letter. *58* is here addressed 'Antisidorensi episcopo' and begins 'Cum
in diocesi' without indication that this is the third section of 'Tua fraternitatis discretio.'

61. One of a small group of decretals which are at the end of the register
of the eleventh year but which, as Baluze noted, do not belong to that year
(cf. Kempf 95-102). This decretal is not found elsewhere in Reg. From its
position in Rotom. III it should belong to the tenth year. Note that Bern.
included it in his collection which claims to be drawn from the registers of
the first ten years (ed. Singer 24, 115) and that Rotom. III and the Harleian MS of Bern. give the address 'Pataviensi episcopo' instead of the reading
of Reg. 11.271: 'episcopo Pictaviensi' (which is that of C.III and X).

68. No address. Von Heckel fails to elucidate Al.'s much corrupted address,
which was probably to the bishop of Ely, dean of Lincoln, and archdeacon
of Northampton. It must be dated late 1200 or early 1201 (cf. S. Kuttner
and Eleanor Rathbone, in *Traditio* 7 [1949-51] 308 n. 30). It seems possible,
therefore, that Rotom. III took this and the next two letters from the lost
register of the fourth year; but neither *68* nor *70* can be found in Theiner's
calendar.

69. Address 'Eliensi episcopo et archidiacono Norhanton' et magistro H.
de Gaherst.' Includes the names of the archbishop's three proctors. A longer
version than Al.

70 and *71* are otherwise unknown (see texts below, pp. 159-160). Their position
suggests that they belong to the fourth year, but this cannot be true of no. *71*,
which names a cardinal promoted in the eighth year. They both have Norman
addresses and both might have been collected in the province.

The last three-quarters of fol. 125ʳᵇ is blank.

86. Title 'de consuetudine.' Address in full as Reg. with a vestigial date:
'Dat' anno octavo.' It is a curious letter to include in a decretal-collection
but is one which would interest a Norman collector.

88. Title 'de privilegiis et excessibus privilegiatorum.' Address 'decano
et cantori London'.' *Incipit*: 'Causam que inter dil. fil. abbatem de Grestein

158

ex una parte et priorem et conventum de Monte Acuto Baston ' [*for* Bato-
niensi] diocesi... ' This appears with the more probable address 'decano et
cantori Lond' et archidiacono Colecestr' ' in Bodleian MS Tanner 8 p. 590 (immediately preceding Collectio Tanneriana). The text of the letter agrees
almost exactly with that printed by Singer under the address 'episcopo
decano Baioc' et magistro H. Nereth' from the appendix to Abrinc. (pp.
399-400). Again we have to do with a letter of Norman interest: the abbey
of Grestain (O.S.B.) was in dioc. Rouen. This and *89-90* would appear from
their position in Rotom. III to belong to the eighth year, but they are not
found in Reg.

89 and *90* are otherwise unknown (see texts below, pp. 160-161).

91. Address 'Dolensi episcopo et dilectis filiis de Savign' et de Ardena
abbatibus, ' which corresponds to Reg. 8.35 (but the latter omits 'dil. fil. ').
A vestigial date: 'Dat' anno viii°. ' Again, a letter of Norman interest.

92 and *93* are otherwise unknown (see texts below, pp. 161-162). *92* is
connected with *91* and ends 'Dat' anno viii°' but is not in Reg. *93* also has
Norman interest; it bears no date. If the final clause is correctly abridged,
the formula suggests a date before 1202 (cf. *Selected Letters of Pope Innoc. III
Concerning England*, ed. C. R. Cheney and W. H. Semple [London 1953]
p. xxi); but it would be dangerous to rely upon this.

94. Written in a slightly later hand: 'Innocentius III episcopo Veronensi. '
The address and text correspond to Al. whereas Reg. 6.202 is addressed
'archidiacono Vicentino' with a note 'scriptum est ... Veronensi (episcopo). '

95. In the hand of *94.* 'Innocentius III Lingonensi episcopo. ' The full
dating clause found in Reg. 9.265 is given with the added words 'pontificatus
nostri' before the year.

Corpus Christi College,
  Cambridge.

TEXTS FROM ROTOM. III
no. 42 (fol. 123ra-b)

[I]dem Prenestino episcopo, apostolice sedis legato, et decano Bunnensi.

Cum dilectus filius magister S. Leodinen' etc. et infra. Sed contra hoc pars
proponebat adversa quod sicut excusatorem ad nos duxerat[1] sic dirigere po-
tuerat responsalem, cum ei non fuisset iniunctum ut ad causam dumtaxat in
propria persona sed vel ipse accederet vel procuratorem[2] idoneum destinaret.
Preterea cum mandatur alicui ut ad certum terminum se iudici representet
duo sub hac forma mandantur: ut ad iudicem veniat et ad diem prefixum ac-
cedat. Unde si venire non possit[3] ad diem assignatum, tenetur tamen nichilominus se iudici presentare sicut ratio suggerit et legitima sanctio manifestat.
Si enim mandatur alicui ut alii ad certum diem rem certam exsolvat,[4] non
ideo erit a mandato solutus si solvere non[5] poterit die data, immo ad solutionem,
elapso etiam die solutioni prefixo, tenetur. Quapropter quia predictus H. nec

venerat nec sufficientem miserat responsalem ad diem sibi statutum vel post, etiam diutius expectatus, nec de vicino eius adventu spes erat, utpote qui per litteras utcunque excusaverat moram suam et calores estivos et insidias sibi positas formidabat, eum de consilio fratrum nostrorum reputavimus contumacem et ad legittimas et moderatas expensas quas adversarii eius fecerant a tempore citationis emisse, quoniam ex tunc expectare inceperant, ipsum curavimus condempnare.

¹ duxxerat.   ² procurarem.
³ *add.* assig.   ⁴ exolvat.
⁵ *om.* non.

no. 56 (fol. 124ʳᵇ)

[I]dem.
Insinuante venerabili fratre nostro Largen' episcopo nostris est auribus intimatum quod quidam nobiles sue diocesis cum ipse pro causis ecclesiasticis aliquas ecclesias rationabiliter interdicto supponit, res et rusticos eius expignorant et per hanc violentiam necessario cogunt ecclesiasticam relaxari censuram. Nolentes igitur ut per huiusmodi presumptores dissolvatur nervus ecclesiastice discipline, discretioni vestre per apostolica scripta mandamus quatinus eos a tali temeritate per censuram canonicam appellatione postposita compescatis.

no. 57 (fol. 124ʳᵇ)

[I]dem eidem.¹
²Cum sicut nobis fuit te significante relatum in ecclesia tua consuetudo reprehensibilis inolevit quod, videlicet, ea que per te pariter et per capitulum ipsius ecclesie disponuntur ex more nequeant habere processum si pauci vel unus solus etiam sine causa rationabili contradicat, volentes huiusmodi maliciis obviare, presentium auctoritate precipimus quatinus quod a te vel maiori et saniori parte capituli provide statuetur, non obstante maliciosa contradictione paucorum debitam obtineat firmitatem.

¹ eisdem, s *expunged.*
² De his que fiunt a maiori parte capituli *added in margin.*

no. 70 (fol. 125ʳᵃ)

Idem W. Rothomagensi archiepiscopo.¹
Devotio nos tue fraternitatis consuluit quid tibi sit de illis agendum qui accedunt ad ordines in quorum celebratione sub excommunicatione generaliter inhibetur ne quis² sine certo titulo aut suo presentatore se ordinandum intrudat et taliter ordinati divina celebrare presumunt. Nos igitur fraternitati tue super hoc breviter respondentes per apostolica tibi scripta mandamus quatinus taliter ordinatos nulla contradictione vel apellatione obstantibus a suscepti officii executione suspendas.

¹ Walter of Coutances, archbishop of Rouen 1184-1207.   ² *om.* quis.

160

no. 71 (fol. 125ra-b)

[I]dem abbati et priori Sancti Petri super Divam et magistro R. priori de Dosulle.[1]
Dilectis filiis W. pro se et R. presbitero,[2] dilectorum filiorum R. cancellarii
et Willelmi Bouuet canonici[3] Baiocensis procuratore in nostra presentia constitutis, dilectum filium nostrum I. sanctorum Cosme et Damiani diaconum
cardinalem[4] dedimus auditorem, et infra. Cumque super hoc inter dictos W.
et R. procuratorem coram cardinali predicto fuisset aliquandiu litigatum et
idem cardinalis que audierat nobis fideliter retulisset, nos audîtis que fuerant
hinc inde proposita intelleximus evidenter quod dicti iudices formam mandati
apostolici sunt transgressi. Cum enim ipsis dederimus in mandatis ut si dictam
excommunicationis sententiam invenerint post apellationem ad nos legittime
interpositam promulgatam, denunciarent eam penitus non tenere, de causa
ipsa iuxta ...arum litterarum continentiam cognituri, alioquin partes remitte-
rent ad examen iudicum predictorum, ipsi motu proprie voluntatis prioribus
iudicibus mandaverunt ut, a dicto cancellario et Willelmo ut ubi debeant
parerent iuri cautione recepta, impenderent beneficium absolutionis eisdem.
Qui nichilominus in apellationis causa postmodum, absente altera parte, procedentes, denunciaverunt dictam sententiam post apellacionem ad nos legitime interpositam minus rationabiliter promulgatam. Propter quod processum
ipsorum iudicum utpote contra nostri formam rescripti et post apellacionem
ad nos legitime interpositam attentatum duximus irritandum, maxime cum
in litteris ad eos[5] apellationis beneficium non fuerit interclusum, discretioni
vestre per apostolica scripta mandantes quatinus suprascriptam excommunicationis sententiam faciatis usque ad satisfactionem condignam inviolabiliter
observari. Cum autem absolutionis beneficium iuxta formam ecclesie meruerint
optinere, audiatis causam et eam iuxta formam prioris rescripti sublato apellationis obstaculo ratione previa decidatis, etc.

[1] The abbey of St. Pierre-sur-Dive (O.S.B.), dioc. Séez, and the priory of Dozulé (O.S.A.),
dioc. Lisieux.

[2] presbiteris.

[3] Roger Bovet appears as chancellor of Bayeux in 1200, William as a canon in 1207.

[4] promoted cardinal in 1205, first subscribes a papal bull 4 May 1206.

[5] litteris repeated.

no. 89 (fol. 126rb)

[I]dem Constantinopolitano patriarche.[1]
[F]uturam infidelibus ecclesiam apostoli predicaverint, et infra. Super eo
quod sedem apostolicam consuluisti utrum scilicet tales debeas venerabili clero
agregare qui propter stature parvitatem risui et merito despectui plebis ...[2]
subiacere dinoscuntur, prehabito fratrum nostrorum consilio breviter respondemus quod licet tales non prohibeantur in sacris canonibus expressim ad sacros
ordines ascendere, tamen cum sacrosancta ecclesia illud solum sibi vendicet
quod reprehensione caret, huiusmodi in Constantinopolitana ecclesia, ne ceteri
per eos scandalum patiantur, institui prohibemus. Si quos tamen quos ita
natura respuit et [3] ad communem statum hominum non erexit, iam institutos et
in sacris ordinibus promotos inveneris, poteris eos sub dissimulatione pati in
minoribus ordinibus ministrare; diligenti tamen cautela adhibita si in eis signa

virilia velud barbam et calvitiem et similia inveneris, scias cum eis facilius dispensandum.[4]

[1] *Title in margin*: De corpore vitiatis.
[2] *Space for a word.*   [3] *om.* et.
[4] The letter can hardly have been addressed to the patriarch before 1205, in which year the pope wrote several times to him (Reg. 8.19-26, 64, 136).

no. 90 (fol. 126rb)

[I]dem Lundensi episcopo.[1]

[Q]uam grave, et infra. A nobis sollicite postulasti an enormiter calvi ad sacros ordines promoveri valeant vel in iam susceptis[2] licite valeant ministrare. Super quo inquisitioni tue taliter respondemus quod licet sic ordinati usque ad hec tempora sint misericorditer tolerati, quia tamen indignum nostris videtur temporibus ut quem natura in principali membro corporis enormiter vitians indignum sui beneficio iudicavit et qui velud hostis nature ab omnibus foribus sequestratur ab ecclesia tanquam filius aprobetur. Potius enim pudenda calvities et tegenda quam populo exponenda. Hoc ergo generali decreto statuimus ut si quos calvities usque ad aures deformavit nec in honore iam suscepto ministrare nec ad maiores aspirare presumant, ne per huiusmodi genus hominum venerabili clero iniuria fiat et sancte matri ecclesie scandalum generetur. Si qui tamen in minoribus reperti fuerint pro necessitate temporis patientes, ex consueta benignitate sedis apostolice sustinebimus.[3]

[1] *Title in margin*: De eodem (cf. no. 89). The address is faulty. If the archbishop of Lund is intended, it is relevant that the pope addressed a series of letters to him in response to consultations in Jan. 1206 (Reg. 8.194-8).
[2] succeptis.   [3] substinebimus.

no. 92 (fol. 126va-b)

[I]dem W. Rothomagensi archiepiscopo.[1]

[C]assatis olim duabus electionibus in ecclesia Baiocensi temere celebratis, venerabili fratri nostro Dolensi episcopo et dilectis filiis de Savigneio et de Ardena abbatibus per apostolica scripta mandavimus ut dilectis filiis capitulo Baiocensi duorum mensium spatium post reditum sociorum suorum qui propter hoc ad presentiam nostram accesserant assignarent infra quod personam idoneam sibi preficerent per electionem canonicam in pastorem. Alioquin extunc ne gregi dominico diu deesset cura pastoris, ipsi auctoritate nostra suffulti talem eis personam concederent in episcopum que tanto congrueret oneri et honori, contradictores et rebelles si qui forsan apparerent per censuram ecclesiasticam apellatione postposita compescendo.[2] Ipsi vero postquam mandatum apostolicum receperunt, eidem capitulo non quidem duorum mensium sed quinque septimanarum et quinque dierum spatium infra quod electionem pontificis facerent assignarunt, pro sue voluntatis arbitrio terminum coartantes. Cum autem idem canonici die ad eligendum communiter assignata convenissent pariter in capitulo, apellatum est ne decanus qui primam vocem in electione debebat habere ad electionem procederet absque consensu capituli vel maioris et sanioris partis ipsius. Sed ipse, singulorum voluntatibus perscrutatis,[3] cum parte capituli non solum numero sed auctoritate minore dilectum filium Saxonem subdiaconum nostrum, canonicum Baiocensem, in episcopum precipi-

162

tanter elegit. Quod cantor cum reliqua parte capituli tam auctoritate quam numero longe maiore contra canonica iura presumptum attendens, protinus nullo interposito actu in eodem loco dilectum filium magistrum R. de Ablegiis, ecclesie Baiocensis canonicum, elegit unanimiter in pastorem, electionis ibidem decretum conficiens, eligentium subscriptionibus roboratum, cuius electionem per te optinuit confirmari. Porro prefatus Dolensis episcopus cum abbatibus memoratis ante terminum per litteras nostras sibi prefixum, post recusationem legittimam et apellationem ad nos interpositam, lite minime contestata post confirmationem electionis, et post ea, utramque predictarum electionum cassavit, iuris ordine pretermisso, et statim dilectum filium . decanum Parisiensem in Baiocensem episcopum nominavit. Quem cum cantor et fautores eius nollent recipere in pastorem, ipse illos de facto excommunicare presumpsit. Partibus in nostra presentia constitutis, cum merita huius cause examinata fuissent, nos de communi fratrum nostrorum consilio tam electionem, quam decanus cum fautoribus suis de predicto subdiacono temere celebrarat, quam electionem a predicto episcopo et collegis suis de Parisiensi decano inordinate presumptam, non propter defectum aut vitium personarum, cum eos idoneos reputemus, duximus irritandam, et electionem de predicto magistro R., a cantore cum maiori, digniori et saniori parte capituli canonice celebratam auctoritate curavimus apostolica confirmare. Quocirca fraternitati tue per apostolica scripta mandamus quatinus eundem electum in temporibus a canone constitutis ordinare procures et consequenter iuxta formam canonicam in episcopum consecrare.[4] Carissimum quoque in Christo filium nostrum Philippum regem Francie illustrem moneas attentius et inducas ut eidem electo reddat regalia que Baiocensis antistes a suo principe consuevit habere, eiusque personam et ecclesiam Baiocensem diligat et honoret. Dat' anno viii°.

[1] *Title in margin*: De eodem (referring to marginal title of no. 91: De electione).
[2] The mandate is no. 91, dated 22 April 1205.
[3] perscruptatis.
[4] Master Robert des Ablèges was consecrated 26 February 1206.

no. 93 (fol. 126vb)

[I]dem episcopo et decano Baioc' et magistro H. Constanc' archidiacono.

Gravem dilectorum filiorum abbatis et conventus Sancte Marie de Augo recepimus questionem quod abbas et conventus Fulcardimontis Cisterciensis ordinis Rothomagensis diocesis quasdam decimas eis expresse ac nominatim a sede apostolica confirmatas ipsis privilegiorum suorum optentu aufferre contra iusticiam presumpserunt, propter quod eorum ecclesia enormiter cognoscitur esse lesa, cum fere omnes ipsius redditus sint in decimis constituti. Cum igitur sic fratribus Cisterciensis ordinis velimus adesse quod alios nolimus indebite agravare, discretioni vestre per apostolica[1] scripta mandamus quatinus fratres predictos moneatis attentius et efficaciter inducatis ut cum dampno ditari non inhient alieno, quia utilitati ecclesiastice nichil deperit si ea que sunt aliena reddantur. Alioquin ipsos ut a predictorum fratrum super prescriptis decimis indebita molestatione desistant et de ablatis satisfaciant ut tenentur, monitione premissa per districtionem ecclesiasticam sublato apellationis obstaculo compellatis. Nullis etc. Quod si omnes, etc.

[1] *om.* apostolica.

ADDITIONAL NOTES

For the structure of Paris,BN ms. Latin 3922A see now Holtzmann,Studies
in the collections of twelfth-century decretals (above, Add. Notes to III)
pp.135-59, and for the analysis of Collectio Rotomagensis I, ibid.pp.160-
207.The construction of the Paris ms. deserves to be compared with that
of Durham C.III.3. Sixteen chapters of Rot.III are found in Dunelm.II
(1-4,11-12,20,22-23,50,52,55-8,74) and twelve more in the Durham annotator (above no.III: 16,23,29,41,45,60,70,73-74,78,85,91),some evidently in the same textual tradition. Cf. Rot.III c.38 (see p.156) with
Durham C.III.3 fo.158b, c.74 (above, III).

P.152 n.15: Rot.III 3 and 6 are on fos.239v of the ms.among the extracts
from Rainer.

P.156 c.42: This is in the calendar of the papal register,probably T.4.
174, and the text as printed on p.158 occurs in C.III 2.7.2 and X 2.14.6.

V

POPE INNOCENT III
Prague University Library, MS XXIII.E.59 (Lobkowitz 439), fol. 46ᵛ

THREE DECRETAL COLLECTIONS BEFORE COMPILATIO IV:
PRAGENSIS, PALATINA I, AND ABRINCENSIS II

This paper concerns three small collections of decretals of Innocent III, two of which have been named and briefly described in print by Professor Stephan Kuttner, who has kindly brought the third to my notice.[1]

---

[1] See Kuttner, *Repertorium* 308 for *Palatina* I, and 'Johannes Teutonicus, das vierte Laterankonzil u. die Compilatio quarta,' in *Miscellanea Giovanni Mercati* V (Studi e Testi 125; 1946) 622 for *Pragensis*. For my study of the collections I have used photostats and microfilms in the possession of the Institute of Research and Study in Medieval Canon Law by the kind arrangement of the Director.

Copyright © 1959 by Fordham University Press

Pragensis is contained in Prague University MS XXIII.E.59 (formerly Lobkowitz 439) fols. 24^r-45^r. It is in a thin folio volume, very well written, which came from the Praemonstratensian abbey of Weissenau.[2] The volume contains the canons of the Fourth Lateran Council (fols. 2^r-23^v) under seventy titles[3] followed by the usual official statement of the composition of the assembly, found in the Chronicle of Ursperg and various other chronicles. Then come thirty-four letters of Innocent III. Fols. 45^r-46^r contain a list of 'Stationes urbis Rome per ecclesias,' and on fol. 46^v is a remarkable full-length drawing of Innocent III, seated, between two attendants, one (left hand) tonsured, bearing a cross, the other (right hand) a layman holding an umbrella over the pope. The pope's right hand is raised in blessing, and his left hand holds a book. Round the frame of the picture is written (reading from the top side): ' + Tercius I. papa lux mundi dux uia | mappa + Visurus Iesse florem iam desinit esse | + Funere priuatur R. | Regia P. dominatur.' Within the frame, on the left, top, and right is written: ' + Ha tarde refero laicus | grex cum grege clero. Arma mouet per que | morti donatur uterque +.' The next page (fol. 47^r) is filled, by another small hand, with short excerpts of theological content. Fols. 47^v-49^r contain, in a handsome large hand, an *Algorismus* (inc. 'Ars ista que ab inuentore dicitur Algorismus ').

The decretal collection is handsomely written in a large book-hand, with inscriptions to the letters rubricated according to guiding marginal notes which have sometimes escaped the binder's shears; the hand must be dated soon after Innocent III's death; but the inaccuracies are numerous and elementary. They occur, we may guess, because the writer of this ornamental copy had before him a canonist's working copy, small and heavily abbreviated, like the existing *Palatina I*. A single example will show what the scribe of *Pragensis* was capable of; in no. 1 we read: 'forticilia stagnum et molendinum accurate sub cuius ecclesia et appellatione obradicetis,' while the copy in the papal register reads: 'fortalicia stagnum et molendinum a comite demolienda sublato cuiusdam contradictionis et appellationis obstaculo iudicetis' (of which the last seven words are abridged in Pal. I to 'sub c' ct^a et ap. ob. iudicetis'). Despite its errors, the texts of *Pragensis* are occasionally nearer to the papal register than are the texts in Compilatio IV and Extra, or supply an inscription where it is lacking in Compilatio IV, or contain a passage omitted in Compilatio IV. The canonistic object of the collection is apparent in the usual reduction of protocols to brief rubrics, the substitution of 'et infra' for narrative (nos. 1, 17, 18), the absence of dates.[4] But no steps have been taken towards systematization: there is no classification by subject-matter and no guide to the subject-matter in the shape of marginal *tituli*.

Palatina I is contained in the Vatican Library MS Palatina lat. 658 fols. 94^v-95^v. This is a small folio, written early in the thirteenth century, of which

---

[2] P. Lehmann gave a brief account in 'Mitteilungen aus Handschriften III,' in *Sb. Akad. München* (1931-32), Heft 6 pp. 21-22, where the canonistic contents are described as 'Compil. IV.' (fols. 2^r-23^v) and 'Formulae litterarum' (fols. 23^v-45^r). Professor Kuttner provided a more accurate description of this section in *Misc. Mercati* 622 n.22.

[3] 43-44 are brought under one title, 46 is divided into two.

[4] Only no. 20 has a date, and that is garbled. See notes to concordance, below, p. 477.

466

the main item of canonistic interest is the 'Glossa Palatina' to the *Decretum*.[5] The decretal collection consists of a mere fifteen letters written, two columns to the page, 105 lines to the column, in a minute hand, heavily abbreviated and unadorned. Like *Pragensis*, it curtails the protocols, sometimes substitutes 'et infra' for narrative, and omits dates; but there are no *tituli*. In another part of the same manuscript (fols. 74ʳ-75ʳ, in the same hand) is a letter of immense length with the inscription: 'Episcopo Perusino.' The first part of this letter is also copied on the last surviving pages of *Abrincensis II*.[6]

Abrincensis II is contained in MS 149 of the Bibliothèque municipale of Avranches. The volume is from the library of the abbey of Mont St.-Michel and consists of various canonistic treatises and collections, among which are interspersed by several hands many letters of popes, legates, and others, concerning the Norman and the English Church, and the acts of various Norman ecclesiastical councils from Lillebonne, 1080, to Rouen, 1231. None of the documents in the volume appears to be later in date than the year 1234. The volume is fairly fully analysed in the *Catalogue général des manuscrits des bibliothèques publiques des départements* 4 (Paris 1872) 502-06, and it was used extensively at an earlier date by Dom Edmond Martène and by Dom G. Bessin for his *Concilia Rotomagensis Provinciae*. The main canonistic sections are the apparatus of Ricardus Anglicus to Comp. I, fols. 7ʳ-77ᵛ; the 'Collectio Abrincensis' which attracted Seckel's notice and was analysed by Singer with the related *Sangermanensis*,[7] fols. 79ʳ-109ʳ; an 'abbreviatio' of the *Decretum*,[8] fols. 136-138ᵛ; the 'Generalia' of Ricardus Anglicus,[9] fols. 139ʳ-147ᵛ; and our collection, which we name *Abrincensis II*, fols. 119ʳ-126ᵛ.

This decretal collection contains thirty-three letters written, two columns to the page, 39/40 lines to the column, in a good small bookhand which can hardly be later than the second quarter of the thirteenth century. The original size of the collection must remain doubtful since it comes to an end abruptly in the middle of no. 33 at the end of fol. 126ᵛ. One or more folios are presumably missing before fol. 127, which begins a new work on a new quire.[10] The initial has been rubricated at the beginning of each decretal, and a space was originally left for an address and/or title. After the first eleven letters (of which only nos. 1, 2, and 5 have addresses noted in the margin) the original scribe has generally written the address in the text each time, immediately following the preceding letter. This does not occupy all the vacant space,

---

[5] See Kuttner, 'Eine Dekretsumme des Johannes Teutonicus,' ZRG Kanon. Abt. 21 (1932) 141-89; idem, *Repertorium* 81-92, where it is shown that although the glosses as a whole are not the work of Johannes, they owe much to him. This deserves to be remembered when the affinities of Pal. I with Comp. IV are considered, below.

[6] See below, notes to concordance, Abrin. 33.

[7] H. Singer, 'Neue Beiträge...,' *Sb. Akad. Vienna* 171 i (1913). For a partial description of the manuscript see pp. 74-80. Singer does not notice our brief collection.

[8] Cf. Kuttner, *Repertorium* 264.

[9] Cf. *ibid.* 417-8; *Traditio* 1.299 n. 40; Kuttner, 'Réflexions sur les brocards des glossateurs,' *Mélanges Joseph de Ghellinck, S.J.* (Gembloux 1951) 779-82.

[10] I have had no opportunity of making a personal examination of the manuscript, but the microfilm shows that fols. 119-126 form a separate quire or quires, smaller in size than the surrounding leaves.

and a second and informal hand inserts (as it has inserted before nos. 4-10) a title, such as the canonists employ in the systematic collections. The titles will be found below, in the notes to the concordance: here we simply note that only eleven titles agree with the titles of Comp. IV or Extra, and where Comp. IV and Extra differ from each other, Abrin. II agrees sometimes with the one, sometimes with the other. While it is impossible to say how soon these titles were added after the making of the collection, the facts that the collection has the appearance not of an original compilation but of a fair copy,[11] and that the titles are not consistently added to all letters,[12] suggest that they were no part of the original compilation.

The justification for treating these three collections together lies in the extent to which they overlap and the purpose which they seem to share. So far as their contents can be accurately dated, the letters mostly fall within the 11th-16th pontifical years, between 1208 and 1213, though there are a few outside this period. Thus they partly fill the gap between *Compilatio* III and *Compilatio* IV, the former having been completed in summer 1209,[13] the latter after July 1216.

Professor Kuttner has pointed out that *Compilatio* IV was based on (i) the canons of the Fourth Lateran Council, (ii) decretals issued after Comp. III, and (iii) earlier decretals of Innocent III omitted from Comp. III and recovered, for the most part, from the collections of Alanus, Gilbertus, or Bernardus Compostellanus antiquus.[14] He has argued that Johannes Teutonicus, in putting together Comp. IV, drew his material not from the papal registers but from private collections which had been formed as supplements to Comp. III, and he has indicated Prag. and Pal. I as examples of such collections.[15] The detailed analysis of these two collections and of Abrin. II makes it clear that they have their place in this development, and there is a family likeness between them.

The disparity of contents alone would suggest that none of the three owes anything directly to either of the others. The possibility that Prag. provided the exemplar for Pal. I or for parts of Abrin. II is excluded by its gross inaccuracies at many points where the other collections follow the papal registers correctly. Likewise, the first fifteen chapters of Prag., which are found in Pal. I, cannot be derived from the latter: at various points Prag. agrees with the register against Pal. I, and it includes a fuller version of no. 12 than Pal. preserves. It can also be proved that Abrin. II does not lie behind Prag. or Pal. I: it does not contain the whole of Prag. 25, or Pal. I 15 (Prag. 17) and it is practically inconceivable that a copyist should have omitted such parts of Abrin. II as are missing from Prag. and Pal. I.

That the three collections are connected is, however, undeniable. The following points may be noted: (i) Out of a total 45 letters, 36 appear wholly or in part in Comp. IV; (ii) Fifteen of these 36 letters are common to all three collections, or — to make the point differently — all the letters in Pal. I are found in both of the other collections and in Comp. IV; (iii) Whereas Prag. has twelve

---

[11] Cf. note to Abrin. II 31 below.
[12] Cf. nos. 2, 3, 4, 27, 31 and 33.
[13] Kuttner, *Misc. Mercati*, pp. 621-2.
[14] *Repertorium* 372, *Misc. Mercati* 617.
[15] *Misc. Mercati* 622.

letters which are not in Abrin. II, and Abrin. II has eleven letters absent from Prag., the twenty-two letters common to both appear in both in approximately the same sequence. The sequence is approximately the same in the fifteen letters of Pal. I ; (iv) In one instance at least a glaring mistake in Prag. is paralleled by a similar misreading in Abrin. II: Prag. 3 begins with 'Non uidimus' for 'Nouimus'; Abrin. II reads 'Non uidemus.' What, then, is the relationship of the collections? We can dismiss at once the idea that they are related by common descent from Compilatio IV. They belong to an earlier stage, before the decretals had been systematically broken up and dispersed under titles in that work, — before, indeed, they had been assigned *tituli* at all.[16] They were, as Professor Kuttner supposed, compiled between 1209 and 1216,[17] and if we look closely at the concordance we can get some impression of the date and method of compilation. The following reconstruction must, however, be regarded as conjectural and tentative.

It is possible to distinguish a common core in Prag. and Abrin. II, which probably also lies behind Pal. I. This consists of Prag. 1-15 and 28-29. All the letters belong to the twelfth or the thirteenth year of Innocent III, except for two (5 and 6) which have not been found in dated copies. Supposing these seventeen letters formed an original collection (which we may call Supplement I to *Compilatio* III) to which were subsequently added the other letters found in Prag., Pal. I and Abrin. II, we must note that the sequence of letters is identical in our three collections, except that two of the letters (28-29) shifted their place in two out of three of the collections. For reasons which will be given later,[18] the order of Abrin. II, where these two chapters (Abrin. II 23-24) follow Prag. 12, is more likely to be the original order than that of Prag. (28-29) or of Pal. I (10-11, preceding Prag. 12).

The first stage in the presumed growth of the collection was the addition of Prag. 17, which is dated 18 August 1212 (i.e., the fifteenth year of Innocent III): this is found in all three existing collections, but only in Prag. and Abrin. II in the abridged form of Comp. IV. Pal. I 15 gives the full letter, and comes to an end with this. In the process of copying the collection, Pal. I had lost three letters and a third of another which we believe to have belonged to the original core: Prag. 3, 5, 13 are missing, and Prag. 12 is abridged. The three chief omissions may perhaps be explained by haplography: for while 2 ends with 'procedi' 3 ends with 'procedendum'; both 5 and 6 begin with 'Cum'; and both 13 and 14 begin with 'Dilectus filius.' If the exemplar was anything like Pal. I itself, it would be easy for the scribe's eye to pass from one letter to the next in these cases. The abridgment of no. 12 must have been deliberate, unless we suppose some complicated confusion in the scribe's mind between the opening clauses of 12 and 11: both begin with the words, 'Cum contingit (contingat) interdum....'

A further addition was made before the compilers of the collections found in Prag. and Abrin. II began to differ. The two collections have in common (and in something like the same position) Prag. 16, which is undated, Prag. 18 and

---

[16] Cf. p. 467 above.

[17] Here I speak of the *collections*, not of the particular manuscripts, which may have been copied at a later date. We may be pretty sure that the Prague MS, at least, is a 'fair copy' of a pre-existent collection.

[18] Cf. below, p. 470.

25, both of the fifteenth year, and Prag. 30, of the eleventh year. Prag. 30 had been omitted from Comp. III and was, like Prag. 16, 18, and 25, included in Comp. IV.

Thereafter, the compilers took separate paths. The eleven letters peculiar to Abrin. II[19] are Abrin. II 1, 4-10, 31-33. Of these, no. 1 belongs to the fifteenth year, no. 4 to the seventh (and was included in Comp. III), no. 5 comes from the seventeenth year, no. 9 comes from early in the pontificate, if not from the pope himself,[20] and the rest are undated. Only four (no. 1 and the three undated letters, 6, 7, and 8) find place in Comp. IV. The twelve final additions which make up *Pragensis* are of a different sort. The last of all (Prag. 34) has the latest date, in the sixteenth year; the rest are either undated or belong to the thirteenth (no. 26) or fourteenth (nos. 19-20) year, except for no. 32, which is of the eleventh year and was included in Comp. III. All of these additions in Prag., except no. 32, find place in Comp. IV. Prag., it will be remembered, also includes the decrees of the Fourth Lateran Council, which form an important part of Comp. IV.

The above conjectures about the development of the collections may be summed up diagrammatically:

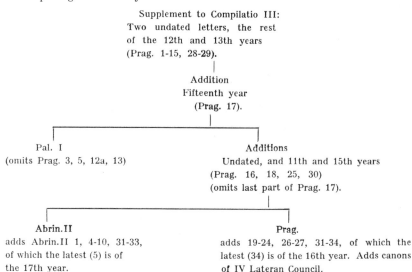

Supplement to Compilatio III:
Two undated letters, the rest
of the 12th and 13th years
(Prag. 1-15, 28-29).

Addition
Fifteenth year
(Prag. 17).

Pal. I
(omits Prag. 3, 5, 12a, 13)

Additions
Undated, and 11th and 15th years
(Prag. 16, 18, 25, 30)
(omits last part of Prag. 17).

Abrin.II
adds Abrin.II 1, 4-10, 31-33,
of which the latest (5) is of
the 17th year.

Prag.
adds 19-24, 26-27, 31-34, of which the
latest (34) is of the 16th year. Adds canons
of IV Lateran Council.

***

Consideration of the foregoing suggests that our three collections, or their exemplars, are connected, though in an indeterminate and unproved way, with *Compilatio* IV.[21] Prag. comes nearest to the later, systematic compilation,

---

[19] i.e. so far as these three collections are concerned.

[20] Cf. p. 472 and notes to concordance, below, p. 479.

[21] For the contents of *Compilatio* IV, see Friedberg's edition, pp. xxxiii-iv, correcting his references to Potthast from 495 to 4195, 1806 to 3663, 1523 to 4523, 4580 to 4577, and

by reason of its contents. It is particularly noticeable that it contains all five decretals ascribed to the years before Comp. III which Comp. IV included and did not find in Alanus, Gilbertus, and Bernardus.[22] Moreover, Prag. offers no others demonstrably earlier in date than Comp. III.[23] But these facts are inconclusive. All that is certainly established is the fact that there must have been many such collections. Yet we may safely infer that they originated in a very few groups of decretals resembling the common core indicated above, and from each group, as the result of accretion and subtraction, many others proceeded.

Whence did the compilers get their stuff? Do these collections provide any clue? The 'core' is almost entirely composed of letters which are found in the papal registers for the twelfth and thirteenth years of Innocent III, the exceptions being Prag. 1, 5, 6, 11.[24] Moreover, although the sequence does not strictly adhere either to chronology or to the order of entry in the register, Abrin. II maintains very close approximation.[25] In the existing collections the dates are missing: but whoever composed this 'core' must have had access to the registers, or at least to dated copies of all the letters. There can really be no doubt that the source lay within the papal chancery if not in the registers themselves. For why should a collector of letters derived from the archives of recipients have confined himself so closely to the products of two years? Is it likely that all the letters would reach him still bearing their exact dates? And if so, is it conceivable that he would wish to arrange what he gathered in chronological order? It is much easier to suppose that these letters were copied (after summer 1211) from the two latest annual volumes of registers by a compiler who began his search for suitable decretals to serve as a supplement to *Compilatio* III. He worked steadily through the two volumes but did not hesitate to return to a page he had overrun: he found his letters in approximately chronological order, but he was not interested in preserving it.

This is plausible, but it does not take account of four letters out of the fifteen in the 'core' which do not occur in the existing registers of the twelfth and thirteenth years. Prag. 1 is dated 'Laterani anno xii'; Prag. 5 and 6 give no clue to their date; Prag. 11 can be dated in the thirteenth year from the complete copy of the letter preserved by Antoine L'Oisel.[26] The case of Prag. 11 is of special interest; for not only does it belong to the thirteenth year and find a place among decretals of that year: it appears — dateless — in the collections in the right chronological order within the year. This could hardly occur unless

---

adding 2360 (3.3.1), 5022 (2.10.1), 5025 (3.1.1), 4143 (5.14.1), 4379 (4.3.2), 4873 (1.2.4). The following letters which occur in Comp. IV come from the years chiefly covered by Prag. and yet are not found in Prag.: 3360, 3886, 3916, 4143, 4312, 4337, 4360, 4400, 4523, 4587, 4598, 4603, 4628, 4722, 4820, 4847. The 'core' of letters of the 12th and 13th years include all in Comp. IV except 3886, 3916, 4143.

[22] i.e., Prag. 1, 13, 16, 27, 30, cf. Kuttner, *Misc. Mercati* 620.

[23] Disregarding no. 32, which is in Comp. III.

[24] See below, notes to concordance, p. 475ff. No. 1 is certainly of the twelfth year, no. 11 is of the thirteenth year.

[25] For this reason the position of Prag. 28-29 in Abrin. II is to be preferred to its position in the other collections (cf. above, p. 468).

[26] *Mémoires des pays, villes, comté, et comtes, evesché et evesques... de Beauvais et Beauvaisis* (Paris 1617) 285. The source of L'Oisel's copy is not stated.

the original compiler of the decretals had all the letters presented to him in approximately chronological order, which he did not bother to disturb. But if so, we are driven to conclude that Prag. 11 was not a later intrusion but one of the original series which he copied. We must infer that he did his work in the Roman curia but did *not* take all his material from the registers we know.[27] The evidence, moreover, points to gradual accumulation, as the letters were drawn up, expedited, and enregistered (in some cases), in the course of the twelfth and thirteenth years. We recall that Comp. III was, on Professor Kuttner's showing, composed of letters up to and including June 1209 (anno 12), and we observe that the first and earliest dated decretal in our series is probably of February-May 1209 and only contains that part of the letter which is omitted from Comp. III, while the rest of our dated series belongs to the period 26 June 1209 - 27 January 1211. These facts point to a decision taken by a curial official soon after the completion of Compilatio III, to bring together a supplement of decretals as they were composed. They might be letters which were enregistered (and these might be copied by the compiler from the register), but others which passed through the chancery without registration might also come to hand at the time of their issue or soon after. The miscellaneous *paperasserie* of the curia must always have been enormous; drafts and duplicates of particular documents would serve the canonist in making his compilation as well as the registers would, especially if the canonist happened to be one of the draftsmen.[28]

This hypothesis explains the presence of the unregistered Prag. 11 in its correct chronological order, and suggests that the unregistered and undated Prag. 5 and 6 both belong to July-August 1209, since they occur between dated letters of those two months. Mere hypothesis, perhaps, but one which seems to do no violence to known facts. Moreover, the idea of composing a decretal collection in the curia from current letters, without depending exclusively on the registers, existed in Rome in 1209. In this very year a canonist had put together the sixteen letters or parts of letters which form quire 13 of Reg. Vat. 7A and which masquerade as letters 262-277 of the eleventh annual register of Innocent III. Baluze long ago recognized that these are not letters composed and enregistered at the end of the eleventh year.[29] They are a decretal collection, drawn from

---

[27] In this connection the disparity between Prag. 1 and the Register may be significant; also the 'et infra' inserted in Prag. 10 where there appears to be no gap.

[28] This hypothesis does not depend on taking one side or the other in the dispute over the nature of Innocent III's registers which Friedrich Bock has recently revived with such force in his 'Studien zu den Originalregistern Innocenz' III (Reg. Vat. 4-7A),' *Archivalische Zeitschrift* 51 (1955) 329-64. I do not think that Bock's arguments for late composition of the registers, between 1213 and 1215, can stand against the objections of various other experts in this field, especially Walther Holtzmann, in *Deutsches Archiv* 12 (1956) 231-2, Friedrich Kempf, 'Zu den Originalregistern Innocenz' III: eine kritische Auseinandersetzung mit Friedrich Bock,' *Quellen u. Forschungen aus ital. Archiven und Bibliotheken* 36 (1956) 86-137, and Othmar Hageneder, 'Die äusseren Merkmale der Originalregister Innocenz' III,' *Mitteilungen des Instit. für österreichische Geschichtsforschung* 65 (1957) 296-339; but the picture which Bock gives of a chancery cluttered up with drafts and copies may have some bearing on the decretal collections even though it does not explain the genesis of the registers.

[29] Cf. H. Singer, 'Die Dekretalensammlung des Bern. Compostell. ant.,' *Sb. Akad. Wien*

472

various years of Innocent III's pontificate, one and all used in Comp. III. True, these letters were not all written in the quire contemporaneously with their issue; but one of them does belong to the early months of the twelfth year; it is not to be found in the register proper; and that part of it which was omitted from Comp. III is precisely the first decretal in Prag. It is a link which implies continuous activity in the curia before and after the preparation of *Compilatio* III.

So much for the common core of Prag., Pal. I, and Abrin. II. The development beyond this is hard to establish. It looks as if the collection made in the curia was put on one side after January 1211 (Prag. 15), only to receive a substantial addition (which agrees with the enregistered copy) in the middle of the fifteenth year.[30] The next stage, we have suggested,[31] was the addition of a group of four of miscellaneous origin, two from the fifteenth year, one from the eleventh, one undated. After this point the exemplars of Prag. and Abrin. II separate. It may be that the Prag. collection was completed at Rome, while Abrin. II received its last additions from other sources; but the evidence is not very strong. For what it is worth we note that of twelve letters peculiar to Prag., seven are found in the registers, whereas Abrin. II contains only two enregistered letters out of its eleven final additions.[32] Abrin. II also contains (no. 9) the decretal 'Miramur non modicum' which Innocent III, according to Bernardus Compostellanus, disowned;[33] it would seem unlikely to be added to a compilation in the curia. All but one (no. 33) of the Prag. additional letters found their way into Comp. IV and Extra, whereas five of Abrin. II's additions (nos. 5, 10, 31-33) did not. These pointers may not be enough to warrant a confident conclusion about the later stages of composition of our collections. It is better to be content with the fairly clear evidence that all three collections had a common core, that the core was compiled in the curia, and that its material was not taken wholly from the registers.

---

171 ii (1914) 24, S. Kuttner, 'La réserve papale du droit de canonisation,' RHD⁴ 17 (1938). 198 n. 5, R. von Heckel, 'Die Dekretalensammlungen des Gilbertus u. Alanus,' ZRGKan. Abt. 29 (1940) 160, O. Hageneder, *loc. cit.* 297, and especially Fr. Kempf, *Die Register Innocenz III* (Misc. Historiae Pontificiae 9 [18]; Rome 1945) 95-101 and 'Zu den Originalregistern,' *loc. cit.* 102-4.

[30] Pal. I 15, of 18 August 1212. Part of this letter was dropped before it reached Prag., Abrin. II, and Comp. IV.

[31] Above, p. 468-9.

[32] One of these (no. 4) is part of the celebrated 'Pastoralis officii,' already included in *Compilatio* III and very widely diffused before then as an isolated addition to legal collections. The other (no. 1) is found as an isolated addition to a few decretals of Innocent III in Reims MS 692 (Rainer of Pomposa: see Kuttner, *Repertorium* 310). Cf. notes on concordance, below.

[33] See Additional Note, below.

Concordance of Decretal Collections and Registers

Pott-hast	Reg.	Date	Incipit et explicit	Prag. I	Pal. II	Abrin.	Comp. IV	X
3663	xi. 265	22 Feb. - 26 May 1209	Cum olim et infra, Ceterum ... obseruari	1	1	11	5.11.un.	—
3775	xii. 81	9 July 1209	Oblate nobis uestre ... procedi	2	2	12	2.12.1	2.28.57
3753	xii.61	26 June 1209	Ex tenore literarum ... procedendum	3	—	13	4.3.1	—
3757	xii. 59	1 July 1209	Significasti nobis ... exequendo	4	3	14	5.6.2	5.12.18
5029	—	—	Cum contra m. Rand-ulfum ... perhibere	5	—	15	2.7.1	2.21.9
3872	—	1206 - 1215	Cum Ioh. heremita ... confirmandam	6	4	16	2.8.un.	2.22.10
3792	xii. 93	4 Aug. 1209	Cum uen. fr. n. ... inponentes	7	5	17	3.13.1	3.36.7
3791	xii. 92	4 Aug. 1209	Cum uen. fr. n. ... absoluendos	8	6	18	2.5.un.	2.25.6
3989	xiii. 72	1 May 1210	Dil. fil. n. P. ˙tit. ... sanctiones	9	7	19	3.2.1	3.5.25
3980-1	xiii. 59-60	24 Apr. 1210	Suscitata super di-uersis ... memorato	10	8	20	1.17.un.	1.41.6
4006	—	17 May 1210	Cum contingit inter-dum ... eterne	11a	9a	21a	2.9.1	2.24.28
»	—	»	Preterea requisisti ... pertinere	11b	9b	21b	3.9.1	3.30.29
»	—	»	Insuper postulasti ... uendicare	11c	9c	21c	2.2.1	2.2.13
4072	xiii. 127	1 Sept. 1210	Cum contingat inter-dum ... confertur	12a	—	22a	1.8.1	1.14.11
»	»	»	Preterea cum quidam ... iudicare	12b	12a	22b	ˆ2.1	1.3.24
»	»	•	Insuper requisisti ... decernatur	12c	12b	22c	ı.12.3	1.29.36
4164	xiii.196	5. Jan. 1211	Dil. fil. Iacobus ... puniri	13	—	25	2.6.1	5.37.11
4163	xiii. 195	5 Jan. 1211	Dil. fil. W. Ymil' ... obtinere	14	13	26	1.7.un.	1.11.15
4174	xiii. 201	27 Jan. 1211	Proposuit olim dil. ... approbandum	15	14	27	5.9.un.	5.27.8
2360	—	—	Accedens ad apost. ... compellant	16	—	28	3.3.1	3.8.14
4577	xv. 156	18 Aug. 1212	(Sicut) scriptum est ... celebratam	17	15a	29	1.3.6	1.6.40
•	»	»	Porro si tam ... mandamus	—	15b	—	—	—

Potthast	Reg.	Date	Incipit et explicit	Prag. I	Pal. II	Abrin.	Comp. IV	X
4401	xv. 7	3 March 1212	Veniens ad presentiam ... prescripsit	18	—	30	5.12.1	2.26.19
4379	xiv. 159	13 Feb. 1212	Tua nos duxit ... inchoarent	19a	—	—	4.3.2	4.14.7
»	»	»	Consequenter autem ... coniugale	19b	—	—	4.1.1	4.1.26
»	»	»	Tertio quesisti ...de rigore	19c	—	—	5.6.3	5.12.19
»	»	»	Ad ultimum ... arcendus	19d	—	—	5.6.3	5.12.19
4195	xiv. 13	10 March 1211	Olim in dil. fil. ... et inane	20a	—	—	2.11.3	—
»	»	»	ac de consensu ... Nulli ergo	20b	—	—	—	—
5025	—	—	Iohannes fil. noster ... tonsuram	21	—	—	3.1.1	3.3.7
—	—	—	Albricus miles nobis ... faciatis	22	—	—	2.7.2	2.20.43
5028	—	—	Sincerum tue deuotionem ... generetur	23a	—	—	3.8.un.	—
»	—	—	Viros quoque et ... compescas	23b	—	—	—	—
5022	—	—	Significauit nobis ... habebimus	24	—	—	2.10.1	—
4614	xv. 184	29 Oct. 1212	Cum in tua ... perceptio	25a	—	2	3.9.2	3.30.30
»	»	»	Sane quia contingit ... contrahentes	25b	—	—	4.1.2	4.1.27
»	»	»	Si uero post ... existat	25c	—	—	4.4.un.	4.18.6
»	»	»	Verum autem si ... casu	25d	—	—	2.7.3	2.20.44
3918	xiii. 4	23 Feb. 1210	Intelleximus quod cum ... expectare	26	—	—	1.8.2	1.14.12
3018	—	—	Causam que inter ... procedatis	27	—	—	2.1.1	2.1.18
4110	xiii. 157	28 Oct. 1210	Dil. fil. (nostro) P. ... contradictores etc.	28	10	23	3.2.2	1.10.5
4136	xiii. 181	27 Nov. 1210	Per tuas nobis ... uxorem	29	11	24	2.6.2	2.19.10
3656	xi. 257	16 Feb. 1209	Non uidimus expedire ... committat	30	—	3	5.16.2	5.40.27
5031	—	—	Ad hoc nos ... amouendus	31	—	—	1.11.1	1.23.7
3526	xi. 167	31 Oct. 1208	Cum olim, frater ... condempnantes	32	—	—	[Comp.III 2.17.8]	2.26.18

Pott-hast	Reg.	Date	Incipit et Explicit	Prag. I	Pal. II	Abrin. IV	Comp.	X
—	—	—	Accedentibus ad nostram ... perhibetur	33	—	—	—	—
4844	xvi. 139	6 Nov. 1213	Constitutis in nostra ... cessante	34	—	—	2.7.4	2.20.45
4628	xv. 191	20 Dec. 1212	Inquisitionis negotium ... existit	—	—	1	5.1.2	5.1.21
2350	vii. 169	19 Dec. 1204	Interrogasti preterea ... derogari	—	—	4	[Comp. III 5.16.9]	5.33.19
4903	—	7 March 1214	De tua prudentia ... obfuscatos (and date)	—	—	5	—	—
5041	—	—	Quoniam sicut nobis ... subiectas	—	—	6	5.12.4	5.33.21
5032	—	—	Cum R. canonicus ... procuret	—	—	7	1.12.2	1.29.35
5021	—	—	Per tuas nobis ... ministrare	—	—	8	5.2.1	5.3.37
—	—	—	Miramur non modicum ... dubitatur	—	—	9	[Alanus 1.14.un.]	1.18.7
—	—	—	Sicut nostris est ... inducas	—	—	10	—	—
—	—	—	Cum in quibusdam ... ?epistolam etc.	—	—	31	—	—
2359	—	—	Cum asperitate merito ... deferre	—	—	32	—	—
—	—	—	Cum cotidie novas ...	—	—	33	—	—

NOTES TO CONCORDANCE

Prag. 1. Without address (which is preserved, though curtailed, in Comp. IV). Abrin. II adds title in top margin: 'De officio iudicis delegati' and *inc.* 'Dum olim et infra.' The confusion introduced by Friedberg into the references to this letter (he confuses Po. 1806 with Po. 3663) was pointed out by Kuttner.[1] Having regard to the probable date of Comp. III, this letter may be dated 26 Feb. - 26 May 1209. The whole letter belongs to the decretal collection added in Reg. Vat. 7A to the register of the eleventh year (cf. above, p. 471). The compiler of these collections only extracted from the letter the portion omitted by Peter Collivaccinus. The most interesting feature of this decretal in our collections and Comp. IV is the difference in the last clause from the text in Reg. Vat. 7A. There this portion is indeterminate; here it reads: 'iamdicta forticilia stagnum et molendinum a comite demolienda sublato cuiuslibet contradictionis et appellationis obstaculo iudicetis, facientes eandem sententiam... inuiolabiliter obseruari.' From the original letter as given in Reg. Vat. 7A we learn that the abbey of Vézelay had objected that the Count of Auxerre had

---

[1] *Misc. Mercati* 620 n. 14.

erected new buildings after the prohibition of new work (cf. *Dig.* 39.1), and the judges were told to aim at a compromise. If either party resisted, the judges were then to deliver sentence 'quam sub bulla nostra uobis mittimus interclusam, facientes eam per censuram ecclesiasticam inuiolabiliter observari.' The order for the destruction of buildings which is found in our collections may have been composed by the compiler of their common ancestor,[2] but may possibly go back to a text of the further instructions which the pope had sent to his delegates under seal.

Prag. 2. Despite errors (Prag. *inc.*: 'Nobis late littere vestre'), Prag. is closer to the Register than Pal. I or Abrin. II, which resemble each other; and all three are nearer to the Register's text than is Comp. IV.

Prag. 4. The title in Abrin. II is 'De homicidio,' which corresponds to the 'De homicidio casuali seu voluntario' of Comp. IV.

Prag. 5. Prag. and Abrin. II both have the address: 'Archiepiscopo Mediolanensi' and *inc.* 'Cum contra magistrum Randulfum de Archa Maurianensi [*Abrin.* Radulfum de Archamarienensi?].' The title in Abrin. II is 'De testibus cogendis.' The position in these collections suggests that the letter may belong to July-August 1209.

Prag. 6. The title in Abrin. II is 'De probatione et fide instrumentorum.' In the address Prag. reads 'Petro Roulanduno ciui Viterbiensi': the surname is 'Relanduci' in Pal. I and 'Relanducii' in Abrin. II. For 'Iohannes Eremita' Pal. I reads 'Ioh. Hermize'(?) and Abrin. II 'Ioh. Heremita.' For 'M. et R. natis tuis' all three read 'Matheo et Rainero (*or* Ranerio) natis tuis.' For 'anno dom. inc. MCCVI... Tabellionem' the three collections read: 'anno inc. dom. MCLXXXVI [*Abrin.* MCLXXXVII] mense Novembris die quarta constitutum [*Abrin.* confectum], in quo profitebaris te propria uoluntate uendidisse ac tradidisse Iohanni Herm' [*Prag.* Emere] domum tuam in ora sancti Blasii sitam cum omnibus utilitatibus et accessionibus eius in integrum et transactum, et postea clxxx librarum pretium recepisse, ita uidelicet quod dictus I. eandem [*Prag. add.* dictam] domum tenendi, uendendi, donandi, uindicandi [*Abrin.* iudicandi] et faciendi quodcunque uellet, haberet [*Pal.* habere] liberam potestatem. Tabellionem.' Kuttner offers reasons for assigning as extreme dates 1206-1215;[3] the position in these collections suggests that the letter may belong to July-August 1209.

Prag. 9. All have the whole letter as in the Register, including 'quod ex eo argui... prebendam uacantem' omitted in Comp. IV. Abrin. II has no address; its title is 'De seruis ordinandis.'

Prag. 10. Address, omitted by Comp. IV, reads 'Terromoreno [*Abrin.* Camorene, *Pal.* Hamorensi] episcopo [*Prag. add.* et] M. archidiacono Toletano et magistro M. canonico Secobiensi [*Prag.* Secorb'].' *Inc.* 'Suscitata super diuersis articulis inter [*Prag.* interuenit] fratrem nostrum [*Pal. add.* G.] Burgon' [*Pal.* Burgensem] episcopum et Omense monasterium questione et infra. Postmodum uero partibus ... manifeste constare [*Prag.* manifestare] dicebat. Et infra.[4] Nos igitur ... indulgendam. Quocirca presentium ... memorato.' This

---

[2] Cf. *Selected Letters of Pope Innocent III,* ed. C. R. Cheney and W. H. Semple (London 1953) xxxi, 76.

[3] *Misc. Mercati* 621 n. 5.

[4] There are no additional words in ep. 59 in the Register at this point (PL 216.251B).

is an *a pari* letter which can only be seen in the Register under two addresses, Reg. xiii.59-60. The address in these collections corresponds to that of ep. 60. Comp. IV omits 'Postmodum ... constare.

Prag. 11. The address 'Beluacensi episcopo' covers the whole letter, but in every manuscript a rubricated initial begins each of the three sections, and Prag. and Pal. I have an initial at 'Cum autem in quibusdam' in no. 11b. Abrin. II has a title for each section: 'De iureiurando,' 'De decimis,' 'De iudiciis.' The text in L'Oisel, *Mém. des pays ... de Beauvais* 285, is presumably drawn from the recipient's archives, though no source is stated. It is noteworthy that the date places it among a group of letters which is found in the Register.

Prag. 12. Prag. has a rubricated 'Idem' to begin 12b and 12c. Abrin. II has three titles: 'De ordinatis ab abbatis [*sic*]', 'De officio iudicis delegati,' 'De sententia excommunicationis.' Pal. I, which omits 12a, *inc.* 'Cum contingat interdum etc. Preterea cum quidam...'

Prag. 13. The address in Prag. 'Ad electum S. Petri ad montes' is manifestly incorrect: this 'addressee' was one of the litigants and the Register gives the judges as addressees. Abrin. II has no address, nor have Comp. IV and Extra. Abrin. II has the title: 'De probationibus.'

Prag. 14. The addresses are all different and all garbled, but none so bad as Comp. IV and Extra: Prag.: 'Laomensi et Scanberen' episcopis et abbatibus'; Pal. I: 'Idem Laoniensi et Sindbarensi episcopis et abbati de Magio Luricen' diac'; Abrin. II: 'Idem Laomensi et Sindbarensi episcopis et abbati de Magio Lumnensis diocesis.' Abrin. II has the title: 'De temporibus ordinationum.'

Prag. 15. This is the letter 'In eumdem fere modum' which is recorded at the foot of Reg. xiii.201. The text departs from the enregistered text wherever the new address demands ('te' becomes 'sepedictum P.' etc.). Abrin. II exceptionally omits to give any title.

Prag. 16. Not found in the Register but printed from Abrin. II in Martène, *Thesaurus* 1.797 (whence Migne, PL 217.277). Potthast places it *s.a.* 1204, Boehmer *s.a.* 1210. Kuttner lists it among decretals dating from before Comp. III (*Misc. Mercati* 620 n. 14), but like others in the group, there seems no reliable evidence and the position in Prag. and Abrin. II suggests a later date. Abrin. II has the title: 'De concessione beneficii non uacantis.'

Prag. 17. Prag. *inc.*: 'Sicut scriptum est... Iohannis etc. et infra. Sane ad hanc....' Abrin. II makes the same abbreviation; but the whole passage omitted is contained in Pal. I. All three collections omit the long passage in PL 216. 677A-80C ('Proposuerunt siquidem ... admittere dignaremur'), and Prag. and Abrin. II omit the final section ('Porro si ... et mandamus'). Abrin. II has the title: 'De electione.'

Prag. 18. The address in Prag.: 'Abbati sancti Martini de Pannonia [*sic, for* Panormia]' is manifestly wrong: it is the title of a litigant in the case (cf. Prag. 13, 24, 27). The other collections have no address. Abrin. II has the title: 'De capellis monachorum et censibus.'

Prag. 19. No address in Prag. The divisions are marked by rubricated initials only.

Prag. 20. The address is in the shortened form of Comp. IV, but Prag. has the latter part of the letter, missing from Comp. IV. The eschatocol is garbled. For the Register's 'Nulli ergo, etc. confirmationis etc. usque incursurum.. Dat' Laterani vi idus Martii p.n.a. quarto decimo,' Prag. reads: 'Nulli ergo hominum omnino etc. stat'. vi idus Martii anno Maguntino *apostolice sedis*

478

legato.' The last four words suggest the record of a letter *a pari* to Siegfried, archbishop of Mainz, though it does not seem that he had the title of legate before 1212.

Prag. 21. The address in Prag. is 'Archidiacono Pictavensi' whereas Comp. IV reads 'Episcopo Pictavensi.' A copy in Troyes, MS 385 fol. 143ᵛ reads 'Pissiac' episcopo' and preserves the full name in the opening words 'Iohannes filius Asconis,' where Prag. reads 'Iohannes filius N.' (Kuttner, *Repertorium* 303).

Prag. 22. No address. This is apparently not otherwise known outside the texts of Comp. IV and Extra.

Prag. 23. The first part only hitherto known, from Comp. IV, without address. Addressed in Prag.: 'Abbati de Sailen*ensi*.' 23b (at fol. 37ʳ and ᵛ) reads: 'Viros quoque et mulieres etatis adulte ad resumendum crucem male dimissam ecclesiastica uolumus censura compelli. Illis autem in remissionem peccatorum dari poterit signum crucis qui ob aliquam causam honestam illud usque ad expeditionis processum uolunt in secreto deferre. Sane cum in cruce signatis crucifixi gloriam et animarum lucra queramus, illos penis legittimis non credimus eximendos qui calcata crucis reuerentia enormia [*Prag.* enormam] non uerentur committere. Ne inde, quod absit, excedendi usurpetur occasio, unde merito debet excessibus aditus intercludi, primo debitores et usurarios ad soluenda debita et restituendas usuras cruce signatis uolumus per ecclesiasticos iudices ordinaria iurisdictione comppelli [*sic*]. Ceterum illos contraditionis [*sic*] et inobedientie filios qui, longe abeuntes a deuotione fidei christiane, tam pium et sanctum negotium impedire presumunt a tanto temerarie presumptionis excessu ecclesiastica censura compescas.'

Prag. 24. The address in Prag. ('Legonum episcopo') is manifestly wrong (cf. Prag. 13, 18, 27). The letter was addressed to regular prelates of the diocese of León at the bishop's instance (cf. Comp. IV).

Prag. 25. No address in Prag. Abrin. II: 'episcopo Beluaciensi.' Prag. has no rubric or divisions to mark the four sections. Abrin. II only contains section a.

Prag. 27. The address in Prag.: 'Abbati et conuentui Vindon' is manifestly wrong (cf. 13, 18, 24): the abbot and convent of Vendôme were a party in this lawsuit. The first clause reads 'archidiaconum Vindocinensem diocesis Carnotensis' where Comp. IV reads 'archidiaconum Carnotensem.' This may be connected with litigation referred to in a grant by Hugh, archdeacon of Vendôme, whereby he renounces procuration fees from certain dependencies of Vendôme after long dispute before 'magistro G. et G. canonicis Parisiensibus.'[5] The decretal, which names other judges, perhaps belongs to an earlier stage in the dispute. Why the archdeacon's grant is dated by its editor 'vers 1205' is not evident: Hugh, archdeacon of Vendôme, was in office as late as Dec. 1223.[6] From the position of the decretal in the Prag. series, it seems to belong to the year 1210.

Prag. 28. Instead of an address (also missing from Pal. I), Prag. reads: 'De presbitero et cardinali S. Marcelli.' Abrin. II has the address as: 'Idem

---

⁵ *Cartulaire de l'abbaye cardinalice de la Trinité de Vendôme*, ed. Ch. Métais (Paris 1893-97) 3.18.

⁶ *Cartulaire de N.-D. de Chartres*, ed. E. de Lépinois and Lucien Merlet (Chartres 1862-64) 2.101-2.

episcopo et cantori San' et abbati de Mor' diocesis Samoensis'; it has the title: 'De electione.'

Prag. 29. Pal. omits the address. Abrin. II has the title: 'Qui filii sunt legitimi.'

Prag. 30. In the address Prag. reads 'Parisiacensi' for 'Parisiensi.' Prag. *inc.* 'Non vidimus'; Abrin. II *inc.* 'Non videmus.' The correct reading is 'Novimus.'

Prag. 31. This is apparently not otherwise known outside the texts of Comp. IV and Extra. Here the first sentence has not been abridged, and reads: 'Ad hoc nos dominus licet immeritos in sacrosancte Romane ecclesie cathedra collocauit ut si in ecclesia dei que per uniuersum orbem longe lateque diffunditur scruspulus [*sic*] dubitacionis emerserit, ad eam a membris suis tanquam ad capud et dominum recurratur, responsum congruum super suis dubitacionibus recepturis [*Prag.* receptis]. Sane consuluit nos...'

Prag. 32. The address in Prag. is 'Abbati sancti Salvat*oris*.' The text in Prag. must be taken, like that of Comp. III and Extra, from Register xi.167 'Lucano episcopo,' for it begins: 'Cum olim, frater episcope'; but the address is that of the next letter recorded in the Register 'in eumdem fere modum.' This is the only decretal in Prag. which is found in Comp. III; and Prag. 32 and 33 are the only two letters in Prag. absent from Comp. IV.

Prag. 33. This long letter, which extends from fol. 40^v to fol. 42^r, is not known elsewhere. Its address is: 'Abbati sancti Martini de Cruthei' but the corruption which pervades the whole text probably begins with the first word; for the letter appears to be directed to the son of a priest who has been presented to the parish church of 'S. Martini de Cruthei.' Mention of various persons concerned in the case point to the diocese of Wurzburg, and we may tentatively identify 'Cruthei' as Krautheim near Tauberbischofsheim, on the Tauber.

Prag. 34. The address is missing from Prag. The last in the Prag. series, it is also the latest in date, so far as dates can be established.

Abrin. II 4. The only decretal in Abrin. which is also in Comp. III. Here it has no address and the title reads: 'Idem pars cap. Pastoralis' which shows pretty clearly that it was taken from a copy in, or added to, a decretal collection (cf. above, p. 472, n. 32).

Abrin. II 5. Printed from this manuscript by Martène, *Thesaurus* 1.847 (whence Bouquet, *Recueil* 19.593). This is a letter of complaint to the legate Robert 'de Corchon' that he has indiscreetly supported the rebellious lay brethren of Grandmont. It is dated 7 March 1214 and is important for the constitutional history of the Order of Grandmont. Here it is given the title: 'De officio legati.'

Abrin. II 6. No address. The title is: 'De officio et potestate iudicii ordinarii.' Has the readings: 'Nefesinus episcopus' and 'sancti Blasii de Flama.'

Abrin. II 7. No address. The title is: 'De officio iudicis delegati.' Has the readings: 'adoptione concessa' for 'optionem relinquas' and 'ad te' for 'a te.'

Abrin. II 8. No address. The title is: 'De qualitate ordinandorum.'

Abrin. II 9. This letter was noted by Bernardus Compostellanus antiquus (ed. Singer, pp. 35, 114) as wrongly ascribed to Pope Innocent III. But it found its way into Lucensis (of which the latest dateable letter is of 6 May 1199) and Alanus, and it must have been composed early in the pontificate or earlier still. Here it has no address and its title is: 'De seruis ordinandis.' Has the *incipit*: 'Miramur non modicum etc. Quomodo...' — See Additional Note, below.

Abrin. II 10. This letter is not known elsewhere. It has no address and its title is: 'De officio iudicis ordinarii.' It reads as follows:
'Sicut nostris est auribus intimatum antecessor tuus [MS cui*us*] plures super possessionibus Livon' ecclesie fecit contractus in ipsius ecclesie non modicum detrimentum. Set quamuis contractus illos ualeas reducere in formam meliorem, archid' et canonici ecclesie tue in instrumentis ipsius subscribere denegant, non commoditatem ecclesie set metum animi potius attendentes. Volentes igitur ipsius ecclesie utilitati prospicere, fraternitati tue mandamus quatinus dictos archid' et canonicos ut pro commodo ecclesie in ipsis instrumentis subscribant [MS superscribant] moneas attentius et inducas. Alioquin auctoritate apostolica tibi plenam concedimus facultatem ut ascitis tibi uiris prudentibus et honestis etiamsi predicti clerici ecclesie tue subscribere noluerint, memoratos contractus in meliorem formam appellatione remota reducas.'

Abrin. II 31. Without address or title. We treat this as a separate item although the greater part is an extract from Prag. 11b (Abrin. II 21b) above. Beginning with the words 'Cum in quibusdam... decimas pertinere' it continues: 'Quocirca mandamus quatinus secundum eandem epistolam etc. d'. in eodem ro. arc̄..' The words 'Quocirca... epistolam etc.' suggest that the extract is not directly from Abrin. I 21b but from another, later letter in which the pope cited 21b. On the other hand, the puzzling abbreviations which follow should perhaps be extended to: '[1]dem in eodem [?titulo] Rotomagensi archiepiscopo,' in which case we might take 'Ro.' as a mistake for 'Re[mensi]' and take the whole phrase to be simply a commentator's reference to Extra 3.30.14.[7]

Abrin. II 32. Printed from this manuscript by Martène, *Thesaurus* 1.796 (PL 217.276). The letter is not known elsewhere. Address: 'Idem Rothomagensi archiepiscopo'; title: 'De qualitate preficiendorum.'

Abrin. II 33. No address, no title. This is an incomplete copy of a letter found complete, though corrupt and with an erroneous address to the bishop of Perugia, in Vatican MS Pal. lat. 658 fols. 74ʳ-75ʳ (cf. above, p. 466). It concerns the claim of a man to be one Palmerius, returned after several years of exciting adventures to Perugia, where Palmerius' wife (now re-married) maintains that she had buried Palmerius and that the man is an impostor.

Additional Note

When Heinrich Singer published his excellent work on *Die Dekretalensammlung des Bernardus Compostellanus antiquus*,[1] he expressed certain reservations about accepting at their face value the statements of Bernard in the Epilogue to the *Breviarium decretalium*.[2] On a cursory view of the epilogue, Bernard seems to say that five decretals (of which he gives the *incipits*) are wrongly attributed to Innocent III, being neither in his registers nor approved by him, as Bernard has heard from the pope's own mouth ('sicut ore ad os ab eo accepi'); and he adds that there are others in the same category. But Singer

---

[7] 'Alex. III Remensi archiepiscopo.' App. Conc. Lat. 26.21; Comp. I 3.26.26. It would be easy for the scribe of Abrincensis to write Ro. for Re., for his next letter is addressed to the archbishop of Rouen: moreover, the book is a Norman book.

[1] Printed in *Sb. Akad. Wien*, 171 ii (1914), under the above title.

[2] *Loc. cit.* 114-15.

saw reason to doubt this condemnation of the five decretals, and although his arguments have not received much attention from later scholars, Professor Kuttner rightly indicated (*Repertorium* 319) that they make it necessary to take Bernard's statement with caution. Not all of Singer's discussion is equally valid, and one piece of evidence he failed to notice. It seems worth while, then, to review what is known about the aspersed documents to see whether a definitive conclusion about them can be reached.

Singer appears to waver between two opinions: that Bernard meant that the letters, though issued by Innocent III, were not to be treated as decretals for the purposes of the classroom or the courts; and that Bernard, whatever he was saying, is not a trustworthy witness. Singer's approach to the matter lay through his admirable discussion of Tancred's words about Bernard's compilation ('in ipsa compilatione quaedam reperiebantur decretales quas Romana curia refutabat').[3] He showed that these words had led critics to confuse letters which the Curia did not treat as decretals with letters which were forgeries. But he advanced from this to suggest that Bernard's statement that specified letters were forgeries really concern letters which the Curia did not treat as decretals. This does not seem cogent reasoning. It is hard to see how Bernard's words can mean other than that the letters were forgeries, in the sense that their ascription to Innocent III was false. (It may be better to call them 'apocryphal,' since some at least may well be genuine products of Innocent's predecessors). For Bernard says they must be rejected *tanquam non suas*; and later, speaking of the fifth in particular, says *sua non est*. The emphasis is not on the 'decretal quality' (or lack of it) of the letters, but on the authorship, which Pope Innocent III, according to Bernard, denies. I am not impressed by the argument (p. 33) that Bernard's statement is just the sort of thing that a Bolognese master would say. That forgeries and falsely-ascribed decretals did circulate is not in doubt. Reg. Innocent. III x.15 makes it clear.[4] Bernard's 'Sic et de quibusdam aliis accipe' was a perfectly reasonable remark to make: ' You may take it that the same is true of some others'; it was true, and neither Bernard nor anyone else could name them all. Singer certainly makes a point when he observes that Innocent's condemnation may have been in general terms, not particularizing the five examples given by Bernard; on this the chances seem to me roughly even, for Bernard's words are ambiguous. But whether the pope named these five or whether Bernard was led to the conclusion that they were apocryphal by other evidence, I see no good grounds for doubting his testimony.

We may now examine briefly the whereabouts and ascriptions of the five texts in question:

i. *Miramur non modicum*. This is the very last document (no. 124) in *Lucensis*, where the latest dated text is of 6 May 1199.[5] It there follows a letter of 7 Feb.

---

[3] *Loc. cit.* 3, 29ff.

[4] The forgery is in the appendix to *Tanneriana*; W. Holtzmann, 'Die Dekretalensammlungen des 12. Jhs. 1. Die Sammlung Tanner,' *Festschrift zur Feier des 200 jährigen Bestehens... Akad. Göttingen* (1951) 144. Incidentally, the pope's words in condemnation — 'eam utpote falsam omnino respuamus' — sound like the sort of thing which Bernard may have heard from his mouth. Cf. Bernard's use of 'respuatis.'

[5] J. D. Mansi, *Stephani Baluzii... Miscellanea* (Lucca 1762) III 391 (cf. Kuttner, *Repertorium* 306).

1199 (Potthast 592) and is said to be of Innocent III, 'datum Laterani in eodem anno' (i.e. 22 Feb. 1198 - 21 Feb. 1199). It reappears in the collection of Alan ascribed to 'Innoc. III in registro,'[6] and in Abrinc. II c.9 without ascription. It is given in Extra 1.18.7 as 'Idem,' following a decretal of Innocent III of 9 June 1207.

ii. *Ex litteris.* This is in *Collectio Halensis* c.80,[7] where it is ascribed to Celestine III, is addressed to the archbishop of Ravenna, and concerns the election of a bishop of Cremona. It re-appears in Gilbert ascribed to Innocent III, without address, reading 'Euoriensis' instead of 'Cremonensis.'[8] It was printed thence by Singer,[9] who, like von Heckel, failed to notice the text in Halensis. Were the Halensis reading, 'Cremona,' correct, the date would be certainly 1185, for in that year Sicardus, the historian and canonist, became bishop of Cremona and remained there until 1215.[10] But this cannot be, for the letter speaks of an election held at Christmas and of reference to the archbishop of Ravenna as metropolitan: Sicardus was elected in August and Cremona was not in the province of Ravenna. Professor Holtzmann, who has recently edited and commented upon the letter, connects it with the bishopric of Cervia, 1193-1198.[11]

iii. *De prudentia.* This is in Comp. II, ascribed to Clement III.[12] But it had appeared in Gilbert, ascribed to Innocent III. It is accepted by Holtzmann and printed by him as a decretal of Clement III.[13]

iv. *Queris.* This is in Comp. II, ascribed to Alexander III.[14] It had appeared in Alan, ascribed to Innocent III.[15] Holtzmann argues that the method of general reference to *sacri canones* is against the plausibility of the Innocentian attribution.[16]

v. *Super consultatione.* This is known only from Alan,[17] who ascribes it to Innocent III. It is of this letter that Bernard says in his epilogue: 'Quinta tamen iuri non repugnat, uerumtamen sua non est.'

Regarding no. i, ascribed by both *Lucensis* and Alan to Innocent III, we note that Alan's reference 'Innoc. III in registro' is in plain contradiction of Ber-

---

[6] 1.10.1 in the Weingarten text, for which see R. von Heckel, 'Gilbertus-Alanus,' ZRG Kan.Abt. 29 (1940) 236; 1.14.1 in the definitive Vercelli text, for which see S. Kuttner, 'The Collection of Alanus: a Concordance of its Two Recensions,' *Rivista di storia del diritto italiano* 26 (1953 [1955]) 39.

[7] As analyzed by F. Heyer, ZRG Kan.Abt. 4 (1914) 592.

[8] 1.9.7 in 'Gilbertus-Alanus' p. 185.   [9] *Loc. cit.* 116.

[10] Cf. O. Holder-Egger, in MGH, SS. 31.24.

[11] W. Holtzmann, 'Kanonistische Ergänzungen zur Italia Pontificia,' *Quellen u. Forschungen aus italienischen Archiven u. Bibliotheken* 38 (1958) 72-73 no. 62.

[12] JL 16589; P. Kehr, *Italia Pontificia* 3.363 no. 45; Comp. II 4.14.1; X 4.20.3. Cf. *Repertorium* 345 on the general absence of Innocentian decretals from Comp. II.

[13] 'Kanonistische Ergänzungen...,' *Quellen und Forsch.* 37 (1957) 91 no. 39; cf. RHE 50 (1955) 452.

[14] JL 13785; Kehr, *Italia Pont.* 6.i.312 no. 15; Comp. II 1.8.1; X 1.14.6.

[15] Anhang 62 (Weingarten), 1.11.1 (Vercelli): 'Gilbertus-Alanus' 321.

[16] *Quellen und Forsch.* 38.196 no. 107.

[17] 2.13.8 and Anhang 80 (Weingarten), 2.15.10 (Vercelli): 'Gilbertus-Alanus' 253, 326. Printed from Alan in Singer, *loc. cit.* 116.

nard's statement that the letters he stigmatized as apocryphal were not in Innocent's register; and Bernard was in a good position to know.[18] Nothing much can be said about no. v: we are faced with the directly opposed statements of Alan and Bernard. For these two letters we have found no text ascribed to anyone but Innocent III.[19] But the remaining three letters (ii-iv) appear to have emanated from Celestine III, Clement III, and Alexander III respectively. The collections which ascribe them to Innocent were not confined to Innocentian material and make numerous other erroneous ascriptions to that pope.[20] Why, then, should we accept their ascription of nos. i and v to Innocent III in the face of Bernard's warning? (He — or the pope — only troubled to warn us because some contemporaries were in error). It is the word of *Lucensis* and Alan against Bernard's word, and it seems very unsafe to regard *Lucensis* and Alan as good evidence. If we accept Heyer's estimate of Bernard's critical faculty,[21] which is confirmed by von Heckel's study of Gilbert and Alan,[22] we shall treat seriously Bernard's warning and exclude *Miramur non modicum* and *Super consultatione*, with the other three which he lists, from the number of Innocent III's letters.

Corpus Christi College,
Cambridge.

---

[18] Cf. 'Gilbertus-Alanus' 170-72 and S. Kuttner, 'Bernardus Compostellanus Antiquus,' *Traditio* 1 (1943) 277-340. Singer observed in favor of no. i that Raymond included it in Extra although he must have known that Bernard had stigmatized it as apocryphal (*loc. cit.* p. 35). But this is susceptible of more than one explanation. Raymond may have been satisfied that the decretal was a genuine papal letter and not repugnant to the law, even though its ascription to Innocent III had been rejected; and if he wished to include it despite Bernard's *caveat*, he had no alternative ascription to offer.

[19] Abrinc. II c.9 has no ascription for no. i, but the fact that the collection is otherwise exclusively of Innocentian decretals suggests that this was copied from a text ascribed to Innocent.

[20] For *Luc.* see Heyer, *loc. cit.* 588-89 (nos. 109, 111, 112, possibly 110 and 113); for Gilbert and Alan see 'Gilbertus-Alanus' *passim.*

[21] 'Den Höhepunkt der Dekretalensammlungen in textkritischer Beziehung bildet das Breviarium decretalium Bernards von Compostella,' *loc. cit.* 608.

[22] 'Gilbertus-Alanus' 171-72.

ADDITIONAL NOTES

A fourth small collection of the same sort (now named Bambergensis II),
with 20 letters of Innocent III, is described and analysed by S. Kuttner,
'A collection of decretal letters of Innocent III in Bamberg', in Medievalia
et Humanistica n.s.1 (1970)pp.41-56, repr. in his Medieval Councils,
Decretals and Collections of Canon Law (Variorum Reprints, 1980)no.VIII.
Bamberg.II c.8 = Abrin.II c.1.

P.465: G.B. Ladner, 'Eine Prager Bildnis-Zeichnung Innozenz' III und die
Collectio Pragensis', Studia Gratiana xi (1967)pp.25-35 and fig.1, and in
his Die Papstbildnisse des Altertums und des Mittelalters (Monumenti di
Antichità Cristiana, ser.II vol.IV, Bd.II (Città del Vaticano, 1970)pp.72-6
and pl.XII(a), supposes the original of the Prague ms. to have been a
short collection written at Rome after 29th Oct.1212 (cf. Pragensis c.25)
and adorned with a portrait of Innocent III in Roman style of the period. It
was carried into Swabia, where the portrait was framed with an inscription which reflected the political situation before the election of Frederick
II on 5 Dec.1212. In Swabia the collection received another decretal(Prag.
c.34, not in Pal.I or Abrin II) dated 6 Nov.1213 [and - I may suggest - the
undated Prag. c.33, otherwise unknown, to a German recipient]. In or
after 1216 a careless scribe copied into the Prague ms. the portrait,
giving it a German late-Romanesque air, the inscription, now out of date,
the decrees of the Fourth Lateran Council, and the decretal collection.

Pp.470 sqq.: For the relationship of the collections to the registers see
K. Pennington, 'The French recension of Comp.III', Bull.Med.Canon Law
n.s.5 (1975) pp.53-71, the same, 'The making of a decretal collection:the
genesis of Comp.III', Proc.Vth Intern. Congress of Med. Canon Law, 1976
(Mon. Iuris Canonici, Series C vol.6. Città del Vaticano, 1980)pp.67-92,
and O.Hageneder, 'Papstregister und Dekretalenrecht', Vorträge und Forschungen xxiii: Recht und Schrift (Konstanzer Arbeitskreis für ma. Geschichte, 1977)pp.319-47, esp. pp.340-1.

P.482: The decretal 'Super consultatione' appears also as a marginal
addition to Gilbert (above, III p.56, cc.39-40) and in 1 Rot.1.65 and 24.7
(Holtzmann, Studies, pp.175,198 cf.168.

VI

A DRAFT DECRETAL OF POPE INNOCENT III
ON A CASE OF IDENTITY

The letter here printed is a remarkable specimen of a familiar type: the pope declares his sentence in a law-suit and, in doing so, summarizes the course of the case, the statements of the parties, and the testimony of witnesses. The detail is copious and picturesque. Where Pope Innocent III and his delegates could not discover the facts, we cannot hope to decide whether the plaintiff was a wronged husband or an impostor; and the many faults in our manuscripts leave some details of time and place in obscurity. But the document deserves to be known and to be placed in its setting in the turbulent Umbria of St. Francis. It only survives, so far as we know, in a complete copy in the Vatican ms. Pal. lat. 658, fols. 74r–75r, where it occupies blank space after c. ult. C. 26 q. 7 of the *Glossa Palatina* on the *Decretum*[1]), and where it is written in the same hand as is the short collection of Innocentian decretals formed between *Comp. III* and *Comp. IV*, known as *Coll. Palatina I*[2]). The text is often corrupt. An equally poor copy of the first, narrative, portion of the letter (paras. 1–2) is found in Avranches, Bibliothèque municipale, ms. 149, fol. 126v, where it is no. 33 of *Collectio Abrincensis II:* with it this collection ends abruptly at the end of a quire[3]).

The events described in the letter, which must have occupied at least five years, probably occurred c. 1200–1205 or c. 1210–1215; two

---

[1]) For the ms. and the *Glossa* see St. Kuttner, ‚Eine Dekretsumme des Iohannes Teutonicus (Cod. Vat. Pal. lat. 658), Zeitschr. Sav. Stift. Rechtsgesch., 52 (1932) kan. Abt. 21, 141–89, especially 143–44.   [2]) Cheney, Traditio 15 (1959) 466, 480.
[3]) Traditio 15, 480.

pieces of internal evidence unfortunately point in opposite directions. The plaintiff, Palmerius, stated that after some three years of wandering he came to Perugia at Easter when Romans went thither to help the Perugians against the Assisans. This suggests April 1203, for we know of strife between the two cities in 1202–1203, the war in which, according to tradition, the young Francis of Assisi became a captive in Perugia[4]). But Palmerius appealed to Rome soon afterwards, and the auditor appointed to hear the case is described as G. cardinal priest of St. Martin. Now cardinal Guala only received this title in 1211[5]). If we suppose that Palmerius arrived in Perugia during the war of 1202–1203, we must emend the initial or the title of the cardinal. The person of Guido de Papa, cardinal priest of S. Maria trans Tiberim suggests itself, although neither he nor any other cardinal is recorded as legate in Umbria during the next two or three years[6]). If we suppose that the letter preserves the correct initial and title of the cardinal auditor and legate, then the litigation took place after 1211[7]), and we must suppose that Romans joined in some unrecorded recrudescence of strife between Perugia and Assisi. We are not disposed to look beyond the pontificate of Innocent III; for Guala was legate in England 1216–1218, and no other letters in *Collectio Abrincensis II* and the related collections appear to be later than 1214[8]).

The story begins with an expedition undertaken by certain knights and others, under the leadership of one Contus or Cortus, from the neighbourhood of Proceno and other parts of the Perugian *contado*, against Pian Castagnaio, a small town across the Tuscan border. On their return journey, laden with booty, Palmerius son of Ranucius

---

[4]) W. Heywood, *A hist. of Perugia* (London, 1910) 55–56 and sources cited.
[5]) The card. pr. of St. Martin from 1190 to 1205 was Hugo; thereafter no one is recorded with the title until Guala, who was cardinal deacon of S. Maria in Porticu 1206–11.
[6]) Guido had been sent to the March of Ancona and the Exarchate early in 1200: A. Potthast, *Regesta pontificum*, no. 959.   [7]) Guala was active in Umbria during 1214–16: H. Tillmann, *Papst Innocenz III* (Bonn 1954) 298, and cf. Philadelfus Libicus (pseudon. of Giuseppe Frova), who says that Guala acted as legate probably between 1211 and 1216, in Tuscany, Piceno, and Flaminia (*Gualae Bicherii presbyteri cardinalis S. Martini in Montibus Vita et Gesta* (Milan 1767) 60).   [8]) Traditio 15, 473–75. Most of the dated letters in the collections belong to 1209–12, but *Coll. Abrin. II* no. 5 is dated 7 March 1214.

Serardini of 'Piçatum'[9]), according to the evidence of some of his companions (paras. 2, 7, 14), was killed near 'Foxatum' and was buried at the church of the hospital of Ponte Rigo[10]). But according to the story of the plaintiff 'Palmerius', he was not killed, but wounded. For nearly a fortnight he was held captive near Arcidosso and then taken to the coast near Corneto-Tarquinia, where he was sold to pirates. After a month with these pirates he was captured by others, and spent eighteen months apparently in Saracen hands before passing to Sicily. There followed an indeterminate space of time occupied by his journey along the north coast of Sicily, through Calabria (Mileto) and Apulia (Barletta) to Ancona. In the following February he went on pilgrimage to Santiago di Compostella, returned to Rome a year later, and after Easter went to Perugia.

It was then that the plaintiff revealed himself as Palmerius to the bishop of Perugia and others, and brought an action in the ecclesiastical court to recover his wife Gilla, to say nothing of his landed inheritance. Gilla had, in the intervening time, married Manerius and refused to recognize the plaintiff as her former husband. Cardinal G. was appointed auditor in the Curia; the examination of witnesses in Umbria was entrusted to the bishop and a canon of Città di Castello[11]), who sent the written evidence to Rome (para. 3). Further investigation was referred, with power to terminate the suit, to Cardinal G. who was by now apostolic legate in Perugia (para. 4). The cardinal, after careful enquiry, sent his report on the case to Rome (para. 6), where all the evidence was reviewed (paras. 6–11). Master P., papal subdeacon and notary[12]), handled the case at this stage (para. 9). But because of the obscurity of the case the cardinal-legate was again told to examine witnesses and make further enquiries, and settle the case or refer it back to Rome. This was two years or more after Palmerius came to Perugia (para. 12). The cardinal returned to the Curia and presented the results of his

---

[9]) ? Picciati, 4 km. SW of Pietralunga, in the diocese of Città di Castello. This would agree with the evidence by men of Pietralunga (para. 7), an incident on the road to Gubbio (para. 13), and the mandate to the bishop of Città di Castello to hear witnesses (para. 6).   [10]) Probably where the medieval road from Radicofani to Acquapendente crosses the R. Rigo.   [11]) Cf. above, n. 9.   [12]) He cannot be identified certainly, but might be the Master Philip who became bishop of Troja in Oct. 1212; cf. Cheney, English Hist. Rev. 63 (1948) 345.

enquiry. The pope weighed the evidence with the cardinals *(fratribus nostris)* and other expert lawyers, and gave judgment for the defendants.

This brief analysis does not do justice to the wealth of detail contained in the letter. Palmerius's dramatic story and the testimony of many witnesses make it a document which may well interest the historian of medieval Italian society. The discursive, loose, construction permits vivid sidelights, which are not impaired by the facts that the testimony is scrappy and much of it untrue.

From the point of view of canonistic principles and procedure the case is hardly of first importance, though one may notice as interesting features the cautious weighing of evidence in paras. 6, 10–11, the setting out of the presumptions in favour of one or other party in paras. 8–9, and the argument in favour of allowing the marriage of Gilla and Manerius to stand, whether or not the plaintiff was an impostor (para. 11). The final stage of taking evidence from witnesses without the knowledge of the parties (paras. 12–14) is also noteworthy. The statement that the cardinal was to take into account everything 'per que formare poterit animi sui motum' (para. 12) and the final remark that 'in absolutione minus quam in condempnatione periculi formidatur' (para. 15) are in keeping with Pope Innocent III's usual cautious approach to complex issues.

The letter has interest of another kind on account of its transmission and its form. Neither this letter nor any other letter on the case appears in the registers of Innocent III. The manuscripts where the letter is found both contain decretal-collections which cannot have been composed (at least, for the most part) from the archives of recipients. It has been argued elsewhere[13]) that the nucleus of both collections was formed in the Curia in the latter years of Innocent III, by somebody who had access not only to the papal registers as we know them, but also to a miscellaneous body of drafts and copies, prepared in the course of curial business but not intended for permanent preservation. This alone seems to account for the arrangement of date-less letters in order of date and for the presence of *a pari* versions of letters which appear in the registers. The inclusion of part of our letter in

---

[13]) Cheney, Traditio 15, 470–72.

Coll. Abrincensis II and its possession by the copyist of *Coll. Palatina I* point to a similar origin. The form of the letter reinforces the conclusion that the copy is derived from a Curial text, and not from the original in the archives of the executors of the sentence. In the first place, the note at the end of the letter ('Scribatur eisdem M. et G. in modum confirmationis') recalls, though with a significant difference of tense, the notes of *a pari* letters in the papal registers. This note could not possibly have had a place in the letter despatched to the executors; it is the memorandum of a draftsman. Secondly, the text of the letter contains various inconsistencies which seem to be explicable only on the assumption that this is a draft. The draftsman had the dossier of the case before him, and in constructing his text he incorporated extracts from the earlier correspondence and written testimony. But he had not revised these extracts to make a coherent whole. As the last clause shows (para. 15) the draft was intended for a letter to the executors of the sentence; if the copy preserves the correct form in 'faciatis', the bishop of Perugia had at least one colleague, although both our texts only name the bishop in the rubric[14]). But the preamble is clumsy and refers to *pars altera* as if one of the parties in the case had already been mentioned or was the addressee. When, in para. 2, the objection of Gilla to the plaintiff is stated, 'ex parte adversa' describes the defendants; but in the very next sentence 'tu, Gilla' is treated as the addressee. Either the draftsman at this stage intended to compose the confirmatory letter for the successful defendants, or else (as seems more probable) he was transcribing this part of his *narratio* from a letter written in the course of the case to Gilla and her second husband. This is the form of paras. 2–4; but para. 5 was based on the cardinal legate's report[15]), and the forms of paras. 5–6 do not suggest a letter to Gilla and Manerius. Gilla appears again as addressee in para. 7 ('testes partis vestre'), but thereafter she is mentioned in the third person. In para. 9 the phrase 'cythara coram vobis accepta', if correctly copied in P, implies that the executors of the sentence are the addressees[16]).

---

[14]) In *Coll. Palatina I* there are several letters with faulty addresses.

[15]) In para. 3 the reading ,transmitteretis' suggests a mistaken copying of the mandate to the bishop of Città di Castello; but it may only be the error of the scribe of P.

[16]) The executors may have included the bishop or the canon of Città di Castello.

34

These inconsistencies explain why the collector of decretals found this letter in a copy outside the register. It is inconceivable that it emanated from the Curia in this form. It is a first draft which, if used at all, was revised and (one may hope) abridged. As it stands, it is too long, too detailed, and too confused to be a satisfactory official record of a papal judgment; and although it seems to have been copied on account of its canonistic interest, the canonists must have been deterred by these features from incorporating the letter in their decretal-collections. For us it provides, none the less, valuable evidence of the way in which a papal letter was constructed and of the material available in the Curia for the canonists.

The text is printed from ms. Pal. lat. 658, fol. 74^r (= P), collated with Avranches ms. 149, fol. 126^v (= A). We are indebted to the Institute of Research and Study in Medieval Canon Law, and to its Director, Professor Stephan Kuttner, for the loan of photostats of P and a microfilm copy of A.

Episcopo Perusino

Dum^a) cotidie novas formas^b) edere natura deproperat^c), nonnulla negotia frequenter emergunt que non^d) sunt iuris laqueis innodata[17]). Verum insolita et inaudita diebus istis materia nobis questionis occurrite^e) que quanto intricatior existebat tanto peritorum faciebat iudicia^f) variari, maxime cum, nonnullis^g) coniecturis et presumptionibus inherentibus, quod pars altera proponebat commentum vel adinventio videretur; propter quod eo^h) plenius^i) investigari mandavimus causam ipsam quo inusitacior erat questio et ob hoc coniugii vinculum maius animarum periculum timebatur. Proposuit siquidem quidam qui se Palmerium nominat, quod dum olim cum Nepoleone, Uguichione, Guidone, Enercede^j) de Castello Artu, et Ranutio Rainerii

a) Cum A.   b) famas P.   c) depereat P.   d) solum *add.* P.
e) occurrurit P.   f) fac. iud. *transp. A.*   g) non nullis *corr. ex* non nullus A; nonnullus P.   h) ea A.   i) plenius *om.* AP, *supplevi.*   j) cūcede A.

[17]) Cf. *Codex Iustiniani*, I. 17, 2 § 18: Multas eten im formas edere natura novas deproperat; non desperamus quaedam postea emergi neg otia quae adhuc legum laqueis non sunt innodata.

in expedictione[a]) versus Planum Castagnarium[b][18]) iverit[c]), et postmodum omnes pariter cum quibusdam[d]) aliis a loco magnam predam abducerent[e]), a militibus demum[f]) et rusticis eiusdem loci amissa preda[g]) fugati fuerunt[h]). Et cum Buccarellus[i]), eiusdem Palmerii scutifer, remansisset, et ipse rogans Uguichionem et alios ut cum eo ad illum perquirendum redirent et eos trahere nequivisset, rediit ipse solus; set invento scutifero, cum reverteretur ad socios, quidam rusticus misso de rupe spiculo eum in latere vulneravit, et cum paululum procedendo voluisset de equo descendere, cecidit, de latere per scutiferum spiculo eodem extracto; cumque propter sanguinis fluxum[j]) iam quasi deficeret, servientem ad revocandum socios cum equo remisit, quibus redire nolentibus[k]) nec scutifer est reversus. Inter nonas autem et vesperas invenerunt eum duo filii Alioti de Archidosso[19]), ut ab eis didicit, qui ad quandam ecclesiam prope Archidossum positam eundem[l]) sustentando duxerunt, ubi per quindecim fere[m]) dierum spacium moram fecit. Set in octavo die nuntium in Castrum Pigati (!)[20]) transmisit ad matrem, ut ad reducendum eum qui sic convaluerat quod redire poterat suos consanguineos destinaret, qui etiam pro liberatione sua custodibus trecentas libras promiserat se daturum. Cum autem id matri nuntiatum fuisset, baraterius[n]) eiusdem[o]) nuntium sicut idem retulit verberavit, quem iterum Uguitio[p]) verberavit in porta. Quo audito captores sui male[q]) tractaverunt eumdem, et ipsum subtus[r]) Cornetum[21]) ad quemdam[s]) portum per tria miliaria a Corneto distantem per nemora deduxerunt, quo vix duobus diebus cum esset debilis potuit pervenire[t]), ubi magistro Vita, Gaietano[u]), et Bonociuso monoculo[v]) piratis inventis ipsum eis[w]) dicti captores receptis pannis[x]),

---

[a]) expeditionem A.   [b]) Castranarium A.   [c]) inierit A.
[d]) quibusdam] quibus AP.   [e]) abducerunt A.   [f]) demum *seq.* rusticis A.
[g]) predam P.   [h]) fuerint A.   [i]) Bucardellus A.   [j]) fluxum *om.* A.
[k]) volentibus P.   [l]) positam eundem P; positum A.   [m]) fere *seq.* dierum A.
[n]) baratenus A.   [o]) eundem A.   [p]) Uguichio A.   [q]) male P; dol'e *vel* tol'e A.   [r]) eb'tus A.   [s]) quemdam (ad *om.*) A; quedam P.   [t]) devenire A.   [u]) Gagetano A.   [v]) Bonoguiso Monacho A.   [w]) eis] ei P; eius A.
[x]) panis A, P.

[18]) Pian Castagnaio, 9 km. SW of Radicofani, in the diocese of Sovana.
[19]) Arcidosso, 13 km. W. of Pian Castagnaio, then in the diocese of Chiusi.
[20]) Presumably the same as Piçatum, above.   [21]) Tarquinia, 20 km. N. of Civitavecchia.

vestibus, et huiusmodi tradiderunt, cum quibus dum per mensis fere[a])
spatium fuerit, Albertus Miliotus pisanus et Albertus Cinamus tam
eundem[b]) Palmarium (!) [fol. 74va] quam supradictorum pirratorum
galeam apud Sardinie[c]) Turres[22]) ceperunt. Set idem P. in galea
ipsorum apud civitatem Tunis in Massimerti[d]) territorio[23]) demum
captus, per annum et dimidium fuit ibi. Qui per magistrum Matheum
Salernitanum exinde liberatus, et ab oculorum curatus infirmitate[e])
quos habere[f]) consueverat lacrimosos, in Syciliam[g]) ad locum qui
Trapolis[h][24]) dicitur est perductus, quem ibi dictus magister M. liberum
dei amore dimisit. Ipse vero per[i]) Panormum transiens et ripariam
venit usque Miletum, et exinde processit terra marique Barletum, ex
quo demum in Anconitanam[j]) transvectus est civitatem. Qui cum
devenisset ad episcopum[k]) Nucerinum[25]), et sicut ioculator[l]) aliquandiu per curias discurisset (!), Melioratum faciens[m]) se vocari, circa
festum Purificationis beate virginis iter aripuit (!) limina beati Iacobi
visitandi, et anno revoluto revertens declinavit ad Urbem, et toto
Quadragesimali tempore moram traxit[n]) ibidem. Set cum Romani
postea ad[o]) Perusinorum auxilium adversus Asinates (!) accederent,
ipse venit Perusium cum eisdem, et tunc primo Perusino episcopo,
Uguitioni[p]) marchioni[26]), et cuidam cognato suo se manifestare curavit.

---

[a]) fere *seq.* spatium A.   [b]) eiusdem P.   [c]) Sardanie A.
[d]) Tunis in Massimerti ?] tiuisinmassimerti P; c'tamass3 merti A.   [e]) infirmitate]
-atem P; instrenuitate A.   [f]) haberes P.   [g]) Siciam A.   [h]) Strapol' A.
[i]) per *om.* P.   [j]) Ansconitanam A.   [k]) episcopum AP, *forte legendum est*
episcopatum.   [l]) sicut ioculator P; sicī oculato A.   [m]) facens P.
[n]) transit P.   [o]) ad *om.* AP, *supplevi.*   [p]) Uguichioni A.

[22]) Porto Torres, Sardinia.   [23]) The place was in Saracen territory (cf. para. 9,
below), but the emendation *Tunis* is doubtful. If A comes nearer to the original reading,
Cirta (= Constantine) is possible; but Tunis seems more likely. *Massimerti* is probably
derived from the Masmūda, the Berber federation which dominated the region; cf. in
1181: Maxamutorum, Malsamitorum, and in 1236: Moadorum, Moadiorum (L. de Mas
Latrie, *Traités de paix . . . concernant les relations des chrétiens avec les Arabes de l'Afrique
septentrionale au moyen âge* (Paris, 1866, ii. 152, 117) and the coins known as Masse-
mutini (*Liber Censuum S. R. E.* ed. Fabre-Duchesne, i (1901) 12[a] note 2). But the
singular ending makes it possible that an individual's name is intended; cf. Robert de
Monte, 1181: Mansamuz rex Malsamitorum (Mas Latrie, op. cit. ii. 117).   [24]) ? for
Trapani, W. Sicily.   [25]) Nocera Umbra.   [26]) Uguccio Marchio made submission to Perugia in 1202: Boll. della Soc. umbra di Storia patria i (1895) 144 cf.
A. Mariotti Saggio di Memorie . . . della città di Perugia (Perugia 1806) ii. 191.

[2] Unde cum idem qui se Palmerium nominat Gillam[a]) mulierem, que matrimonium contraxerat cum Manerio, tanquam uxorem
propriam petiisset, fuit ex adverso propositum quod Palmerius qui
Gille maritus extiterat, et ex ea[b]) filiam dignoscitur suscepisse, dudum
in expedictione predicta percussus et mortuus extitit, et apud ecclesiam hospitalis de Ponte Rigo[27]) presentibus pluribus tumulatus. Et
cum hoc Gilla[c]), mater, et alii consanguinei Palmerii, septima et
quibusdam aliis sicut moris est pro anima eius ympletis[d]), processu
temporis tu, Gilla, dicto Manerio te[e]) in facie ecclesie matrimonialiter
copulasti[f]). Unde petebatur ex parte vestra[g]) illum qui per quorundam
confictiones[h]) ad hereditatem que fuerat dicti Palmerii aspirantium per
excogitata commenta se Palmerium nominabat ab huiusmodi maliciosa
presumptione conpesci.

[3] Lite itaque inter partes apud sedem apostolicam legitime
contestata[i]), venerabili fratri nostro episcopo et dilecto filio G. canonico
Castellano[28]) dedimus in mandatis[j]) ut, recipientes testes quos in causa
matrimonii que inter dictum Palmerium ex parte sua[k]) et vos ex altera
vertebatur, pars utraque perduceret, diligenter examinarent[l]) eosdem,
et ad nos eorum dicta transmitterent[m]) suis litteris interclusa. Qui,
receptis iuxta mandatum apostolicum testibus et prudenter exami-
natis, depositiones eorum ad nostram presentiam sub suis transmisere
sigillis[n]) inclusas.

[4] Quia vero merita dicte cause dilecto filio G. titulo sancti
Martini presbitero cardinali tunc apostolice sedis legato[29]) erant ex
maxima parte nota, qui dudum partibus auditor datus extiterat, et in
loco in quo manebat, apud Perusium scilicet, investigare commodius
poterat negotii veritatem, ei[o]) causam ipsam cum attestationibus
utriusque partis sub bulla nostra fideliter interclusis duximus com-
mittendam, mandantes[p]) eidem ut, te Gisla (!) si fieri possit ad suam
presentiam evocata, et indagata veritate[q]) diligentissime, de qua dicen-

---

a) Giliam A.   b) eam P.   c) Guilla A.   d) impletis A; *forte addendum est* fecissent.   e) Gilla . . . te P; Guilla .i. A.   f) copulati A.
g) ex parte vestra ?] aperte AP.   h) confectiones A.   i) contestatam P.
j) *hic desinit* A.   k) sua] tua P.   l) examiarent P.   m) *corr. ex* transmitteretis P.
n) singulis P.   o) ei *om.* P, *supplevimus.*   p) mandates P.   q) veritatem P.

27) See p. 31 above.   28) Città di Castello, Umbria.   29) See p. 30 above.

da patrare te faceret iuramentum, eandem causam fine debito terminaret. Qui tam ab eadem demum in sua presentia constituta quam a
prefato Palmerio de veritate dicenda patrare fecit corporaliter iuramentum; sed, eodem Palmerio a prefata narrationis serie[a]) minime
recedente, tu ipsum esse Palmerium omnino negasti, cum signa que in
Palmerio videras, qui cythariçare ac cantare tam gallice quam latine
necnon ad scacos aleasque ludere noverat, et qui faciem, manus, pedem,
et occulos (!) grossos habuerat, in illo qui se dicebat Palmerium non
videres.

[5] Cum autem ad eiusdem cardinalis instantiam, qui pro investi-
ganda plenius veritate rimari singula satagebat, a se invicem mediante
cardinali iamdicto qui, audita secreto narratione unius cauta inter-
rogatione formata, responsionem audiebat alterius, de secretis que
solent inter coniuges fieri requisisset, quibusdam licet paucis hinc inde
recognitis que suis etiam tunc familiaribus poterant[b]) esse nota, super
aliis nichil scire penitus asserebat.

[6] Porro, cum idem cardinalis eandem causam, quam propter
sui novitatem decidere noluit, ad nos remisisset instructam, dicto
Palmerio sententiam postulante[c]) ac altera parte minime conparente
per se vel aliquem responsalem, attestationes utriusque partis et
acta inspeximus, et invenimus[d]) quod multi testium a Palmerio produc-
torum expresse deponere videbantur quod iste qui se dicit Palmerium
et inter quem et Gislam questio vertebatur est Palmerius filius Raynutii
Serardini de Piçato[30]) et domine Gentile[e]) cui dictus Ranucius tanquam
proprio filio hereditatem suam in morte reliquit, quam idem Palmerius
post eius mortem aliquandiu in pace possedit, quodque idem P. G. in
uxorem duxerat et filiam susceperat ex eadem; quorum aliqui quibus
magis videretur esse credendum causam huiusmodi testimonii sui
reddiderunt: quod Palmerius sinistre manus digitum lesum ab asture
habuerat[f]); dicunt[g]) quidam quod in virga nervum habuerat, et
plerique quod quandam in facie habuerat cicatricem. Sophia quoque
soror eiusdem Palmerii asseruit quod duos digitos in utroque pede magis
coniunctos habuerat quam in homine alio naturaliter coniugantur; que

---

[a]) ferie P.   [b]) poterat P.   [c]) postulantem P.   [d]) invenimus *om.*
P, *supplevimus.*   [e]) *add.* hoc eas? P.   [f]) habuerat *om.* P, *supplevimus.*
[g]) dic P.

[30]) See p. 31 above.

utique signa reperiuntur in[a]) isto qui se Palmerium esse fatetur; quamquam dicta Sophia dixerat quoddam falsum quod videlicet iste Palmerius curvum per asturem habeat digiti[b]) manus dextre, quod
falsum per inspectionem[c]) apparet, cum in digito manus sinistre
habeat huiusmodi curvitatem. Benedictus quoque presbiter dixit quod
cum Palmerius antequam in predictam expedictionem ivisset, quoddam sibi confessus fuisset peccatum; postea rediens illud sibi ad memoriam revocavit; quamquam longe minus sit peccatum commissum
quam confessionem super peccato factam ad memoriam revocare. Alii
vero testes qui eundem esse Palmerium asseruerant alias sciencie sue
causas assignant, quorum multis sunt in causis quas exprimunt singu-
lares.

[7] Ceterum, testes partis vestre quorum aliqui se familiares et
amicos Palmerii extitisse fatentur et conversationem habuisse diu-
tinam cum eodem, istum non esse illum Palmerium protestantur.
Preterea, duo testes eiusdem partis, Uguitio videlicet et Enercede,
probare videbantur expresse quod in expeditione predicta Palmerius
de quo agitur interfectus extitit, et demum ab ipsis et quibusdam aliis
tumulatus. Et interrogatus Enercede de sciencie sue causa respondit
quia viderat dictum Palmerium mortuum, qui ab ipso et Uguitione ac
quibusdam aliis apud ecclesiam hospitalis predicti circa ingressum
hostii fuit a latere dextro sepultus. Uguitio quoque qui Palmerium
occisum supradicto modo firmavit, de sciencie sue causa interrogatus,
respondit quod cum invenisset iamdictum P. mortuum, ipsum super
quodam equo posuit per transversum, ita quod capud ab uno latere ac
ab alio latere pedes erant, adiciens quia ideo sciebat illum fuisse Palmerium quia vivum et mortuum novit eum. De sepultura vero idem
fere asseruit quod Enercede. Plures quoque testes deposuerunt quod
cum is qui se Palmerium nominat venisset ad castrum quod dicitur
Petra longa[31]), dicentibus ei loci hominibus: Tu es Palmerius de Piçato,
respondit: Non sum, et quod ille non esset corporale super libro prestitit
iuramentum. Oddo preterea et Bernardus testes ipsius partis dixerunt
quod ipsi cum quibusdam aliis[d]) hoc consilium invenerunt ut iste de

___

a) in *om.* P, *supplevimus.*   b) digitus P.   c) inspectione P.   d) aliis]
alii *seq.* consilium P.

31) Pietralunga, 16 km. E. of Città di Castello, in that diocese.

quo agitur, qui Melioratus tunc temporis dicebatur, Palmerium se
vocaret, pactum inter se invicem facientes ut podere seu bona Palmerii
equis inter se portionibus partirentur, quamquam isti suam videantur
turpitudinem[a]) revelare. Quidam quoque testes dixere quod iste Palmerius aliquandiu ad modum ioculatoris se habuit priusquam moveret
huiusmodi questionem.

[8] Presumptiones quoque ac coniecture pro utraque parte mul-
tiplices apparebant. Pro isto quidem qui se dicit Palmerium huiusmodi
presumptio prima facie occurrebat quia si factum quod ab ipso
narratur esset adinventio vel commentum, vix potuisset tanto tempore
duravisse, maxime cum habuit cum multis postea super bonis Palmerii
questionem, qui si possent figmentum huiusmodi detexissent et obti-
nuerint in iudicio contra quosdam. Preterea, ydioma regionis illius,
locorum et personarum nomina, et cognationes multorum, et ea que
cum quibusdam dixerat feceratque Palmerius, quomodo tam subito
didicisset. Secreta insuper quedam que fecisse Palmerius asseritur[b])
eadem recognovit et signa in eodem apparent[c]) que testes in Palmerio
fuisse fatentur; quamquam obici posset ab aliquo quod testes prius
signa in isto viderant, et postea illa fuisse in Palmerio sunt testati. Ex
eo etiam quedam presumptio pro eodem P. contra predictam G. merito
potuit suboriri[d]), quia postquam de morte Palmerii rumor invaluit,
superveniente demum quodam nuntio, Rubeo nomine, qui Palmerium
vivere nuntiavit, deposita veste lugubri vestes quas deposuerat reas-
sumpsit. Item, interrogata utrum Palmerius signum in manu habuerit
quod fecerat sibi astur, licet id primo negasset, ad multam[e]) interrogan-
tis instantiam postea recognovit. Item, interrogata respondit quod a
Manerio[f]) instructa fuerat ne istum confiteretur esse Palmerium qui
olim extitit vir ipsius; quamquam eadem subsequenter adiecerit quod
quicquid a Manerio[f]) vel fratribus fuerit preceptum eidem, ipsa tamen
non diceret nisi quod puram crederet veritatem.

[9] Similiter contra sepe dictum Palmerium presumptiones vali-
de insurgebant; quia non est verisimile quod sorores aut consanguinei,
vel uxor saltem aut mater, audito de vita eius eum cum omni diligentia
non quesissent, maxi-[fol. 74[vb]]me cum unus ex captoribus eius ad

---

[a]) turpitudine P.   [b]) asserit P.   [c]) appareret P.   [d]) suborri P.
[e]) multa P.   [f]) Manecio P.

matrem post spacium septem dierum accessit, sicut idem Palmerius
recognovit, vel quod de magno vulnere absque medico fuerit sicut dixit
infra xv dierum spatium fere curatus, et quod de die prope Cornetum
transiens coram occurrentibus sibi minime reclamarit. Nec etiam
inmemor esse debuit temporis in quo fuit a captivitate Sarracenica
liberatus, presertim cum confessus fuerit se per annum et dimidium in
eadem fuisse detentum, vel utrum cum prefata G. nuptias celebraverit
hyeme vel estate[a]). Presummebatur (!) insuper contra eum quia, cum
multas haberet ut dicit sorores et consanguineos nobiles et potentes, ad
nullum eorum postquam ad partes illas rediit declinavit, immo non
solum in illis partibus sed etiam Sycilia more se habuit ystrionis; item,
quia iamdicta Gisla ipsum suum esse virum minime recognovit, cum
mulieres primos viros magis diligere consueverint quam secundos,
maxime cum is qui dicit se Palmerium, ex quo illa prolem susceperat,
iunior sit Manente (!). Preterea, Micoola testis eius, que ipsum Palmerium sicut dixit lavit, fasciavit etiam et lactavit eundem, rosam in
spatula et utriusque pedis digitum minimum alii superpositum digito
asseruit habuisse, que utique signa minime inveniuntur in isto. Item,
cum dicta G. dixerit quod Palmerius bene cytharicare noverat et iste
P. fateretur quod cytharicandi peritiam quam habuerat eidem abstulerat exercicium, . . .[b]) cythara[c]) coram vobis accepta eam pulsare sive
digitos ducere iuxta cytharicantium artificium nesciebat, cum utique,
sicut asseritur a plerisque, vix id dedidicisset[d]) omnino ex quo aliquando id bene scivisset. Ex eo quoque presumebatur quodam modo
contra ipsum quod cum mares secreta que cum uxoribus faciunt invere-
cunde quandoque revelent, maxime cum utilitas id deposcit, iste
Palmerius requisitus de secretis que fecerat cum uxore cui iuvenis
iuveni cohabitasse dicitur novem annis nulla fere, ut dicitur, dignoscitur explicasse que aliis nequiverunt esse nota. A dilecto quoque filio
magistro P. subdiacono et notario nostro sollicite requisitus de his que
ad instructionem negotii permanebant, nichil voluit respondere, debil-
itate se laborare pretendens. Protinus ab eodem requisitus de hiis que
in sua narratione prius expresserat ea tanquam notam fabulam per-
currebat.

[a]) etate P.   [b]) *spatium unius unciae* P.   [c]) cytharam P.
[d]) didicisset P.

42

[10] Cum ergo prefatus Palmerius qui vice actoris sustinet inten-
tionem suam per testes quibus nichil obicitur, sacerdotes videlicet et
milites, sorores, consanguineos, nutricem et alios, fundasse legitime
videretur, pro eo videbatur sententia proferenda non obstantibus ad-
verse partis probationibus super morte ac sepultura predicti P. ac
articulis aliis, cum sint pauciores numero et auctoritate minores,
maxime cum unus eorum qui super morte[a]) ac sepultura deponit unum
agrum et iiii[or] familias de bonis Palmerii habere se dicat in pignore
quodque sperat de bonis eius habere, ac alius asserat quod de pon-
dere (!) Palmerii habet aliquot homines in Castro Gonusci[32]), non
obstantibus etiam probationibus super iuramento ab[b]) eodem P. pre-
stito cum publice confessus extiterit se non esse Palmerium, cum id
videatur officere non debere ad uxorem propriam repetendam propter
matrimonialis cause favorem[c]); sed nec fides illorum dictis est adhibenda quod dum super commento et fraude deponunt suam non eru-
bescunt turpitudinem revelare[33]).

[11] Ad hec autem taliter respondebatur e contra quod cum
testes omni exceptione maiores, qui super Palmerii morte ac sepultura
deponunt, super re sibi certa de scientia testimonium proferant et de
visu, illud debebat proculdubio prevalere, presertim cum id fame
publice ac communi credulitati concordet que invaluerant longe ante,
non obstante quod pro parte adversa plures testes deponunt: quia illi,
etsi deponere de scientia videantur, verba tamen eorum ad credulitatem
videntur potius referenda, ex eo quod videlicet[d]) cum hii qui efficatius
dixisse creduntur causas testimonii sui redderent, adiecerunt se ideo
scire illum esse Palmerium quia illa signa que in Palmerio fuerant
inveniuntur in isto; nam certum est quod etsi per signa huiusmodi
poterunt credulitatem firmam concipere quod esset ille Palmerius,
certitudinem tamen sive[e]) scientiam habere minime potuerunt, maxime cum talia sint illa signa que exprimunt que preter subiecti cor-
ruptionem et abesse possunt pariter et adesse; unde facta fide de signis
huiusmodi, de persona vel corpore per consequentiam non fit fides.

a) mortem P.   b) ad P.   c) favore P.   d) quod *add.* P.
e) sine P.

32) ? cf. Madonna di Canoscio, 8 km. S. of Città di Castello.   33) Cf. Reg.
Innoc. III xi. 270, *Comp. III*, III. 18, 4, *Extra*, III. 24, 8 (and see glos. com.).

Preterea, cum idem P. se non esse illum Palmerium de quo agitur corporali iuramento firmaverit non coactus, videbatur quod non esset in anime sue dispendium contrarium asserens audiendus, cum nimis indignum sit ut quod quisque voce dilucide protestatus est id in eundem casum proprio valeat testimonio infirmare[33a]), iuxta legitimas sanctiones. Nec obstare posse videtur quod dicitur quia esse (!) idem Palmerius in favorem matrimonii, nam matrimonii talis occasione quod dubium est fuisse contractum modicum illi favoris accrescit, cum ex adverso re vera favor copule maritalis obsistat in ecclesie conspectu contracte. Cum etiam in dubiis tollerabilius sit aliquos copulatos relinquere quam coniunctos quomodolibet separare[34]), tutius videbatur eundem Palmerium repellendum quam pro eius instantia[a]) in casu tam obscuro et novo separare in ecclesie facie copulatos; cum sive[b]) sit iste Palmerius sive non[c]), sine scrupulo conscientie videatur illos remanere posse coniunctos. Si enim in veritate iste non est ille Palmerius de quo agitur inter illos[d]), nisi forsan aliud obviet[e]), est revera vinculum coniugale; si vero esset in veritate ille Palmerius, cum hoc ipsi omnino non credunt[f]) sicut iurati testantur, absque scrupulo conscientie insimul remanerent. Set si mulier illa isti Palmerio iungeretur in eo casu cum iste Palmerius non existeret, nunquam eam sana posset conscientia re tinere.

[12] Quia vero supradicti Gisla et Manerius non venerant nec responsalem miserant ad sententiam audiendam, et tam ex[g]) signis et coniecturis quam ex gestibus partium, necnon et de circumstantiis que circa personas testium attenduntur ut sciri posset quanta fides esset testibus adhibenda, et de quibusdam[h]) aliis negotium contingentibus ad plenum non fueramus redditi certiores[i]), tam insolitam et obscuram non nisi adhibita omnimoda diligentia voluimus terminari. Unde dicto cardinali dedimus in mandatis ut de circumstantiis omnibus que pertinebant ad enucleandam negotii veritatem inquireret[j]) diligentius que inquirenda videret[k]), ita quod absque conscientia partium a testibus

---

^a) instantiam P.   ^b) sine P.   ^c) non *repetit* P.   ^d) vos *add.* P.
^e) oviet P.   ^f) creditis P.   ^g) tam ex ?] tandem P.   ^h) quibus P.
ⁱ) causam *forte addendum est.*   ^j) inquirent P.   ^k) viderent P

^{33a}) Cf. Codex Iustiniani, IV 30. 13.   ³⁴) Cf. Reg. Innoc. III xii. 61 (26 June 1209), *Comp. IV*, IV. 3, 1; also in Coll. Prag. no. 3 and Coll. Abrin. II no. 13 (Traditio 15, 473). The same form of words was used in C. Lateran IV c. 52, *Extra*, II. 20, 47.

44

iam productis utrinque qui deposuisse super eadem[a]) causa efficatius
videbantur investigaret diligentissime universa, prout eidem negotio
congruebat, inquirendo prudenter an sepefatus Palmerius ita familiari-
ter et secreto cum hiis quas suas sorores asserit moraretur ut eoipso
eius presumerentur esse sorores; per aliquem discretum virum inquiri
faciens an in Archidosso fuerint hiis temporibus aliqui filii Alioti qui
Leo et Gaufreducius, a quibus idem Palmerius captum dudum se
asserit, fuerint nominati; et hiis et aliis per que formare poterit animi
sui motum diligenter investigatis[35]), vel eandem causam per sententiam
terminaret vel ad nos eam remitteret sufficienter instructam, partibus
peremptorium terminum assignando quo per se vel responsales ydoneos
nostro se conspectui presentarent sententiam recepture.

[13] Cum autem, postquam cardinalis prefatus de premissis,
omnibus ignorantibus partibus, inquisivit, ad nostram presentiam redi-
isset, explicatis nobis negotii circumstantiis depositiones testium nobis
obtulit quas iuxta mandatum nostrum recipi fecerat super negotio
memorato. Quas cum inspici fecissemus diligenter, invenimus quod
supradicta Sophia soror Palmerii de familiaritate quam cum Palmerio
habuerat requisita respondit quod postquam rediit is qui se Palmerium
nominat cum ea stetit per duos annos et ante in domo patris atque
mariti familiaritatem cum ea habuerat quam frater cum sorore consuevit habere, comedens[b]) cum ea in una mensa et bibens cum ea in uno
cypho. Dixit etiam dicta Sophia quod iste Palmerius de quo agitur
huiusmodi facultatem habuerat cum Gisla sorore ipsius, scilicet quod
comedebat et sedebat cum ea tanquam cum sorore germanus et hoc
vidit post reversionem[c]) ipsius P. fere per sexaginta vices et ante per
centum; et dixit quod vidit quando eadem G. dedit Palmerio camisiam
atque bracas. Iuilla[d]) quoque, soror ipsius P., interrogata respondit
quod iste de quo agitur est Palmerius frater suus qui cum ea priusquam
exisset de suo et postquam reversus est mansit et modo manet cum ea
in una domo utpote cum sorore, et statim quod rediit[e]) recognoscens
ipsum amplexata et osculata est eum, quia in veritate scit quod ipse est
Palmerius frater suus. Preterea dominus Mannus iuratus dixit quod

---

[a]) eandem P.   [b]) comodes P.   [c]) resisionem P.   [d]) Iuilla ?] In
illa P.   [e]) rediens P.

[35]) Cf. *Digesta* XXII. 5, 21 § 3 and *Extra*, I. 9, 6 and II. 20, 27.

vere iste de quo agitur est Palmerius de Piçato, quem ideo noverit quia familiarem conversationem habuit cum eodem et quia quedam secreta que inter ipsum solum et dictum Palmerium sacramento[a]) firmata fuerunt cum quadam vice idem Mannus esset Perusii, hic Palmerius in reversione sua eidem M. reduxit ad memoriam seriatim[b]). Presbiter Fides dixit quod ideo scit quia iste de quo agitur est Palmerius de Piçato, quia longam conversationem cum eodem habuerat et quia cum hic Palmerius rediit ad memoriam reduxit eidem qualiter quendam mantellum rubeum ei abstulerat quem habet[c]) idem presbiter in ecclesia de Piçato, et qualiter cum Eugobio quadam vice uterque veniret per fontem de Ragio[36]) via publica ludendo predictum presbiterum in capite percusserat Palmerius ferula, et idem presbiter tunc iratus fuerat contra eum.

[14] Ab hominibus etiam de Preceno[37]) quibus dicebatur idem negotium esse notum idem cardinalis fecit partibus insciis veritatem inquiri. Unde Tancredus iuratus et in remissionem suorum peccaminum obtestatus respondit quod ipse fuit in expedictione seu cavalcata predicta, et tunc ipse[d]) ac Saxulus de Caraiola[38]), Thedericus filius Saxuli, Mannus de Callatore, ac Cortus cuius erat negotium apud Serviognianum convenerunt primitus et cum Palmerio cenaverunt. Et dixit quod ex parte sua nullus nisi Palmerius fuit mortuus illa vice; et quando fuit vulneratus Palmerius erat iuxta[e]) Foxatum, et Uguitio de Valle Arni, germanus eiusdem P., scilicet qui iam pridem testis inductus fuerat a Manente (!), et alii milites secum fleverunt[f]); et quod Palmerius habuit gunellam sanguineam et equum sorum et ille fuit vere Palmerius de Piçato, adiciens quod probam faceret quia iste qui se dicit Palmerium non est Palmerius de Piçato. Bartholomeus Petritorti de Archidosso, quem Uguitio supradictus in suo testimonio dixerat in sepultura Palmerii fuisse presentem, de loco in quo[g]) vulneratus fuit Palmerius, et quod Uguitio cum militibus suis flevit cum vulne-[fo. 75r]ratus extitit, et de gunella et equo Palmerii, et quod nullus ex parte ipsius cuius

---

[a]) sacramenta P.   [b]) feriatim P.   [c]) habeat P.   [d]) ipsa P.
[e]) iusta P.   [f]) flenerunt P.   [g]) in quo *repetit* P.

[36]) Raggio, on the road from Pietralunga to Gubbio.   [37]) Proceno, 7 km. W. of Acquapendente, in the diocese of Sovana.   [38]) ? Carnaiola, 22 km. NE of Acquapendente.

fuerat expeditio nisi Palmerius mortuus fuerat, et quod ille fuit Palmerius de Piçato, dixit etiam idem per omnia quod Tancredus. Çoppus
de Preceno, quem Uguitio supradictus in testimonio suo dixit in morte
Palmerii fuisse presentem, iuratus dixit quod cum fuisset missus ab
Uguitione ac sociis eius ad videndum an mortuus esset Palmerius,
mortuum invenit eundem et fuit vulneratus inter flanccum et la garese,
et nullus alius nisi Palmerius mortuus extitit in conflictu predicto,
adiciens quod cum occisores concessissent corpus ad preces Willelmi,
ipse Willelmus et Ianusus portaverunt corpus, et primo portabant in
clippeo (!) et postea super equum sive iumentum imposuerunt illud et
portaverunt ad hospitale Pontis Henrici[39]) et fuit ante ianuam ecclesie
a latere dextro sepultum. Et dixit quod Obertus castellanus de Plano
dedit Roberti . . .[a]). Willelmus dixit quod Contus cuius erat negotium
et qui convocationem fecerat et ipsius socii eundem miserunt ut videret
an Palmerius vivus esset aut mortuus, et si eum vivere inveniret non
relinqueret eum pro centum libris nec etiam pro ducentis. Qui cum
ivisset, invenit ipsum apud inimicos spirantem; et cum occisores
concessissent corpus eidem, ipse ac socii sui, scilicet Çoppus et Ianusus,
posito corpore super equum portaverunt illud ad hospitale predictum.
De sepultura et loco plage atque gunella et qualiter portabatur[b]) corpus, necnon cui data lorica fuerit, dicit idem quod Çoppus. Robertus
vero W. secutus est per omnia in predictis, adiciens quod probam
faceret quod ipse qui se dicit Palmerium non est Palmerius de Piçato.
Eçulus de Preceno super eo quod occisores ad preces Willelmi conces-
serunt corpus Palmerii, et quod positum extitit a Çoppo, Ianuso, et
Willelmo super equum sive iumentum, et quod sepultum fuit corpus a
dextro latere ante ecclesiam hospitalis, et de lorica, idem dicit quod
Çoppus. Iohannes iuratus respondit quod fuit in loco quando Palmerius vulneratus fuit et mortuus. De loco, plage, tunica, et sepultura,
dixit idem quod testes iamdicti. Adamus de Hospitali dixit idem per
omnia quod iamdictus Iohannes. Bonus Filius iuratus dicit quod sua
mala fortuna iaculo percussit Palmerium in posteriori quam in longa
sive in illa parte, et vidit vivum et mortuum Palmerium, scilicet sicut

---

[a]) *spatium verbi brevis* P.   [b]) potabatur P.

[39]) The *hospitale de Ponte Rigo* in para. 2.

dicebatur a suis, et ipse spoliavit eum sanguinea gunella[a]) et calligis quas postmodum cuidam distraxit. Benedictus de Plano dicit quod vidit Palmerium vivum et mortuum, et spoliavit eum gunella sanguinea et lorica. Rogerius et Piganutius dixerunt per omnia illud idem. Bonus Homo, quem Daniel Brunetus et Bonasera secuntur, inter cetera dixit quod Bonus Filius cum iaculo occidit Palmerium et quod Palmerius iaculum aliquantulum portavit in carne sua sicut in humero[b]). Presbiter Stephanus de Archidosso, quem presbiter Iohannes, Tonsus, Petrus, et Pepe secuntur, iuratus dixit quod a XL annis non fuit quisquam in Archidosso qui Aliottus vocatus fuerit vel aliqui qui Leo et Gaufredutius Aliotti filii fuerint nominati, et quod hec que dicebantur penitus falsa erant.

[15[Nos igitur habita super hiis cum fratribus nostris et aliis iurisprudentibus deliberatione multimoda et diligenti tractatu, quia cum iura partium sunt obscura tutius est sententiare pro reo[40]) et in absolutione minus quam in condempnatione periculi formidatur[41]), ut[c]) superius expressum est, prefatos Manerium et Gislam ab inpetitione dicti Palmerii super causa matrimonii duximus absolvendos, super hoc ei perpetuum[d]) silentium inponentes. Quocirca mandamus quatinus quod a nobis[e]) est sententialiter diffinitum faciatis appellatione remota firmiter observari, contradictores etc.

Scribatur[f]) eisdem Manenti (!) et Gisle in modum confirmationis.

---

[a]) sanguineam gunellam P.   [b]) in humero ?] innumero P.   [c]) ut *om.* P, *supplevimus.*   [d]) perpetuam P.   [e]) quod. a nobis *repetit* P. [f]) Scribantur P.

[40]) Cf. *Digesta*, L. 17, 125: Favorabiliores rei potius quam actores habentes; Reg. Innoc. III ii. 37 (16 Apr. 1199), *Comp. III*, II. 13, 1, *Extra*, II. 22, 6: Cum obscura sunt iura partium, consuevit contra eum qui petitor est iudicari; *Sext*, V. 12 de reg. iuris xi: Cum sunt partium iura obscura reo favendum est potius quam actori.   [41]) Cf. Alex. III., J. L. 13845, *Extra*, II. 19, 3: Cum promptiora sint iura ad absolvendum quam ad condempnandum.

VII

The fragment of a decretal collection
from Bury St Edmunds*

Professor Rodney Thomson, writing on 'The Library of Bury St Edmunds Abbey in the eleventh and twelfth centuries', commented on the legal texts in the twelfth-century book-list and noted the existence of one or two law-books from St Edmunds. He remarked on the interest in law and administration which characterizes the chronicles of the house in the late twelfth and early thirteenth centuries and quoted the famous words of Jocelin of Brakelond in which Abbot Samson (1182-1211) tells how he equipped himself to act as a papal judge dele-gate.[1] Legal books from Bury are scarce. If the *Liber penitentialis* of Bartho-lomew of Exeter counts as one, we may note a thirteenth-century copy in B.L. MS Royal 7 E i; while MS Royal 6 B x (also s. XIII in.) contains, along with the *Summa de penitentia* of Raymond of Peñafort parts of a treatise of civil law and the *Summa titulorum decretalium* of Damasus. Another book which may il-lustrate interest in canon law at Bury is Lambeth Palace MS 105, if the second part (fols. 134-294), like the first, belonged to the abbey library. It can be dated *c.* 1200. This begins with *Compilatio prima* and a few additions, followed by a collection of forty-two decretals now named *Collectio Lambethana*.[2] It also con-tains a text of the decretal collection of Gilbertus Anglicus, a formulary for English ecclesiastical courts, the *Regulae iuris* (Dig. 50.17) with Azo's two commentaries, and the *De verborum significatione* (Dig. 50.16).[3]

Though these manuscripts provide only doubtful evidence, it can be supplement-ed by surviving fragments which do service in bindings of Bury books. True, it

---

* I am grateful to J. P. Brooke-Little, Esq., Richmond Herald of Arms, and to Mrs Louise Campbell, formerly archivist of the College, for the facilities which they accorded me to study Arundel MS 30. Richmond Herald, on behalf of the College of Arms, kindly permits me to publish my findings here.

[1] *Speculum* 47 (1972) 617-45 at 641. *The chronicle of the election of Hugh abbot of Bury St Edmunds*, ed. R. M. Thomson (Oxford Medieval Texts; 1974) gives a vivid account of some of the legal issues and processes which absorbed the energies of the monks of Bury a few years later, leading rival parties to litigate before papal judges delegate.

[2] Kuttner, *Repertorium* 305, cf. W. Holtzmann, *Studies in the collections of twelfth-century decretals* (forthcoming). Prof. Kuttner kindly points out additions to Comp. I: on fol. 138r, upper margin (tit. *De rescriptis*) JL 13846 and WH 641 (b), which occur in this order in Sang. 7.16-7 (Singer 288-9), Abr. 7.2.3-4, Tann. 6.2.5-6, Pet. 3.2-3; on fol. 213vb, after the end of Comp. I, in the same hand, JL 14179, which is often added to texts of Comp. I (see *Reper-torium* 300-02). Then comes 'Finito libro reddatur / / /'. *Collectio Lambethana* follows on fol. 214ra in another hand.

[3] Kuttner, *Repertorium* 311 and n. 1. The information on Azo's two commentaries and De verb. sign. was supplied by Prof. Kuttner.

2

is possible that the bindings were not all made at Bury or that the binders got the waste parchment they needed elsewhere; but there is surely a presumption in favor of regarding these leaves as the remains of volumes discarded from the abbey library, a presumption strengthened when we find evidence that they were at Bury in their re-used condition at an early date. Professor Thomson calls attention to the end flyleaves of Oxford, All Souls Coll. MS 49, a fourteenth-century Italian copy of the Digest, which are from a late twelfth-century Bury manuscript of the same work. The preliminary leaves of the Bartholomew of Exeter just noted contain canonistic *quaestiones*. Two more Bury manuscripts in the same collection (10 B xii and 12 F xv) contain flyleaves taken from thirteenth-century copies of the Digest.[4] The flyleaves of Cambridge, Pembroke Coll. MS 62, a glossed book of Daniel, yield diocesan statutes of archbishop Stephen Langton of Canterbury, 1213 × 1214.[5]

Finally, we come to MS Arundel 30 in the College of Arms, London. This was written at Bury St Edmunds, s. xiii-xiv, and contains a chronicle by the cellarer, John of Eversden, and historical, legal, and administrative miscellanea which include an abridgment of the Decretum of Gratian,[6] a 'Regulae iuris' (Dig. 50.17.1-211), a 'Legum medulla',[7] and other pieces which were described by William Henry Black in his careful *Catalogue of the Arundel manuscripts in the library of the College of Arms* (London, 1829: 'not published').[8] All this comes from a later period. What is of present concern is that the contents must have been bound at Bury in the thirteenth century (though the existing leather cover is later) and the binder used earlier waste to fill out the book at its ends with no less than nineteen leaves. Several large leaves are included, which have been cut down, defaced, and in some cases turned sideways, to fit a book which measures roughly 135 × 215 mm. M. R. James noted some of the contents of these leaves (which include part of a palimpsest glossed Vergil in Anglo-Saxon script, s. x in.), but he failed to mention that there is legal matter on fols. 1, 4, 213a-16. Fols. 213a-16 may be briefly noted: they are parts of a

---

[4] For more details of the Royal MSS see the *Catalogue* by G. F. Warner and J. P. Gilson. Notes on fol. 56ra of MS Royal 7 E.i are extracts from Gratian, D.50, and not *quaestiones*, as stated in the *Catalogue*.

[5] C. R. Cheney, 'The earliest English diocesan statutes', EHR 75 (1960) 1-29 and *Councils and synods of the English Church*, ed. F. M. Powicke and C. R. Cheney (Oxford 1964) 23-36.

[6] 'Concordantia decretorum' in red crayon, s. XVI. *Inc.* (fol. 76r) 'Hec decretorum concordia sacra sacrorum / Que confusa fuit sub brevitate cluit. Tractaturus Gratianus de iure canonico orditur ab altiori a iure . . . (fol. 88r) *Expl.* In duobus c. de spiritu sancto operi suo concludit'.

[7] No original title; 'Legum medulla' in red crayon, s. XVI. *Inc.* (fol. 92r): 'Disce quid humanum ius divinumque vocatur'.

[8] M. R. James, *On the abbey of St Edmund at Bury* (Cambridge Antiq. Soc. 8vo publications 28; 1895) 55, described the MS briefly, without mentioning the part which interests us. He remarked that 'it is very like the Liber Albus.' (= B.L. MS Harl. 1005, another Bury miscellany, s. XIII-XIV, actually quite different in character).

well-written book of *c.* 1200 in a small Italian (?) hand. It was written on two columns to the page and the leaves have been inserted sideways into Arundel 30 to make two bifolia. The scribe left ample margins which, after the manuscript's degradation, were filled with writing, and fols. 213v and part of 214r were erased. Enough of the original is legible to show that the leaves come from a text of the Codex Iustiniani and contain parts of Cod. 1.1.1-1.1.8 and of 1.4.19-1.5.3.[9]

The object of the present enquiry is the remains of canon law on fols. 1r, 1v, and 4v. They prove to be much disfigured parts of a decretal collection. The collection was written in a small neat hand by an English or Northern French scribe, *c.* 1200, on two columns of about 53 lines to the page. The few inscriptions and incipits which have survived the savage ill-treatment accorded to the manuscript are adorned with fairly small and simple capitals, in red and green and blue. The original size of each leaf can be estimated to have been as much as 200 mm. wide by 340 mm. deep, and the original written space was about 106 × 180 mm. A scrutiny of the contents of what remains shows, as we shall see, that the two leaves were in all probability consecutive. The top third of each leaf has been removed; the remainder has been trimmed, so that a third of the text remaining on fol. 1ra, after its decapitation, is missing, a third on fol. 1vb, and about three-quarters on fol. 4va. The fragments have also suffered further indignities. On fol. 1r the right-hand margin and the deep bottom margin were filled (s. xiii in. et med.) with miscellaneous and disorderly notes which have no bearing on the canonistic texts. Not long afterwards the remainder of the second column of decretals was totally scrubbed out; verses with the title 'De sancto Benedicto' were written on the space thus provided. Fol. 4r is filled with a collection of verses on scriptural subjects which may well conceal the erasure of a column of decretals (though this is not absolutely certain). On fol. 4v the original text was untouched, but the inner margin and the foot of the page were covered with thirteenth-century additions, beginning with 'Pronosticacio Lombardorum' and continuing with 'Pronosticacio Merlini'. The additions were briefly noted by W. H. Black, whose description of the original canonistic contents reads: 'Ff. 1 and 4 are part of a fine manuscript of the thirteenth century, on the last page of which may be read a copy of an entire bull of absolution entitled "Clemens papa G. Claremonten. episcopo" besides fragments of other letters and documents'. Walther Holtzmann remarked in 1930 that 'die Vorsatzblätter fol. 1, 4, 213-216 sind aus einer Dekretalenhs. genommen';[10] but he apparently failed to follow up this observation, and nobody else did so.

---

[9] The order in which they must be read is fols. (214ra), 215va, 214rb, (215vb), 214va, 215ra, 214vb, 215rb, 213ra, 216va, 213rb, 216vb, (213va), 216ra, (213vb), 216rb. Columns in parentheses are wholly or partially erased. For the over-writing on fols. 213-16 see Black's *Catalogue*, pp. 56-7 and James, *op. cit.* p. 203, who also transcribes many of the additions to fols. 1-4.

[10] *Papsturkunden in England* 1 (Abh. Akad. Göttingen NF 25(i); Berlin 1930) 204. For fols. 213-16 see above.

4

At first sight, this mutilated pair of folios is no very attractive addition to the literature of canon law. Only one of the texts — that described by Black as a 'bull of absolution' — survives in its entirety, and two more are nearly complete. The other pieces, some of them represented by only one or two words from each line of a papal letter, can be identified but contribute nothing of textual value. However, their very survival in one series enables us to associate them with others in similar series. In this context they acquire some evidential importance. For, on inspection, the Arundel fragment shows a family resemblance to decretal collections which Holtzmann distinguished as the Lucensis group (after the *Collectio Lucensis*, published *in extenso* by Mansi in 1762). It comes, in short, from a lost 'unsystematic collection of the second phase' which followed *Compilatio prima* and preceded *Compilatio secunda*, composed around the year 1200. A table will show the similarities and occasional divergences between our fragment and several of the chief collections of this group in the matter of general contents and of sequence. The closest resemblance is to Lucensis, in that all the eleven decretals of the fragment are found in Lucensis; but 'unsystematic' collections more recently discovered — Monacensis, Cracoviensis, and Seguntina — are obviously related.[11] There are also notable similarities of content (not sequence) with a 'systematic' collection of the same period: *Rotomagensis prima*, compiled in Rouen as a supplement to *Collectio Francofortana*. As Holtzmann insisted, I Rot. drew on just such collections as those of the Lucensis group, and not on one source only. Both he and Adam Vetulani called attention to the evidence for dossiers of recent decretals circulating among canonists at the close of the twelfth century (though the two scholars disagreed about the ways of diffusion).[12] It is therefore of some interest to find a fragment of just such a collection written in England or Northern France at about the time when the Rouen canonist put together his collections in Paris, B.N. MS lat. 3922A.

With the clues at our disposal, we turn to investigate the extent of the losses suffered by the Arundel fragment through erasure and excision. Naturally, nothing definite is discoverable about the original contents of the collection outside these two folios; but what of the gaps within them? The heads of fol. 1ra and 1rb are gone, the rest of fol. 1rb, the heads of fol. 1va and 1vb, probably the whole of fol. 4r, the heads of fol. 4va and 4vb. The gap left between fol. 1va and 1vb is most instructive. Because it falls entirely within a single chapter (Council of Tours, c.10), we can calculate its length. Probably nineteen lines are missing

---

[11] For these, and for *Collectio Rotomagensis I*, see Holtzmann's list in *Kanonistische Ergänzungen* 9-10 = QF 37 (1957) 63-4 and the revised list in his forthcoming *Studies*.

[12] Holtzmann, 'La "Collectio Seguntina" et les décrétales de Clément III et de Célestin III', RHE 50 (1955) 401-5, 418-9 and *Studies*, forthcoming; A. Vetulani, 'L'origine des collections primitives de décrétales à la fin du xiie siècle', *Congrès de droit canonique médiéval, Louvain et Bruxelles 1958* (Bibliothèque de la RHE 33; Louvain 1959) 66-72 and 'Collectio Cracoviensis', *Studia źródłoznawcze: Commentationes* 8 (1963) 81-2.

as a result of the decapitation of the leaf, and this finding can be applied to all the other pages. When the gaps are compared with the sequence of Lucensis a striking fact appears. All gaps are accounted for if they were filled with the chapters which occur in Lucensis at those points where the fragment is imperfect. As a result we can confidently reconstruct a group of eighteen items, instead of the eleven which alone remain. In the comparative table below, asterisks against items in the Arundel manuscript mark those which are now entirely lacking, but of which the presence there originally may be presumed.

The fact that all the surviving texts (and probably seven others) also appear in Lucensis, mostly in the same order, may encourage the idea that Lucensis was the main, perhaps the only, source of the collection. But this hypothesis is not acceptable. In at least four chapters the Lucensis text is inferior to the fragment (cc. 4, 16, 17, 18). The analysis shows this to be so in the inscriptions of cc. 17, 18, and other parts of the text have better readings than Lucensis: c.16 'statutus numerus' (Luc. 'statutis uestris'), c.17 'traditionis pallii continetur' (Luc. 'tradenda pallii retinetur'), c.17 'indutum' (Luc. omits), c.18 'Claremonten' (Luc. 'dare monitum'). Other collections of the Lucensis group show close correspondence (though not complete). Cracoviensis has sixteen of these eighteen chapters and Monacensis has fifteen. The sequence in Monacensis at one point (cc.49-51) matches the fragment better than the sequence in Lucensis (87, 42, 88). This all serves to underline a fact already stressed by Holtzmann and Vetulani and others: that we possess only a fraction of the canonical collections compiled by individual practitioners and teachers in this period before the official collections were made, and cannot hope to establish the pedigrees of our manuscripts. The fate of this particular fragment is a reminder that the unsystematic decretal collections before *Compilatio secunda* and *Compilatio tertia* were very soon superseded, and before long must often have been regarded as so much waste parchment.

The collection represented by the fragment was probably written at or for the abbey of St Edmunds c. 1200, perhaps by one of those clerks, *legis periti*, whom abbot Samson summoned to his side to assist him in hearing lawsuits. But it shows no sign of hard wear as a law book.[13] Within a decade or so, enterprising clerks and teachers would have better tools at hand. When this manuscript was written, more than two thirds of each page had been left blank after the usual fashion of canonistic texts, to receive cross-references and other glosses. In the fragment this space was never used for the purpose. It never came into the hands of a keen canonist such as those who worked on Paris B.N. MS lat.

---

[13] This is in contrast to *Collectio Lambethana* (see above, p. 1), also perhaps from Bury, which is heavily annotated. That collection includes 37 pre-Innocentian decretals of which all but three occur in Lucensis. Although all the contents of our fragment are in Luc., only one (the last of the fragment) is in Lamb. c.1. Cf. Holtzmann, *Studies*, pp. 217-8 and above p. 1.

6

3922A and Cracow Cathedral MS 89 and Durham Cathedral MS C III.3, bringing up to date collections which were falling short of contemporary needs. These wide open spaces were evidence of neglect, and an invitation to the monks of St Edmunds to turn the parchment to other uses.

Corpus Christi College,
Cambridge.

Comparative table

Only a selection of the collections which contain these decretals is shown. Every chapter appears in Comp. II and the references are in JL. For other references see the index to Holtzmann's *Studies in the collections of twelfth-century decretals* and his *Regesta decretalium*, both forthcoming in 'Monumenta iuris canonici'.

JL	Arundel 30	Luc.	Mon.	Crac.	Seg.	I Rot.
17655	1	95	63	74	-	-
14083	2	76	-	-	-	17.14
-	3	77	-	96	-	9.8 etc.
17645	4	78	39	97	-	-
17614	5	79	40	98	-	31.33
17615	6	80/90	41	99	-	-
16078	7*	81	42	100	-	22.6
16578	8*	82	43	101	19	-
16607	9*	83	44	88	69	10.20
16603	10*	84	46	102	80	-
16549	11*	85	47	103	49	10.22
16563	12*	86	48	-	50	1.46
16608	13	87	49	23/36	55	10.18
(= 16554)						
16941	14	42	50	14	93	-
16594	15*	88	51	104	100	31.24
16558	16	89	-	89	90	10.21
17049d	17	32	52	18/105	106	4.2
16568	18	58	12/53	40	22	22.4

Analysis of the Arundel fragment

The inscription, incipit, and explicit of each letter is given. Where (as commonly) these elements or any of them are missing, the words are supplied within square brackets and the words with which the fragment begins and ends are also given. No attempt is made to indicate all gaps in the body of the text.

1. [Idem (Celestinus) fidelibus in Messanensi provincia constitutis. Non est in potestate] — (fol. 1ra) saluis priuilegiis ecclesie [Romane decim] -as ecclesiis ad quas pertinent cum [integritate debi]-ta persoluatis. JL 17655. Cf. Holtzmann, *Kan. Erg.* no. 215.

VII

2. [Alexander III Fulconi] decano et magistro R. cano-[nico Remensi. Cum causam que inter] P. ciuem Remensem et A. presbiterum — in quibus archiepiscopus iniungebamus ut — [in expensis aliquatenus condempnetis]. JL 14083.

3. [Concilium Turonense sub Alexandro III.
Quoniam nouis superuenientibus] — (fol. 1va) reclamatores. Si quis autem — a christianitate suspensis (fol. 1vb) — cognitum fuerit aliquem — anathematis sententia feriatur. Con. Turon. (1163) c.10. *Comp. II*, 3.27.1.

4. [Celestinus III] suffraganeis et decano [Rotomagensi] aliter Cantuariensi.
Per falsarios qui nuper — uolumus reuocari. Dat' Lat' [xii kal. Ian.] pontificatus nostri anno primo. JL 17645.
Luc. does not give the date, which is preserved fully in Crac. 97 and 2 Berolinensis 15; nor does Luc. give the alternative address, only found elsewhere in Crac. 97.

5. Idem Cantuariensi archiepiscopo.
An sit deferendum — appellanti deferendum [esse censemus]. JL 17614.

6. Idem eidem.
[Si] matrimonii causa — ab aduersa parte — [calculum procedatur]. JL 17615.
Cc. 7-12 are missing: see above, p. 5.

13. [Idem.
Fraternitatem tuam etc.] (fol. 4va) — scanda-[lum non modicum] — et ecclesiarum [utilitas — extendetur.] JL 16608 (16554).

14. Idem abbati [et conuentui Liriniensi in ii libro registri. Certificari uoluisti] — illa clau-[sula que solet] — diuersita-[(fol. 4vb)te attendatur. Dat' Laterani 4 i. Mart. p.n.a. ii]. JL 16941. Cf. SG 1 (1953) 335.
C.15 is missing: see above, p. 5.

16. [Idem Asturicensi episcopo.
In ecclesia uestra] — laicis computatis qui in — ut canonicos admittatis. JL 16558.

17. Idem Tran[ensi? *om.* archiepiscopo MS]
Ut [(C?) VR MS] super aliqua re et infra.
Quesiuisti etiam quomodo — uti minime debeas. JL 17049. Cf. Holtzmann, *Kan. Erg.* no. 194d.
The address in Luc. is to Ravenna, that to Trani occurs in Mon. 52, Crac. 18, 105, Seg. 106, 1 Rot. 4.2, etc.

18. Clemens papa G. Claremontensi episcopo.
Cum te audierimus — tibi duximus indulgendas. JL 16568.
No inscription in Luc. 'G. Claremontensi' in Seg. 22 and 1 Rot. 22.4.

VIII

A NEGLECTED RECORD OF THE CANTERBURY ELECTION OF 1205-6

T H E circumstances in which Stephen Langton became archbishop of Canterbury are imperfectly reported, and it is unlikely that much will be discovered to amplify Professor M. D. Knowles's recent account.[1] We know that the monks of Christ Church, Canterbury, elected Reginald, their subprior, to be archbishop at some time shortly after Archbishop Hubert Walter died on 13 July 1205 and that the election was irregular for three reasons: (1) The royal licence to elect had not been sought;[2] (2) the election was made pending appeals to Rome;[3] (3) the election was made conditional upon a contingency which did not arise.[4] We know that before the truth of this matter became public, the monks abandoned this, their first candidate, and proceeded on 11 December 1205 with royal licence to postulate John de Gray, bishop of Norwich. Although a complication was introduced by the claim of the suffragans of Canterbury to participate in the election, this scarcely affected the main issue:[5] the pope was called upon to decide between the two archbishops-elect who had come to the Curia for confirmation, each accompanied by monks and documents to testify to his election by the convent of Canterbury. We know the legal grounds on which Innocent III quashed both elections and ordered a fresh election in his presence: this time Stephen Langton was elected, on or before 21 December 1206. We do *not* know precisely how or when Reginald the subprior was elected; and we do *not* know (however much we may be inclined to guess) what caused the monks to change their tune and elect John de Gray. Nor do we know the whole truth about Langton's election in the Curia. It is easy for modern writers to copy medieval partisans and expatiate on the unfair pressure brought by king and/or

---

[1] 'The Canterbury election of 1205–6', *Eng. Hist. Rev.*, liii (1938), 211–20.

[2] The pope naturally did not call attention to this irregularity, which was not a canonical impediment. The obtaining of *congé d'élire* was none the less established custom, which the pope accepted when he ratified John's charter to the Church in 1215.

[3] For record of the appeals, see *Rot. lit. pat.* (Rec. Comm.), i. 56*b*.

[4] The contingency provided for in the election of Reginald, as alleged in March 1206 by Master Honorius of Richmond and the other Canterbury proctor, is stated in Innocent's letter of 30 March 1206 (*Register*, lib. ix ep. 34, Migne, *Patrol. latina*, ccxv. 837). He was to use the decree of election only if the envoys of the king and the suffragans in the Curia had obtained papal letters in favour of a certain person.

[5] The pope gave formal hearing to this claim, and formal judgment, in December 1206 (*Reg.*, lib. ix ep. 205, Migne, ccxv. 1043, and Matt. Paris, *Chron. Maiora*, ii. 495). How this came about is not evident, for both parties had renounced their appeals to Rome on this issue twelve months earlier (*Rot. lit. pat.*, i. 56*b*).

pope upon the electors.[1] But the only clear reflection on the conduct of the parties in the case concerns the monks of Canterbury. They acted dishonestly, and their duplicity earned hard words from the pope when in March 1206 he heard of the second election.[2]

The letter printed below[3] does not much enlighten our ignorance, but it merits careful study and adds slightly to our knowledge of the first reception of the subprior Reginald at the Curia. The original at Canterbury was quoted in 1876 by J. Brigstock Sheppard, and described in the following terms: 'A peremptory letter from Innocent III to King John, requiring him to consent to the promotion of Reginald, the subprior, to the archbishopric of Canterbury. This letter, the tone of which is very characteristic, hardly supports the account of the pope's wishes on the subject of this election as it is recorded by Paris'.[4]

Since 1876 this seems to have been unnoticed by those who have written about the Canterbury election. It shows that Reginald the subprior and his companions had been at the Curia for some time before 1 December 1205 and that the pope was at this time satisfied that Reginald had been chosen by the unanimous will of the convent. Secondly, the terms of the letter suggest that the canonical examination of the fitness of the elect had already taken place and that Reginald had passed the test. Thirdly, the pope—while he recommends Reginald to the king—makes it clear that the question of confirmation is still *sub judice*. Moreover, the pope is already aware that there is opposition to the elect (probably on the part of the suffragans) and that King John favours the opposition. We might suppose that he is only anticipating a possible objection in the future ('quatinus . . . non solum non impedias . . .'), were it not for the clause 'te desistente nostris monitis ab incepto'. On the other hand, we may infer from the vagueness at this point that while Master Peter of Anglesham,

---

[1] Professor Knowles accepts the view that King John used threats to intimidate the electors (*loc. cit.*, p. 218, and notes 1, 3). He fails to observe that in December 1206 the pope expressly cleared the king of this charge: 'Sicut in examinatione praedicti negotii nos et fratres nostri comperimus evidenter, nullam super electione monachis iniuriam aut violentiam irrogasti, quin potius tanquam benignissimus princeps et christianissimus rex circa eos in omni benignitate ac mansuetudine processisti'. (*Reg.*, lib. ix ep. 206, Migne, ccxv. 1048).

[2] 'Ubi est illa religionis honestas, discretionis prudentia, veritatis sinceritas, et virtutis constantia, quae claris late titulis de vobis solebant hactenus praedicari! Mutatus est color optimus, et aurum in scoriam est conversum . . .' (*Ibid.*, lib. ix ep. 34, Migne, ccxv. 834–5).

[3] It is published here by permission of the Dean and Chapter of Canterbury, to whom I wish to express my best thanks, as also to Mr. W. P. Blore, Chapter Librarian, for his help. The letter has many stains upon it and the last five lines cannot be read without special lighting appliances. Through the kindness of the Dean and Chapter, who deposited the manuscript temporarily in the Library of the University of Manchester, it has been possible to recover most of the obliterated passages. I am obliged to the University Librarian, Dr. Moses Tyson, who placed the resources of his photographic department at my disposal, to Dr. F. A. Vick, of the Department of Physics, for technical help, and to Professor W. H. Semple for advice about conjectural readings.

[4] Hist. MSS. Commission, *Fifth Report*, Appendix, p. 429.

the bishops' proctor, had probably lodged the appeal of the suffragans,[1] the king had not yet lodged an official complaint at the Curia. The letter of 1 December, like the letter to the suffragans dated 8 December,[2] was sought as a safeguard by Reginald and his fellow-monks in Rome; they knew, better than the pope knew, how much opposition their action would arouse, for they knew how irregular it was. In trying to arm their candidate against trouble, they may well have conveyed to the pope an inkling of the king's displeasure. At the same time, the traffic between England and Rome in the latter part of 1205 was so intense that the pope probably had more than one source of information.

This document was despatched from the Curia in the form of a 'letter close'. As original letters close of Innocent III are far from common,[3] the external features of this specimen deserve to be noted. It measures approximately $10\frac{1}{4}$ ins. by $7\frac{7}{8}$ ins. (depth), is written upon 19 lines, about $\frac{3}{8}$ in. apart, with a rather deeper margin at the bottom than at the top and no margin at the sides. The calligraphy is outstandingly fine, without being fussy or ornate. It is better writing than that of some other letters close of Innocent III. The initials are unadorned, and the abbreviations (few in number) are indicated by straight lines, as in ordinary *mandamenta*, except for one aberration, where the scribe used the ꝑ or tittle, for the suspended part of Cantuariensis. A double *u* (*tuum*) is marked with two hair-strokes above, after the fashion of the double *i* (in *consilii*). The single *i* and combinations as in *cuius* are not marked. The greater part of the word *subprior* is written over erased letters which cannot be read. There can be no doubt that this correction was made in the papal chancery.[4]

[1] As described in Innocent's letter of 11 December 1205, *Reg.*, lib. viii ep. 161, Migne, ccxv. 740 (where the name appears as 'Englosam', cf. *ibid.*, 835). This letter is preserved in the papal register, not in Matthew Paris's chronicle as stated by Knowles, *loc. cit.*, p. 217, n. 4.

[2] Preserved by Matthew Paris, *Chron. Maiora* (Rolls series), ii. 490. It is significant that neither of these letters appears in the papal register. Letters issued at the instance of litigants would not be enregistered as a matter of course and probably not without special payment. (Cf. R. von Heckel, in *Festschrift Albert Brackmann* (1931), p. 436).

[3] Delisle observed, 'Les lettres closes d'Innocent III dont nous avons les originaux sont d'une excessive rareté: la seule que j'ai vue est à la Bibliothèque Impériale'. 'Mémoire sur les actes d'Innocent III' (*Bibl. de l'Ecole des Chartes*, xix (1858), 20). I have only traced 5 originals in English archives: at Canterbury, Chartae antiquae A. 187 and A. 191 and Christ Church letters vol. ii, no. 14a; at the Public Record Office, Papal bulls 52/1 and 52/3. A. Teulet, *Layettes du Trésor des Chartes*, i (1863), 249, no. 712, prints a letter close from the Archives Nationales. E. Winkelmann, *Acta imperii inedita* (1880–5), ii. 676, no. 1009, prints one from Munich. A. Brackmann, *Papsturkunden (Urkunden u. Siegel*, ed. G. Seeliger, Bd. ii. 1914), Tafel vi c–d, prints in facsimile another from the same source. W. Diekamp, 'Zum päpst. Urkundenwesen des xi, xii u. der erstem Hälfte des xiii Jhs.', *Mitteilungen des Inst. für oesterr. Geschichtsforschung*, iii (1882), 599, 607, signals an original at Graz. Earlier examples preserved in England are Canterbury, C.A., C. 1284 (Urban III) and three of Alexander III printed by W. Holtzmann, *Papsturkunden in England*, I. ii. 430, II. ii. 312, 329. The Public Record Office contains some 24 originals for the period 1216–1303 (cf. P.R.O. *Lists and indexes* no. xlix (1923)). Cf. R. L. Poole, *Lectures on the history of the papal chancery* (1915), p. 121.

[4] Erasures, the mark of careful correction, are not uncommon in earlier products of the papal chancery. Of 28 originals (1160–96) edited by Holtzmann, *op. cit.*, vol. i, pt. ii, thirteen show

This letter close was fastened in the usual fashion,[1] by the making of one vertical fold and two horizontal folds in the parchment. The seal-cord was then passed through holes pierced through the six thicknesses thus brought together, and the leaden seal was suspended. Seal and cord have disappeared, and the six slits on each side of the parchment show how the cord was removed. On the dorse, in the usual position, is the address written in the papal chancery: 'J. regi Anglorum illustri', below this in large letters 'cant', and below that, in a very small hand 'de commendacione Electi'.[2] We may argue from a remark of Innocent III himself[3] and from similar marks on other papal letters that 'Cant' indicates the person who sought the letter and became responsible for its delivery: it was the archbishop-elect or the monks who accompanied him.

Two other chancery marks outside the text are visible: (i) On the dorse, in the top left-hand corner, are the letters "Mil' ". Dorsal notes in this position are not very common on early letters of Innocent III, and it so happens that the earliest noted by Diekamp dates from 17 November 1205 (a fortnight earlier than our example) and consists of ". . . mil', c."[4] Diekamp opined that notes in this position indicate the responsible notary or the datary. More evidence seems to be needed to confirm this suggestion. (ii) On the face of the document is a tiny letter p, written lightly but unmistakably, just under the top edge of the document in the very middle. Diekamp observed the same mark in the same place on an original letter close of 1 December 1209 preserved at Graz; it is also visible (though Brackmann does not comment on it) in Brackmann's facsimile of a letter close of 14 May 1214 at Munich.[5] I have also found it on two letters close of 15 March and 18 November 1214 in the Public Record Office.[6] Students of diplomatic do not seem to have noticed this mark and it is apparently not found on letters close of other popes. The form of the letter p varies from one example to another, so that it can scarcely be a scribe's signature: it may be

corrections, usually involving erasure. Cf. Alexander III in *Decretales*, ii. 22. 3. In Innocent III's time erasures seem to be rarer than before, but the pope did not regard them as raising a presumption of forgery (*Reg.*, lib. i ep. 405, Migne, ccxiv, 382 and *Decretales*, v. 20, 9).

[1] For facsimiles of a letter close of Innocent III, see Brackmann, *op. cit.*, Tafel vi c–d, Text pp. 12–13. For earlier examples cf. *ibid.*, Tafel vi a–b (A.D. 1120), G. Battelli, *Acta pontificum* (Exempla scripturarum, fasc. iii, Vatican, 1933), pl. 9b (A.D. 1181), and A. de Bouard, *Manuel de diplomatique*, i (1929), Album, pl. 3 (A.D. 1188). On the method of closure, see also E. Berger, *Les registres d'Innocent IV*, i (1884), p. xxxviii.

[2] Immediately below the address is the endorsement made at Canterbury c. 1300: 'J. Regi Angl', ut acceptare velit electum nostrum'.

[3] *Reg.*, lib. x ep. 80 (Migne, ccxv. 1178 and *Decretales*, iii. 7. 7), cited Delisle, *loc. cit.*, p. 33, n. 2.

[4] Diekamp, *loc. cit.*, pp. 602–3. This was apparently sent open; the original is at Vienna. An earlier open letter (12 July 1201), Lambeth Palace MS. 644, no. 1, has 'Rus' in large letters endorsed in the top left-hand corner.

[5] Brackmann, *op. cit.*, Tafel vi c–d.

[6] Papal bulls, 52/1, 52/3 (Potthast, *Regesta pontificum rom.*, nos. 4911, 4325).

tentatively suggested that it was the chancery's signal to the *bullator* that the letter must be closed: *p(lica)*. In each instance the vertical fold follows the downstroke of the *p*.

Why is this document found among the archives of Canterbury Cathedral? By the time that the monks of Canterbury could have brought it to England it was already out of date. The community of Christ Church had repudiated Reginald, and so the letter was never delivered to the king. Its survival at Canterbury is a lucky chance, for it served no useful purpose as a muniment. Perhaps some sentimental or historically-minded archivist of the thirteenth century thought it worth preserving on account of the memories it evoked: the exile of the monks and the interdict of England.

Christ Church, Canterbury, Chartae antiquae, A. 187.

Innocentius episcopus servus servorum dei carissimo in Christo filio illustri regi Anglie salutem et apostolicam benedictionem.

Si regias petitiones libenter admittimus, et eas quantum honestas patitur efficaciter promovemus, indignum existeret si nostras preces et monita recusares admittere, presertim cum nostri propositi non existat, te aliquando interpellare pro aliquo quod te non deceat exaudire. Quantum autem in negotio Cantuariensis ecclesie regie curaverimus serenitati deferre, quantumque ipsa ecclesia dispendium patiatur in dilatione substituendi pontificis, tua sicut credimus prudentia non ignorat, que quanto vicinius tanto facilius necessitates eius et gravamina intuetur. Verum cum ad ipsius gubernationem et regimen de totius conventus unanimi voluntate dilectus filius R. subprior[1] eiusdem ecclesie sit electus, quem sue probitatis, litterature, ac honestatis intuitu nos et fratres nostri carum habemus plurimum et acceptum, de cuius quoque conversatione ac moribus indubitate certitudinis argumenta tenemus, celsitudinem tuam monemus attentius, et affectuosa prece deposcimus, quatinus nostris precibus et consiliis acquiescens, ipsius personam electi habeas propensius commendatam, et quod factum est circa ipsum non solum non impedias vel perturbes, sed alios quantum in te fuerit ab ipsius facias inquietatione desistere, ut si forte iustitia exigente obtinuerit quod intendit, a te recognoscat exhibitum, quod te desistente nostris monitis ab incepto, tua sibi non fuerit potentia impeditum. Licet enim tuam velimus magnificentiam honorare, ac in hiis exaudire propensius que tue sint beneplacita voluntati, quia tamen deferre deo magis quam hominibus nos oportet, nullius precibus vel amore declinabimus in dexteram vel sinistram, sed via regia procedentes, quantum nobis dominus dignabitur inspirare, quicquid postulaverit ordo iuris investigare curabimus, et non habentes respectum ad hominem sed ad deum, ipso duce studebimus adimplere. Cum igitur tua circumspectio non ignoret quantum commodi et honoris tibi ac regno tuo ex *persona ipsius*[2] electi valeat provenire, si te promovente vel potius non obstante, Cantuariensis *ecclesia suo*[2] de *ipso desiderio gaudeat, nostris salubribus monit*is[2] et consiliis acquiescas,

[1] The letters 'subp" and the preceding full stop are written in a darker ink than the rest, over an erasure.

[2] Italicized words and letters are almost obliterated; the reading 'gaudeat' is conjectural; cf. the letter of 11 December 1205: 'Sic Cantuariensi ecclesie . . . quantum de iure poterimus providere curabimus quod optata deinceps poterit tranquillitate gaudeat'. Migne, ccxv. 742.

et in huius ambiguitatis discrimine, viam eligas . . . .*m per quam ad sp . . . . st.s . . . ibus* *. . s . . . . nullum regno tuo*[1] generari valeat detrimentum. Eligas ergo fili carissime post *tam dulces preces et monita nostris consiliis acquiescere et non deneges nobis*[2] quod in tuum potius quam nostrum credimus commodum redundare.

Dat' Rome apud Sanctum Petrum kal.[2] Decembris pontificatus nostri anno octavo.[3]

---

[1] Italicized words and letters are almost obliterated and, apart from 'nullum regno tuo' the readings are doubtful. Dots indicate the space of wholly illegible passages.

[2] Italicized words are almost obliterated.

[3] For measurements and early endorsements of the document, see above, p. 235. An endorsement of ?xvii cent. reads: 'Pope Innocent 3ᵈ Letter to King John commending to him to confirm the Election of R. the subprior to the Archbishopric. 1205.' A later endorsement in red ink gives the pressmark: 'A 187'.

/

ADDITIONAL NOTES

Pp.233-4 : On the Canterbury election see Cheney, Innocent III and England (Stuttgart,1976)pp.76,147-54.

Pp.235-7 : A letter close of Adrian IV to Theobald of Canterbury (1157 x 1159) is printed by Holtzmann, Papsturkunden in England ii p.290 no.104, and cf. Letters of Innocent III, ed. C.R. and M.G. Cheney (Oxford,1967) p.xv. I have elsewhere suggested that the use of this form in the thirteenth century was certainly more common than survivals suggest and may have been greater than is usually supposed (Eng. Hist. Rev. lxxix (1964)p.367); but see P.Herde, Beiträge, 2 ed. (1967)pp.72-8. Cf. above Add. Notes to II and p.8.

Pp.236-7 : My hypothesis that connects the note 'p' exclusively with letters close is untenable: 'p' is also found on one letter close to Philip II of France, 30 May 1204 (Barbiche, Les actes,i no.51, see above, Add. Notes to II) but it is also found on letters patent,22 Nov.1204 (ibid. no.52) and 12 March 1215 (J. del Alamo,Coleccion diplomatico di San Salvador de Oña (Madrid,1950)ii facs. opp. p.498).

IX

KING JOHN AND THE PAPAL INTERDICT.[1]

ON Sunday 23rd March, 1208, an Interdict was pronounced
in England and Wales, with the effect that these lands lay
under the ban of the Church from the Monday next following
for more than six years, until 2nd July, 1214.[2] This fact—that
there was a prolonged ecclesiastical strike in England—is a
schoolboy's commonplace. And although this particular Interdict has not been the subject of any special monograph, all
scholars who have written about the reign of King John have had
to discuss it.[3] Yet it remains amazingly obscure. Even in
stating the precise date of its beginning, I am at variance with
some of the pundits, and if we proceed to enquire into the terms
of the Interdict, its application, the king's counterstrokes, the
effect on popular opinion, we immediately run into darkness and
contradictions. It is down this dark path that I wish to go
exploring this afternoon ; I can do no more than assemble, at

[1] A lecture delivered in the John Rylands Library on Wednesday, the 14th
of April, 1948.

[2] There are numerous independent witnesses to the fact that the Interdict
began on Monday, but the solemn pronouncement could only be effectively
published on a Sunday, when all churchgoers would hear it, and publication on
Sunday would explain the date given by several chroniclers (*Memoriale Fr.
Walteri de Coventria* (Rolls series), ii. 199, *Annales monastici* (Rolls series), i. 29
iii. 30 ; F. Liebermann, *Ungedruckte anglo-normann. Geschichtsquellen* (1879),
pp. 146, 168). The Winchcomb annals in Cottonian MS. Faustina B. i (fo. 24 r)
say ' Veniente igitur dominica qua cantatur officium *Iudica me deus*, iubentur
omnes sacerdotes per Angliam accensis candelis pulsatis campanis omnes excommunicare qui in personas ecclesiasticas vel res aut possessiones earum manus
violentas inicere presumerent. Igitur per totam Angliam et Walliam interdictum
feria secunda subsequenti districtissime observatur.' It may be noted that in
accordance with liturgical usage a ban pronounced for Monday might take effect
on Sunday evening after vespers.

[3] The most elaborate essay is that of J. Armitage Robinson, on ' Bishop
Jocelin and the Interdict ', *Somerset Historical Essays* (1921), pp. 141-159 ; and
the best general survey is in the admirable pages devoted to the Interdict by
Sir Maurice Powicke in *Cambridge Med. Hist.*, vi. (1929), 233-237.

296

various points along the track, a few illuminating facts, many of them familiar, a few of them less well known.

Let us begin with the one feature which stands out clearly : the cause of the Interdict. The archbishop of Canterbury had died in July, 1205. The monks who had to choose his successor had made two irregular elections and then, in December 1206, under papal guidance, elected Stephen Langton at Rome.[1] Pope Innocent III consecrated Langton as archbishop ; but John would have none of him, refusing to confirm the election or let Langton enter England. He maintained that Langton was unfit to be archbishop and that, in accordance with the approved English custom, the king's consent to Langton's election should have preceded consecration. The pope entreated and then threatened : he demanded unconditional surrender. John hardened his heart and the pope's delegates laid the Interdict on England as punishment for the king's resistance.

An interdict constituted a serious disturbance of the normal life of the Church. Why, then, did the ecclesiastical authorities impose interdicts? They were, after all, not uncommon. Innocent III had already been responsible for an interdict on the kingdom of Leon which lasted from 1198 to 1204,[2] for interdicts on Normandy and on the kingdom of France in 1199,[3] for another interdict on France in 1200[4] and another on Normandy in 1203.[5] Besides papal sentences, there were countless interdicts imposed on smaller areas by bishops. From the eleventh century onwards, when the local interdict was clearly distinguished from personal forms of ecclesiastical censure, it had been applied to all sorts of infringements of ecclesiastical rights, whether committed by laymen or clergy.[6] Men recog-

---

[1] The only good account of these elections is by Professor David Knowles, *Eng. Hist. Rev.*, liii. (1938), 211-220.

[2] E. B. Krehbiel, *The Interdict, its History and its Operation* (American Hist. Assoc., 1909), pp. 104-106.

[3] Roger of Hoveden, *Chronica* (Rolls series), iv. 94.

[4] A. Cartellieri, *Philipp II August*, IV. i (1921), 27-33.

[5] F. M. Powicke, *The Loss of Normandy* (1913), p. 248.

[6] An excellent discussion of interdicts in general will be found in P. Hinschius, *System des kathol. Kirchenrechts*, vols. iv and v (1888, 1895). W. Richter, *De origine et evolutione interdicti* (Textus et documenta : series theol. 12 and 13; Pontificia Universitas, Rome, 1934) is a useful collection of early texts.

nized that it weighed on the innocent as well as on the guilty, but this very fact made it more effective. For the interdict not merely deprived the guilty of spiritual consolations, it was designed to make the innocent sufferers hostile to the guilty party. By the time of Innocent III it was a diplomatic weapon, and the pope used it as a diplomatic weapon when he ordered that it be imposed on England. Doubtless he hoped for an immediate result : the acceptance of Langton by King John. In fact, he misjudged his adversary. John treated the Interdict as tantamount to a declaration of war, and war between king and pope, *regnum* and *sacerdotium*, continued for five years before an armistice was made in May 1213. Even then the Interdict, the occasion of the war, could not be lifted. The different interests of the pope, who had gained a vassal by the armistice, and of the English clergy, who had suffered heavy material losses during the preceding five years, confused and prolonged negotiations for more than a twelve-month.

The time of the Interdict may be regarded, then, not merely as a period when England was subject to a peculiar kind of ecclesiastical censure, but as a period of war between pope and king. As in many medieval wars, hostilities did not prevent constant efforts from both sides to negotiate a peace, nor should we describe it as ' total war ' ; but war it was. It follows that, if we would measure the effects of the Interdict on England, we must look not only at its terms and its application, but also at the king's retaliatory measures. The two aspects of the matter are brought out by Giraldus Cambrensis when he speaks of the Interdict as a double wound involving both the withdrawal of divine service and the plundering of the clergy's possessions.[1]

The first question is : what was involved in the withdrawal of divine service ? The pope's original instructions to the three bishops who were told to promulgate the sentence were brief. The bishops were to permit no church-service (*officium*) to be celebrated in England except the baptism of children and the penance of the dying.[2] Everyone understood this to exclude in

---

[1] *Opera* (Rolls series), viii. 311.

[2] Migne, *Patrologia latina*, ccxv. 1210. Also in Gervase of Canterbury, *Hist. works* (Rolls series), ii. p. lxxviii.

general all celebration of the mass, all marriage-services and burial-services ; but there was plenty of room left for doubt. For instance, what was the position of the religious Orders with privileges which mitigated interdicts ? How were infants to be baptized with chrism, if chrism was not to be consecrated ? [1] There was as yet no common law of interdicts ; and it is curious to observe that, despite Pope Innocent III's great reputation as a lawyer, he allowed his draftsmen repeatedly to draw up mandates for interdicts which the administrators of those interdicts found to be insufficient. Time after time, prelates of France, of England, of Italy, have to write to the pope for interpretations or amplifications of an earlier papal mandate.[2] The prevailing uncertainty in this particular case is reflected in the ambiguity and contradictions of the records which have come down to us. The two fullest surviving mandates for the application of the interdict are both of doubtful authority. The first is a *Forma interdicti*, printed in the eighteenth century from a manuscript at Mont-St-Michel, which may have emanated from one or all of the bishop-executors.[3] Our second source, not in all respects compatible with the first, is an interpolated version of Innocent III's supplementary instructions of 14th June, 1208 ;[4] who composed it we cannot guess. These point to divergent practices in different parts of the country. The annals of Dunstable, which probably represent the practice in the diocese of Lincoln, give another not wholly identical picture.[5] While the *Forma interdicti* provides that children should be baptized at home, our second source provides for baptism within the church, behind closed doors, and this harmonizes with the practice reported by the annalist of Dunstable. The exclusion of laity from the churches seems, indeed, to have been variously applied. According to the *Forma*, no layman might enter unless he were some influential person who was not excommunicate and devoutly sought admittance and could not be refused without evil

[1] Migne, ccxv. 1423.
[2] Cf. Krehbiel, pp. 116-117 ; Migne, ccxv. 1423, 1582 ; *Decretales*, V. 38, 11.
[3] E. Martène and U. Durand, *Thesaurus novus anecdotorum* (1717), i. 812, reprinted, Migne, ccxvii. 190.
[4] Gervase of Canterbury, ii. p. xcii.　　　[5] *Annales monastici*, iii. 30.

KING JOHN AND THE PAPAL INTERDICT 299

consequences : such a person might be admitted simply to hear a sermon. On the other hand, the Dunstable annalist says that priests granted access to the altars to those who wished to make offerings. In one place the priest might be advised not to distribute *panis benedictus* or holy water ; elsewhere he might receive contrary instructions. An unpublished letter of Peter of Blois, archdeacon of London, shows that the bishop of Salisbury looked to the chapter of St. Paul's for guidance and that in some particulars the advice he received left discretion to the parish-priests themselves.[1] Peter of Blois knew of a letter which Innocent III had written on another occasion to the bishop of Paris, mitigating the severity of an interdict, but he did not know whether the pope intended this to apply to England.[2] Again, although Innocent III, in 1209, told the bishop of Ferrara that baptized children might be confirmed, no such decision is known to have reached England, and we do not know how the English Church acted in this matter.

Early in 1209 the pope permitted conventual churches to celebrate mass once a week behind closed doors ;[3] but, again, his brief mandate left much unexplained, including the precise meaning of ' conventual church '. Peter of Blois proceeded to put to the bishop of London no less than eight separate questions on the matter. Late in 1212[4] a further mitigation of the Interdict's hard terms was granted : the *viaticum*, or last communion, was to be permitted to the dying. But still the terms were hard. Most people were still deprived of all sacraments save baptism and *viaticum*, and were confronted everywhere with closed and silent churches. Nobody at all was permitted Christian burial

---

[1] The two letters of Peter of Blois cited in this paper are contained in the Erfurt Amplonian MS. F. 71 fos. 194v, 196r. I am indebted to Mr. R. W. Southern, who discovered them, for transcripts.

[2] It is in *Decretales*, V. 38, 11 without address. Peter probably knew it in the collection of Alanus (V. 20, 1) where it is addressed to the bishop of Paris (*Ztsch. Savigny-Stiftung für Rechtsgeschichte*, Kanon. Abt. xxix (1940), 301-302).

[3] Migne, ccxv. 1529 and Gervase, ii. p. xcvii.

[4] Probably after 1st July, 1212, when Mauger, bishop of Worcester, died, since the permission was communicated by the bishops of Ely and London (Rad. de Coggeshall *Chronicon* (Rolls series), p. 165). The Reverend T. M. Parker tries unsuccessfully to connect this with Innocent's letter of 14th June, 1208 (' The terms of the Interdict of Innocent III ', *Speculum*, xi (1936), 260).

until the Interdict was lifted in July 1214. So far as can be seen, the clergy obediently observed what they believed to be the terms of the Interdict. The Cistercians, it is true, maintained, until called to order by the pope, that their privileges exempted them ; but this may have been due to a genuine misunderstanding. While there may have been some grumbling at the policy the pope had adopted—for this is hinted at by Matthew of Rievaulx [1]— we hear of no large-scale evasion of the interdict, as occurred in France in 1200 and in London in 1216.[2] Positive evidence is admittedly scanty ; there are, however, records from several monasteries and from the city of London of the setting aside of special unconsecrated ground for cemeteries.[3] Bishops who died in England during the Interdict are recorded as having shared the common fate in this respect. Ralph of Shrewsbury, bishop of Bangor, was buried at his own request in Shrewsbury market-place in 1213.[4]

This was the pope's way of waging war. Now let us look at the other side. King John's immediate reaction to the Interdict remains unknown, for his orders were conveyed to the county-courts by word of mouth. We cannot attach much importance to Roger Wendover's picturesque account of the king's passionate outburst against the bishop-executors, of his threat to slit the noses and tear out the eyes of all Italians and papal clerks in

---

[1] A. Wilmart, ' Les mélanges de Mathieu préchantre de Rievaulx ', Revue Bénédictine, lii (1940), 83 : ' Ceterum non bene sapit quisquis ex nostris precipitanter et insolenter derogat et diiudicat actus apostolici. Non etenim expedit os in celum ponere et de huiusmodi loqui '. Stephen Langton administered a similar rebuke to critics in the sermon he preached at St. Paul's on 25th August, 1213 : ' Vos enim cum sitis laici, vestros prelatos tales esse debetis credere ut omnia discrete agant et cum consilio. Dominus papa christianitatis dominus est et ei oportet obedire.' (G. Lacombe, ' An unpublished document on the Great Interdict, 1207-13 (sic)', Catholic Hist. Rev., xv (1929-1930), 417).

[2] Cartellieri, op. cit., IV. i. 30-31 ; Matthew Paris Chron. maiora (Rolls series), ii 644-645. We cannot be sure how it was observed in Wales. Cf. Cheney, ' Alleged deposition of King John ', in Studies in mediæval history presented to F. M. Powicke (1948), pp. 103-4, 115-6.

[3] Liebermann, op. cit., p. 172 (St. Albans) ; Chron. abbatiae de Melsa (Rolls series), i. 351 (Meaux) ; Krehbiel, op. cit., p. 61 (St. Bartholomew's, Smithfield, and London). Cf. Book of Fees, i. 197.

[4] Annales monastici, ii. 273 ; Hist. dunelmensis scriptores tres (Surtees Soc.), p. 26 ; H. Wharton, Anglia sacra (1691), ii. 347.

KING JOHN AND THE PAPAL INTERDICT

England, of his amnesty to a highwayman who had killed a priest; but there is nothing incredible in it. Two of the bishops certainly left the country in a hurry, and the third, Mauger of Worcester, disappears from John's court early in the month of May. Some luckless Roman moneylenders had their property seized and were themselves turned out of the country.[1] It is not impossible that John pardoned some violence to the clergy, for he was a cruel and capricious man. But here the evidence is contradictory; for while we have a royal precept, dated 11th April, 1208, which expressly forbids action against monks or clergy, the *Annales londinienses*, of the early fourteenth century, which show a particular interest in legal procedure, say that during the Interdict the king ordered that no coroner in England should hold enquiries into the murder of clerks, in consequence of which many clerks perished.[2] John, abbot of Ford, writing in 1210, implies that the clergy had to fear personal violence as well as loss of property.[3] ' Benefit of clergy ' was generally respected. During the Interdict felonous clerks were handed over to the church courts as before, and the recorded infringements of privilege are few. There was the famous case at Oxford in 1209 which caused the dispersal of the University. Two other cases, of Master Honorius, archdeacon of Richmond, and Geoffrey of Norwich, are examples of the arbitrary imprison-ment without trial of persons whom the king may have suspected of treason.[4]

John chiefly adopted what we may call ' economic sanctions ' to dissuade the English clergy from obeying the pope. On 18th March, 1208, he sent letters to the bishoprics of Lincoln and Ely to say that royal custodians would take into their hands on Monday, 24th March all the lands and goods of abbots and

[1] *Chron. abb. de Evesham* (Rolls series), p. 225.

[2] *Rotuli litt. clausarum* (Rec. Comm.), i. 111a (and in *Foedera* (Rec. Comm.), I. i. 101); *Chron. of Edward I and II* (Rolls series), i. 8.

[3] Balliol Coll. MS. 24, containing the sermons of John of Ford, has two sermons (no. 41 fo. 99r and no. 76 fo. 173v) which bear on the Interdict, written respectively in 1210 and 1212. I am obliged to Professor R. A. B. Mynors for indicating these writings to me, and to the Librarian of Balliol for furnishing photographs of them.

[4] *Rot. litt. claus.*, i. 115a; Liebermann, *op. cit.*, p. 155.

302

priors and all religious and clergy of these dioceses who would not celebrate divine service.[1]   We may safely assume that orders of this sort covered the whole country.   The monastic chroniclers almost all speak of a general seizure or confiscation of ecclesiastical property at this juncture.   The work may have been left in some part to the sheriffs, but generally special custodians were detailed to take possession of both the landed property and the movables of the clergy.   John can hardly have found enough officials to do more than supervise the performance of this enormous task.   It involved the substitution of new personnel for the monastic obedientiaries in charge of estates and the appointment of controllers for the sale of the clergy's farm-produce and the provision of their daily bread.   This work was entrusted to local men.   ' Four legal men ' of each parish or vill were appointed to assess the maintenance-allowance or ' estovers ' of the clergy, and they, it seems, actually took possession of the clergy's barns in the king's name and administered the supplies which were contained there.[2]   It was a thankless (and presumably unpaid) task.   The men fell under sentence of excommunication for laying hands on ecclesiastical property, and had to render account to royal officials.[3]   The letter written by Peter of Blois early in 1209, to which reference has been made, discusses the circumstances in which absolution might be given to ' the groups of four villagers (*rustici*) wickedly standing guard over the clergy's barns '.   Opinion in the chapter of St. Paul's was divided, he says, ' but we are agreed in this, that if any of them come to your eminence [the bishop of Salisbury] in a state of penitence and devotion and humbly seek absolution, he might be absolved . . .   Doubtless such as these ought to be brought into the embrace of the Church, for so long as the Church militant endures, there may be found sheep and goats in Jacob's flock, good fish and bad in Peter's net, thorns and lilies in the garden of Abraham.'   Ralph Niger's continuator in a passage on these years where his chronicle adds to the printed chronicle

---

[1] *Rot. litt. patentium* (Rec. Comm.), p. 80*b*, cf. p. 80*a*.

[2] *Gesta abbatum S. Albani* (Rolls series), i. 236; *Annales monastici*, ii. 260-261; *Rot. litt. claus.*, i. 109*b*, 111*b*.   I cannot subscribe to Professor A. B. White's interpretation of the procedure (*American Hist. Rev.*, xvii (1911-1912), 12-16).

[3] Migne, ccxvii. 191-192 ; *Annales monastici*, ii. 261.

of Coggeshall tells us that in 1209 ' the four men of each vill who last year had taken charge of the clergy's movables by the king's command were now called upon miserably to answer for their stewardship '.[1]

It is not easy to estimate all the implications of this measure. There are few detailed instructions to show how it was applied, no reports or accounts of custodians, no record (save in comparatively few cases) of how and when the king relaxed his hold. Both the Close Rolls and Fine Rolls of chancery are missing for the tenth and subsequent years of King John, and the other classes of chancery and household records are fragmentary for the period of the Interdict.[2] The Pipe Rolls of the exchequer are almost silent on the matter. Yet it deserves investigation. If this measure was widely applied for five years (until the king made submission to the pope) it must have brought great wealth to the king and at the same time strained his administrative staff to the uttermost. It must have been a constant irritation to the clergy and must have limited their activity in various directions. Actually, the royal policy seems to have changed. The first confiscation was general. But very soon, in many cases within a few weeks, the king relinquished control of much of the Church's property. Although, in these cases, he restored administration of the property but not its profits, he may in fact have abandoned both. The evidence is scrappy and cannot be analysed in the course of a single lecture, but it points in this direction. Certainly, if John continued for five years to take the revenues of the bulk of the clergy and the monasteries, it is hard to explain the silence of the records. The royal receipts from this source might, indeed, have gone to swell the resources of the *camera regis* without being accounted for at the exchequer ;[3] but the

---

[1] British Museum, Royal MS. 13 A. xii fo. 89r. Niger records a second seizure of the clergy's crops in 1209 (*ibid.*) ; cf. *Ann. mon.*, ii. 264.

[2] The Close Rolls begin again on 3rd May, 1212, the Fine Rolls a year later. The Charter and Patent Rolls are missing from May 1209 to May 1212. The only Misae Rolls run from May 1209 to May 1210 and from May 1212 to May 1213.

[3] Cf. Pipe Roll 10 John (Pipe Roll Soc., n. s. 23, 1947), p. xii. But the renders to the chamber recorded in the next Pipe Roll all concern ecclesiastical property which was in the king's hand by reason of vacancies. P.R.O., Pipe Roll 11 John rot. 1 m. 2 (Chichester), rot. 6 m. 2d. (Lincoln), rot. 8 m. 1d. (Exeter).

304

chancery records of 1212 and 1213, the returns of sheriffs in 1212, and the papal correspondence seem only to be concerned with the property of the exiles. According to Adam of Eynsham, who wrote his life of St. Hugh of Lincoln during the Interdict, almost all the rectors of England redeemed their property.[1] The many who accepted confiscation passively during the first few weeks of the Interdict may well have groaned under their custodians as weeks lengthened into months and years; and as the prospects of peace receded they may have fined with the king to regain control of their property.

Adam of Eynsham's remark about the rectors of England was intended to present a contrast with the noble self-denial of Raymond, archdeacon of Leicester, who preferred to go into exile and forfeit his revenues. The king's animosity, in fact, was directed against those who fled, not those who stayed. It is indeed possible that he presented the clergy with the plain alternative of redeeming their confiscated property or forfeiting it by flight. (In 1210 he set about the tallaging of the Jews by a somewhat similar method.) Many undoubtedly fled, especially after the excommunication of the king in November 1209. Early in 1211 John ordered (if the Waverley annalist can be trusted) ' that all bishops and clergy with revenues in England and dwelling abroad should return within a fortnight of the feast of St. John the Baptist, or be deprived of their revenues in England '.[2] A year later (5th June, 1212) the king ordered the seizure of all churches and revenues of clerks who had been instituted by the authority of the exiled prelates, and the expulsion of the persons so instituted.[3] The returns of the sheriffs

---

[1] *Magna vita S. Hugonis* (Rolls series), pp. 303-304.

[2] *Ann. mon.*, ii. 266. Coggeshall (p. 164) says that the exiles ' vocitantur . . . per edictum publicum in vicecomitatibus '. This suggests the process of outlawry which John renounced at his submission in 1213 (Rot. litt. pat., p. 100*a* and *b*). It may have been as a result of this action that the Pipe Roll 14 John (1211-1212) includes in the account of the bishopric of Lincoln ' £92 8s. 8d. de exitibus ecclesiarum que fuerunt hoc anno in manu regis unde nomina et particule sunt in rotulo qui est in thesauro ' (rot. 1 m. 1) ; also under York, ' £308 7s. 2½d. de ecclesiis et prebendis archiepiscopatus existentibus in manu regis ' (*ibid.*) ; also under Bath, ' £85 7s. 3d. de exitibus ecclesiarum et prebendarum ' (rot. 1 m. 1d).

[3] *Rot. litt. claus.*, 1. 130*b*. The editor of the *Book of fees*, i. 53, failing to note the official enrolment, quotes Wendover's slightly garbled version. Cf. *Ann. mon.*, iii. 33.

KING JOHN AND THE PAPAL INTERDICT 305

to the king's writ have only survived for five counties. They record institutions to the deanery of Wells, the archdeaconry of Bath, and only nine parishes.[1] The returns do not generally state what action has been taken to seize the property or expel the parsons, but in two cases the execution of the writ had apparently been anticipated. First, ' Elias ', to whom the bishop of Lincoln had given the church of Sleaford, was ' overseas and the church has been seized into the king's hand by the servants of Brian de Lisle '.[2] Secondly, the bishop of Bath had given the deanery of Wells to Master Ralph of Lechlade, ' but it is in the lord king's hand '.[3] These were now the objects of the king's displeasure, and it was for them that special provision was made in the armistice terms of May, 1213.

The dramatic confiscation of property in March 1208 was only applied to a limited extent. All sections of the clergy, nevertheless, were obliged to pay large sums to the king during the Interdict. We may take it that they normally recovered possession of their property on paying a fine ; in the case of St. Albans, this amounted to 600 marks, with a *donum* of 500 marks into the bargain.[4] Besides this, the clergy was taxed. In the year 1211 the secular clergy of the Northern province paid more than £3,700 as gifts (*dona*), and the monasteries (especially the Cistercians) were very heavily mulcted.[5] Finally, bishoprics and monasteries were left vacant for years on end so that the Crown might enjoy their revenues. By May 1213 there were seven vacant bishoprics and more than a dozen headless abbeys. But these two last sources of royal income, *dona* and vacancies,

---

[1] *Book of fees* (H.M.S.O., 1920-1931), i. 70, 81, 141, 149, 197.

[2] *Ibid.*, i. 197.

[3] *Ibid.*, i. 82. This fact gives a fact in the career of Ralph of Lechlade unnoticed by Armitage Robinson, *Somerset Hist. Essays*, p. 188. Ralph had been precentor, and is said to appear as dean in 1217 (*ibid.* and Le Neve, *Fasti*, i. 150), but can this be substantiated ? He was not dean between 30th Sept., 1213 and 11th July, 1215 (Hist. MSS. Comm. *Report on . . . Wells*, i (1907), 53, 67, 490), when Leonius was dean. Ralph acted as dean when overseas with Bishop Jocelin (*ibid.*, i. 58) and he was probably abroad in March 1213 (*Rot. litt. claus.*, i. 128*b*).

[4] *Gesta abbatum S. Albani*, i. 241-243.

[5] S. K. Mitchell, *Studies in Taxation under John and Henry III* (Yale, 1914), pp. 106-108.

should not strictly be placed to the account of the Interdict. They were only incidentally part of the king's reaction to the pope's anathemas. English kings (John included) had not needed the stimulus of an interdict to make money from vacancies deliberately prolonged. In 1203 Innocent III had complained to King John that he was preventing an election to the wealthy see of Lincoln in order to enjoy the revenues the longer.[1] *Dona* were demanded from the clergy in 1199, 1203, 1204, and 1205 ; taxation of the clergy in a more formal way began with the income-tax of 1207, and was soon to lose all air of novelty. The chronicles of the time and modern historians have tended to represent all these measures too exclusively as the depredations of a king at war with the Church rather than as the financial devices of a ruthless fiscal expert.

One ' economic sanction ' applied by the king is in line with other indications which point to a certain roguish humour in John's temperament. He gave orders, we are told, to the officials charged with confiscating the clergy's goods, that they were to lock up the mistresses, housekeepers, and lady-loves (*amasiae*) of priests and clerks and hold them to ransom.[2] It was a piquant stroke at ecclesiastical authority. The clergy's women-folk caused a scandal which the canon law denounced but which disciplinarians had long rebuked in vain. The king now traded on the ill-success of the Church in controlling its ministers, and contrived to do so without infringing clerical immunity. Abbot John of Ford, preaching in 1210, condemns those priests who account this privation the worst feature of the Interdict, and who hasten to devote the churches' revenues to the ransom of their mistresses.[3] How much this action profited the Crown we cannot say. The Pipe Roll of 13 John shows that Hugh de Nevill was to be charged with receipts ' de sacerdotissis et rebus clericorum '.[4]

[1] Migne, ccxiv. 1176.
[2] *Ann. mon.*, ii. 261. The Bury annalist, Wendover, Coldingham, and Niger also report this action.
[3] Balliol Coll. MS. 24 fo. 100r.
[4] P.R.O., Pipe Roll 13 John, rot. 14 m. 2. No sum is stated, but the corresponding entry next year gives it as 100 marks (Pipe Roll 14 John, rot. 16m. 2d.). This sum was still outstanding in 1215 (Pipe Roll 17 John, rot. 5 m.2).

I have suggested that John treated the Interdict as a declaration of war. But his war was against the pope, not against the English Church or the Christian religion. His economic sanctions and his threats of violence were designed to discourage the English clergy from obeying the pope, not to wreck the ecclesiastical system in England. The king himself, whether or no he had earned his reputation for impiety, continued active in devotional works and promoted Christian piety among his subjects. His excommunication in 1209 made no difference. Not only do the exchequer records show that the regular accounts of ' elemosine constitute '—royal subscriptions for charitable purposes— continued as before. We also find in 1212 a long list of fresh gifts to religious houses.[1] Although the king regularly neglected the fasts enjoined by the Church, his household accounts were as regularly charged with the expense of his penance : a hundred poor people were fed at Tewkesbury on 31st July, 1212, at a cost of 9s. 4½d, because the king had eaten twice on the preceding Friday at Ludgershall, and so on many more occasions.[2] The household accounts contain more convincing evidence of the king's observance of religious propriety in expenditure during 1212 on candles to be set upon coffers of relics.[3] In the same year sumpter-horses were hired and bought to carry relics in the king's train, and he visited the relics of St. James at Reading Abbey (in which he had always taken special interest). On Good Friday, 1213 the king made his offering of 13d. at the Cross ; and, what is more, paid 8d. for the knights who offered with him.[4] Thus he advertised his orthodoxy, though excommunicate.

In view of this, we need not be surprised that the everyday administration of the Church was allowed to proceed as usual. Within the last twenty years the publication of the Curia Regis Rolls has enabled us to see more clearly how the king's court dealt with the clergy. When the Interdict began, the curia regis sometimes postponed a suit *sine die* because one of the litigants

---

[1] *Rot. litt. claus.*, i. 123b. Cf. H. Cole, *Documents illustrative of English History* (1844), pp. 233-234, 240, 247.

[2] Cole, *op. cit.*, p. 236, cf. *ibid.*, 231-235, etc. and *Rotuli de liberate ac de misis et prestitis* (Rec. Comm.), pp. 110-111, 117, 120, 122, 136, etc.

[3] Cole, *op. cit.*, p. 237.

[4] *Ibid.*, pp. 231, 233, 246, 258 (cf. *Pipe Roll 2 John*, p. xviii).

308

was a religious house whose property was in the king's hand; but it did not do so always. After the summer of 1208 the plea was not admitted as a cause of postponement.[1] The clergy, secular and religious, continually appear in court as plaintiffs and defendants in disputes over advowsons and landed property. Final concords concerning them are continually executed at Westminster and at assizes in the shires. Nowhere is there the least suggestion that the scales are weighted against an ecclesiastical litigant. The chroniclers of Worcester, Dunstable, and Peterborough, each reports a successful lawsuit in which his house engaged during the Interdict.[2] The honorial courts of bishops and abbeys (through their custodians) successfully contest the jurisdiction of the king's court in several cases.[3]

It is never easy in the early thirteenth century to find out how the church courts worked, but so far as we can see their work was not interrupted by the Interdict. The king's court hears of cases which have been improperly called into the court christian, and allows felonous clerks to be removed to the court christian. On one occasion, Aubrey de Vere, earl of Oxford, is told not to impede the process of a tithe-case before the archdeacon of Colchester.[4] But this freedom was seriously restricted in one respect. In 1210 (if we may believe the chroniclers)[5] John forbade the hearing of ecclesiastical law-suits on the authority of papal mandates. The cessation of papal jurisdiction is confirmed by the record of several cases which show otherwise inexplicable delay. For instance, a papal commission to judges delegate dated 20th May, 1210, is recorded in a report by the judges in 1216, and a commission of 28th July, 1210, leads to a judgment late in 1214 or after. A composition reached in October 1214 is based

---

[1] The only case between Trinity Term 1208 and the end of the Interdict concerns the abbot of Waverley, in Michaelmas Term 1210, and then a later day was appointed ' because it is not known whether the abbey is in the lord king's hand or not ' (Curia Regis Rolls, vi. 69). This was an exceptional occasion, when the heavy taxation of the Cistercians had led to the temporary dispersal of the convent and the flight of the abbot (Ann. mon., ii. 265). And the case went on.

[2] Ann. mon. iii. 33, iv. 397 ; Hist. Anglicanae scriptores varii, ed. J. Sparke (1723), ii. 106.

[3] Curia Regis Rolls, v. 317, vi. 8, 206.   [4] Rot. litt. claus., i. 124a.

[5] Ann. mon., iii. 33, iv. 54 ; Walter of Coventry, ii. 202.

KING JOHN AND THE PAPAL INTERDICT 309

on a mandate dated 30th November, 1212.[1] Other papal commissions survive from 1209, 1210 and 1212, but there is no
indication of the date at which they were executed, and they are
strikingly few in number.[2] Moreover, there is no evidence that
English suitors carried their cases to Rome during this period.
By a letter dated 29th October, 1210, Innocent III stopped a case
until the storm in the English Church should have ceased.[3]

Apart from litigation, a good deal of routine business had to
be done. Vacancies on the episcopal bench had to be filled ;
and although the king was frequently obstructive, he did not
impose a veto on all elections. Following papal letters of January
1209, elections took place at Chichester, Exeter, Lichfield, and
Lincoln.[4] Throughout the Interdict, rectors and vicars were
instituted in livings, and we hear of nuns receiving solemn benediction, religious houses entering into confraternity. The prebend of Ogbourne was created in the church of Salisbury in May
1208, and a vicarage was established in the Sussex church of
Henfield in 1209.[5] In 1210-1211 Peter FitzHerbert arranged

---

[1] *Monasticon Anglicanum* (1817-1830), VI. ii. 908 ; Hist. MSS. Comm. *Report on
MSS. of Duke of Rutland*, iv. 33 and *Cartulary of Darley Abbey*, ed. R. R. Darling-
ton, ii. 439-440 (cf. *Rot. litt. pat.*, p. 125ab) ; Westminster, Dean and Chapter
muniments, 15684. A writ of prohibition was issued in 1210 or 1211, probably
directed to judges delegate of the pope : ' Stephanus de Ebroic' debet vi canes de
mota pro habendo precepto regis ad abbatem de Evesham et priorem (sic) de
Davintr' et de Ely ne procedant in loquela ' (Pipe Roll 13 John, rot. 12 m. 2d.).

[2] *Coucher Book of Kirkstall Abbey* (Thoresby Soc.), p. 254 (Nov. 2nd, 1209) ;
Migne, ccxvi. 374 (Dec. 13th, 1210) ; Westminster, muniments, 2596 (17th Dec.,
1210) ; *Cartulary of St. Frideswide's* (Oxford Hist. Soc.), ii. 50 (Apr. 25th, 1212) ;
Hist. MSS. Comm. *Report on var. Collections*, iv. 64 (May 7th, 1212). A case
which had lasted a long time (*diutius*) between St. Guthlac's, Hereford, and
St. John's, Brecon, was settled by judges delegate on Apr. 9th, 1214 (*Archaeologia
Cambrensis*, 4th series, xiv (1883), 26-27).

The statement of the Waverley annalist, s.a. 1207 (*Ann. mon.*, ii. 259) : ' Facta
est hoc anno prohibitio domini regis ne placita domini papae in Anglia teneantur '
is probably misplaced. Cases were conducted in England on papal mandates in
1208 and 1209 (Brit. Mus., Cotton MS. Vesp. E. xx fos. 92 and 240, and Migne,
ccxv. 1504) ; in the exchequer year ending Michaelmas 1209 Master John de
Rammesbiri offered three palfreys to have royal letters to judges delegate ordering
them to proceed in a case (Wm. Salt Soc. *Collections*, ii. 148, 154, 161 ; cf. *Curia
Regis Rolls*, vi. 189).

[3] *Memorials of Fountains Abbey* (Surtees Soc.) i. 172.

[4] Migne, ccxv. 1528-1529 ; *Ann. mon.*, iii. 31, iv. 54.

[5] *Register of St. Osmund* (Rolls series), i. 189 ; *Victoria County Hist. Sussex*, ii. 7.

with Robert de Ros to divide between them the advowson of a Yorkshire church 'if it could be done with the archbishop's agreement'; if the archbishop would not give his assent, the two parties were to present alternately to the living.[1] The archbishop for whom this nice regard was shown was the exile, Geoffrey Plantagenet. We cannot assume (as is often done) that church-building was at a standstill. Dunstable Priory built a new almonry during 1208. In January 1209 the canons of Lincoln had the king's permission to transport without hindrance the timber and lead which they had bought for the work on their church. A little later we hear of appeals for repairs to the church of St. Mary and St. Chad at Lichfield, and for work on the church of St. Andrew's Northampton. In the same year the church of St. Mary Overey, Southwark, was rebuilt after the fire of 1207. These records all belong to the early part of the Interdict. But early in 1213 King John subscribed to building operations at Barlings, Beaulieu, and Romsey Abbeys.[2]

Scanty as our evidence is, it suggests that there was no deliberate obstruction of ecclesiastical business, with the important exception of appeals to Rome in and after 1210. This immediately raises the question : was business indirectly impeded by shortage of personnel ? Were the exiled clergy so numerous and so important that their absence precluded sound administration ? This is one of the hardest questions connected with the Interdict. For we can neither discover the names of all who left England, nor measure their importance. A few facts may, however, dispel a few illusions. As regards the episcopate,

[1] P.R.O., Pipe Roll 13 John, rot. 4 m.l: 'Petrus filius Hereberti reddit compotum de 500 marcis pro habenda alia medietate ville de Wichton' cum pertinentiis, ita quod capitale mesagium cum gardino remanebit predicto Petro sed faciet Roberto de Ros rationabile escambium mesagii illius de parte sua in eadem villa. Medietas autem advocationis ecclesie de Wichton' si fieri possit de assensu archiepiscopi remanebit predicto Roberto et alia medietas predicto Petro, et si de assensu archiepiscopi ita fieri non possit, predictus Robertus dabit ecclesiam illam cum vacaverit una vice et predictus Petrus alia vice '. Ecclesiastical authorities opposed this division of livings (cf. *Curia Regis Rolls*, ii. 211 and Council of Oxford (1222), c.xiii, Wilkins, *Concilia*, i. 587).

[2] *Ann. mon.*, iii. 30, 451 ; *Rot. litt. pat.*, pp. 88*b*, 90*a* ; Cole, *op. cit.*, pp. 251, 257. In the year ending Michaelmas 1212 he had spent no less than £354 2s. 7d. on work at Beaulieu, his own foundation (P.R.O., Pipe Roll 14 John, rot. 11 m.l).

KING JOHN AND THE PAPAL INTERDICT 311

none of the chroniclers is a safe guide. Until November 1209 the only absent diocesans out of a total of seventeen in England were the two primates and the bishops of Ely, Hereford, London, and Worcester. But the sees of Durham and Lichfield fell vacant during 1208, and Chichester, Exeter, Lichfield, and Lincoln were filled by bishops unconsecrated in November 1209. The excommunication of the king seems to have been a signal for further desertions : the bishops of Bath, Lincoln, Rochester, and Salisbury all went abroad. Thereafter, most of the episcopal bench were absent from England until the summer of 1213. This state of affairs was, beyond doubt, unhealthy ; but it may not seriously have impaired the workings of diocesan government. Just as the government of England went on in the king's absence during the reigns of Richard I and John, so also in the dioceses of England administration had reached an impersonal stage where the diocesan's presence was not absolutely necessary. Archbishops Baldwin and Hubert can have spent comparatively little time in the personal conduct of diocesan business. Archbishop Geoffrey of York was absent from his see as often as he was present—and perhaps, in view of his fiery Plantagenet temper, that was just as well. The secular activities of bishops and long vacancies of sees had caused a great deal of diocesan business to devolve on the officials and the archdeacons. The *officialis* had emerged in most English bishoprics by the beginning of the thirteenth century—in time to take over during the Interdict all the routine work connected with the parochial clergy. He is constantly mentioned in royal letters of presentation. We have letters of the exiled Mauger, bishop of Worcester, to his two officials, Robert, prior of Worcester, and Master Robert of Clipston, in 1211,[1] and the notice of Langton's appointment of the prior of Worcester to be official after Mauger's death.[2]

Concerning cathedral dignitaries, regulars, and the inferior clergy, we cannot hope for the whole truth. Richard Poore, dean of Salisbury, and Raymond, archdeacon of Leicester, were at Paris during the Interdict. Benedict of Sansetun, precentor of St. Paul's, and Robert Grosseteste, may have been there

[1] Brit. Mus., Harl. MS. 3650 fo. 47v. Miss K. Major kindly drew my attention to these documents. [2] *Ann. mon.*, iv. 401.

312

too.[1] Among those found abroad with the brothers Jocelin and Hugh, bishops of Bath and Lincoln, are the dean of Wells, several canons of Wells, and the celebrated Master Elias of Dereham.[2] In the early part of the Interdict Adam, monk of Eynsham, biographer of St. Hugh, visited France, but he was back in England in 1211 or 1212. We also find English monastic prelates in Ireland and Scotland, but we cannot assuredly count them among the exiles. The impression we gain is that the clerical exiles were comparatively few in number : some clerks who had incurred the king's displeasure, some who were men of unbending character and high principles, some scholars who could pursue their studies most satisfactorily abroad ; they could be counted in dozens, not in hundreds. Their absence meant a diminution but no dearth of ecclesiastical lawyers and administrators in England. With the exception of Poore and Grosseteste and Sansetun, nearly all the bishops of the next generation seem to have lived under the Interdict in England, many of them as trusted servants of the king ; they include Walter de Gray, the chancellor, Henry de Londres, Richard de Marisco, Simon of Apulia, William of Cornhill, Ranulf of Wareham, Walter Mauclerk, Eustace of Fauconberg, Geoffrey de Burgh. There were others, too, who, although they never reached the episcopate, held cathedral dignities and archdeaconries and had responsibilities as churchmen. One may name among them Master Roger of Rolveston, dean of Lincoln, William de Monte, chancellor of Lincoln, Peter of Blois, archdeacon of London, Thomas of Chobham, subdean of Salisbury, John of Brancaster, archdeacon of Worcester, Robert of Gloucester, archdeacon of Stafford, William of Wrotham, archdeacon of Taunton.

To sum up with a guarded opinion on this ill-recorded subject, we may say that ecclesiastical government was undoubtedly disturbed by the Interdict. There could be no appeals to Rome, and if synods and visitations could, theoretically, be held by the bishop's deputies, in fact they were less likely to occur,

[1] Benedict was in the schools at Paris when elected bishop of Rochester in Dec. 1214 (Wharton, Anglia sacra, ii. 386). Grosseteste suggests that he heard the exiled Langton in France (Matt. Paris, Chronica maiora, v. 404).

[2] J. A. Robinson, Somerset Hist. Essays, p. 154.

and we have no trace of them. In the notorious cases of the exempt abbeys of Evesham and Westminster much-needed disciplinary action had to await the coming of a papal legate. There was also the imponderable depressing effect of the Inter-dict itself and the fear of the king's tyranny, tending to produce pessimism and inertia in church government. The normal routine of diocesan administration went on, but at a somewhat reduced tempo.

This paper has already touched on enough doubtful matters, but before I close I shall make bold to raise a still more difficult question, which is also perhaps the most interesting of all : What was the effect of the Interdict on the religious life and practices of the people of England ? Here again I can only offer a few shreds of information which cannot always be interpreted with confidence. Contemporary comment on the Interdict is for the most part the comment of monks, from their own special standpoint ; not a single layman's opinion of these events is on record.

The first reaction of the people of England to the solemn pronouncement of the Interdict must have been confused by John's propaganda. The king anticipated the sentence by send-ing his agents to the shires to give his version of the dispute with Innocent III. In appealing to the custom of England, he had a plausible case, and never once admitted that he was wrong, until his submission in 1213. The laity, in so far as they thought about the matter, might be expected to take his side rather than adopt a high 'ultramontane' point of view. The clergy, too, were in a great measure the products.of the system which the pope opposed, and there was room (if not so much room) for honest disagreement about the rights of the case as there was in the case of Becket, which had divided the English clergy a genera-tion earlier. The Cistercian annalist of Margam Abbey makes the remarkable statement that all the laity, most of the clergy, and many religious were on the king's side at the outset of the dispute over the Canterbury election.[1] The Interdict, by

---

[1] *Ann. monastici,* i. 28 : ' Pro cuius electione quia facta fuit contra profanas illas consuetudines, quas vocant avitas leges et regias libertates, orta est statim discordia inter Papam Innocentium et Iohannem tyrannum Angliae, faventibus

emphasizing a conflict of loyalties, must have bewildered many. When the king was excommunicated, matters became worse ; many of his subjects now had to decide between ignoring the sentence and going into exile. The majority seems to have ignored the sentence. The lay magnates remain at court attesting the king's charters and participating in government, and although the clerical element in the royal circle is reduced, it still includes two bishops, two Cistercian abbots, various members of the two orders of the Temple and the Hospital, and a large number of secular clerks.

All this must have been demoralizing to the persons immediately concerned and to the onlookers. Their orthodoxy was tested in another way by the removal of the usual stimuli to devotion. In the margin of Matthew Paris' *Chronica maiora*, at the year 1208, is a drawing of a church-bell, with the bell-rope looped up so that it cannot be used.[1] The cessation of bell-ringing was a minor evil, but symbolic of the silence which had descended on the churches. Abbot John of Ford, in a sermon preached in 1210, remarks on the danger that Christian piety will expire if help is not brought by the Father of Mercies, because the sacrament of the Last Supper has been withdrawn. ' To a few of us ' he says, ' by the mercy of God, is left a modicum of refreshment with the Bread of Life, but the masses have waited in continual fasting for nearly two years now, denied all participation in the sacraments. And there is no doubt that they will die on the road and completely cease to remember their fatherland if their hunger goes on increasing.'[2] The denial of the sacraments was a check upon religious devotion which was likely to have permanent results. Some ninety years later Pope Boniface VIII recognized that as a result of the denial of the sacraments during interdicts ' the indevotion of the populace grows, heresies pullulate, and infinite spiritual dangers arise '.[3]

ei et consentientibus omnibus laicis et clericis fere universis, sed et viris cuiuslibet professionis multis, sicut plenius habetur in quodam libello qui inscribitur *De symonia.*' I have failed to identify this book.

[1] Facsimile in M. R. James, ' The Drawings of Matthew Paris ', *Walpole Soc. Publications*, xiv (1925-1926), pl. 7.

[2] Balliol Coll. MS. 24 fos. 99v, 101r.   [3] *Sext*, V. 11, 24.

KING JOHN AND THE PAPAL INTERDICT 315

The mitigation in favour of the conventual clergy (1209), to which Abbot John refers, by which they might celebrate mass once a week behind closed doors, caused scandal rather than comfort to the rest of the people, who saw in it unjust discrimination.[1] There was added the discouragement to men who wished to enter the priesthood; for they could not receive ordination in an interdicted land.

On the other hand, the local ecclesiastical authorities tried to keep alive religious practices which were not positively prohibited by papal mandate. Priests were exhorted to say their hours in private, to preach regularly to the people, to announce the feast-days, and open their church-doors to their parishioners on the patronal festivals. Confession was to be encouraged, although the penitent could not be given absolution (save *in articulo mortis*). On Good Friday, priests might set up, outside the church, a cross for the customary adoration of the parishioners.[2] At London there was no blessing of candles at Candlemas, but ashes were blessed in the chapter-house of St. Paul's on Ash Wednesday, 1209, for distribution to the canons and cathedral clergy.[3] In 1210 an attempt was made to kindle the Londoner's faith by the burning of a heretic, if we may believe the jejune and solitary record of the *Liber de antiquis legibus*.[4]

Adversity sometimes produces a state of mind favourable to religious observances. Some of those who took hardly the cessation of church-services, or who experienced the oppressiveness of John's arbitrary rule, regarded the Interdict as a divine judgment, an encouragement to works of penance. John of Ford expatiates on the wickedness of the clergy and concludes, ' What wonder if the hand of the Lord has been stretched out

---

[1] Peter of Blois writing to the bishop of London about March 1209, says : ' Primores nostre civitatis graviter scandalizantur et murmurant quod cum per episcopos et clericos sicud asserunt procuratum sit interdictum et ipsi ab hoc penitus sint immunes, clericis aliqua relaxatione gaudentibus illi sine causa remanent obligati.' Cf. Innocent III's letter to the Cistercians, Migne, ccxvi. 20.

[2] These details are from the sources mentioned above, p. 298, notes 3, 4, 5.

[3] From the letter of Peter of Blois to the bishop of Salisbury.

[4] *Liber de antiquis legibus*, ed. T. Stapleton (Camd. Soc.), p. 3 : ' Hoc anno concrematus est quidam Ambigensis apud Londonias '. Maitland, *Roman canon law*, p. 161 accepts this story. Mr. H. G. Richardson remarks that the victim was ' presumably a foreign merchant '. *Eng. Hist. Rev.*, li (1936), 1.

against all these ?' Matthew of Rievaulx, another Cistercian, attributes the Interdict to sin. He discusses the evil of lay influence on elections of prelates and says : ' This is the original reason and the definite apostacy which explains why the voice of the turtle-dove—that is, Mother Church—is not heard in our land. For this reason chiefly the Lord of Sabaoth has closed the mouths of those who praised him and abandoned us to scorn and derision, so that people and priesthood are deprived of sacred rites and sacrifices.'[1] Religious exercises were stimulated by these considerations. We need not be surprised if pilgrims flocked to the shrines of saints during the Interdict, and if signs and wonders ensued. (Whereas most churches remained shut, monastic churches which were frequently visited by pilgrims were told to admit visitors by a side door.[2]) The annalist of Waverley tells us that in 1211 one ' St. Simon was martyred in the Isle of Wight, and very soon miracles were worked at his tomb.'[3] In 1212 a miraculous cure at the tomb of St. Wulfstan brought to Worcester a substantial grant of land in Ireland.[4] At Eastertide in 1213 ' the miracles of God and St. Frehemund, king and martyr, so increased in the church of Dunstable that the news of them spread far and wide and the people gave thanks abundantly.'[5] Giraldus Cambrensis, in his life of St. Hugh of Lincoln, gives a detailed account of five miracles worked at this saint's tomb during the Interdict and of another at Worksop Priory.[6] Many years afterwards, in 1228, when evidence was collected towards the canonization of St. Osmund of Salisbury, Master Thomas of Chobham and other witnesses told of two miraculous cures effected at Osmund's tomb in the old cathedral, which could not be adequately signalled and celebrated by the ringing of bells because of the General Interdict which lay on England at the time.[7] I do not wish to over-emphasize the significance of these incidents. They do, however, show that the normal expressions of religiosity were not lacking.

[1] *Revue Bénédictine*, lii. 83.
[2] Gervase of Canterbury, ii. p. xcii. cf. above, p. 6.
[3] *Ann. monastici*, ii. 266.   [4] *Ibid.*, iv. 401.
[5] *Ibid.*, iii. 39.   [6] *Opera* (Rolls series), vii. 137-147.
[7] A. R. Malden, *The canonization of St. Osmund* (Wilts Rec. Soc., 1901), pp. 37-8, 40.

KING JOHN AND THE PAPAL INTERDICT 317

The Interdict left a mark on English society which was not easily forgotten, particularly by the clergy. Did it fulfil its purpose ? The clergy suffered material losses ; the laity lacked in great measure the clergy's ministrations. But for five years King John—the sole object of the pope's displeasure—remained unmoved. In Stubbs's words, ' he grew richer and stronger as he grew more contumacious '.[1] When at last he submitted, his submission was a diplomatic move, prompted by fear of rebellion at home combined with invasion from abroad. These political circumstances may conceivably have been due in part to the Interdict, but this cannot be demonstrated. Still, Innocent III, by maintaining the Interdict for five years, had exhibited his tremendous authority over the English Church. He was able to go on enforcing this spiritual punishment until political cir-cumstances led John to want a papal alliance ; then the king accepted the terms which the pope had offered in 1211 and admitted Langton to the see of Canterbury. It was a con-siderable victory for the pope, but it was a victory without the prospect of peace. It did nothing to relax the tension which the conflicting claims of Church and State had created in medieval society.

[1] *Constit. Hist. of England*, ch. xii. § 153.

ADDITIONAL NOTES

References to additional evidence, drawn from fresh published sour-ces, are in my Pope Innocent III and England (Stuttgart,1976) pp.108-109, 298-356. For interruptions to judicial business see J.E. Sayers, Papal judges delegate in the province of Canterbury 1198-1254 (Oxford 1971) pp.268-70. The management of confiscated estates is illustra-ted by Interdict documents, ed. P.M. Barnes and W.R. Powell (Pipe Roll Soc. n.s.34. 1960).

P.298 n.2:   Breton bishops voiced doubts in May 1200 (see Potthast 1350a) and the pope had to reply to questioning from Portuguese pre-lates in 1199 on the nature of a general interdict (Potthast 592).

P.299:   The letter to Ferrara is III Comp. 5,21,12 and Extra 5.39.43

P.301:   Mr. Honorius apparently bought his release by Michaelmas 1208 (Pipe Roll 10 John p.54,cf.p.xix). He was alive two years later (Pipe Roll 12 John p.153).

P.301 :   The dispersal of scholars was not complete. Some masters were punished by the legate in 1214 for having continued to lecture, Med. archives of the univ. of Oxford (Oxford Hist. Soc. lxx, 1917) i.4.

P.301 n.3 :   Both sermons of John of Ford were probably delivered in 1210: see C.J. Holdsworth, Eng. Hist. Rev. lxxviii (1963) 713. They are ed. by E. Mikkers and H. Costello in Corpus Christianorum continuatio medievalis, pp.17-18 (1970).

P.316 :   The miracles of St Frehemund cannot be confidently ascribed to Eastertide 1213, in view of the doubtful chronology of the Dunstable annals (Cheney, Medieval texts and studies (Oxford, 1973) p.226).

X

KING JOHN'S REACTION TO THE INTERDICT
ON ENGLAND

GIRALDUS CAMBRENSIS observed that the interdict laid on England in 1208 inflicted a double wound, involving as it did both the withdrawal of divine service and the plundering of the clergy's possessions.[2] The eagerness of King John in exploiting the situation for his financial profit does not admit of doubt. The estimate of reparations for *ablata* and *dampna* arrived at in 1214 was 100,000 marks ; this did not satisfy the clergy, and probably the sum was too small to cover all that the king had received by confiscations, prolonging of vacancies, *dona*, and fines.[3] Although even an approximately correct estimate is now unattainable,[4] an enquiry is still worth while to discover the king's policy and his methods of exaction during the interdict. This paper is primarily concerned with his general seizure of church property in 1208.

King John's reaction to the threat of interdict, of which he received final warning from Simon Langton on 12 March 1208, was swift and violent. The precise orders which he gave in the first moment of fury are unfortunately not preserved by any reliable witness. All we know is that on 14 March he

---

[1] This paper is an amplified version of part of the paper read by Professor Cheney on 11 December in place of the Presidential Address which Professor Seton-Watson was prevented by illness from delivering. [ED.]

[2] *Opera* (Rolls Series), viii. 311.

[3] See S. J. Mitchell, *Studies in taxation under John and Henry III* (New Haven, 1914), pp. 93–109. Further discussion of the reparations will be found in an unpublished thesis (M.A., Manchester, 1947) : 'Anglo-papal relations 1213–1216', by Miss Stella M. Whileblood.

[4] The list of King John's receipts which is found in *Red book of the exchequer* (Rolls Series), ii. 772–3 is of unknown origin, provides no analysis to show what items of income are included, and is almost certainly incomplete. The total, as printed, amounts to £100,000, 5 *marks*, 5s. 3d., but this should probably be read as 100,055 *marks*, 5s. 3d. ; the total of the separate items should be 113,412 *marks*, 12s. 5d. The details of this list do not appear to agree with the figures recorded by the Dunstable annalist for the diocese of Lincoln and Christ Church, Canterbury (*Ann. monastici* (Rolls Series), iii. 39). The sum of £53,474 3s. 9d. added up by Mitchell (*op. cit.*, pp. 106–8) as profits of church lands in hand is, as he observes, not exhaustive. It must also be noted that the sum represents gross receipts, from which considerable deductions must be made to discover the real profit to the Crown. Out of two years' gross revenues of Whitby amounting to £412 12s. 6½d., £181 18s. 6d. was spent on the abbey. At Ramsey, in one year, gross revenues were £1,219 0s. 8½d., and internal expenditure £156 12s. 2d. (P.R.O., Pipe Roll 14 John, rot. 1, m. 2 and m. 1d). Moreover, these profits cannot be regarded wholly as consequent upon the interdict.

sent Reginald of Cornhill with a letter to the men of Kent ; the letter announces the breakdown of negotiations with Langton and orders the men of Kent to credit what Reginald of Cornhill shall tell them on the king's behalf, concerning what has been done and what is to be done in this business. In the course of the next week, other officers of the Crown were sent with oral instructions to half the bishoprics of England. The people of the diocese of Bath were told to obey Gerard de Aties as the king's bailiff for the bishopric on and after Monday, 24 March. Robert of Vieuxpont was told to do what had been enjoined upon him concerning the clergy and their goods and possessions in the diocese of Durham.[1] The king's messengers apparently denounced the executors of the interdict (the bishops of London, Ely, and Worcester) and ordered the expulsion of Italians [2] ; it is doubtful whether, apart from this, they threatened the persons of the clergy.[3] Their chief business was of a different sort. The king's letters sent to the bishoprics of Lincoln and Ely on 18 March explicitly say that the royal custodians will take into their hands on Monday, 24 March, all the lands and goods of abbots and priors and all religious and clergy of these dioceses who will not celebrate divine service. We may assume that, as the monastic chroniclers say, this order was applied to the whole country. In some places the sheriffs, but in many places special custodians, took charge of both the landed property and the movables of the clergy. They were to hold these possessions in the king's name and give the owners a mere subsistence-allowance. So great an undertaking must have taxed the man-power of the adminis- tration to the utmost, and the burden of local management must have fallen in large measure on local men. According to an order directed to Hugh de Nevill on 6 April 1208, the estovers, or reasonable maintenance, allowed to the regular and secular clergy was to be assessed by ' four legal men of the parish ' [4] ; and this is confirmed by a similar order to Reginald of Cornhill, dated a week later.[5] Several unofficial sources speak of the locking up of the clergy's barns,[6] and it seems

[1] *Rotuli litterarum patentium* (Record Commission), p. 80a, b.
[2] Gervase of Canterbury, *Works* (Rolls Series), ii, 101, 107 ; *Chron. abbatiae de Evesham* (Rolls Series), p. 225 ; Roger Wendover, in Matt. Paris, *Chron. maiora* (Rolls Series), ii. 522.
[3] Cf. C. R. Cheney, ' King John and the papal interdict ', *Bulletin of the John Rylands Library* (hereinafter, *B.J.R.L.*), xxxi (1948), pp. 300–1.
[4] *Rotuli litterarum clausarum* (Record Comm.), i. 109b. Sir Maurice Powicke is the only historian who has noted the importance of this as a precedent for the summons to St. Albans in August 1213 (*Cambr. Med. Hist.*, vi. 235, n. 1).
[5] *Rot. lit. claus.*, i. 111b : ' per visum iiii legalium hominum de eadem *villa* ',
[6] *B.J.R.L.*, xxxi. 302.

to be clear that the ' four legal men ' actually administered the supplies which were contained there. A letter written by Peter of Blois early in 1209 speaks of ' the groups of four villagers (*quaterni rustici*) wickedly standing guard over the clergy's barns '.[1] The continuator of Ralph Niger records that in 1209 ' the four men of each vill who last year had taken charge of the clergy's movables by the king's command were now called upon by the king's bailiffs to answer miserably for their custody '.[2]

How generally and for how long did this state of affairs last ? A complete answer to this double question, while it would not by any means tell us all we want to know about King John's spoliation of the churches, would be a valuable contribution to the subject. To supply a partial and provisional answer is the object of this paper. We approach the question without hope of doing more. Not only are we baffled by paucity of evidence ; we are puzzled by the apparent contradictions in the little that we have. The chancery rolls for the period are distressingly incomplete, and the Pipe Rolls of the exchequer, which ought to be a principal source, throw, as will be seen, singularly little direct light on the problem. The monastic writers provide some details but wrote in some instances long after the event, with bitterness and imperfect recollection, and at best could seldom describe more than the vicissitudes of their own monastery. Of non-monastic writers there is none of importance.

To take first the evidence for a single abbey. The annalist of St. Edmunds was probably contemporary, and may even have been writing during the interdict. He belonged to a famous and wealthy Benedictine house in the thick of affairs. According to him, the king ' arranged to confiscate (*confiscare disposuit*) all ecclesiastical revenues and converted them for the most part to his own use. But out of reverence for St. Edmund, at Guildford where he had celebrated Easter, he granted St. Edmund's abbey its former liberty in all respects.' [3] Easter fell on 6 April 1208, and on 7 April, as we learn from the Close Roll, the king informed the Earl of Oxford that he had committed to the abbot of St. Edmunds all the lands, revenues, and goods (*res*) of his abbey which were seised into the king's

---

[1] Erfurt, Amplonian MS. F. 71, fo. 194v. I am indebted to Mr. R. W. Southern, who discovered the letter, for a transcript.

[2] Brit. Mus. Royal MS. 13 A. xii, fo. 89r. The Dunstable annalist says that the church property was put in the charge of constables (*Annales monastici* (Rolls Series), iii. 30). ' Constabularius ' can have the general meaning of warden or controller (cf. A. L. Poole, *Obligations of society*, p. 50) and may here refer to the four legal men.

[3] *Ungedr. anglo-normannische Geschichtsquellen*, ed. F. Liebermann, p. 146.

hand by reason of the interdict, because the abbot will be answerable for the proceeds at the king's will, saving his reasonable estovers.[1] So it seems that St. Edmunds suffered confiscation, in common with other monasteries, on 24 March, and recovered the administration but not the free disposal of its property within three weeks. One would not infer from the royal letter of 7 April that the abbey would thereafter enjoy ' its former liberty ' ; but the annalist was perhaps thinking of the abbot's legal rights within the Liberty of St. Edmund. A lawsuit between the abbot of St. Edmunds and the bishop of Ely, which came before the royal court on or about 23 April, was postponed *sine die* because all the property (*res*) of the two litigants was in the king's hand ; later in the same Easter term the abbot was awarded seisin in a case in which the plaintiff failed to appear.[2] King John's devotion to St. Edmund (independently recorded by Jocelin of Brakelond) was unlikely to prevent him from taking an opportunity to make money, and we may guess that Abbot Samson purchased this freedom with a great sum. But if he made fine with the king, the Fine Roll of 9 John contains no record of it ; nor do the Pipe Rolls of ensuing years indicate that the king ever called upon the abbot to answer for the abbey's revenue. All we know is that when the king's exactions from the abbey were discussed after the interdict, in December 1214, the monks presented a bill for 4,000 marks on account of *ablata* [3] : this is not at all helpful.

Was the position of St. Edmunds exceptional during these years ? That is the question. Most of the chroniclers who record the confiscation have no more to say about it, but we cannot safely argue from their silence. The historian of the Cistercian abbey of Meaux, in the East Riding, says that at this time all religious houses made fine with the king for their possessions, save only Abbot Alexander of Meaux, who refused to pay the thousand marks which Richard de Marisco demanded for the king.[4] The annalist of Worcester says briefly that ' the king disseised all ecclesiastical persons of all their goods and possessions, but afterwards made restitution to the religious '.[5] So far as Worcester Cathedral Priory is concerned, the Close Roll shows that the priory regained control on or about 12 April

---

[1] *Rot. lit. claus.*, i. 110a.
[2] *Curia Regis Rolls*, v. 157, 207. Four years later the abbey successfully claimed its jurisdiction when the plaintiff tried to get a hearing in the king's court (*ibid.*, vi. 206).
[3] *Memorials of St. Edmunds* (Rolls Series), ii. 111.
[4] *Chron. abbatiae de Melsa* (Rolls Series), i. 326 ; cf. 351-2.
[5] *Annales monast.*, iv. 396.

1208.[1] And the case of Worcester is but one among many. Between 27 March and the middle of May (when, alas, the record stops), the Close Roll records over a hundred licences to prelates, clergy, and others to have custody of their own property or of some other ecclesiastical property taken into the king's hand by reason of the interdict. Some are in the form used for the abbot of St. Edmunds, providing that the recipient will be answerable to the king ; others modify or omit the clause. This is the distinction which was common enough in the exercise of royal wardship in the early thirteenth century. Wardship might be committed to a custodian who held the property for the royal profit, or granted outright to a custodian who rendered no account. In the cases under consideration commission was much commoner than grant. Even where the word *commisimus* is not used, some phrase implies that the grant was not absolute. Thus, the sheriffs are told to let the archdeacon of Stafford have his property and his revenues in peace, ' because he will answer to us therefor if we should so wish ', and they are to let the king know what remains in the archdeacon's custody and what it is worth.[2] The canons of Exeter, who are to have their lands, revenues, and possessions in peace, have bargained with the king to remove nothing, waste nothing, and take nothing beyond their reasonable estovers, through which damage to the king might occur.[3]· In only fifteen cases is a grant without further obligation on the grantee implied. Certain clerks are to hold their property until further orders,[4] or to hold it in peace,[5] and William of Cornhill, archdeacon of Huntingdon, is to have in peace his corn from Awelton and sell it or do what he likes with it.[6] The letters in favour of the bishops of Winchester, Norwich, Bath, and Hereford refer to grants, not commissions: *reddidimus* is the word used[7]; likewise with the Cistercian Order[8] and a few individuals who are recognizably men with influence at court.[9]

The commissions may be divided into two categories according as they commit the property to the ecclesiastical owners or to other persons. In the second category are the notifications that the king has committed to Adam de Portu

[1] *Rot. lit. claus.*, i. 111b.
[2] *Ibid.*, i. 107b (26 March).   [3] *Ibid.*, i. 110a (7 April).
[4] *Ibid.*, i. 108b (4 April : Peter of Blois).
[5] *Ibid.*, i. 108a (2 April), and cf. 110a, 111b, 113a.
[6] *Ibid.*, i. 109b (7 April).
[7] *Ibid.*, i. 108b, 111a, 113b (the word is not used in the case of Hereford).
[8] *Ibid.*, i. 108b (4 April).
[9] *Ibid.*, i. 108b (Philip de Lucy), 110b (prior of Frampton), 113b (Humphrey de Bassingbourne, archdeacon of Salisbury). Also grants for Hugh de Nevill (i. 111a) and Richard de Marisco (i. 111b).

the custody of his priory of West Sherborne, and that Brian de Lisle is to have the property of Alexander of Dorset, ' our clerk'.[1] In several instances, the custodian is brother or father of the clerk concerned.[2]

All told, these licences cover a larger proportion of English church property than their number suggests. Comprehensive grants were made, for instance, to the prior of the Hospital in respect of all the Hospitallers' property[3]; to the monks of the Cistercian Order of all England[4]; to the master of the Order of Sempringham[5]; to the bishop of Winchester to have his episcopal lands, those of the cathedral priory, and those of St. Mary's Abbey and the churches of his fee and gift.[6] In three separate grants the chief justice, Geoffrey FitzPeter, obtained custody of the monasteries in his patronage (Walden, Shouldham, and Hurley), the property of the clergy of his demesne and wardships and of clerks of his household, and the property of the Order of the Temple throughout England.[7] The bishops whose property was returned to them all obtained custody of their cathedrals' property. The cathedrals of two of the four vacant sees also recovered their possessions.[8]

These grants and commissions raise a good many problems. Whether they were generally given for a consideration we cannot say with certainty ; but this is suggested by the remark of the historian of Meaux and also by Adam of Eynsham, biographer of St. Hugh, who states that most rectors redeemed their property from lay hands with money.[9] In the case of St. Albans—if we may believe Matthew Paris—the king first took a fine of 600 marks and shortly afterwards, through his agent, the notorious Richard de Marisco, demanded a present of 500 marks.[10] At Peterborough, where the sheriff, Robert de Braybrook, had accounted at Michaelmas 1210 for £1,000 15s. 2d. as the gross receipts of six months,[11] a presumably new arrangement was recorded in 1211, whereby the prior farmed the abbey for an annual payment of £600.[12]

---

[1] Rot. lit. claus., i. 108b, 109a.
[2] Ibid., i. 109b (William Malet), 110b (William of Huntingfield and Henry Hosatus), 114a (William de Sancto Iohanne and Ralph Hareng).
[3] Ibid., i. 108a (1 April).   [4] Ibid., i. 108b (4 April).
[5] Ibid., i. 112a (13 April).   [6] Ibid., i. 108b, 111a (1, 10, 12 April).
[7] Ibid., i. 107b, 110a (26, 27 March, 9 April).
[8] Ibid., i. 110a, 112a (Exeter and Lincoln).
[9] Magna vita S. Hugonis (Rolls Series), pp. 303-4.
[10] Gesta abbatum S. Albani (Rolls Series), i. 241-3.
[11] P.R.O., Pipe Roll 12 John rot. 19, m. 1d.
[12] Pipe Roll 13 John rot. 17, m. 1d.   To this sum was added 400 marks and 100 measures of corn and 100 measures of oats for possession of the abbot's portion during vacancy.   T. Madox, Hist. of the Exchequer (2nd ed., 1769), i. 411, note t, quoting this entry, reads 300 for 400 marks.

One confusing feature of the situation is the incompatibility of certain grants. Whereas the Gilbertine priory of Shouldham was committed to its patron, Geoffrey FitzPeter, on 26 March 1208,[1] the whole possessions of the Gilbertine Order were committed to its master on or about 13 April.[2] And a few days after two canons of Hereford were granted their lay fees and chattels, their bishop was granted ' all the lands, tenements, property, and revenues of his cathedral church and of his canons '.[3] In the absence of financial accounts, there seems no way of discovering how these difficulties were resolved. On the other hand, the apparent conflict between the mandate issued in favour of the Cistercians on 4 April 1208 [4] and the statement already cited of the historian of Meaux is explicable on the supposition that the general grant of 4 April was a reward to the Cistercians for their refusal to observe the interdict.[5] When, early in 1209, the pope called them to order, the Cistercian abbeys probably had to fine separately for the custody of their lands ; but we have practically no record of this for lack of Close Rolls after the middle of May 1208. At Michaelmas 1210 Roger de Lacy, constable of Chester, owed the king two good palfreys for the abbot of Stanlaw, that he might hold all his property in peace.[6] A year later Brian de Lisle rendered account of £100 ' de abbate de Basingewerc pro habenda benevolencia regis et pro habendis terris et redditibus suis captis in manu regis occasione malivolencie quam rex versus eum habuit '.[7] On the same Pipe Roll, under *Nova oblata*, the abbot of Strata Florida accounted for 1,200 marks, without reason stated.[8] The ambiguous forms of the last two records and their date (1211) suggest that they arose from John's taxation of the Cistercians in the autumn of 1210.[9]

We are now brought to the question : do the hundred or so licences recorded on the Close Roll represent all, or nearly all, that were issued ? If so, the king had an enormous amount of ecclesiastical property on his hands. Among the great

---

[1] *Rot. lit. claus.*, i. 107*b*. Described as the Abbey of Shouldham.
[2] *Ibid.*, i. 112*a*.
[3] *Ibid.*, i. 113*a* and *b* (about 20 April and 28 April).
[4] *Ibid.*, i. 108*b*.
[5] On this episode see Innocent III's letters of February–March 1209 in Migne, *Patrologia latina*, ccxv. 1563, 1564, ccxvi. 19, 21 ; Wendover in Matt. Paris, *Chron. maiora*, ii. 524 ; Walter of Coventry, *Memoriale* (Rolls Series), ii. 199 ; *Statuta capitulorum gen. ord. Cisterc.*, ed. J. M. Canivez, i. 351.
[6] *Lancs. Pipe Rolls*, ed. W. Farrer, p. 237. They were the equivalent of £10 (*ibid.*, p. 241).
[7] Pipe Roll 13 John rot. 14, m. 2d.
[8] *Ibid.*, rot. 7, m. 2d. There were possibly special political reasons for a heavy fine on Strata Florida : cf. *Rot. lit. claus.*, i. 122 (17 August 1212).
[9] Cf. Mitchell, *Studies in taxation*, p. 105.

Benedictine houses Westminster, St. Augustine's, Canterbury, Glastonbury do not appear on the Close Roll as recipients of licences ; nor do the cathedral chapters of Carlisle, Durham, York, Chichester, Ely, Lichfield, London, or Rochester. The Order of Prémontré is almost entirely missing,[1] the unmentioned monasteries of other orders are numerous. The list of secular clergy is very short. In one case, at least—that of St. Albans— there is external evidence that the abbey fined with the king at some date unspecified to recover possession of its property.[2] Some more scraps of information in the public records bear upon the question. They may be considered according as they throw light on three matters : fines for the resumption of property, administration of property by its owner during the interdict, and continuance of royal custody.

For traces of fines one naturally turns to the Pipe Rolls. They do not, it must be admitted, abound in evidence. Lady Stenton has recently commented upon the roll for 1208 and noted ' very little evidence ' of the fines made by ecclesiastical persons and institutions in consequence of the interdict in order that they might farm their own possessions : in fact, she produced no instance, and considered it possible ' that all the numerous fines due from ecclesiastical persons and institutions, as well as from laymen, for being allowed to farm church lands were never entered on the Pipe Rolls '.[3]

On this matter of fines for right to farm or to obtain an unrestricted grant, the later Pipe Rolls are almost equally unrewarding. The roll for 1209 has a solitary entry which may be connected with the general confiscation : ' Prior de Plinton' [Plympton, Devon] reddet compotum de uno palefrido pro habendo prioratu suo et rebus ad illum pertinentibus que fuerunt in manu regis '[4] ; even here the disseisin is not explicitly stated to have been occasioned by the interdict. The prior of Plympton, be it noted, was among those monastic

---

[1] Durford was committed to its patron and Langley to its abbot in April 1208 (*Rot. lit. claus.*, i. 110b).

[2] *Supra*, p. 134. We may credit the statement of the *Gesta abbatum* that Abbot John de Cella recovered custody of his abbey, apparently by grant (*in pace*). But when this happened is doubtful. Whereas Matthew Paris says that Robert of London was granted the custody (before the abbot recovered seisin) as a reward for his embassy to Morocco, placed in 1213, the letters patent appointing Robert of London and Matthew Mantell to be custodians are dated 29 March 1208 (*Chron. maiora*, ii. 564 ; *Gesta abbatum*, i. 241 ; *Rot. lit. pat.*, p. 81a).

[3] *Pipe Roll 10 John*, ed. Doris M. Stenton (Pipe Roll Soc., N.S. xxiii, 1947), pp. xi–xii. In references hereafter in the text to the Pipe Roll of a particular year, the year is the one in which the account was made up (at Michaelmas and after). In footnotes P.R. = Pipe Roll.

[4] P.R. 11 John, rot. 8, m. 1d.

prelates who were able to litigate in the king's court in the Easter term of 1208. Again, the Pipe Roll of 1211 records that the prior of Ystleswrd' (Isleworth, Middlesex) owes 200 marks and four palfreys 'pro habenda seisina terrarum et reddituum suorum in comitatu Essexie ',[1] but we do not know the cause of the disseisin. Payments by ecclesiastical persons or communities to have the king's goodwill or favour [2] cannot with any certainty be laid at the door of the interdict, for similar payments frequently occur in earlier years and ecclesiastics are not the only debtors. Nor can we include the large sums charged against the monks of Peterborough, Battle, St. Edmunds, and St. Augustine's, Canterbury, for having custody of their abbeys during vacancy.[3] On the other hand, the case of Peterborough, already cited, is significant. Here, in 1211, when the prior fines for custody of the whole house during vacancy, the clerk of the exchequer notes that the prior will render to the king annually £600 for the farm of the abbey.[4] Peterborough had evidently recovered its property recently, and only administered it by commission, not by grant, at the cost of a heavy farm. No other mention of this transaction has been found, and if the prior paid the farm, it must have gone direct to the royal camera. Clearly, then, the argument from silence cannot be used to prove that monasteries did not fine with the king to regain custody of their possessions. The evidence so far examined leaves the possibility of these transactions occurring at any time during the interdict.

We may next consider such evidence as exists for the administration of ecclesiastical property by its owners during the interdict. The Pipe Rolls show that monasteries (concerning which we have no positive record that the king had relaxed his hold) had been disseised of lands, not on account of the interdict but for some other reason. On the roll for 1209 the abbot of Croyland owes four palfreys to have the lands, revenues, and chattels of which he was disseised because he was said to have excommunicated the king's servants.[5] On

---

[1] P.R. 13 John rot. 5, m. 2d. There was perhaps a cell of S. Valéry here. The remaining half of this fine was pardoned to the prior in 1214, ' pro dampnis sibi factis per preceptum regis ' (P.R. 16 John rot. 1, m. 2).

[2] P.R. 11 John rot. 11, m. 1 (chapter of York) ; P.R. 12 John rot. 4, m. 2 (Geoffrey, archdeacon of Suffolk) and rot. 12, m. 1d (prior of Blyth) ; P.R. 13 John rot. 3, m. 1d (Laurence, clerk of Wilton) and rot. 21, m. 2 (Roger, archdeacon of Suffolk).

[3] P.R. 13 John rot. 17, m. 1d ; rot. 17, m. 2 ; rot. 21, m. 2 ; P.R. 14 John rot. 2, m. 2d.

[4] *Supra*, p. 134. ' Et idem prior etiam reddet singulis annis regi de firma eiusdem abbatie £600.'

[5] P.R. 11 John rot. 4, m. 1d ; P.R. 12 John rot. 1, m. 1d ; *Red book of the exch.*, iii. 822.

the roll for 1211 six English priories of Le Bec Hellouin owe fines of one hundred marks apiece for seisin of their lands, and in the case of St. Neots the occasion of the disseisin is plainly stated as the death of the abbot of Le Bec.[1] The inference is that these lands, which were not in the king's hand on account of the interdict, had been released since the first general confiscation. We have seen that four wealthy Benedictine houses which had lately lost their abbots were prepared to pay large sums to have custody of the abbot's portion during the vacancy.[2] They would scarcely have done so if, at the time, all their property lay in the king's hand.

At this point the Curia Regis Rolls deserve examination, although they are far from providing a solution of the problem. The records of the king's court for Easter and Trinity terms 1208 yield a small crop of cases like the one concerning the abbey of St. Edmunds which has been already cited : there is postponement *sine die* because the property of one or more of the litigants is in the king's hand.[3] In no case is a secular clerk the litigant in question ; only in the cases of St. Edmunds and Sempringham does the postponement follow the commission of custody to the prelates concerned ; and while the abbot of St. Edmunds is again in action in the court before the end of the term, the master of Sempringham appears in a case in Easter term 1212.[4] So far, so good. We might suppose that these two cases were postponed because the release of the lands had only followed the commission on the Close Roll after some few weeks' delay. But other cases concern religious houses for which no release is recorded (before 19 May 1208, when the Close Roll fails us), and these cases show variety of practice. The prioress of Clerkenwell, who had *licencia concordandi* in one case, saw another case in which she was defendant postponed ' sine die quamdiu prioratus fuerit in manu domini regis ' ; yet a little later she obtained a quitclaim of land in

---

[1] P.R. 13 John rot. 8, m. 2.   Cf. Ogbourne and Ruislip, *ibid.*, rot. 9, m. 1d ; Goldcliff, *ibid.*, rot. 12, m. 1d ; Steventon, *ibid.*, rot. 17, m. 2 ; Stoke, *ibid.*, rot. 21, m. 1.   William II, abbot of Le Bec, died 18 September 1211 and his successor was elected and consecrated within a fortnight (A. A. Porée, *Hist. de l'abbaye du Bec*, i. 523, 544).   Cf. *Pipe Roll 10 John*, p. xiv.

[2] *Supra*, p. 137.   In July 1213 the king wrote to the priors and convents of St. Augustine's, Canterbury and Peterborough and Battle, whereas he addressed the custodians of St. Benet's Holme and Whitby (*Rot. lit. claus.*, i. 150).

[3] *Curia Regis Rolls*, v. 157 (St. Edmunds), 158 (Peterborough, Croyland, Sempringham), 161 (Dereham, Lewes ; cf. p. 174 (about 27 April) : ' quia prioratus est in manu comitis Warenn' ', and *Rot. lit. claus.*, i. 112b), 188 (Thornholm), 199 (Clerkenwell), 202 (Osney), 271 (St. Benet's Holme).   Cf. C. T. Flower, *Intro. to the Curia Regis Rolls* (Selden Soc., lxii, 1944), p. 458.

[4] *Curia Regis Rolls*, v. 207, vi. 251, etc.

court.[1]   While a case concerning Peterborough was stopped in the early days, the abbot was in action again before term had ended.[2]   Had the abbey meanwhile recovered custody of its property ?   Our evidence suggests the contrary.   Eight or nine other monastic prelates are parties to litigation without hindrance during Easter term 1208 and yet, according to the Close Roll, they had not recovered custody.   Moreover, among the many cases concerning clerks and religious in Trinity term 1208, only two show ecclesiastical property in the king's hand.[3] Thereafter, no case was postponed *sine die* on this account. The only mention of royal custody that appears between Trinity term 1208 and the end of the interdict concerns the abbot of Waverley, in Michaelmas term 1210, and then a later day was appointed ' because it is not known whether the abbey is in the hand of the lord king or not '.[4]   This synchronized with the heavy taxation of the Cistercians, when the monks of Waverley dispersed for a time and the abbot fled by night from the abbey.[5]   And the case went on.

The sole postponement *sine die* in Trinity term 1208 deserves more attention for its sequel.   Peter de Alto Bosco had sued Abbot Ralph of St. Benet's Holme in an assize of novel disseisin and the case was reopened in Michaelmas term 1213 with a new abbot of St. Benet's as defendant.   The new abbot said that there was no novel disseisin because the king had given him seisin of all lands of which his predecessor had died possessed [6] :   these included the lands in question.   To this the plaintiff replied that in 1208 the king's writ respited the action for the very reason that Abbot Ralph had not then seisin of the disputed land or of any other of the abbey's land. The abbot, in his reply to this, said ' that the lord king admittedly had placed a custodian in the abbey as he had done in all the religious houses in England ; but he made no disseisin of lands or tenements and took nothing therefrom (*nec aliquid inde cepit*) '.[7]   This *ex parte* statement may not be very good evidence for the events of 1208, but, with all allowance made

[1] *Ibid.*, v. 189, 199, 223.
[2] *Ibid.*, v. 158, 187, 188.   The abbot appoints an attorney.   The king tells the justices to postpone an advowson case between the prior of Thornholm and the abbot of Peterborough ' quamdiu *prioratus* fuerit in manu sua '.
[3] *Ibid.*, v. 271 (St. Benet's Holme), 283 (St. Bartholomew's Hospital, London).   In the second case—one of mort d'ancestor—the defendant produced the prior to warranty ' et petit pacem per hoc quod domus S. Bartholomei est in manu domini regis.   Nichil dictum est quare assisa remaneat.'   The defendant lost his case.
[4] *Ibid.*, vi. 69.   [5] *Ann. monast.*, ii. 265.
[6] He died 4 February 1210 (*Chron. Ioh. de Oxenedes* (Rolls Series), pp. 296, 434).
[7] *Curia Regis Rolls*, vii. 6 ; cf. 24, 40.

140

for special pleading, it still supports the inference we should draw from other cases on the Plea Rolls. When the interdict began, the Curia Regis sometimes regarded royal custody as an obstacle to litigation ; but not always. The court may simply have admitted the plea, as a justification for postponing the case, when it was advanced by one of the parties.[1] It was soon seen, however, that financial control over the clergy could be maintained without interference with their rights and obligations as litigants,[2] and after the summer of 1208 the plea was not admitted as a cause of postponement. We cannot allege this as proof that royal custody was everywhere abandoned in 1208 (though these facts would be compatible with that conclusion), but rather that the judges' attitude towards the monasteries in custody was undefined during the first three months of the interdict and then achieved definition.

Our third line of enquiry is directed to examples of positive evidence that the king retained custody. Here a modicum of information is provided by the clerks who drew up the Pipe Rolls, and this can be supplemented slightly from other sources. Again the question will arise : is the record complete ?

When the interdict was published the sees of Canterbury, Chichester, Exeter, and Lincoln lay vacant in the king's hand, while York was administered by royal custodians as a result of King John's quarrel with his half-brother, Archbishop Geoffrey. During the next few months Durham and Lichfield fell vacant. Of these, Canterbury, Durham, and York were not filled until after John's submission in 1213 ; elections were made in 1209 to the bishoprics of Chichester, Exeter, Lichfield, and Lincoln.[3] The remaining English sees include those of the three executors of the interdict—London, Ely, and Worcester —and of Hereford, whose bishop followed the others into exile in the spring of 1208.[4] The bishops of Winchester and

---

[1] In probably all the recorded cases of postponement (above, p. 138, n. 3), it was the defendant's house which was in custody.

[2] Cf. *B.J.R.L.*, xxxi. 308.

[3] *Ann. monast.*, iii. 31 ; iv. 54. Hugh de Wells was bishop-elect of Lincoln by 14 April 1209 (*Rot. chartarum*, p. 185*b*) ; Henry de Londres was elect of Exeter by 8 August (Gervase of Canterbury, *Works*, ii, p. ci) ; Walter de Gray appears as elect of Coventry on P.R. 12 John rot. 16, m. 2 ; Master Nicholas de Aquila is apparently described as bishop of Chichester in a document of 1 June 1209 (Dallaway, *Hist. of W. Sussex*, II. ii (1830), 270). The elections of Londres and Gray were quashed in 1211 (*Ann. monast.*, iv. 399 ; cf. *Monasticon angl.* (ed. 1817–30), viii. 1242–4).

[4] Giles de Braose had not recovered possession of the castles of the see of Hereford, and these, with all the other property, was committed to Gerard de Aties on 23 May 1208 (*Rot. lit. claus.*, i. 113*b*, and *Rot. lit. pat.*, p. 83*b*).

Norwich, and possibly Carlisle,[1] remained in England through-out the interdict; there remained with them until the autumn of 1209 the bishops of Bath, Lincoln, Rochester, and Salisbury.

Were all these sees, vacant or full, retained in the king's hand ? Or did the Crown discriminate, and if so, how ? The Pipe Rolls show no accounts for Winchester or Norwich, whose bishops were the king's trusty servants ; and the Close Roll shows that their possessions were released as early as 5 April 1208.[2] Bath, Salisbury, and Hereford also regained possession of their property within a few weeks, but the bishop of Hereford had forfeited control by 23 May 1208.[3] While Hereford leaves no trace on the Pipe Rolls, John FitzHugh answered in 1209 for £184 11s. 6d. which he had received from the sale of stock of the bishopric of Salisbury.[4] He continued to collect revenue from this see in the next three years.[5] Bath appears on the Pipe Roll in custody in 1211, when Thomas Peverel is named as *custos*, and he renders full account in 1212.[6] Canterbury, Chichester, Durham, and Exeter are fairly completely accounted for on the Pipe Rolls between 1208 and 1212.[7] Accounts for London, Worcester, and York first appear on the Pipe Roll in 1212.[8] There are no accounts for Carlisle, Ely, Lichfield,[9] or Rochester.

These facts may be supplemented by two records on the Misae Roll of 1209–10. On 17 May 1209 Ralph Parmentarius was entrusted with £1,000 from the profits of four bishoprics : Lichfield (? £189), Ely (£55), Durham (£220), and

---

[1] Bishop Bernard of Carlisle is not mentioned by any of the chroniclers of the interdict and his movements are uncertain. An agreement between the abbeys of Furness and Fountains which he witnessed in 1211 (*Fountains chartulary*, ed. W. T. Lancaster, i. 61, no. 74) may have been made at Melrose (*Chron. of Melrose*, ed. A. O. and M. O. Anderson, p. 55).

[2] *Rot. lit. claus.*, i. 108b.

[3] *Ibid.*, i. 111a, 113b.

[4] P.R. 11 John rot. 13, m. 2.

[5] P.R. 13 John rot. 5, m. 1d ; 14 John rot. 5, m. 1.

[6] P.R. 13 John rot. 7, m. 1d ; 14 John rot. 1, m. 1d ; cf. 16 John rot. 7, m. 2d, and *Rot. lit. claus.*, i. 135b.

[7] The accounts for Chichester, Exeter, and Lincoln for the years 1208 and 1209 were not recorded at the exchequer because they were returned to the camera (P.R. 11 John rot. 1, m. 2 ; rot. 6, m. 2d ; rot. 8, m. 1d).

[8] P.R. 14 John rot. 1, m. 1 ; rot. 1, m. 2d ; rot. 6, m. 2d. The London account extends from 24 June 1211 ; it also covers arrears and the proceeds of Stortford and Maldon for three years before this date. An entry on 13 John rot. 10, m. 2, relating to the scutage of Wales shows Giun de Chancels answering for a debt of the bishop of Worcester.

[9] Lichfield was committed to Master John of Ramsbury and Robert Lupus on 9 October 1208 (*Rot. lit. pat.*, p. 86b). On P.R. 16 John rot. 14, m. 1d, is the unsatisfying item : ' Idem R. [Robertus Lupus] (*space*) de exitibus episcopatus Cestrie.'

142

London (£536).[1] On 28 June following Reginald of Cornhill received £90 from the bishopric of Exeter.[2] Three of these bishoprics were vacant at the time ; the other two (Ely and London) were full, but the bishops had left England early in 1208.

The first impression derived from these details about the bishoprics is disheartening, for the accounts on the Pipe Rolls have omissions and gaps which make the rolls an imperfect guide to the duration of royal custody. We are warned against arguing confidently from the silence of the Pipe Rolls. At the same time it is to be remarked that bishoprics only prove to be in royal custody (a) when the see is vacant, (b) when the bishop-elect is not known to have been confirmed,[3] or (c) when the bishop was probably abroad.[4]

The evidence for monastic houses next demands attention. We have seen that a great many monasteries fined to recover control of their property within a few weeks of its confiscation, and that others evidently obtained free disposition of their property. Nevertheless, the Pipe Rolls witness to a great deal of property being in the king's hand in the latter years of the interdict, and the circumstances are significant. The numerous accounts for religious houses on the rolls from 1208 to 1214 concern seventeen monasteries, almost all of which were demonstrably headless, or at least were headless in 1213 and may have been so during the whole period of account.[5] Christ Church, Canterbury, whose prior, Geoffrey, was in exile with his monks from 1207 until his death in June 1213, is obviously a special case. The two other possible exceptions are Tewkesbury and Battle. The succession of abbots of Tewkesbury

[1] *Rot. de liberate ac de misis et praestitis* (Rec. Comm.), p. 110. The missing figures for Lichfield (' Cestr ' . . . et ix *l.*') are probably *c iiii^xx*, which brings the total to the £1,000 mentioned in the margin of the roll.

[2] *Ibid.*, p. 115.

[3] Hugh de Wells received the possessions of the see of Lincoln when elected, according to Wendover, and lost them when he was consecrated at the end of 1209 (Matt. Paris, *Chron. maiora*, ii. 526, 528).

[4] Salisbury may provide an exception, since John FitzHugh accounted for ' venditio instauri episcopatus ' on the Pipe Roll for 1209, but it is not impossible that this represents a seizure late in Michaelmas term. Bishop Herbert was in Scotland about Martinmas (*Chron. Melrose*, p. 54). He may have returned later on, for a letter of presentation was directed to him on 19 April 1212 (enrolled out of order, *Rot. lit. pat.*, 95*b* ; cf. *Rot. chart.*, i. 189*a*). His property was then in the custody of John FitzHugh, who received orders of 13 December 1212 to hand over to Ralph of Winesham. Ralph was closely associated with the bishopric (cf. *Salisbury charters and docs.* (Rolls Series), pp. 66–8, and *Curia Regis Rolls*, vii. 124).

[5] Abbotsbury, Battle, St. Aug. Canterbury, Ch. Ch. Canterbury, Chertsey, Eynsham, Grimsby, Kenilworth (with Stone and Calwich), Malmesbury (no amount stated), Middleton, Peterborough, Ramsey, St. Benet's Holme, St. Edmunds, Sherborne, Tewkesbury, Whitby.

shows no vacancy during the interdict [1]; but the Pipe Roll contains accounts for the house for three and a half years from Easter 1208.[2]   For Battle Abbey we have custodians' accounts for the years 1210 and 1211,[3] and an arrangement dated 18 December 1211 [4] whereby the prior and convent were to get custody of the abbatial portion during any vacancy.   No further accounts of custodians appear on the Pipe Roll except in respect of the abbey's manor of Bromham.[5]   We might infer that the abbot died in 1211 and that the monks then obtained and retained custody of the abbey in the same way as Peterborough had done.[6]   Against this we must set Browne Willis's statement that Abbot John of Dover (who succeeded in 1200) died on xii *kal. Jul.* 1213.[7]   The abbacy was indubitably vacant on 24 July 1213, when the prior and convent were instructed to elect an abbot.[8]   There remains some doubt whether the vacancy had occurred in 1211.

With these exceptions, the monastic accounts on the Pipe Rolls apparently concern none but headless houses.   Interdict or no interdict, these would have been in the king's hand. There is, however, one marked difference from earlier practice in the method of accounting to the exchequer for vacancies during the interdict.   Long before the reign of John, many English religious houses had made division of their revenues between the abbot's *mensa*, or portion, and the convent's.[9] At a vacancy, the king or other patron had, by old custom, custody of the abbot's property, but he was supposed to leave the convent undisturbed in the enjoyment of property and rents specially assigned to it.   This arrangement is reflected in the Pipe Rolls of Henry II, Richard, and John, by the record of the royal custodian's receipts.   He is said to render account of a sum ' de exitu abbatie de S. Ædmundo de parte

---

[1] Abbot Walter, who succeeded in 1202, is said to have died in 1214 (*Ann. mon.*, i. 61 : Winchcomb annals in Cotton MS. Faustina B. i supply the abbot's name at this point).   An entry on *Rot. lit. claus.*, i. 206, confirms this.   The entry of Abbot Walter's death under 1203 in the Winchcomb annals is therefore probably an error ; it has produced an unintelligible note on Abbot Walter in the Tewkesbury annals under 1203 (*Ann. mon.*, i. 57).

[2] P.R. 13 John rot. 17, m. 1d.

[3] *Ibid.*, rot. 13, m. 2d.

[4] *Cal. Charter Rolls*, i. 25, and *Monasticon angl.*, iii. 247b ; cf. P.R. 13 John rot. 17, m. 2.

[5] P.R. 14 John rot. 16, m. 1 and 2.

[6] *Supra*, p. 137.   P.R. 14 John rot. 10, m. 2, records the payment of the remainder of the monks' fine : ' Monachi de Bello, R. de Cornhull' pro eis reddit compotum de 1000 marcis sicut supra continetur '.   I am unable to suggest why Reginald de Cornhill was responsible for this debt.   He was not *custos* in the preceding year.

[7] *Hist. of the mitred parliamentary abbies* (1718), i. 35.

[8] *Rot. lit. claus.*, i. 150b.

[9] M. D. Knowles, *Monastic Order in England*, pp. 435 ff.

144

abbatis preter victum monacorum ',[1] or ' de redditibus et exitibus et perquisitionibus de his que pertinent ad cameram abbatis '[2]; or some formula of similar import is used.[3] In other abbeys the accounts suggest that there was no division of revenues and that the custodian had charge of all : for here, while the record of receipts makes no distinction, the expenses side of the account shows sums paid ' in necessariis expensis monachorum . . .',[4] or, more explicitly, ' in victu et vestitu monachorum . . .',[5] or ' ad vestimentum monacorum . . . et in victu monacorum . . .'.[6] During the interdict this difference in treatment vanishes. In one headless house after another we find the custodian charging expenditure ' in victu et vestitu monacorum '. We may infer that the estates of the convent as well as those of the head of the house had come under the custodian's control.[7]

The abbey of Ramsey, which had come into royal custody when Abbot Robert resigned or was deposed in the early part of 1206, presents clearly this contrast in methods of accounting. In the account for the twelve months ending 24 June 1207 we read : ' Iohannes archidiaconus Wigorn', magister Hubertus ut custos pro eo, reddit compotum de £508 0s. 1d. de omnibus exitibus eiusdem abbatie preter hoc quod pertinet ad victum et vestitum monacorum.' That this account only includes the abbatial *mensa* is confirmed by the expenditure : ' in necessariis expensis infra abbatiam preter cameram et cellarium monacorum . . .'.[8] Compare this with the first comparable accounts rendered during the interdict : those of Michaelmas 1211.[9] ' Robert de Braibroc, Henricus filius eius pro eo, ut

---

[1] *Pipe Roll 27 Henry II* (Pipe Roll Society, xxx, 1909), p. 93. Cf. *Pipe Roll 8 John*, p. 190 (Malmesbury).

[2] *Chancellor's Roll 8 Ric. I* (Pipe Roll Soc., N.S., vii, 1930), p. 175 (St. Mary's, York).

[3] At Whitby and Glastonbury the accountants in 1194 and 1195 made a further deduction : ' preter victum monachorum et necessarias expensas et operationes factas in abbatia ' (*Pipe Roll 6 Ric. I*, p. 10 ; *Pipe Roll 7 Ric. I*, pp. 28, 48).

[4] *Pipe Roll 8 John*, p. 46 (Hyde).

[5] *Pipe Roll 7 Ric. I*, p. 57 and *Chanc. Roll 8 Ric. I*, p. 207 (Winchcomb).

[6] *Pipe Roll 1 Ric. I* (Rec. Comm.), p. 6 (Sherborne).

[7] True, the expenditure on food and clothing is sometimes so small as to preclude the possibility that it covers the whole cost of the monks' maintenance. The account for Eynsham on P.R. 12 John rot. 1, m. 1, points to an explanation : ' Et in victu et vestitu monachorum *preter blada horreorum* £20 2s. 4d.'

[8] *Pipe Roll 10 John*, p. 189. The preceding roll gives details of receipts (totalling £586 16s. 8d.) and specifies the manors from which the monks draw their portion.

[9] P.R. 13 John rot. 13, m. 1d. A copy is printed in *Cartularium mon. de Rameseia* (Rolls Series), iii. 215–17. From June 1208 to December 1209 John of Brancaster answered to the king in his camera, and on P.R. 12 John rot. 19, m. 1d, Robert de Braibroc answered for nine months, to Michaelmas 1210.

custos, r.c. de . . . £1,320 18s. 9d.' The details of these receipts show no exclusion of the convent's manors and include the item ' de superplusagio celarii £280 15s. 3d.', which suggests that the custodian received the revenues of the cellar, even if the cellarer collected them.[1] Moreover, among the expenses now appear fairly large sums for the monks' clothing (£46 13s. 4d.) and for the monks' kitchen (£38 12s.). Naturally enough, in these circumstances, the division between the abbot's *mensa* and the convent's might become obscured ; and Bishop Hugh de Wells of Lincoln later certified that this had happened in respect of the manor of Lawshall. He obtained for Ramsey in August 1213 a royal writ to Roger de Nevill to give the monks full seisin, ' si vobis constiterit quod manerium de Laushall' spectet ad victum et vestitum prioris et mona-corum '.[2]

It seems, then, that a monastery which remained headless during the interdict commonly suffered thoroughgoing exploita-tion by the Crown.[3] At the same time, when all allowance has been made for the incompleteness of the Pipe Rolls, it is surely significant that we find there hardly any accounts for a house while its abbot was alive. The few exceptions—Tewkes-bury and Battle—show, however, that there was no rigid rule whereby only the headless houses were answered for at the exchequer.

The other records at our disposal provide little more direct evidence of monasteries submitting to continuous confiscation between 1208 and 1213. A writ of 8 July 1215 restored to the abbot and canons of Cirencester the seven hundreds of Cirencester with all their appurtenances, of which Gerard de Aties had disseised them.[4] If the disseisin occurred when Gerard was sheriff of Gloucester (1207–9),[5] it may have been incidental to the general confiscation in March 1208 and not have been revoked when the abbot recovered his abbey in

---

[1] In the preceding nine months this item was £226 9s. In the year ending Michaelmas 1212 it was £183 6s. 7d. That the cellarer continued to administer the convent's estates and simply paid the profits to the custodian is suggested by the fact that the sum for farms, rents of assize, and sale of works does not rise very steeply between 1207 and 1212.

[2] *Rot. lit. claus.*, i. 148ab ; *Cart. mon. de Rameseia*, ii. 195–6.

[3] After John's submission, the older procedure significantly reappears ; cf. P.R. 16 John rot. 9, m. 2d : ' Ricardus de Mariscis (episcopus donolmensis *on erasure*) reddit compotum de £20 9s. 5½d. de exitu abbatie de Scireburne de tribus partibus anni preter victum et vestitum monacorum preter neces-sarias expensas. Et de £33 0s. ½d. de exitu abbatie de Abbodesbir' preter victum et vestitum monacorum et necessarias expensas de dimidio anno . . .' This reversion to earlier practice suggests that the change involved more than the method of accounting.

[4] *Rot. lit. pat.*, p. 149a.

[5] *Rot. lit. claus.*, i. 649 ; cf. *Patent Rolls 1216–25*, p. 474.

the next month.[1] Similar proceedings had resulted in the disseisin of woods belonging to Cerne and Dore Abbeys, and had caused Meaux to lose possession of a house in York and Brecon to lose the tithes of certain royal castles.[2] These particular losses may indicate the evil consequences of royal custody ; they do not prove that custody endured for long.

Finally, there is the scanty evidence of continuous royal custody of the property of the cathedral dignitaries and prebendaries and the inferior clergy. The Pipe Rolls show that the deanery of Chichester was in the sheriff's hand at least from Easter 1210 to Michaelmas 1212,[3] while Master Robert of Gloucester accounted for the archdeaconries of Chichester and Lewes with the bishopric.[4] Brian de Lisle was due to account in 1210 for Oxton, a prebend of Southwell, for three years past [5] ; in 1212 he accounted for some £400 in respect of the year's proceeds of churches and prebends in the king's hand in the bishopric of Lincoln and the archbishopric of York.[6] In the same year Thomas Peverel accounted for £85 7s. 3d. from churches and prebends of the diocese of Bath.[7] Meanwhile, in 1211, John FitzHugh accounted for nearly one hundred marks from tithes of the churches of Wingham, Ickham, Peckham, Cliffe, and Wrotham [8]—churches in the peculiar jurisdiction and gift of the archbishop of Canterbury. He also charged expenditure in collecting the corn of Hugh de Gayhurst (104s.) and in paying Hugh's vicar (40s.).[9] In 1212 John FitzHugh accounted for the proceeds of Hugh's churches of Odiham and Witney and Sonning (£71 10s. 1½d.).[10] In this year also occurs another small account for corn sold ' de ecclesia de Duueliz '.[11]

These facts must be seen in the setting provided by evidence from other sources. We may first consider the references by the continuator of Ralph Niger to the great seizure as it affected the rank and file of the clergy. He speaks particularly of the

---

[1] *Rot. lit. claus.*, i. 113a. The abbey came into the king's hand again in 1213 when Abbot Richard died (*Ann. mon.*, ii. 273 ; cf. *Rot. lit. claus.*, i. 146b) and was returned to the new abbot, Alexander Neckam, in May 1214 (*ibid.*, i. 204b). Another disseisin by Gerard de Aties (of property of the lepers of St. Lawrence of Bristol) is reported in August 1215 (*ibid.*, i. 227a).

[2] *Ibid.*, i. 148b, 150a, 155b.

[3] P.R. 14 John rot. 10, m. 2.

[4] *Ibid.*, rot. 1, m. 1d. Cf. a small sum of 2s. ' de exitu terre Iohannis archidiaconi capte pro eodem ' in P.R. 13 John rot. 9, m. 2.

[5] P.R. 12 John rot. 12, m. 1d. The record was not completed.

[6] P.R. 14 John rot. 1, m. 1.   [7] *Ibid.*, rot. 1, m. 1d.

[8] P.R. 13 John rot. 22, m. 1.   [9] *Ibid.*, rot. 22, m. 2.

[10] P.R. 14 John rot. 5, m. 1.

[11] *Ibid.*, rot. 13, m. 1d. In 1214 there is an account of 9 marks ' de blado ecclesie de Kingewaldestowe vendito ' (P.R. 16 John rot. 6, m. 2d).

stores locked up in the clergy's barns, derived from the glebe-
land and tithe.   ' Niger' tells us that in 1209 ' the clergy's corn
was plundered a second time by the king's servants and put up
for sale in the markets and also sold at a price to the clergy
themselves '.[1]   It was a comparatively simple business to put
the clergy's barns in the care of local custodians :   much less
difficult than attempting to administer their lands and revenues
in detail.   We recall that several of the entries on the Pipe
Rolls give nothing but receipts ' de decimis ' and ' de blado
vendito '.   Is it not possible that royal custody was commonly
limited to this particular form of wealth ?   We may go farther
and question whether even this limited custody generally
prevailed.[2]   For Adam of Eynsham says that nearly all the
rectors of England redeemed their property and, though he
may have exaggerated, he is not likely to have erred grossly.
Moreover, certain royal mandates issued in 1211 and 1212 are
powerful arguments against the view that most of the clergy
still suffered confiscation.   In 1211, according to the annals of
Waverley,[3] the king gave orders throughout England that all
bishops and clerks having revenues in England and dwelling
outside the realm should return within a fortnight of the feast
of St. John the Baptist or be deprived of their revenues in
England.   A year later, a writ went forth, dated 5 June 1212,
ordering the seizure of all churches and revenues of clerks
instituted by authority of the exiled prelates ;   persons so
instituted were to be expelled.[4]   Unfortunately, as we do not
know who or how many of the clergy were abroad,[5] we cannot
estimate the effect of the first measure.   As for the writ of
5 June 1212, only five sheriffs' returns have survived. .   They tell
of institutions to the deanery of Wells, the archdeaconry of

---

[1] Brit. Mus., Royal MS. 13 A. xii, fo. 89r : ' Bladum clericorum iterum a
regis satellitibus diripitur, et venum in mercatis exponitur, ipsis quoque
clericis sub certo precio venundatur.'
[2] Some mitigation of it is implied in an undated memorandum on the dorse
of the Close Roll for 1207–8 : ' Mandatum est omnibus vicecomitibus Anglie
quod permittant archiepiscopos, episcopos, abbates, priores, et omnes viros
religiosos et omnes clericos vendere blada sua per summas usque ad festum
S. Katerine [25 Nov.] ' (Rot. lit. claus., i. 114b).   But I am unable to
relate this to the evidence already cited about the custodians of barns in
1209.
[3] Ann. mon , ii. 266 ; cf. Rad. de Coggeshall, Chron. anglic. (Rolls Series),
p. 164.   The chancery rolls for this year are all missing.   In this year, the
Waverley annalist says, the king ordered all the woods of the archbishopric
of Canterbury to be sold and granted away and rooted up, so that not a tree
remained (Ann. mon., ii. 265).   According to Coggeshall (loc. cit.) the lands
of the bishop-executors of the interdict had suffered in 1209.   Ralph Niger's
continuator refers to the destruction of the bishop of London's castle at
Stortford in 1211 (Brit. Mus., Royal MS. 13 A. xii, fo. 89r).
[4] Rot. lit. claus., i. 130b.   [5] Cf. B.J.R.L., xxxi. 310–12.

148

Bath, and nine parish churches.[1]   One thing at least is evident. These measures against the exiles and their protégés need scarcely have been framed had the bulk of the English clergy's possessions been still in royal custody.   As with the bishops, so with their subject clergy, the king's policy was to make matters worse for the exiles than for those who stayed at home. Two letters on the Close Roll emphasize this discrimination. On 28 October 1212 the king ordered the sheriff of Hereford to return to the dean and chapter those prebends which had been seized because it was said that the bishop of Hereford had granted them after he went overseas.   A writ of 17 March 1213 provides for the chapter of Wells to receive back the prebends and revenues of those canons and clerks who are resident.[2]   It is impossible to tell whether this order indicates a new relaxation of old instructions or whether the custodian had been exceeding his powers.   In either case, the original policy of 1208 had been modified.

The chancery rolls of the period of reconciliation (13 May 1213 to 2 July 1214) are significant in what they lack concerning restitution to the clergy.   Shortly after John's submission, letters patent were issued, telling the tenants of the exiled bishops to obey the proctors appointed by the bishops for the acceptance and custody of their bishoprics.   A similar mandate went to the tenants of Christ Church, Canterbury.[3]   Apart from these there is practically no order for the restitution of lands under the terms of the settlement of 13 May.   In addition to a few re-seisins of woods and tithes noted above,[4] in July 1213 Master R., parson of Alveston, received a wood belonging to his church, ' unde disseisitus fuit occasione discordie que fuit inter nos et anglicanam ecclesiam ', and in September Master Henry of Nottingham received his church of Bulwell with its appurtenances.[5]   Both of these parsons may have been overseas : we have no proof.

This enquiry has of necessity been concerned with a great many details of doubtful import.   The records on which we principally rely are lamentably incomplete.   Apart from the big gaps of whole years in the chancery rolls, there are shorter periods of a few weeks in which nothing was written on the

---

[1] *Book of fees*, i. 70, 81, 141, 149, 197 (Surrey, Somerset, Worcs., Notts. and Derbyshire, Lincs.).
[2] *Rot. lit. claus.*, i. 126a, 128b.
[3] *Rot. lit. pat.*, p. 99b, 101a.
[4] *Supra*, pp. 145–6.
[5] *Rot. lit. claus.*, i. 146a, 150a (the reason for Master Henry's disseisin is not stated).

Close or Patent Roll.[1] The Pipe Roll of the Exchequer is missing for the crucial year, 1213, and the rolls which survive contain the evidence of their own incompleteness, in the notice of accounts rendered to the camera and in the appearance of arrears hitherto unrecorded. In the matter of fines paid to the Crown they are notoriously incomplete.[2] Ought we to suppose that royal custodians of church property were exempt from accounting to the exchequer ? ' John ', suggests Lady Stenton, ' may well have been content with accounts made up within the royal household.'[3] This is indeed possible ; but we have seen that the administrative line was not carefully drawn between the ordinary run of confiscated church property and that which was in the king's hand because of the vacancy of a see or an abbacy. Although the accounts for the latter are somewhat incomplete, they generally leave their mark on the Pipe Rolls in the course of years.[4] It would be dangerous to assume that possessions of important churches lay for long in the king's hand without leaving some trace behind, and we may take it that the Pipe Rolls give a fairly complete indication of the scope of royal custody. If, then, this material is insufficient for a statistical estimate of the king's revenue from the Church—and its insufficiency cannot be too clearly stated—it is still possible to use it, with non-official sources, to throw light on the trend of royal policy in the years 1208 to 1213. The material is not easy to manipulate in its unprinted form, and there are many obscurities which may be variously interpreted. The present conclusions, therefore, are tentative and indeed likely to require correction.

To sum up our findings ; after the first general seizure of the churches' property, the king immediately relinquished his hold over much of it by grants and commissions from which he derived a profit, the amount of which it is now quite impossible to ascertain. Thereafter, he kept in his hands for the whole period the property of the bishops who were in exile, together with the vacant bishoprics. As for those monasteries which did not recover their lands in the first two months after confiscation, they only continued long under royal control if and when they fell vacant : the exceptions are Christ Church, Canterbury, Battle (? until 1211), and Tewkesbury. The king treated vacancies, however, as opportunities for more than

---

[1] No letters close between 10 January and 5 March 1213, no letters patent between 27 June and 17 July 1213.

[2] Cf. Hilary Jenkinson, ' Financial records of the reign of King John ', *Magna Carta commemoration essays*, ed. H. E. Malden, pp. 290, 297–8.

[3] *Pipe Roll 10 John*, p. xii.

[4] Of the vacant sees, Lichfield is the least recorded (*supra*, p. 141).

ordinary exactions. The secular clergy as a whole were probably left to administer their estates and collect their revenues, so long as they remained in England, although for an undetermined period (perhaps only two years) they may not have had free disposal of their crops and tithes. But as the interdict dragged on, the resident clergy resumed possession, so that few if any besides the exiles were still disseised of their property when peace was restored between king and pope.

ADDITIONAL NOTES

The Pipe Rolls of 11-14 and 16 John are now printed in Pipe Roll Soc. n.s. vols.24,26,28,30,35 (1949-1962), with introductions by D.M. Stenton and P.M. Barnes. Interdict documents (Pipe Roll Soc. n.s. vol.34,1960), ed. by P.M. Barnes and W.R. Powell, contains two royal surveys concerning Wiltshire during the Interdict from the Exchequer, and documents from Canterbury muniments concerning Christ Church, 1207-13.

Pp.142-3: 'The succession of abbots of Tewkesbury...Easter 1208',cf.p.149. The passage in PR 13 John rot.17 m.1d is printed in Pipe Roll 13 John, where D.M. Stenton points out (p.xvi) that the account concerns the town, not the abbey.

A recent view of the General Interdict on England, 1208-1214

In recent years there have been several obvious places where an enquirer might learn about the interdict laid by Pope Innocent III on England and Wales. Powicke in the Cambridge Medieval History, Poole in the Oxford History, and Painter in *The Reign of King John* all described this episode in the history of the English Church and discussed its bearing on political affairs. People who wanted more detail could go to two papers, published in 1948 and 1949, and would find additions to their knowledge in fragmentary documents discovered recently in the Public Record Office and the Canterbury archives, and edited by Dr Powell and Dr Barnes for the Pipe Roll Society in 1960.[1] From all these places they would receive roughly the same impression. But last year Messrs Richardson and Sayles published the first volume of *The Governance of Mediaeval England*. In it they enlarge upon the Interdict and, as in the rest of their stimulating book, are not content to repeat received views. Since they are very learned, and very clever, and widely read, it is desirable to ask what is the evidence on which their view is formed. For—I may as well admit at once—their picture strikes me as a picture compounded of true and important views

---

[1] C. R. Cheney, 'King John and the papal interdict,' *BJRL*, XXXI (1948), 295-317 (and separately), and 'King John's reaction to the interdict on England,' *TRHS*, 4th series XXXI (1949), 129-50. *Interdict Documents*, ed. P. M. Barnes and W. R. Powell, Pipe Roll Society, New series XXXIV (1960); another fragmentary account of some interest, headed 'Exitus de maneriis episcopi Saresberiensis per manum Rogeri de Molend','is contained in P.R.O., E. 216.

and of imperfect, misleading ones. While it ought to be welcomed, it needs to be scrutinized.

The authors treat the Interdict in some dozen pages (pp. 343-55). Well aware of the paucity of reliable information and the danger of generalizing about conditions during the Interdict (pp. 343, 348), they open their discussion by pointing out how clumsy and ineffective the weapon of interdict had been when it was applied or threatened in the Angevin Empire. 'In 1208,' they say, 'the king was highly experienced in the appropriate tactics to counter it' (p. 346). This leads them to claim that 'the king's counter-attack, though it could not be made effective everywhere at once, was not relaxed. The probabilities are therefore that the Interdict was progressively less and less effective' (p. 347). In short, the Interdict did not work. Its 'horrors,' of which Stubbs spoke, are 'elusive' (p. 343) and it caused little 'hardship', though 'to the governing classes the position was unquestionably irksome' (p. 351). The Interdict must be regarded as a political measure, and as 'political blackmail' which failed (p. 354). It had been imposed by the pope as a result of the election of Stephen Langton to Canterbury; when it was lifted, 'it was as though the disputed Canterbury election had never been' (pp. 354-5). John's submission was a pyrrhic victory for the pope (p. 352). 'Politically John had made substantial gains' (p. 356). 'John, after his quarrel with Innocent III had been resolved, remained in possession of the ancient right for which he had contended' (p. 314).

That last remark may seem a dubious estimate of the situation when one remembers that the king received Langton as archbishop, paid many thousands of marks to the aggrieved clergy, and saddled himself and his successors with an annual charge of a thousand marks' tribute to Rome. But I do not wish to dwell on mere extravagant expressions. The authors have taken up a legitimate point of view which has been too often neglected: they look at the Interdict from the angle of Westminster, not Canterbury,[1] and the result is instructive.

[1] Cf. *The Governance of Mediæval England from the Conquest to Magna Carta*, Edinburgh 1963, 294.

A recent view of the General Interdict on England, 1208-1214

Perhaps they moralize rather more about the impropriety of interdicts than their predecessors have done (at least, since the days of Dean Hook); but they are at one with earlier writers in declaring that the Interdict on this occasion proved to be only a blunt weapon. It cost the clergy much in material wealth, and probably diminished their popularity, and it failed in its main purpose. It was Stubbs, not Richardson and Sayles, who wrote that King John 'grew richer and stronger as he grew more contumacious.'[1] John's submission to the pope, in the sixth year of the Interdict, was made when it suited him. For him, as Powicke wrote, the Interdict had been 'an opportunity no less than a menace.'[2] Thus far, Messrs Richardson and Sayles hardly depart from former opinions, though their estimates of the chief actors—John, Innocent III, and Langton—are their own. Where they differ from others is in their view of the enforcement of the Interdict. They argue that not only was it a bad thing, not only did it fail to achieve its object; they declare that, so far as the evidence goes, the pope's authority was flouted and the rules of the Interdict were not obeyed. Here their argument seems to me to be neither self-consistent nor at harmony with some known facts.

One can best approach this problem of how the Interdict worked by asking two questions: How was it *meant* to work? To what extent did the king wish to hinder its operation or succeed, by intimidating the clergy, in so doing? Richardson and Sayles are not very clear on these points. True, on the first point they quote the terms of an interdict threatened by Alexander III, involving the denial of all the services of the church save baptism and the absolution of the dying (p. 344), and they quote approvingly Stubbs's observation to the effect that the Interdict did not preclude all religious exercises (p. 346). But when they talk of the failure of the Interdict, they seem to be labouring under the same misapprehension as produced the old highly-coloured pictures: that it aimed at a total ban on pious

---

[1] *Constitutional History of England*, ch. XII, para. 153 (fourth edition, 1883, I. 559).
[2] *Cambridge Medieval History*, VI (1929), 235.

practices and organized ceremonial. It is therefore necessary to insist that the interdict was essentially a ban upon celebration of the mass, upon sacramental ceremonies and liturgical practices in church, and upon the administration of sacraments elsewhere, except for baptism, which was always allowed, marriage, which was a sacrament even when it could not be solemnized by a priest, and the absolution of the dying. The application of this ban and its possible extension or mitigation was very largely left to the discretion of the executors; this is made clear by letters of Innocent III, various reports on the terms of the Interdict, and two letters of the archdeacon of London. What is equally clear is that the ecclesiastical authorities raised no objection to sermons by the clergy in churchyards, organized processions outside the churches, observance of the Church's fasts, the blessing of candles at Candlemas, the distribution of ashes on Ash Wednesday, the special treatment of public penitents on Maundy Thursday. The pope himself formally sanctioned mitigations of the Interdict, for conventual churches in 1209, and for persons *in articulo mortis* in 1212. Moreover, he left much to be decided by the executors, thereby giving rise to doubts and questions and diverse practice.[1] Bearing this in mind, do we find evidence that the clergy willingly or unwillingly broke the terms of the Interdict as they understood them?

Richardson and Sayles look at this under various heads. They speak of the observance of the Interdict by the monasteries, and by the secular clergy, and of the attitudes of the laity and of the king himself.

So far as monasteries are concerned (they say) there seems to have been no uniformity of observance as between one house and another, even within the same order: we can select none as typical. *We may be sure, however,* (italics mine) that nowhere was a zealous obedience given to the pope's command. From the outset the Cistercians, for example, held that their privileges entitled them to disregard the Interdict, and though their claim was disallowed by the pope, it is

[1] *BJRL*, XXXI, 299; PL, CCXV, 1423, 1455; *Selected Letters of Pope Innocent III concerning England*, ed. C. R. Cheney and W. H. Semple (1953), p. 109 n. 17.

A recent view of the General Interdict on England, 1208-1214

far from certain that in any Cistercian house there was more than the minimum of compliance. If we may trust what appears to be a contemporary narrative of the monastery of Meaux, the Cistercians there adhered to their ordinary routine except for closing their doors and burying their dead in an unconsecrated cemetery. The chronicler asserts that this was the extent to which the Interdict was observed by other exempt and privileged houses. (p. 348).

We may perhaps overlook the incompatibility of this with a remark made later in the book (p. 367 n. 1) about the Cistercians: 'While at first they ignored the Interdict, they later complied with the pope's mandate.' Nor need I insist that the 'example' of Meaux provides no clue to the practice outside the Cistercian Order. But what do the authors mean by 'the minimum of compliance?'

In January 1209 religious houses were permitted to celebrate mass once a week behind closed doors [1]; and although the Cistercians were then refused this mitigation because of their early disobedience, they were allowed it by a papal letter of 6 March.[2] A Cistercian chronicler writing after the Interdict was over might well pass under silence the comparatively short period during which the White Monks did not enjoy this privilege. That they were not disobedient on principle, or out of fear of the king, seems to be indicated by the Meaux chronicler's account of unconsecrated ground set aside for burials.[3] And this particular practice can be paralleled in other monasteries, Cistercian and Benedictine (Waverley, St Albans, St Benet's Holm, Snelshall).[4] Evidence of exclusion from consecrated cemeteries is, as one would expect, scanty; but it is widespread. The bodies of the bishops of Durham, Rochester, and Bangor, and of William de Monte, chancellor of Lincoln, are all

---

[1] PL, CCXV, 1529.
[2] PL, CCXVI, 21.
[3] *Chronica Monasterii de Melsa*, ed. E. A. Bond, RS, 1866-8, I, 351.
[4] *Annales Monastici*, ed. H. R. Luard, RS, 1864-9, II, 282; *Ungedruckte Anglo-normannische Geschichtsquellen*, ed. F. Liebermann (Strassburg, 1879), 172; *The Cartulary of Snelshall Priory*, ed. J. G. Jenkins, Buckinghamshire Record Society, X (1952), 7; *Chronica Johannis de Oxenedes*, ed. Henry Ellis, RS, 1859, 296.

reported to have been buried in unconsecrated ground.[1]

As regards the observance of the Interdict by the secular clergy Richardson and Sayles interpret the records in a way which I find implausible. 'Instructions (they say) were given' to the king's servants, just before the Interdict started, 'to sequestrate the lands and chattels of those *qui divina extunc celebrare noluerunt*' (p. 346 n. 5). '*It follows* (they say) that sequestrations would be relaxed only when the offender agreed to celebrate.' But does it follow? What we know is that between 27 March and the middle of May (after which the Chancery Rolls are missing) the Close Roll records over a hundred licences to prelates, clergy, and others to have custody of their own property or of some other ecclesiastical property taken into the king's hand by reason of the Interdict.[2] What we do not know is the consideration for these grants; but it seems highly probable that it took the form of money. The *Magna vita Hugonis* says that most rectors redeemed their property from lay hands with money. Those who had mistresses ransomed them when they, too, were seized by the royal officials.[3] There is no suggestion in the records or narratives that these bargains involved disregarding the terms of the Interdict. If Richardson and Sayles conclude that 'in general, the clergy made their peace with the king *and continued to officiate*' (p. 346, italics mine) their conclusion is only reached by ignoring two letters of Peter of Blois and a complaint of the monk Matthew of Rievaulx [4] and by unreasonably depreciating the evidence of Langton's sermon in July 1213 (p. 350). All these, in different ways, show that churches were closed, and that parish-priests were denying their flocks some at least of the usual ministrations. The resident parochial clergy, like the monks, probably fined to be quit of royal sequestration and interference and were probably then free to observe the Interdict as they saw fit.[5]

[1] *BJRL*, XXXI, 300 and *Chronicle of Melrose*, ed. A. O. and M. O. Anderson (1936), p. 57.
[2] *TRHS*, 4th series XXXI, 133.
[3] *BJRL*, XXXI, 304, 306.
[4] Ibid., 299, 316.
[5] Ibid., 304-5, *TRHS*, 4th series XXXI, 131-6.

A recent view of the General Interdict on England, 1208-1214

Richardson and Sayles would draw a parallel with the interdict laid on the city of London in 1216. Except for a few religious houses, that interdict, they observe, was disregarded. 'The citizens and parish clergy were encouraged in their defiance by the barons and the canons of St Paul's' (p. 349); in the earlier Interdict, they think, 'the menaces of the king' will have produced similar defiance. As to this, one must first note that the circumstances of the two interdicts were utterly different; secondly, however unpopular the Interdict of 1208 may have been among the London laity, they had no say in the matter. One of Peter of Blois's letters shows them to be complaining precisely because they remained bound by the Interdict while bishops were untouched and the clergy's lot eased by authorized mitigations. Richardson and Sayles are convinced that the Interdict was ineffective largely because the king wished it so. 'We have every reason to suppose (they say) that the king's authority was steadily and continuously exerted, wherever it might stretch, to check any attempt at a public manifestation of compliance with the pope's command' (p. 349). Yet they recognize that in the summer of 1213 the Interdict was in a considerable measure still effective: Langton then had to meet the criticism that, though a reconciliation had taken place, the voice of the Church was silent and the churches were shut (pp. 349-50, 353).

In this connexion it is significant that the authors' account of the Interdict never alludes to those clergy other than the bishops who chose to go abroad. We do not know how many the 'exiles' were; though probably a small minority, they were not negligible. The chroniclers' statement that many fled has a little support from the records.[1] It seems to have been these 'exiles' and their nominees who became the objects of the king's displeasure as the years of interdict wore on.[2] The king was apparently prepared to leave the residents alone in return for money.

The authors reinforce their view that the king intimidated

[1] *Rotuli Litterarum Clausarum* ... (1204-27), ed. T. D. Hardy, Record Commission, 1833-4, I. 130*b* of 5 June 1212.
[2] *BJRL*, XXXI, 304-5, 311-2; *TRHS*, 4th series XXXI, 147-8.

the clergy to be disobedient towards their ecclesiastical supe-
riors with the view they hold of John's own conduct. 'The king's
interest and pride were touched and he was determined that so far
as in him lay, religious ceremonies should continue unimpaired'
(p. 347). Maybe; but they go further: 'We can confidently
deny that the Interdict was respected in the king's household.'
What does this confident denial rest on? 'The household
accounts for the year 1212-13 are conclusive.' What do the
accounts show? First, they show that the king gave lavish
alms, 'notably when, as was his practice, he broke a fast day.'
This, incidentally, in the authors' view, constitutes 'fulfilling
religious duties with a regularity beyond praise'! Secondly,
they show that he distributed his maundy to thirteen poor men
on Holy Thursday. Thirdly, they show that 'he crept to the
Cross with his knights on Good Friday.'[1] Fourthly, they say:
'If we are not directly told that he communicated on days of
obligation, there is the significant fact that, like his predecessors,
he had a bath before each of the great feasts.' The first
three points have no bearing on the respect paid to the
Interdict. Almsgiving and other works of mercy were to be encouraged. The rules for the Adoration of the Cross 'sine
sollempnitate' and 'extra ecclesiam' are set out in the version of
the pope's letter of 14 June 1208 contained in the Canterbury
collection.[2] So we are left with the king's baths as evidence.
Nobody reading the sentence I have just quoted from *The
Governance* would suppose that there was only one feast of
obligation for a layman (though communion three times a year
was considered more fitting) or that King John took two baths
in May and June 1212 and three between 5 August and 30
November [3]: none of them can be connected with a feast of

---

[1] The entry on the *Misæ* roll shows simply that an offering was made *ad
crucem* on behalf of the king and his knights (*Documents illustrative of
English History in the Thirteenth and Fourteenth Centuries*, ed. Henry Cole,
Record Commission, 1844, 258).

[2] *Historical Works of Gervase of Canterbury*, ed. W. Stubbs, RS, 1879-80,
II, xciii: 'Presbiteri in die Passionis sine sollempnitate crucem extra ecclesiam ponent, ut parochiani ipsam cum consueta devotione adorent.'

[3] *Documents*, ed. Cole, 237, 249.

A recent view of the General Interdict on England, 1208-1214

obligation. Turning to earlier records, we find twelve baths between January and November 1209 and eleven in the next six months.[1] Do the authors (who know all these facts perfectly well) really suppose that the king bathed only or specially ceremoniously when he intended to communicate?[2] In fact, the evidence of the household accounts on the subject of the king's communion amounts to exactly nothing.

They continue: 'Elsewhere, too, there are indications that he did communicate.' They refer to instructions of the pope to the bishops in March 1213, in which he tells them to suspend from office and benefice 'clericos et viros religiosos qui publice communicaverunt prefato regi, et aliis excommunicatis auctoritate apostolica nominatim, in casibus non concessis.' I must here make public confession of a regrettable error of translation in the edition which Richardson and Sayles cite.[3] The words 'communicaverunt prefato regi' were taken to mean 'given the sacrament to the king'; but this is not admissible, and the words 'in casibus non concessis' make it clear that this really refers to the intercourse with excommunicates for which the canons provided in certain cases.[4] This provides, therefore, no indication that the king ever took communion.

Richardson and Sayles conclude these comments on the king's intentions by saying: 'While the circumstances may have been exceptional, it is not to be overlooked that Stephen Langton himself celebrated mass publicly in the king's presence on 20 July 1213, a year before the Interdict ended.' It is not, indeed; and Innocent III implied that Langton, in so doing, exceeded his instructions.[5] But again, this is no evidence that the king communicated, nor does it enlighten us about his general demeanour in the face of the Interdict.

Let me conclude with an apology for a querulous paper. As I

---

[1] *Rotuli de Liberate ac de Misis et Praestitis regnante Johanne*, ed. T. D. Hardy, Record Commission, 1844, 115, 137, 170.

[2] In a footnote they say: 'Some of his other baths, not precisely dated, may have been taken before he communicated' (p. 347).

[3] *Selected Letters*, 139-40.

[4] Cf. *Decretum*, C. 11 q. 3 c. 102-3.

[5] *Selected Letters*, 172; PL, CCXVI, 954.

suggested at the outset, Richardson and Sayles have much to say about the Interdict which agrees with what has been current among historians for the past generation. It is not always so novel as the authors' method of exposition would suggest. If I have dwelt on points of difference it is because the uninstructed reader of *The Governance of Mediaeval England* may not easily disentangle what opinions command general assent and what are novel or peculiar to the authors. And if, with my talk about baths and burials, I have laboured points which strike you as trivial, it is because the picture which Richardson and Sayles created is composed of many small details; their accumulations of recondite learning are impressive, but do not always provide very solid support for their conclusions. That is why their words deserve close study.

XII

THE ALLEGED DEPOSITION OF KING JOHN

THE protracted trial of strength between King John and Pope Innocent III has been so often studied that one might suppose that the events would have been clarified long since.[1] But just as, a few years ago, Dr. Knowles showed that the beginnings of this struggle are usually misrepresented,[2] so we find that its ending is still not clear. Modern historians generally agree that after John was excommunicated personally in November 1209, and after negotiations had broken down in the summer of 1211, the pope proceeded to release John's subjects from obedience and invited, or rather exhorted, Philip Augustus to come and take the English crown by force. Sometimes the release from obedience and the offer of the crown to Philip are represented as two distinct stages, sometimes the latter act is apparently deemed to include the former. The modern narratives do not agree in detail and often they are a trifle vague; but they mostly concur in telling us how Innocent III delivered a formal sentence of deposition in the winter of 1212–13 and bade Philip Augustus execute that sentence.[3] The dissentients among modern scholars are few,[4] but it is the object of this essay to amplify and justify their reasons for dissent.

[1] I am obliged to Professor V. H. Galbraith for reading this paper in manuscript and making valuable comments.

[2] 'The Canterbury Election of 1205–6', *Eng. Hist. Rev.* liii (1938), 211–20.

[3] Stubbs in *Memoriale fr. Walteri de Coventria* (Rolls series, 1872), ii. lviii–lix; Paul Meyer in *Hist. de Guillaume le Maréchal* (Soc. Hist. France, 1891–1901), iii. 200, n. 3; C. Petit-Dutaillis, *Étude sur la vie et le règne de Louis VIII* (1894), pp. 35–7, and *La Monarchie féodale* (1933), p. 252; C. Bémont, *Chartes des libertés anglaises* ('Collection de textes . . .', 1892), p. xvii; Kate Norgate, *John Lackland* (1902), pp. 161, 167–8, 175; Else Gütschow, *Innocenz III und England* (1904), p. 164; G. B. Adams, *Hist. of England 1066–1216* (1905), p. 422; A. Luchaire, *Innocent III: les royautés vassales du s. siège* (1908), pp. 212–21; W. S. McKechnie, *Magna carta* (2nd ed., 1914), pp. 24–6; A. Cartellieri, *Philipp II. August*, iv (1921–2), 341–2; F. M. Powicke, *Stephen Langton* (1929), p. 78, and in *Camb. Med. Hist.* vi (1929), 317; S. Painter, *William Marshal* (1933), p. 175; W. E. Lunt, *Fin. relations of the Papacy with England to 1327* (1939), p. 134; J. Haller, *Das Papsttum*, ii. ii (1939), 383.

[4] J. H. Ramsay, *The Angevin Empire* (1903), pp. 430–1, 436–9; H. W. C. Davis, *England under the Normans and Angevins* (7th ed., 1921), p. 367 (but cf. p. 369); H. Tillmann, *Die päpstl. Legaten in England* (1926), p. 96, n. 130. Professor Powicke implied some doubt about the version of events which he had accepted elsewhere, in reviewing volume v of Carlyle's *Med. Pol. Theory in the West* (*Eng. Hist. Rev.* xliv (1929), 299), when he wrote: 'Innocent III . . . threatened to depose John of England.'

We need not be surprised that historians say that John was deposed, for a mass of contemporary or sub-contemporary witnesses said so; but it is a little surprising that historians have not been more concerned about the difficulty of accepting this testimony. The evidence for John's deposition comes entirely from chroniclers, and they vary; no record material of any kind has been adduced in support. In reconsidering the matter we shall do best to let the chroniclers speak first, then note their inconsistencies, and finally confront them with the evidence of records.

No chronicler implies that, when sentence of excommunication on John was published in the churches of northern France, this specifically released his subjects from obedience or included any incitement to revolt.[1] Although the excommunication of a ruler in a Christian country would, strictly interpreted, make his position untenable and although canonists inferred that the pope's right to excommunicate kings gave him the right to depose them,[2] the canon law was careful to provide for occasions when it was expedient for the faithful to co-operate with excommunicates,[3] and cases in which a ruler was excommunicated without being deposed are too common to need enumeration. In condemning Otto IV, it is true, Innocent III speaks of excommunicate and tyrannical rulers as being unable lawfully to exercise jurisdiction;[4] but perhaps Otto's offence was greater than John's, for Otto had encroached on the Patrimony of St. Peter whereas John had not; and, as Innocent once told the king of Portugal, God particularly dislikes attacks on the rights of the Apostolic See.[5]

We may assume, then, that the pope did not, when he excom-

---

[1] Innocent's letter threatening John with excommunication, in Jan. 1209, does not state the temporal consequences of anathema, though we may find a veiled threat in the words: 'adhuc cum altissimi adiutorio contra te multipliciter processuri, si nec sic tuum corrigere festinaris errorem.' *Reg.*, lib. xi, ep. 211; Migne, *Pat. lat.* 215, col. 1528.

[2] See R. W. and A. J. Carlyle, *Med. Pol. Theory in the West*, i. 278–80, ii. 204–6, v. 161–2.

[3] Cf. Gregory VII in *Decretum*, ii. 11, 3, 103; Innocent III in *Decretales*, v. 39, 30.

[4] 'Cum tales legitime nequeant iurisdictionis officium exercere ab unitate fidelium separati.' *Reg.*, lib. xv, ep. 31; Migne, 216, col. 566. Cf. *Reg. super neg. imp.*, ep. 21 (Migne, 216, col. 1019): 'Unde iuxta sanctorum patrum canonicas sanctiones ei qui talis [i.e. excommunicatus] existit non obstante iuramento fidelitatis est obsequium subtrahendum', and Honorius III in *Decretales*, v. 37, 13. See also the letter threatening interdict on England. *Reg.*, lib. x, ep. 113; Migne, 215, col. 1209.

[5] 'Qui, etsi de aliarum ecclesiarum iniuriis graviter offendatur, tanto gravius adversus eos qui apostolicae sedis iura illicite detinent commovetur, quanto fortius peccare videntur qui eius quae caput est omnium et magistra non sine praesumptione sacrilega jura invadere non formidant.' *Reg.*, lib. i, ep. 448; Migne, 214, col. 425.

102   ALLEGED DEPOSITION OF KING JOHN

municated John, declare him to be deposed. Whether subsequently and in secret he advised the king's subjects to withdraw
allegiance or to depose John by a formal constitutional act[1] is a
question which cannot be answered; the question now under
discussion is whether the pope himself, by virtue of his plenitude
of power, ever passed sentence of deposition on John.

A papal sentence of deposition (as it may for convenience be
described) usually took the form of a statement that the pope
absolves the ruler's subjects from fealty and forbids them to obey
him.[2] Rarely was emphasis laid on the ruler's loss of office.[3] In
the political theory of the time there was doubtless a distinction
between release from obedience and deprivation of office;[4] but
if the two acts had different theoretic origins, they were both
designed to nullify the ruler's authority and were equally acts of
supreme papal power. After either act the pope withheld from
the ruler the title of his office.[5]

The earliest occasion on which, on any showing, Innocent III
deposed King John was when the nuncios Pandulf and Durand
met the king at Northampton on 29 or 30 August 1211.[6] Most of
our sources confine themselves to saying that negotiations broke
down, either because John refused to pay damages to the exiled
bishops or because he argued about his royal dignity. The *Annals
of Burton*, on the other hand, know all about it and are able to
give a verbatim report of the discussion between king and nuncio.[7]
A violent argument culminated in a declaration by Pandulf, of
which the crucial words are: 'We absolve, from to-day onwards,

[1] On the theoretical rights of the subjects in this respect see Carlyle, op. cit. v.
112–19 and F. Kern, *Kingship and Law* (trans. S. B. Chrimes, 1939), pp. 83, 86–8.
Langton's view is expressed in a letter of 1207: *Gervase of Canterbury*, ii, p. lxxxii,
and Powicke, *Stephen Langton*, p. 97.

[2] e.g. Alexander III on Frederick Barbarossa, 4 Apr. 1160 (Migne, 200, col. 90);
Innocent III on Otto IV, 22 Dec. 1210 (*Reg.*, lib. xiii, ep. 193; Migne, 216, col.
361, cf. P. Hinschius, *System des kath. Kirchenrechts*, v (1895), 46, n. 8); Gregory IX
on Frederick II, 20 Aug. 1228 (*M.G.H. Epp. saec. xiii*, i (1883), 399); Boniface VIII
on Philip IV, 8 Sept. 1303 (A. Baillet, *Hist. des démêlez du pape Boniface VIII avec
Philippe le Bel* (1718), p. 388).

[3] Gregory VII, passing sentence on Henry IV (1076), said: 'Heinrico . . . totius
regni Teutonicorum et Italiae gubernacula contradico' (*Registrum*, ed. E. Caspar, i.
270); Innocent IV, denouncing Frederick II (1245) said: 'memoratum principem . . .
ne regnet vel imperet, est abiectus' (*M.G.H. Leg.*, sect. iv, *Const.* ii. 512).

[4] Cf. Carlyle, op. cit. v. 116.

[5] See below, p. 112.

[6] Annales S. Albani (*Ungedruckte anglo-norm. Geschichtsquellen*, ed. F. Liebermann (1879), p. 169) say, 'iiii kl. Septembris', while the Waverley annals (*Annales
monastici* (Rolls Series), ii. 268) say: 'die Martis proxima post festum S. Bartho-
lomaei' (wrongly *s.a.* 1212, cf. ibid., p. 266).

[7] *Ann. mon.* i. 209–17.

the earls, barons, knights, clerks, and lay freemen and all Christians
in the lands subject to you, from the fealty and homage by which
they are bound to you. . . . The Lord pope proposes to send his
army into England.' Different but obviously related versions of
the dialogue occur in the chronicles of two Cistercian abbeys as
far apart as Waverley (Hants)[1] and Meaux (E. Riding, Yorks.).[2]
Another Cistercian chronicle, from Margam in south Wales, and
a Benedictine chronicle from Durham, describe Pandulf's visit
in terms which suggest knowledge of the dialogue.[3] But in all
these narratives we have evidently to do with a common literary
tradition and not a number of unconnected writers independently
recording an event of common knowledge.

The next witness to be called is Roger of Wendover. He
describes the visit of Pandulf and Durand in words borrowed
from the earlier Annals of St. Albans and he knows nothing of
any absolving from fealty by Pandulf.[4] But he, alone among the
chroniclers, tell us that

'in the same year Pope Innocent, since the English king, John, had scorned
to accept the warnings of his nuncios, and being amazed beyond measure
at his manifold contumacy, absolved from fealty and subjection to the king
those kings and all others, great and small, who owed obedience to the
crown of England; and he ordered all and sundry, strictly and under pain
of excommunication, to shun King John carefully at board and council
and assembly.'[5]

This action by the pope must be dated very late in 1211.
The annalists provide more evidence *s.a.* 1212 to support
Wendover's account. The *Brut y Tywysogion* (probably of
Cistercian origin) says:

'That year, Pope Innocent absolved the three princes, namely Llywelyn,
son of Iorwerth, and Gwenwynwyn, and Maelgwn son of Rhys, from the

---

[1] *Ann. mon.*, ii. 268–71. This would appear to be a later addition to are cension
of the chronicle which had already recorded the nuncios' mission briefly in its
proper context on the preceding folio (p. 266).

[2] *Chronica mon. de Melsa* (Rolls Series, i. 387–9).

[3] *Ann. mon.* i. 30–1; *Hist. dunelm. scriptores tres* (Surtees Soc., 1839), pp. 26–7
(Geoffrey of Coldingham). Stubbs (*Gervase of Canterbury*, ii. 107, n. 1) speaks of
the 'best and oldest account' of the nuncios' visit as being contained in the Cotton
MS. Tiberius A. ix. He is apparently referring to the version of the dialogue given
on ff. 49r–51r, and not to the brief notice recorded by the Osney chronicler in the
same volume at f. 58v (printed, *Ann. mon.* iv. 55). A version of the dialogue is said
to be contained in the episcopal register of John Gynwell, bishop of Lincoln,
1347–62 (W. E. Lunt, *Financial Relations*, p. 135, n. 4).

[4] Wendover, *Flores historiarum* (Eng. Hist. Soc., 1841), iii. 235–6; Annales
S. Albani (loc. cit.), p. 169.

[5] Wendover, iii. 237.

XII

104   ALLEGED DEPOSITION OF KING JOHN

oath of fealty which they had given to the king of England. And he commanded them, for the pardon of their sins, to give a sincere pledge of warring against the iniquity of the king. And the interdict, which he had ordered five years previously in England and Wales, was remitted by the pope to the three princes afore-mentioned within their dominions, and to all who were united with them. And they, with one consent, rose against the king and bravely wrested from him the midland district which he had previously taken from Llywelyn son of Iorwerth.'[1]

The *Annals of Waverley* (also Cistercian) say that

'in this year Wales was absolved from interdict and from the yoke of servitude to John, king of England, and also received an order to attack him with all their might, as one who behaved not as a son of Holy Church, but as her enemy, abrogating his predecessors' laws.'[2]

Precisely the same story is told by the Barnwell chronicler, who also reports the rumour that at a meeting of English magnates a letter absolving them from allegiance was read.[3] The Bury annalist has the same report of a letter,[4] and Wendover speaks of the rumour without mentioning the letter.[5] Matthew Paris, in his *Gesta abbatum*, says that some of the nobles began to rebel against the king (now the open enemy of the lord pope and the Church) by command of Pope Innocent III.[6]

The final stage of John's condemnation is most fully described by Wendover, in the following terms:

'About this time [end of 1212] Stephen, archbishop of Canterbury, William, bishop of London, and Eustace, bishop of Ely, went to Rome . . . and humbly besought the lord pope to deign, of his pious mercy, to help the English Church, now reduced as it seemed to the last extremity. Then the pope, . . . with the advice of the cardinals, bishops and other wise men, definitively decreed (*sententialiter definivit*) that John, the English king, should be deposed from the throne and another, deemed more worthy, should with the pope's help succeed him. And for the execution of this sentence, the lord pope wrote to the mighty king of France, Philip, to the effect that he should undertake this task for the remission of all his sins and that, once the English king had been expelled from the throne, he and his successors should possess the kingdom of England lawfully and in per-

---

[1] *Brut y Tywysogion* (Rolls Series), p. 273. Similarly, *s.a.* 1211, the related 'Cronica de Wallia', *Bull. Board of Celtic Studies, Univ. Wales*, xii (1946), p. 34.

[2] *Ann. mon.* ii. 268. The (later) Osney annals also say that the Welsh were incited to rebel by the pope's order (ibid. iv. 56).

[3] *Memoriale fr. Walteri de Coventria*, ii. 206–7.

[4] *Ungedr. anglo-norm. Geschichtsquellen*, p. 154.

[5] Wendover, iii. 239. The *Historia anglicana* of Matthew Paris is a little more explicit (Rolls Series, ii. 128); cf. the Worcester annals (*Ann. mon.* iv. 400).

[6] *Gesta abbatum S. Albani* (Rolls Series), i. 228.

petuity. He wrote, moreover, to all the magnates, knights and other warriors of diverse nations, to take the Cross to overthrow the English king and, by following the French king as their leader in this expedition, strive to avenge the injury done to the Universal Church. He ordered, furthermore, that all those who gave money or aid towards overthrowing this contumacious king should, like pilgrims to the Holy Sepulchre, rest secure in the peace of the Church, both temporally and spiritually.

'This done, the lord pope sent the sub-deacon Pandulf as his representative to France with the above-named archbishop and bishops, so that he could carry out in his presence all that has been described above. But Pandulf, when he was about to leave the pope and the others were absent, in a private interview asked what the pope wished to be done if perchance the English king showed the fruits of repentance and wanted to satisfy God and the Roman Church and the persons concerned in this business. Then the pope declared clearly to Pandulf a form of peace by assent to which the king might win the favour of the Apostolic See.'

Wendover goes on to describe the arrival of Pandulf and the prelates in France in January 1213, and the calling of a council in which the papal sentence and mandate were solemnly published to the French king, bishops, clergy, and people. Philip's levying of an army of invasion, to assemble on 21 April, is described as a direct consequence of this. John was frightened into submitting to the pope on 13 May, and Philip's invasion was thereupon prohibited by Pandulf.[1]

No other contemporary tells of this definitive sentence issued by advice of the cardinals and others, or of the council held in January 1213 in France. But support for Wendover's statement that Innocent invited Philip to conquer England is found in the Winchester–Waverley group of annals and the *Annals of St. Davids*;[2] the statement is also made in a later London chronicle[3] and in an addition made by the Lanercost chronicler to the words of the Melrose chronicle.[4] Corroboration from the Continent is

---

[1] Wendover, iii. 241–3, 246–8, 256–7. The *Historia anglicana* (ii. 129) gives a brief account which, though couched in different terms, is probably derived from Wendover.

[2] Winchester annals (*Ann. mon.* ii. 82): 'Philippus rex Francorum promissione domini papae . . . .' The 'Winton–Waverley' annals (*Ungedr. a.-n. Geschichtsquellen*, p. 186) reads *permissione* and the Waverley annals (*Ann. mon.* ii. 274) *ex praecepto*. The Annales Meneviae (*M.G.H. Scriptores*, xxvii. 443, cf. *Annales Cambriae* (Rolls Series), p. 69) also reads *ex praecepto* and perhaps derives from the Waverley source.

[3] *Liber de antiquis legibus* (Camden Soc., 1846), p. 201: *ad monitionem praedicti papae*.

[4] 'Philippus rex Francorum *ex praecepto domini papae* [Melrose omits] haud dubium *et* [Melrose *quin*] divina dispositione adversus *regem Angliae excitatus* [Melrose *eum*] cum omni impetu exercitus sui [Melrose adds *insurgens etiam*]

perhaps even more noteworthy. This is provided by William, abbot of Andres, in the county of Guînes (dep. Pas-de-Calais), whose contemporary chronicle is specially valuable for the events of the Flemish border in the early thirteenth century. The abbot describes Philip Augustus's preparations for invasion and Pandulf's order to him to desist, after John had made submission to the Church:

'Then the French king, who had first been aroused to do this by the authority of the Roman Curia, being afterwards impeded by the nuncio of the said Curia, altered his plans and led his whole army into Flanders.'[1]

One other author remains to be cited. The Barnwell chronicler who, under the year 1212, described the release of the Welsh from their allegiance to John as a fact and the release of John's English subjects as a rumour, begins the year 1213 with the statement that the exiled English bishops persuaded the pope to put an end to their ills: the pope 'wrote to the French king Philip and the princes of those regions to say that unless the English king straightway recovered his senses (*nisi . . . resipisceret*), they should deliver England from him with armed force'.[2]

If we conflate all this testimony, we shall put the first sentence of deposition (i.e. the release from allegiance) into the mouth of Pandulf in summer 1211. It was confirmed by the pope at the end of that year and repeated solemnly by him a year later, when he also deprived John of his office. Then Innocent III, who had already urged John's subjects to rebel in the early part of 1212, summoned Philip Augustus to lead an attack on the deposed monarch. But it is to be noted that, excepting the last act, the chief papal pronouncements in this story are each vouched for by one source or group of sources, and never by more than one. Moreover, the Barnwell chronicler, one of the most judicious and best informed of contemporary writers, expresses the pope's invitation to Philip II as conditional upon John's continued resistance.

Let us take the incidents one by one: first, the John–Pandulf

usque ad mare anglicum pervenerat.' (*Chronicon de Lanercost* (Bannatyne Club, 1839), p. 11; cf. *Chronicle of Melrose* (ed. A. O. and M. O. Anderson, 1936), p. 58, f. 30ᵛ). The line in *L'histoire de Guillaume le Maréchal: Quer pormise li ert la terre* (14498), does not say that *the pope* promised Philip the land of England, and may refer to Philip's alleged negotiations with the English magnates.

[1] *Recueil des hist. de la France*, xviii. 575. This is repeated in slightly different words by Jean Le Long, abbot of St. Bertin in the fourteenth century, in a passage of his chronicle which is evidently taken from William of Andres (*M.G.H. Scriptores*, xxv. 829–30, cf. p. 739).

[2] Walter of Coventry, ii. 209.

dialogue. Not only is this dialogue suspicious in unessentials—it is surely odd to find an Italian, who had never been in England before, lecturing the English king on the wickedness of William the Conqueror's laws—it is incompatible with other chronicles on the matter of excommunication. For Pandulf is made to say:

'You may know that the lord pope has excommunicated you, but the sentence was suspended until our arrival in these regions subject to you. Henceforth, however, you may know that you are excommunicated and the sentence passed on you has effect.'

Now we are told by three apparently independent chroniclers that sentence of excommunication on John was published solemnly in churches of northern France in November 1209,[1] and this was presumably not known by the composer of the dialogue. If Pandulf declared sentence in this dramatic fashion it is surprising that Roger of Wendover, who is so fully informed of later events, knew nothing about it. There are, as we shall soon see, other good reasons for regarding the whole thing as pure fiction.[2] Proceeding for the moment to compare the two sentences decreed by the pope, according to Wendover, late in 1211 and late in 1212 respectively, we may find it hard to understand why a year should separate these two acts. Modern historians have apparently found some difficulty in this, and the former sentence is usually not mentioned. But those who reject and those who believe the story of the acts of 1211 nearly all accept and give a full account of the deposition declared in December 1212 and the consequent invitation to Philip Augustus. There is only one source for the whole of this episode: Roger of Wendover. One may read the story in the English of Kate Norgate, the French of Charles Petit-

---

[1] Powicke, *Stephen Langton*, p. 77, citing Jean Le Long. Cf. Dunstable annals (*Ann. mon.* iii. 32): *mense Novembri* and John of Oxenedes (*s.a.* 1210, *Chronica* (Rolls Series), p. 126): 'die dominica proxima post festum Omnium Sanctorum'. The pope's commission to the bishop of Arras and the abbot of St. Vaast to publish the sentence when requested by Archbishop Stephen, was probably dated 21 June 1209 (*Reg.*, lib. xii, ep. 57; Migne, 216, col. 64). The excommunication is mentioned by the continuator of Gervase of Canterbury and by Ralph of Coggeshall, and is implied by the annalists of Bury and Winchester. John's later absolution is recorded by the Merton-Southwark-Winchester-Waverley group and by the annalists of St. Albans and Tewkesbury.

[2] Sir James Ramsay offered reasons, mostly good, for rejecting the story *in toto* (*Angevin Empire*, p. 430). Stubbs (*Walter of Coventry*, ii, p. lviii, n. 4) and Tout (*Dict. Nat. Biog.*, s.v. Pandulf) had already expressed grave doubts. Chroniclers who mention the unsuccessful mission of the nuncios, without any of the details contained in the dialogue, are Wendover, the continuator of Gervase of Canterbury, Thomas Wikes, the annalists of Osney, Worcester, Winchester, Southwark, Merton, and Bury.

108   ALLEGED DEPOSITION OF KING JOHN

Dutaillis, the German of Alexander Cartellieri, but it is always Wendover in translation.

There are episodes of medieval history which we can only reconstruct by piecing together the reports of various chroniclers who are complementary rather than corroboratory; each contributes something, sees events from an individual point of view, ignores one part of the story and illuminates another part.[1] But the historian's conflation of this sort of testimony is not altogether convincing if important chronicles make absolutely no contribution to the story. In this case the singularity of Wendover's account of the two papal sentences is highly significant; and both this and the other chroniclers' reports command less respect when the complete silence of other reputable writers is taken into account. Ralph, abbot of Coggeshall, had much to say about King John's misdeeds and was well placed to know about papal sentences upon him; but while he explicitly says that John was excommunicated, nowhere does he hint at deposition. So also Richard de Morins, prior of Dunstable (or whoever put together the Annals of Dunstable in their present form) and the continuator of Gervase of Canterbury. The omissions of the episode, in whole or in part, by some of the best narrative-writers of the time cannot be overlooked; they represent a real conflict of testimony. They do not in themselves invalidate the positive statements,[2] but they should make us treat these statements with extreme reserve.

Fortunately, we have other evidence as well, the evidence of official records, and they enable us to settle the matter. The difficulties of reconciling the story of deposition with the records seem insuperable. The papal registers of the thirteenth century provide ample material for observing by what procedure and with what effect the popes usually excommunicated ruling monarchs. The practice, after all, was not uncommon. In the winter of 1212–13 no less than four kings lay under the ban of the Church: the Emperor Otto IV, John of England, Alfonso II of Portugal, Leo II of Armenia; and Otto was deposed. We need not enter into the details of procedure, which naturally varied according to the exigencies of the case, but we ought to remember that it was elaborate, was conducted with careful attention to forms, and usually left abundant records. In the present case we know

---

[1] Cf. the remarks of F. M. Powicke, *Eng. Hist. Rev.* xxi (1906), 295, 630–3.

[2] Neither Ralph of Coggeshall nor the Dunstable annalist makes any mention at all of the nuncios' visit in 1211.

that John's excommunication was publicly pronounced in the churches of northern France in November 1209.

Extant papal letters arrange for the pronouncement and refer to John as excommunicate, but not one letter is known in which he is said to be, or to have been, deposed. The registers of Innocent III contain no document recording John's deposition in 1211 or 1212, no document freeing the Welsh from interdict and allegiance in 1212, no document inciting the English magnates to rebel,[1] or bidding Philip Augustus to act against John.

Stubbs was the first to account for this big gap by a letter which Innocent III directed to Nicholas of Tusculum in October 1213.[2] This is a mandate requiring the legate, after relaxing the interdict, to order the archbishop of Canterbury and his suffragans to hand over all the letters (both the former and the latter) which they had obtained from the pope against the king in case he should not accept the form of peace, and particularly those which begin with the words *Expectantes hactenus expectavimus*, which were to be sent (*destinandas*) to the archbishops and bishops throughout France, England, Scotland, and Ireland and the bishops of Liége and Utrecht. The legate was to have the letters chopped up small or burned. The ominous *incipit 'Expectantes'* and the intended distribution of the letter certainly suggest that it may have conveyed a sentence of deposition which was not to come into force unless John rejected the peace terms offered to him in the spring of 1213. But while this is a matter for conjecture, the terms of Innocent's mandate make it clear that the letters had not in fact been communicated to their addressees: they were still in the hands of Langton and his colleagues, from whom they were to be collected.[3] The mandate to Nicholas of

---

[1] Late in 1212 John obtained letters patent from magnates of England and Ireland proclaiming their loyalty to the king and expressing grief and surprise that the pope should propose to absolve the king's subjects from allegiance. (H. S. Sweetman, *Cal. Docts. relating to Ireland* (1875), i. 73; cf. *Ungedr. a.-n. Geschichtsquellen*, p. 155, and Norgate, *John Lackland*, pp. 172–3.) This, of course, only indicates that the pope had threatened deposition or that a rumour to this effect was abroad. The crucial words of the Irish magnates' letter are: 'sicut nuper accepimus dominus papa proposuit omnes fideles domini regis Angl' a sua absolvere fidelitate pro eo quod ipse restitit iniurie sibi illate super facto Cantuar' ecclesie' (Public Record Office, Red Book of the Exchequer, f. 180ᵛ). John probably obtained these letters to counteract rumour and to impress the pope with a picture of English solidarity when he sent his messengers to Rome in November 1212.

[2] *Reg.*, lib. xvi, ep. 133 (Migne, 216, col. 926) dated 31 Oct. 1213, and Rymer, *Foedera* (Rec. Com.), i. i. 116, wrongly dated 22 Oct. 1213. Cf. Stubbs, Walter of Coventry, ii, p. lviii, n. 4, and Powicke, *Loss of Normandy*, p. 475.

[3] As Ramsay hesitantly suggested (*Angevin Empire*, p. 431, n. 1). Langton and his fellow exiles were the natural bearers of such letters. Two of the letters may be

110   ALLEGED DEPOSITION OF KING JOHN

Tusculum, therefore, cannot be taken as evidence that an act of deposition was ever published, and the absence of any such act in itself justifies doubts about the chroniclers' stories. We need not rely on arguments from silence. The letters which stand under the number 234, in the Register of Innocent III's fifteenth year, provide enough positive evidence to demolish a whole series of fictions.[1] The first of these letters is addressed to King John, beginning with the words: *Auditis verbis nuntiorum tuorum*. This has an appendix beginning: 'Exposiciones autem et explanaciones sunt iste',[2] and is terminated by the date: 'Dat' Laterani iii kal. Marcii pontificatus nostri anno xvi°' (27 February 1213). The first letter refers to the form of peace which had been transmitted to the king by Pandulf and Durand in August 1211 and this *forma* follows in the shape of the pope's original letter to Pandulf and Durand. It bears no date, but we know from an English copy of the original that it was dated 'xviii kal. Maii pont. nostri anno xiiii' (14 April 1211).[3] The form of the commission to the nuncios is particularly interesting because it destroys all faith in the John–Pandulf dialogue. As Ramsay pointed out: 'Pandulf and Durand had no authority to utter any sentence against John. They were directed if he proved obdurate to leave the prosecution of the struggle in the hands of Langton and

those issued late in February or early in March 1213 which stand at the end of Innocent III's register of the fifteenth year, nos. 238 and 239 (Migne, 216, cols. 781–2). The letter *Expectantes* is unfortunately not found with them; it may have started on the lines of Innocent III's letter 'Expectans expectavit diutius apostolica sedes', ordering the deposition of the archbishop of Bordeaux, addressed to the archbishop of Bourges and others on 31 Oct. 1205 (*Reg.*, lib. viii, ep. 150; Migne, 215, col. 725). Cf. a letter written about June–November 1214, which begins: 'Satis actenus expectavimus si forte duritia Narniensium per nostram posset patientiam emolliri' (ed. by K. Hampe, *Mittheilungen des Instituts für österreichische Geschichtsforschung*, xxiii (1902), 553). Cf. also Potthast, nos. 1753, 1769.

    [1] Vatican Archives, Reg. Vat. 8, ff. 132ᵛ–133ᵛ. Whereas most of the registers of Innocent III are the originals, this volume, containing letters of the pontifical years thirteen to sixteen, is a copy made in the time of Urban V (cf. H. Denifle, in *Archiv für Literatur- und Kirchengesch. d. Mittelalters*, ii (1886), 21, 43, 74, n. 2). The earliest numeration of the letters (not original) attaches the numbers 232–4 to the three documents beginning respectively with the words *Auditis*, *Exposiciones*, and *Forma*. According to a later numeration (corresponding to the printed editions) all three are placed under the number 234. Printed in Baluze, *Epp. Innoc. libri undecim*, ii (1682), 727 and Migne, 216, col. 772. The undated text of the letter *Auditis verbis nuntiorum* preserved by the Burton annalist (*Ann. mon.* i. 217) gives the names of the six king's messengers, of whom only two are named in the papal register.

    [2] The title *Pacis et reconciliationis leges* given in the printed editions of the register is not in Reg. Vat. 8.

    [3] Gervase of Canterbury, II, pp. cxiii–cxiv from Brit. Mus. Cotton MS. Cleop. E. i.

ALLEGED DEPOSITION OF KING JOHN   111

return to Rome.'¹ On the other hand Pandulf was authorized to absolve the king from excommunication if he were penitent, and this confirms our other information that excommunication had been published before this date.

Returning to the letter *Auditis verbis* and its appendix, we have first to note that although in 1635 the original editor François Bosquet gave the correct date, later editors have persistently misdated it *anno quintodecimo*;² although the book of the register in which it appears professes to concern the fifteenth year of Innocent III, this letter and the following six letters belong properly to the beginning of the sixteenth year.³ Next, we see from its text that Innocent III has received John's representatives (who had been dispatched in November 1212)⁴ and offers the king the choice of blessings or curses. The royal envoys have agreed provisionally to the terms which Pandulf and Durand had put forward in 1211; now it is for the king to confirm the agreement with pledges from his magnates. If he will not receive peace while he may, he will not be able to when he wishes and repentance will be useless once he is ruined. He is given until 1 June (1213) to ratify his envoys' agreement. It seems inconceivable that Innocent III should write in this strain to a king whom (if we believe Wendover) he had solemnly deposed some two months earlier. *Ruina* spells deposition. This letter contains a threat, and a threat of deposition, but only to take effect if John does not submit within three months.⁵

---

¹ Op. cit., p. 430.
² What is more, Achille Luchaire failed to note this fact in his critical analysis of Potthast ('Les Registres d'Innocent III et les *Regesta* de Potthast', *Troisièmes mélanges d'histoire du moyen âge*, Bibliothèque de la Fac. des lettres, Univ. de Paris, 1904, p. 77). W. H. Bliss (*Cal. of Papal Letters*, i (1893), 37, put the letter in its right place but did not indicate the terms of the dating clause in Reg. Vat. 8. The manuscript from which Bosquet took his text was probably the original register copied in Reg. Vat. 8 (cf. Luchaire, loc. cit., pp. 20–3).
³ Innocent III's pontifical year began on 22 Feb. The correct date of 'Auditis verbis' has long been recognized (Stubbs, Walter of Coventry, 11, p. lviii, n. 4) but the editors' misdating has been ascribed to the papal registrar (cf. preceding note). There is no need to dwell on the error, but it must be mentioned, since Rymer prints the letter with the date 'Kal. Mart. anno 15' (while setting it under A.D. 1213, *Foedera* (Rec. Com.), I. i. 108–9) and Potthast (*Regesta pontificum*, no. 4395) assigns it to 1 Mar. 1212. Luchaire falls into the trap (*Innocent III: les royautés vassales du saint-siège* (1908), p. 215) and Miss Gütschow tries to justify the date 28 Feb. 1212 (op. cit., pp. 164–5).
⁴ *Rot. lit. clausarum* (ed. T. D. Hardy), i. 126; cf. Walter of Coventry, ii. 207.
⁵ 'Alioquin, eius exemplo qui populum suum de servitute Pharaonis in manu valida liberavit, anglicanam ecclesiam in forti brachio de servitute tua studebimus liberare' (Migne, 216, col. 773). The phrase 'eritque inutilis penitentia post ruinam' (ibid.) is reminiscent of the threat in an earlier letter to the excommunicate

That Innocent did not regard John as already legally deposed is proved by the address and greeting of the letter: 'Johanni illustri regi Angliae spiritum consilii sanioris.' This is the address for an excommunicate but not for a man deposed from his office. The usual formula of apostolic benediction is withheld,[1] but the king is not denied his title. Both here and in a letter dated 7 March 1213[2] to Langton and his colleagues, John is *rex*. Another letter, probably of the same date, provides that if, after peace is made, the *king* does not make proper satisfaction, the *king* and *his* kingdom are to revert to the same state of interdict and excommunication in which they were before the peace.[3] It was not thus that the popes spoke of rulers who were deposed. Otto IV, once deposed, becomes 'dictus imperator, maledictus et excommunicatus'.[4] Frederick II becomes *quondam Romanorum imperator*, with various unpleasant epithets besides.[5] Nor was John

king, preserved only in an undated copy: 'quanquam tibi merito sit verendum ne sera sit penitentia post ruinam' (*Gervase of Canterbury*, II, p. cxiii).

[1] While Innocent III observed in 1205 that his chancery might sometimes, in error or in ignorance of the facts, give the apostolic benediction to excommunicates (*Reg.*, lib. vii, ep. 224; Migne, 215, col. 542, and *Decretales*, v. 39, 41), the formula *spiritum consilii sanioris* was usual. The only other surviving letter of Innocent to John while the latter was excommunicate bears the same greeting; other examples are *Reg.*, lib. vi, epp. 38, 39, 149, 230; vii, ep. 18; ix, ep. 96; xv, ep. 122; xvi, epp. 22, 114 (Migne, 215, cols. 43, 44, 160, 260, 301, 911; 216, cols. 635, 810, 909), and *Foedera*, I. i. 136. Sometimes the pope took the trouble to explain why he wrote thus. On the very next day after writing to King John, he wrote to the excommunicate king of Armenia, saying: 'Inviti ac dolentes tibi negamus apostolicae salutationis et benedictionis alloquium, cui benedictionem et salutem aeternam in domino affectamus. Verum id exposcit tuorum excessuum magnitudo' (*Reg.*, lib. xvi, ep. 2; Migne, 216, col. 784). Cf. other letters of Innocent III (*Reg.*, lib. i, ep. 574; vi, epp. 39, 93; Migne, 214, col. 527; 215, cols. 44, 97), and the original of a letter of Alexander III to the Serbian prince Miroslav (1181), in which the usual 'Dilecto filio . . . salutem et apostolicam benedictionem' has been erased, and the following clause explains the reason (G. Battelli, *Acta pontificum* (Exempla scripturarum, fasc. iii, Vatican, 1933), pl. 9*b* and p. 11, n. 1). The papal chancery also coined formulas of greetings for infidels: see letters to the sultans of Aleppo and Damascus (*Reg.*, lib. xiv, ep. 69; Migne, 216, col. 434, and *Neues Archiv*, xxxi (1906), 592–3). The thirteenth-century writers on dictamen take account of these peculiar types of salutation: see L. von Rockinger, *Briefsteller und Formelbücher des XI. bis XIV. Jh.* (Quellen zur bayer. u. deut. Geschichte, ix, 1863–4), pp. 261, 366, 463, 731.

[2] *Reg.*, lib. xv, ep. 236; Migne, 216, col. 780. The 'Datum ut supra' (i.e. iii kal. Mart.) of Migne does not appear in Reg. Vat. 8, where no date is given. The copy, taken from the original by Nicholas of Tusculum, is dated 'nonis Martii anno xvi°' (i.e. 7 Mar. 1213. *Essays in History Pres. to R. L. Poole* (1927), pp. 280–1).

[3] *Reg.*, lib. xv, ep. 238; Migne, 216, col. 781.

[4] *Reg.*, lib. xv, ep. 193; lib. xiv, epp. 78–9; Migne, 216, cols. 361, 439, 440.

[5] *Registres d'Innocent IV* (École franç. de Rome, 1884–1919), Index, p. 167 *passim*. Alexander III referred to Frederick Barbarossa consistently as *dictus*

denied his royal title by his enemies Philip Augustus and Frederick II when they made a treaty on 19 November 1212: they observe the formal distinction between 'Otto formerly called emperor and John king of England'.[1] Again, Prince Louis's pledge to his father, drawn up early in April 1213, speaks of John as king of England.[2] We can only conclude that when Innocent III directed *Auditis verbis* to John on 27 February 1213, he had not yet pronounced sentence of deposition and did not intend to do so before 1 June.

In the event, John submitted well within the time allowed. The documents connected with the submission nowhere suggest that the king had lost his royal title. It is, indeed, difficult to see how the transactions of 15 May 1213 could take place—how John could surrender the kingdom—if, according to the papal theory, he had no kingdom to surrender. Had John been deprived of his office some document must have recorded his reinstatement, but none survives; and of all the chroniclers who tell of his absolution, not one speaks of his restoration to the throne.

King John, then, was never formally deposed by the pope. But if that be so, what of the report that Philip Augustus prepared to invade England under papal auspices? The evidence of the English chroniclers must be discounted, since they have been discovered in error on the other point, and there is practically no other positive evidence.[3] French chroniclers are completely silent about the meeting in January 1213 which Wendover describes; and the Council of Soissons (early April) at which Philip Augustus

---

imperator from the time when he released Frederick's subjects from allegiance (April 1160) to the reconciliation in 1177 (e.g. Jaffé-Löwenfeld, *Regesta pont.*, nos. 10655, 10750, 11747, 12737). Supporters of the popes took their cue from the papal chancery. To John of Salisbury, Frederick I is *teutonicus tyrannus* and *ex-augustus* (cf. *Materials hist. Thomas Becket* (Rolls Series), vi, *passim*. Étienne de Gallardon, canon of Bourges, speaks scurrilously of Frederick II as 'Mederi-cum imperatorem, nominalem non realem' (*Bibl. de l'Éc. des Chartes*, lx (1899), 18).

[1] *M.G.H. Leg.*, sect. iv, *Const.* ii. 55.

[2] *Foedera*, I. i. 104. The date 'April 1212' is in modern terms April 1213; since the French chancery reckoned the year of grace from Easter, its year 1212 ran from 25 Mar. 1212 to 13 Apr. 1213.

[3] William, abbot of Andres (cf. p. 106 above), provides the only evidence from the Continent (if we exclude such a late and unreliable writer as Ptolemy of Lucca). William was well placed to pick up an English rumour. In 1211 he was at Paris, engaged in a lawsuit in which, out of three judges delegate, Richard Poore, dean of Salisbury, favoured William's cause (L. D'Achery, *Spicilegium*, ii (1723), 849; cf. *Innoc. III Reg.*, lib. xi, ep. 205; lib. xiv, ep. 19; Migne, 215, col. 1519; 216, col. 396). Some of the exiled English prelates may well have stopped at Andres during these years and may have passed that way on their return to England in July 1213.

formally announced his intentions, is reported at length by William le Breton in both his prose chronicle and his poem, without any suggestion that the pope was concerned. Philip, is indeed, represented as piously inclined to the invasion (*innata motus pietate*) and he poses as the defender and avenger of the Church, but the invasion is all his own idea (*mens mea proponit*).[1] If Pandulf had conveyed to Philip a formal commission to invade England, the French king could hardly fail to be aggrieved at the turn of events in May 1213. But there is no evidence of this worth having. In keeping with their account of Soissons, the French chroniclers report no recrimination by Philip Augustus against the pope when Innocent accepted John's submission: that was left for Wendover and the modern French historians who copy him. There is no official correspondence of Philip to suggest that he wanted or relied on papal backing; and when Innocent wrote to him on 5 July 1213, announcing the reconciliation of John to the Church, he wrote only a brief letter of credence for the legate[2] and not the sort of grandiloquent epistle with which this pope habitually justified his changes of policy. Again it proves impossible to reconcile Wendover's story with the evidence from other sources. We are under no obligation to believe that the pope behaved inconsistently at this juncture, treating with a deposed king, while he urged an enemy to dispossess him.

Maybe this verdict on the story of John's deposition and Philip's commission does not seriously alter our view of the events of 1211–13, but it tends to a toning down of the colours of the picture. It confirms the impression gained from other sources that the interdict and excommunication did not seriously impede royal government and that John's difficulties were of different origin, though they were aggravated by the displeasure of the Church. As the events of these years now appear, the pope was more of a statesman than he seemed when we believed in the various unheeded sentences of 1211, 1212, and 1213. He measured his words according to his means and did not declare deposition when he could not enforce it. On the other hand, this episode suggests that John was still strong enough in 1212 and 1213 to

---

[1] *Œuvres de Rigord et Guillaume le Breton* (Soc. Hist. France, 1882–5), i. 244–53, ii. 247–8, 255.

According to the *Histoire des ducs de Normandie et des rois d'Angleterre* (Soc. Hist. France, 1840), p. 120, the idea of invading England came suddenly to Philip early one morning, as he lay in bed!

[2] *Reg.*, lib. xvi, ep. 83; Migne, 216, col. 884–5.

choose the time and manner of his reconciliation with the Church. The pope was more anxious to pardon a prodigal than the king to solicit the forgiveness of his spiritual father. John's final acts of submission and homage were not the fruit of sudden desperation; they were the consequences of an embassy sent to Rome six months earlier. If it is true, and it may well be, that John acted on his own initiative when he made England and Ireland vassal states of the papacy, he made his intention known in Rome before Pandulf left for England; the formula of surrender shows that the act was premeditated. The terror-stricken tyrant and the domineering priest disappear from a story of well-calculated diplomacy by two men, each of whom had many qualities of greatness.

The inquiry has also a subsidiary interest. It has been concerned about a matter of fact: did Pope Innocent depose King John? The negative answer leaves us with a lot of bad evidence on our hands, which must be accounted for.[1]

The various chroniclers did not manufacture this evidence out of nothing. The truth seems to be that while the deposition of John was not a fact it was, in the years 1211, 1212, and 1213, a widespread and persistent rumour. The rumour flourished in the atmosphere of distrust which prevailed in an England labouring under tyrannical government and the shadow of four years' interdict. We know from various sources that the countryside was teeming with rumours, which set people's nerves on edge and probably worked powerfully on the imagination of the king.[2] It was widely known that John's nephew, the emperor, had been deposed as well as excommunicated and that a crusade was being directed by Simon de Montfort,[3] claimant to an English earldom, against the king's brother-in-law, Raymond VI of Toulouse. There were those in England and Wales who would use this information to start a 'whispering campaign' against the king. The failure of the nuncios' mission in 1211 encouraged a belief

---

[1] 'If every piece of news that reached an English abbey and is recorded could be traced to its source we should find their errors as natural and instructive as their accuracy.' F. M. Powicke, 'Roger of Wendover and the Coggeshall chronicle', *Eng. Hist. Rev.* xxi (1906), 295.

[2] See especially the Bury annals (*Ungedr. a.-n. Geschichtsquellen*), p. 153, and Walter of Coventry, ii. 206. The unsettled state of mind that prevailed in England in 1212 and early in 1213 is constantly remarked by the Barnwell chronicler (ibid. 207–11).

[3] According to the well-informed annalist of Dunstable, the rumours of conspiracy which reached John in August 1212 included the news that his barons had chosen Simon to be king of England (*Ann. mon.* iii. 33).

in deposition, the Welsh princes welcomed it as an excuse for throwing over a treaty very recently established, and finally, Philip's preparations for invasion were associated with the pope's calls to arms against enemies of the Church. Although the chroniclers cannot be trusted to tell us precisely what happened, they can therefore be trusted to report what the people of England (particularly in monasteries) felt and believed about current affairs. This at least is probably true of the Cistercian sources and the Barnwell chronicler: we must put the John–Pandulf dialogue[1] and Wendover's narrative in a class apart. As regards Wendover (and it is he whom modern historians have followed), the scrappy reports of other chroniclers seem to be not corroboration of his elaborate, circumstantial account, but the very material out of which he, or someone else, invented it. The rumours of 1212 may indeed have been magnified soon after John's submission if Langton let it be known that he had the letter 'Expectantes hactenus expectavimus' up his sleeve.[2] Be that as it may, the details of Wendover's narrative cannot be other than products of imagination. In the last few decades Wendover's work has come under close scrutiny and his reputation as an historian is sinking.[3] He had great opportunities at St. Albans to collect historical materials and he misused them, as he is reported to have misused the goods of Belvoir Priory. Inaccurate in small matters, when he tried to copy exactly, he seems to have been quite without the power of discriminating between true news and gossip. But if he is a poor historian, as a writer of dramatic narrative he shows very considerable ability. It is by his art that, in the history of this episode, fiction has successfully masqueraded as fact for more than 700 years.

---

[1] I take this to be a literary exercise composed after John's submission and probably after his death.

[2] Cf. above, p. 109.

[3] Cf. V. H. Galbraith, *Roger Wendover and Matthew Paris* (David Murray Lecture, Glasgow, 1944). In 1903 Sir James Ramsay wrote: 'Wendover is a careless, inaccurate writer, on whom, however, we are dependent for a great mass of matter' (*Angevin Empire*, p. 524).

ADDITIONAL NOTES

The evidence set out in this paper was re-considered by Sidney Painter
(The reign of king John (Baltimore,1949) pp.190-2 and by W.L. Warren
(King John (1961) pp.203,310),who interpreted it somewhat differently.
Richardson and Sayles (Governance of medieval England (1963) p.351 n.1)
while accepting that 'there is no evidence that the pope formally deposed
John', judged my argument 'perhaps rather academic'. In Innocent III
and England (pp.320-1,326-7,339-41) I have tried to clarify the object of
my original paper, which simply aimed at disproving that the pope ever
deposed the king, or publicly incited his subjects to rebel, or invited the
king of France to invade. I hope that my later remarks give a more nuancé
picture of the situation as a whole.

P.109 n.1:   The letter of the Irish magnates is edited by Richardson and
Sayles, The Irish parliament in the middle ages (Philadelphia,1952) pp.
286-7, where it is dated Jan. 1213.

Pp.112 n.1:   The withholding of a greeting is found as early as pope Gregory VII (e.g. Registrum, lib.IV ep.16,cf.I ep.67,II ep.6). The English
chancery used the formula in addressing excommunicate rebels ,1216-7
(e.g. Rot .lit.pat. p.184b,Patent rolls,p.4).

XIII

THE EVE OF MAGNA CARTA [1]

A LTHOUGH Magna Carta has been a household word in England for more than seven centuries, it is less than two hundred years since the scientific study of the great charter of King John was initiated by one of England's most celebrated lawyers, William Blackstone. Writing in 1759 he said : " There is no transaction in the antient part of our english history more interesting and important, than the rise and progress, the gradual mutation, and final establishment of the charters of liberties . . . and yet there is none that has been transmitted down to us with less accuracy and historical precision. . . . This want of authentic materials, or neglect of recurring to such as might be easily had, . . . has often betrayed our very best historians and most painful antiquarians into gross and palpable errors, as will in some measure appear from the following deduction." [2] He concludes by leaving the last word on the Charter to " some masterly and comprehensive genius ", but opines that such a one may be wanting in " critical attention to dates, and names, and other minuter circum-stances ".[3]

Blackstone's care and acuteness cleared away some of the muddle surrounding the Magna Carta of 1215 ; and from his day to ours the Charter has been continuously studied. It is, however, many years since anyone attempted a chronological account of the weeks which preceded its issue. That is my object : to establish dates. I am not concerned with the constitutional importance of the Charter : I am trying to find the order of preceding political events. Even so, I shall not

[1] A lecture delivered in the John Rylands Library on Wednesday, the 11th of May 1955, printed with some additions and changes. I am indebted to Professor V. H. Galbraith, Mr. Eric John, and my wife for criticism and advice.

[2] William Blackstone, *The Great Charter and the Charter of the Forest* (Oxford, 1759), p. i.   [3] Ibid. p. lxxvi.

© *The John Rylands University, 1956*

312

attempt to include all relevant events, but only to provide a chronological framework in which they will fit. Our sources are inadequate, and a plausible conjecture is often all that can be offered instead of a certain conclusion. Nevertheless the attempt is worth making. The "critical attention to dates" of which Blackstone spoke should not be beneath the dignity of serious students of history. I invite you, then, to follow me along a somewhat arid track of facts and dates. As we go we may gain incidental light upon the situation, besides preparing the chronological path for some future "masterly and comprehensive genius" to tread.

The period which I wish to study and which I have described as "the eve of Magna Carta" begins in Easter Week 1215 and comprises some nine weeks. A rather protracted *eve*, you may think : but Mr. H. G. Richardson, in an important contribution to the BULLETIN in 1944, made the "morrow of the Great Charter" last a full three months.

I

Now, in January 1215, Low Sunday, that is the Sunday next after Easter, 26 April, had been appointed as the day when King John would answer a request for redress of grievances which an important group of barons had made. These barons had come armed to the king's council in London on 6 January. Although most of the earls stood aloof, the party clearly was a political and military force to be reckoned with. It included a strong north-country element, but we cannot guess its numbers or composition. Eustace de Vescy, Richard de Percy, Robert fitzWalter were among the leaders. They had asked the king to confirm their ancient liberties, as contained in his predecessors' charters and implicit in his coronation-oath.[1] The king had reacted violently. He had tried to make the malcontents withdraw their demand and give security that they would not renew it. This they would not do. Eventually, the king had

---

[1] Cf. the report of Walter Mauclerc from the Curia in March 1215 (T. Rymer, *Foedera* (Record Commission ed.), I. i. 120). Roger Wendover and "Walter of Coventry" both say that the coronation-charter of Henry I was brought to the fore at this stage.

THE EVE OF MAGNA CARTA 313

promised to give them safe-conduct to and from Northampton, where, on Low Sunday, 26 April, he would give his answer. John had played for time, and the records show that between January and April he was not inactive. He was fetching troops from abroad, stocking his castles with food and ammunition, making siege-weapons and, in short, preparing for war. The business of the law-courts diminished and the enrolment of charters in chancery ceased entirely for ten weeks.[1] Chroniclers suggest that the king's court was deserted by most of those prelates and nobles who usually frequented it. But meanwhile, the king was making concessions to individuals, which might detach them from the opposition, and he used Archbishop Stephen Langton and the bishops and the veteran William Marshal, earl of Pembroke, to negotiate with the " northerners ", as the malcontents are almost invariably described. One meeting may have taken place at Oxford on 22 February, another at the same place on 13 April.[2]

Both sides recognized (better than some modern historians have done) the importance of interesting the king's new overlord, Pope Innocent III. They had sent their respective envoys off to Rome soon after the meeting in January. But these *démarches* could only produce results later on, for the journey to and from Rome in winter-time would scarcely take less than three months and, in this instance, took longer. We must leave them, for the present, on the path to Rome. Then, on 4 March, King John took a step which all acknowledged to be a master-stroke of diplomacy. He took the Cross as a Crusader. It put him and his possessions under the special protection of the Church and rendered liable to anathema those who interfered with him.

II

By the time Easter came both the king and his opponents apparently were dubious of settling the matter peaceably. If we may credit " Walter of Coventry ", the harsh reply which

---

[1] Between 9 February and 22 April.
[2] *Rotuli litterarum patentium*, ed. T. D. Hardy (Record Comm.), p. 129a ; *Memorials of St. Edmund's Abbey* (Rolls Series), ii. 124-5.

314

the king had returned to the barons' proposals in recent parleys made them hurry to fortify their castles, look for allies, and prepare horses and arms. So they came armed to the appointed meeting-place, Northampton, on Low Sunday, 26 April. We hear from chroniclers of a first assembly of northern barons at Stamford in Easter week.[1] Thence they moved to Northampton where they were joined by Giles, bishop of Hereford, Geoffrey de Mandeville, Robert fitzWalter, and many others—presumably those whose strength, like these great lords', lay in East Anglia. The opposition came chiefly, though not entirely, from the north and east of the country.[2] The king made no attempt to keep the appointment. Having gone as far north as his stronghold of Nottingham late in March, he came southwards at the beginning of April and stayed in the Thames valley and farther south. Easter he spent at London, and during Easter-week moved through Hampshire to his hunting-box of Clarendon, near Salisbury. Nevertheless, before leaving London on Thursday, 23 April, he issued letters of safe-conduct for those who should come with the archbishop of Canterbury or bearing letters from him to speak with the king.[3] The safe-conduct was to last for five weeks—until Ascension day, 28 May.

Stephen Langton was still working for a peaceful settlement, but for the course of his negotiations there are few clues.[4] Our account of the fortnight after 26 April, therefore, may well be faulty in detail.

According to Roger Wendover, on the day after Low Sunday the malcontents moved to Brackley, some twenty miles to the south-west of Northampton. There (or nearby)[5] they met the

---

[1] Wendover, in Matthew Paris, *Chronica maiora* (Rolls Series), ii. 585 and "Walter of Coventry", *Memoriale* (Rolls Series), ii. 219. Sir James Ramsay (*The Angevin Empire* (1903), pp. 470–2) places this and succeeding events much earlier. His arguments for dating the barons' diffidation about 13 April are not cogent. Professor Sidney Painter, *The Reign of King John* (Baltimore, 1949), p. 288, puts the meeting at Stamford in mid-April.

[2] Painter, op. cit. pp. 287–90.　　　　　　　[3] *Rot. lit. pat.* p. 134a.

[4] He was engaged in the negotiations of 22 February and 13 April, and between those two dates he is found in Norfolk (Gaywood, 31 March) and Herts (Little Wymondley, 6 April): see *Acta Stephani Langton*, ed. K. Maior (Canterbury and York Soc., 1950), nos. 13, 14.

[5] "Walter of Coventry", ii. 219.

THE EVE OF MAGNA CARTA 315

archbishop, the earl of Pembroke, and other representatives of the king. The malcontents had now set down in writing their demands, largely for " old laws and customs of the realm ", which were to be found in the coronation-charter of Henry I and the so-called Laws of Edward the Confessor. They asked that the document embodying their demands should be confirmed at once by the king's seal ; otherwise they would resort to force. Wendover is not a writer on whom we can rely for accuracy in describing a transaction of this sort : but it is altogether prob- able that at this juncture a demand was made in writing. To suppose, with Sir James Ramsay, that the demand was " doubt- less the Articles subsequently produced at Runnymede " is to go far beyond the evidence, but we can best explain the impasse which was reached if we suppose that the baronial document included a demand for a restrictive council of some sort.

This demand, which may be dated 27 April, had to be con- veyed to the king, who was then making his way rapidly from Corfe, through Clarendon and Marlborough, to Wallingford. He reached Wallingford (if the chancery-roll can be trusted to give the king's itinerary) late on Thursday, 30 April. Walling- ford is about thirty-four miles from Brackley. There, I suggest, he received the malcontents' demand and threat. On the same day, as the patent roll shows, he wrote to Walter de Lascy, John de Monmouth, Hugh de Mortimer, Walter de Clifford, and " other barons at Gloucester ", requesting them to be at Ciren- cester on Monday next, well equipped with horses and arms and all the men they could muster, there to await the king's command. Without going into questions of military strategy I may point out in passing the importance of Cirencester at a key-point east of the main Cotswold ridge.

At this critical juncture an event occurred which prompted the king, if he needed prompting, to reject the malcontents' demands and make counter-proposals. The evidence points to this week after Low Sunday—about the end of April—as the moment when the king's messengers returned from Rome. Precisely when they arrived and what they brought with them are far from clear ; but we shall not be wrong in placing their

316

arrival in this week [1] and in making them the carriers of two
letters, which were later transcribed upon the dorse of the patent
roll. Both these letters are dated at the Lateran, 19 March.[2]
One letter, addressed to the magnates and barons of England,
ordered them to abandon conspiracies and show of force against
the king, to render their due service to him, and, if they had
requests to make, to make them respectfully. The second surviving letter was directed to Archbishop Stephen and his suffragans.
It upbraided them for failing to mediate in the dispute between
king and barons, and stated that they were suspected of giving
help and favour to the king's opponents : they were to condemn
conspiracies and forbid them under pain of excommunication.
In both these letters the Pope said that he had written to the king
asking him to treat the barons kindly and hear their just petitions
graciously. The letter to the king on behalf of the barons does
not survive ; presumably it was brought by the barons' messengers at about the same time.[3] Besides these three hortatory
letters the Pope, it seems, also sent to the disputants terms of
agreement which he had propounded and to which the barons'
messengers at the Curia had agreed.[4] A few months later the
Pope's commissioners spoke of these " three-fold peace-terms
(*triplex forma pacis*) which were thoroughly honourable and
reasonable and worthy of acceptance by God-fearing men ".[5]
From later letters of the Pope we learn that one of the proposals
was for the king to " grant the barons full safe-conduct, . . .

[1] A writ of *computate* in favour of Thomas of Erdinton suggests that he was
back to his normal activities by 7 May (*Rotuli Litterarum Clausarum*, ed. T.D.
Hardy (Record Comm.), i. 199a), completed by an unpublished fragment of the
roll. Brother Alan Martel appears on 14 May (*Rot. lit. pat.*, p. 135b). Sir
Maurice Powicke suggested that the letters might not have reached England
before the seizure of London on 17 May (*Stephen Langton* (Oxford, 1928), p. 131
and n. 4), but the terms of the later papal letter ("interim prefatis nuntiis
revertentibus ") seem to date their arrival much earlier.

[2] *Selected Letters of Pope Innocent III Concerning England*, ed. C. R. Cheney
and W. H. Semple (1953), pp. 194, 196 (and in *Foedera*, I. i. 127).

[3] See Walter of Coventry's evidence, below.

[4] This agreement is stated in the Pope's letter of 18 June (*Magna Carta
Commemoration Essays*, ed. H. E. Malden (1917), p. 44).

[5] *English Historical Review*, xliv (1929), 92. Mr. Painter has pointed out
that this cannot refer to Magna Carta, as Powicke and Richardson supposed
(*The Reign of King John*, pp. 345-6, and cf. my remarks, *ante*, xxxiii (1950), 35-6).

so that if they could not arrive at agreement the dispute might be decided in his court by their peers according to the laws and customs of the kingdom ".[1] This proposal, although made by the Pope, must surely have been inserted in the papal *triplex forma* at the instance of the barons' messengers. But what more was included we cannot say.

John told the Pope that he offered to accept these terms and that the barons refused to agree to them.[2] Wendover says nothing of this, but since his object was to make a dramatic story and to represent the king as wholly intransigent, his silence is not fatal. It is to be noted that " Walter of Coventry " says that the Pope's letters, to the king " pro baronibus " and to the archbishop " pro rege ", were produced in the discussions between the king's representatives and the barons before the latter defied the king. He does not mention the letter to the barons " pro rege " or the *triplex forma,* but it seems most probable that when the first two letters came under discussion, the third letter and the *forma* were also produced. This is borne out by the words of the Pope's commissioners in England who afterwards said that the barons defied their lord *contra triplicem formam pacis.*[3]

We may assume, then, that the offer was made. We can only guess why the barons rejected the king's offer and what part of their earlier proposal was objectionable to the king. The impasse is explicable if the barons were already insisting upon the sort of supervision over the Crown which was eventually effected by the security clause of Magna Carta.[4]

The malcontents had sent their demands to the king by the hands of the archbishop and the earl of Pembroke in the week

---

[1] *Selected Letters*, p. 214 (24 August) and the letter of 18 June cited above.

[2] *Foedera*, I. i. 129. Objection may not only have been raised by the " opposition " barons.

[3] " Walter of Coventry ", ii. 219 ; *Eng. Hist. Rev.*, xliv. 92. Note that the Pope's letter of 24 August suggests that before the messengers bearing the *forma* reached England, the barons had defied the king. But the English chronicles and the Pope's commissioners in England may have been better informed of the sequence of events.

[4] Painter, op. cit. pp. 315–6. Dr. A. L. Poole takes a different view in *From Domesday Book to Magna Carta* (Oxford, 1951), p. 473.

318

following Low Sunday. I have suggested that he received and rejected them on Thursday, 30 April at Wallingford. If the barons waited at Brackley, they can hardly have received the king's reply and counter-proposals before 1 or 2 May. Another day may well have been spent in discussing the situation and then the barons took the decisive step of diffidation : they " defied " the king, in the sense of formally renouncing their homage and fealty. It was a declaration of war.

The annals of Southwark report that war broke out between the king and the northern barons about the feast of the Invention of the Holy Cross (that is, about Sunday, 3 May), and that the barons defied the king by an Austin canon at Reading on 5 May.[1] It must have been an uncomfortable mission, best undertaken by someone who had the protection of the monastic habit. On receiving the barons' diffidation, the king declared that he held the land as patrimony of St. Peter (in other words, as a fief from the Pope) and that as a Crusader he should benefit from the Crusaders' privilege. He appealed against disturbers of the peace through the earls of Pembroke and Warenne.[2]

Meanwhile, the malcontents marched back in battle-formation to Northampton, where they laid siege to the royal castle whose castellan was a Poitevin soldier, Geoffrey de Martigny. As the attackers had no siege-weapons, they sat before the castle in vain for a week or two.[3] If we may trust Wendover, the rebels straightway appointed the great East Anglian lord Robert

[1] M. Tyson, " The Annals of Southwark and Merton ", *Surrey Archaeol. Collections*, xxxvi. 49. Tewkesbury annals say that " turbatio magna " arose on 1 May (*Annales monastici* (Rolls Series), i. 61). If the canon left Brackley on 3 May to go to the king where he was last known to be, i.e. Wallingford, he would find on arrival that the king had left for Reading (18 miles away) on 2 May. The Dunstable annals say that a canon of Dereham (O. Praem.) was sent to the king at Wallingford (ibid. iii. 43). Praestita Roll 16 John m. 6 confirms the evidence of the chancery rolls that John was at Reading on 5 May.

[2] This is how I interpret the king's letter to the Pope of 29 May which does not, however, mention the diffidation (*Foedera*, I. i. 129). The earls of Pembroke and Warenne were with the king on 5 May (*Rotuli chartarum*, ed. T. D. Hardy (Record Comm.), p. 206b) ; neither attests a charter of 6 May ; Pembroke does not witness charters of 7 and 9 May.

[3] Wendover says : a fortnight, but a writer who puts the capture of London a week too late cannot be trusted here.

THE EVE OF MAGNA CARTA   319

fitzWalter as their commander-in-chief and he took the high-sounding title of " Marshal of the army of God ".[1] Did Robert or any of his fellows really believe that they were about to wage a holy war ? The title is intriguing. In 1212, to be sure, Robert had associated his opposition to John with the grievances of the Church against an excommunicate king. It was less easy to take this line in 1215 when the king was the Pope's vassal and a Crusader. But the rebels had one of the bishops committed to their cause and they found in Langton a sympathetic mediator with the king.

III

With 5 May, then, civil war seems to have broken out. Northampton castle was besieged by rebels and we might expect the king to take violent action. But he still held his hand. The records show that the earlier preparations for war were continuing ; one would never guess from them that hostilities had begun. Not until 9 May does the chancery take note of the state of affairs by referring to " the barons opposed to us " (barones nobis adversantes), and a fragmentary copy of a letter of the same day shows the first hostile act on the king's part : Philip of Worcester is to have possession of " the manor of Ditton, which belonged to Geoffrey de Mandeville ".[2]

Why did the king hold his hand ? There may have. been adequate military reasons which are obscure to us, and John and his advisers may still have had hopes of settlement. He was evidently persuaded to go a long way towards meeting reasonable complaints. His own version of what followed, as

[1] M. Paris, Chronica maiora, ii. 586. Coggeshall gives Robert the same title and Robert uses it officially a little later (Foedera, I. i. 133, cf. Eng. Hist. Rev. xliv. 92). Walter of Coventry speaks of the appointment of " marshals of the army of God ", and the London chronicle (De antiquis legibus (Camden Soc., 1846), p. 201) says that Robert fitzWalter and Geoffrey de Mandeville were appointed marshals.

[2] Public Record Office, Close Roll 16 John (C. 54/9) m. 1. Mr. Jolliffe notes that Geoffrey's lands had been taken in hand in July 1214 for failure to keep his terms at the Exchequer in the matter of the Gloucester inheritance (Angevin Kingship (1955), p. 333). But Geoffrey regained seisin by writs of 9–10 August 1214 (Rot. lit. claus. i. 209b–210) and the record of 9 May must relate to a new disseisin if we interpret it correctly.

320

contained in a letter of 29 May to the Pope, is anything but clear. Fortunately, the chancery rolls enable us to confirm and date his proposition, conveyed to the rebels by the archbishop and two or three bishops, that each side should choose four arbiters who, with the Pope as president, should settle all complaints about liberties which the rebels might bring forward. A charter to this effect was drafted, with the date 9 May.[1] This document, seldom quoted, is of interest for two reasons. It refers to " questionibus et articulis que petunt a nobis et que ipsi proponent ", which recalls the title : " Capitula que barones petunt et dominus rex concedit " which heads the Articles of the Barons. Also, it reserves to the king interim rights to fines and debts and services which he enjoyed " before the dis-agreement (discordia) arose ". But this charter did not protect the barons from the king's displeasure pending arbitration. Next day it was re-drafted as letters patent with the proviso (made famous later on by the words of Magna Carta) that the king would not take the barons or their men nor dispossess them nor go against them with force and arms except according to the law of the realm or by judgement of their peers in the king's court until the arbitrators should give their decision.[2] At the same time the king offered Geoffrey de Mandeville and Giles de Braose, bishop of Hereford, the judgement of his court respecting the enormous sums charged upon them as reliefs for the Gloucester and Braose inheritances.[3] The king also granted his fifth charter to the citizens of London, empower-ing them to appoint their mayor by annual election ; but simul-taneously he pressed forward the fortification of the city [4] and the manning of his castles throughout the country.

He had every reason to do so. By Tuesday, 12 May, he

---

[1] *Rot. Chart.* p. 209b (the dorse of the roll). Note the connection with the *triplex forma.* If the *forma* only reached the king after the barons' diffidation, the fact might help to explain these continuing negotiations. But see p. 317 n. 3.

[2] *Rot, lit. pat.,* p 141a (the dorse of the roll).

[3] Ibid.

[4] The two documents printed by Mary Bateson from " A London municipal collection " (*Eng. Hist. Rev.* xvii (1902), 726–8) may well belong to this time when the citizens were being encouraged to look to the defences and were themselves framing their *desiderata.*

THE EVE OF MAGNA CARTA 321

heard that his latest proposal to the rebels was rejected.[1] This is implied by the writ of that date to all sheriffs of England ordering them immediately to seize the lands and chattels of the king's " enemies " and to submit returns and valuations to the king. Two days later the king began to grant the lands of rebels to his supporters : William de Mandeville's estates in Devon to Henry fitzCount, the lands of Robert de Vere in Devon to Reginald de Vautort, and so on. In the case of all but the most important rebels this action may have been a threat in order to recall them to loyalty. Thus, Simon of Pateshull's manor of Wasden (Bucks) was granted to Robert de Courtenay on 15 May ; but within a week, on the intercession of the abbot of Woburn, Simon had a royal letter of safe-conduct to come and make peace with the king. Henry of Braybrook's manors of Horsendon and Corby were also seized ; but on 17 May Henry had safe-conduct offered to him to come and speak with the king.[2] At this stage, indeed, John may still have entertained hopes of dividing and pacifying the rebels. For on 16 May he instructed Geoffrey of Martigny and the others to observe a truce if the archbishop of Canterbury should announce one, to be effective until Thursday 21 May or later.[3]

But no such truce was made. For early on Sunday morning, 17 May,[4] some of the rebels arrived at London, having come from Northampton through Bedford, where the castle was delivered to them by its castellan, William de Beauchamp. The rebels had friends in the city, who aided their entry, and there was little resistance by the Londoners. Doubtless a strong element sympathized with the barons or saw in their

[1] If the proposals of 10 May were sent to the barons at Northampton there must have been some hard riding in both directions : Windsor to Northampton and thence to the king at Wallingford. These proposals may explain the note " v idus Maii ad Norhamtun " added in the margin to the poetic account of negotiations in the *Chronicle of Melrose*, facs. ed. by A. O. and M. O. Anderson (1936), pl. 60 (fo. 3lv) ; but it is the wrong date, if we are right in putting the barons' diffidation on 5 May.

[2] *Rot. lit. claus.* i. 200a and *Rot. lit. pat.* pp. 136b, 138a. It is unlikely that either Simon or Henry availed himself of the offer ; their reconciliation only came later. Martin of Patteshull had safe-conduct on 2 June.

[3] *Rot. lit pat.* p. 136b.

[4] *Foedera*, I. i. 121.

322

alliance an opportunity to realize civic ambitions. William, earl of Salisbury, who had been directed to London on the day before it fell, was too late to intervene, likewise some Flemish soldiery under Robert de Bethune and others.[1] London already had the prestige of a capital city and the news of its capture must have made a deep impression in the country. Wendover is not likely to have fabricated the story that from London the rebels sent persuasive and minatory letters, urging the other barons to join them.[2] The king's situation must have seemed critical; and John's material superiority in wealth, trained soldiery, and fortified places over the scattered resources of an ill-organised opposition is perhaps more evident to us than it was to contemporaries. There were sporadic outbreaks in other parts of the country, at Lincoln and at Exeter, and on the North Welsh march a raid in considerable force by Llewellyn ap Iorwerth surprised the town and castle of Shrewsbury.[3] The rebels felt strong enough to attempt some sort of shrieval organization in the counties where they were predominant. The king, deprived of much of his normal revenue, left his castellans to maintain their garrisons by levying protection-money from the countryside. He was at a severe disadvantage because he did not know on whom to rely. Thus, on 29 May the king ordered that " if Hugh de Beauchamp is our enemy and with our enemies, then his lands in Cornwall are granted to Hasculf de Suleny ".[4] Two days later he apparently still counted on the loyalty of John de Lascy, the young constable of Chester,[5] whose heavy debts he had remitted over two months ago. But within three weeks John de Lascy was sufficiently deeply implicated with the rebels to be chosen as one of the council of twenty-five.

[1] R. de Coggeshall, *Chronicon anglicanum* (Rolls Series), p. 171; *Rot. lit. pat.* p. 136b; *Histoire des ducs de Normandie et des rois d'Angleterre*, ed. F. Michel (Soc. de l'hist. de France, 1840), p. 147.

[2] M. Paris, *Chron. maiora*, ii. 587–8; cf. Coggeshall, loc. cit.

[3] Reginald de Braose made trouble in the southern march, but whether this synchronized with these other events is doubtful (*Brut y Tywysogion*, trans. T. Jones (Cardiff, 1952), p. 90; cf. J. Lloyd, *History of Wales*, ii. 643–5).

[4] *Rot. lit. claus.* i. 213b.

[5] *Rot. lit. pat.* p. 142b, cf. 129b. Mr Painter doubts Wendover's statement that John de Lascy was with the barons at Stamford (op. cit. p. 288).

THE EVE OF MAGNA CARTA   323

After the fall of London on 17 May neither party embarked on hostilities on a big scale.[1]   On 29 May another royal proposal was made to the rebels. This we learn from a letter addressed by King John to the Pope.[2]   A clerk of the papal camera had arrived at the king's court at Odiham that same day, the Friday after Ascension Day ; he brought (almost certainly) the Pope's reply to John's announcement that he had taken the Cross. The bishops of Worcester and Coventry were present at court and Saer de Quincy, earl of Winchester, was probably there under safe-conduct, representing the rebels.[3]   In the presence of the papal clerk the king offered (so he says) to submit to the Pope's arbitration in the matter of all the petitions the rebels were making, so that the Pope, holding the plenitude of power, might order what should be just.   The barons, he says, refused this offer.   " Therefore, pious father," concludes John's letter, " we have thought fit to tell you all this in order that you, with your customary kindness, may order things as seems expedient to you."   This invitation to the Pope (dated 29 May) is not without interest in the light of the next few months' events.

Stephen Langton is not named as being present at this encounter of 29 May.   Where he was during these weeks is not known, but he was still actively working for peace.   As on 16 May, so on the 27, various of John's captains were told to keep truce with the king's barons according as the archbishop of Canterbury should require by his letters patent ; and on the same day the archbishop had safe-conduct with all those whom he should bring to Staines to treat of peace between the king and his barons.[4]   If this safe-conduct was immediately used, the fact is not recorded ; but according to the king's itinerary John was near at hand, at Windsor, from 31 May to 3 June.   Thence he went to Winchester for Whitsun,[5] but may have been brought back by fresh proposals for a meeting.   On Monday, 8 June,

[1] There was disorder in London, and at the end of May John took reprisals against the citizens of Northampton (Walter of Coventry, ii. 220 ; *Rot. lit. claus.* i. 214a).

[2] *Foedera*, I. i. 129.   For a letter probably enclosed in the Pope's letter to which John's letter was the reply see *Selected letters*, pp. 203–4.

[3] *Rot. lit. pat.* p. 138b.

[4] Ibid. p. 142a.   [5] Apparently without taking the great seal.

324

being at Merton, he issued safe-conduct for those who should come next day to Staines on behalf of the barons to make peace, the safe-conduct to last until Thursday the 11th. The king followed up this letter two days later by announcing to his captains that " the aforesaid truce " was extended from Thursday to the following Monday, 15 June.[1]

And so we reach the last stage in the preparation of Magna Carta.

IV

It is, of all the stages, the most debated and the hardest to establish. We shall never know the whole truth about these days of mid-June. But the generally accepted chronology will, I am convinced, repay scrutiny.

What may be called the orthodox view can be briefly stated.[2] The rebels did not come to the king until the last day for which their recorded safe-conduct was valid : 15 June in the meadows of Runnymede, between Windsor and Staines. There they presented their proposals which were written on a sheet of vellum (about 20 in. × 10½ in.) which still survives, with the title : " These are the articles (capitula) which the barons request and which the king grants." The document received there and then the royal seal whereby it became a warrant for the chancellor to issue Magna Carta. The charter is dated 15 June ; but, it is argued, it is too lengthy a document to have been prepared and engrossed all in a day and it varies in some particulars from the Articles. Therefore, the date when it was actually completed and handed over must be 19 June, which is the day upon which (according to several royal writs) " firm peace " was made between the king and his barons.

On this view one or two preliminary observations must be made. First, the Articles do not constitute a chancery warrant.[3]

[1] *Rot. lit. pat.* pp. 142–3.
[2] See W. S. McKechnie, *Magna Carta*, 2nd edn. (Glasgow, 1914) and C. G. Crump, " The execution of the Great Charter ", *History*, n. s. xiii (1928), 251 ; J. C. Dickinson, *The Great Charter* (Historical Association pamphlet G.31, 1955), pp. 13, 16 ; cf. A. J. Collins, " The documents of the Great Charter 1215 ", *Proceedings of the British Academy*, xxxiv. 234, 244, 248, 258.
[3] Cf. V. H. Galbraith, *Studies in the Public Records* (1948), p. 135. As Mr. Collins observes (loc. cit. p. 224), the chancery could not be responsible for all the differences between the Articles and the Charter.

The affixing to them of the Great Seal simply amounted to a promise by the king that a charter would be made on the basis of the Articles' demands and suggestions. Secondly, the assignment of the date 19 June to the Charter—that being the day when " firm peace " was proclaimed—assumes that the completion of a charter was an essential preliminary to the announcement of firm peace. This seems to me a big and unwarrantable assumption. Documents describe the peace which has been made without mentioning the charter.[1] It was needed, certainly, to confirm the promises made when the king set his seal to the Articles, and to provide a document to be permanently preserved ; but its completion was not the most urgent need, from the point of view of a group of extremist barons of whom each had his own grievances and of whom probably none believed that the king's good faith was guaranteed by a piece of vellum. They understood better a system of oaths, hostages, and sureties.

With these considerations in mind, let us look at the positive evidence, such as it is.

The Articles of the Barons are undated. We do not know either how long the document existed before it received the seal or when the sealing took place. So far as internal evidence goes, it reflects other interests besides those of the extremist barons. With its reference to London and merchants and trade it is highly improbable that it could have been finally framed before London joined the opposition in the second half of May ; and the careful draftsmanship and breadth of scope suggest that Langton and other negotiators of moderate opinions had said their say.[2] On the other hand, the security clause, which set up twenty-five barons to control the king, was a

---

[1] It is only mentioned in the draft writ dated 19 June which orders its publication (cf. below, p. 326). As will be seen, copies of this writ were delivered out of the chancery in advance of copies of the Charter.

[2] Mr. Collins's important discovery that the sealed Articles found their way into the Canterbury archives adds to the probability that the archbishop played a leading part. But while ch. 46 of the Articles provided for arbitration by the archbishop and his nominees, the Charter (ch. 59) requires, instead, judgment by the king's court. This looks like a change made by the king or his advisers who mistrusted Langton.

326

condition most obnoxious to the king, who can hardly have accepted it at sight.

Then we have Magna Carta itself, which is dated in the meadow called Runnymede between Windsor and Staines on 15 June. McKechnie explained this by asserting that in John's reign "elaborate charters, which occupied time in preparation, usually bore the date, not of their actual execution, but of the day on which occurred the transactions they record ".[1] It may be so ; but McKechnie produced no evidence, and studies of the chancery's practice in John's reign have so far failed to reveal what system was used for dating either original instruments or their enrolments.

What other record-evidence is there? Hundreds of chancery writs were enrolled during the month of June. None shows the king to have been at Runnymede before 18 June: only Magna Carta (whose real date is dubious) declares him to be there on the 15th. Moreover, the only writ dated at Runnymede on Thursday, 18 June, is the letter patent to Stephen Harengod announcing that firm peace has been made on Friday, 19 June ![2] All other letters given on 18 June are dated, like those of 10–17 June, from Windsor. Then for six days the activity of the chancery was divided between Windsor and Runnymede. The latest writ from Runnymede is dated 23 June.

Among these writs several refer to the "firm peace" made between king and barons on Friday, 19 June. One of them[3] also informs sheriffs and other royal officers that a charter has been made and that it is to be read publicly and firmly maintained. Arrangements are then made for implementing certain regulations common to the Articles of the Barons and Magna

---

[1] McKechnie, op. cit. pp. 40–1, cf. Mr. Collins's caveat, loc. cit. p. 235, n. 1.

[2] McKechnie brushes aside the discrepancy ; assuming the error of " xviii " for " xxiii " in the date as a " certainty " (p. 41, n. 1), he prints the text with the date 23 June (p. 493). Mr. Collins tacitly accepts this emendation (p. 244, n. 2). But the error, if it be an error, was not made at enrolment, for this letter appears on a chronologically-arranged roll between letters of 18 and 19 June (*Rot. lit. pat.*, p. 143b. Cf. ibid. p. 142a, where a receipt is dated 28 May for property received on 29 May).

[3] *Rot. lit. pat.* p. 180b and McKechnie, p. 494. Facsimile in Collins, pl. 14.

THE EVE OF MAGNA CARTA   327

Carta.[1] The date is Runnymede, 19 June. Following the enrolled copy of this writ, which is on the dorse of the roll, is a memorandum that certain named persons received copies of the aforesaid " draft " (*forma*) and copies of the Charter. No date is assigned to the record of the first twenty-one deliveries (all of them writs) ; then comes a dated record of delivery of both writs and charters to the bishop of Lincoln on St. John the Baptist's day (24 June). This is followed by other undated entries until the last : " Also at Oxford on Wednesday the feast of St. Mary Magdalen (22 July) were delivered to Master Elias of Dereham six charters." In all, thirty-five writs and thirteen charters had been issued by this date, if this memorandum is complete. It is to be observed that the writ, though fully dated, has a generalized address. Either it is a draft or it is copied from a draft. If 19 June saw firm peace established that was certainly the day to compose such a letter as this for general distribution. But we cannot assume from the date on the draft that the letter was actually despatched on that day.[2] All we can safely say is that twenty-one writs were delivered out of chancery before 24 June, the date at which we have clear official evidence for the first time that copies of the charter were in existence, for two were then handed over to the bishop of Lincoln.

Do the thirteenth-century narrative-writers throw light on the events of June 1215 ? Very few of them are sufficiently precise to be of service and when they are precise they are not always convincing. Modern historians have gone for details as a rule to Roger Wendover. Wendover describes the king's meeting with the barons in the meadows on 15 June ;[3] but he does so in a context which suggests that his narrative is simply embroidery upon the dated charter which he had before him. The Annals of Melrose [4] contain a rhymed poem about the

---

[1] The word *prave* is applied to *consuetudines* as in Articles, ch. 39, not *male* as in Charter, ch. 48. On the other hand, the reference to abolishing (*delendis*) customs resembles the Charter more than the Articles.

[2] Mr. H. G. Richardson says cautiously: " some perhaps were actually despatched on that day " (" The morrow of the Great Charter ", *ante*, xxviii (1944), 428).

[3] M. Paris, *Chron. maiora*, ii. 589.　　　[4] Facs. edition, pl. 60 (fo. 3 lv).

328

troubles of this year. It says that peace-terms (*forma pacis*) were presented to the king and that the king refused to accept the terms until, being forced, he conceded everything. Against the words " formam pacis " the contemporary annotator puts the date : 18 June in the meadow of Staines.

The Annals of Dunstable [1] do not discuss or even mention the charter, but simply say that peace was made at Runnymede on the feast of SS. Gervase and Protasius (i.e. 19 June).

The Annals of Southwark [2] give a later date for the making of peace : Tuesday before the feast of St. John the Baptist (i.e. 23 June) ; and the Annals of Waverley [3] say that it was on this day that the king, archbishops, bishops, magnates, and barons met at Runnymede, where the king made the charter of liberties they wanted.

Finally, there is the story of the *Histoire des ducs de Normandie et des rois d'Angleterre*, which represents the information available to the mercenary troops brought over from Flanders for the king's service. [4] It is confusing in the extreme. It tells of an expedition headed by Earl William of Salisbury and Robert de Bethune to put down a rising in Devonshire. They turned back once on hearing of the rebels' superior strength. Their departure from Winchester for the second time can be probably dated 6 or 7 June. [5] They marched to Exeter (a distance of about 112 miles), spent four days there, and then returned to the king. In their absence, the king (says the author) met the barons at Staines without waiting to consult his half-brother, the earl, or the Flemings, and he made a shameful peace (*vilaine pais*). Now Earl William appears in the preamble of Magna Carta as one of

[1] *Ann. monastici*, iii. 43.

[2] Loc. cit. p. 49. The Merton annals and the London " Liber de antiquis legibus " agree, as was to be expected.

[3] *Ann. monastici*, ii. 283.

[4] pp. 147–9.

[5] Miss Norgate reckoned that the first expedition set out from Freemantle (Southampton) c. 19–20 May and the second, from Winchester, on 24 May. But the troops had only landed in Kent on 16 May and this scheme seems to allow too little time. The king was at Winchester also 5–8 June and on 6 June ordered Faukes de Breauté to send to the earl of Salisbury 400 Welshmen, to be at Salisbury on 9 June (*Rot. lit. claus.* p. 214 a). On 8 June the king was already arranging an immediate truce (above, p. 324).

the king's counsellors by whose advice the charter was granted. But if William went to Exeter on 6 June he could not be at Runnymede by 15 June; he could, indeed, hardly have reached this point by the 19th, and a letter from the king of that date confirms the presumption that he was still absent from court.[1]

What does all this evidence amount to? It gives no certainty about the genesis of the charter but it suggests other possibilities besides (and in preference to) the usually proposed sequence : the Articles sealed on Monday 15 June, the charter sealed on Friday the 19th.

First, the hypothesis of an earlier dating of events must be considered, even if we have later to reject it. The datelessness of the Articles permits the hypothesis that they were the result of discussions between the king's representatives and the rebels towards the end of May,[2] and that they were presented to the king about Whitsun (7 June). The king, having decided by 8 June to agree to them, summoned the barons to be at Staines on 9 June : there and then he signified his agreement by having the great seal affixed to the Articles.[3] (It may be added that probably the king would not deign to negotiate in person or, at the most, would only meet the rebels to ratify the articles which his representatives had accepted on his behalf.) But much remained to be done before either the Articles were turned into the charter or the immediate conditions for peace were fulfilled. So the safe-conduct of the barons was prolonged, discussions continued, and the Charter was hammered out of the Articles on Monday, 15 June, as the charter itself proclaims.

I do not see how this hypothesis can be disproved. It has the advantage of requiring no elaborate explanation of the date set upon the charter. That date is taken at its face-value. On the other hand, there is no record-evidence that the rebels came to Staines or to Runnymede before Monday, 15 June; except for Wendover, no narrative-writer who provides dates regarded

---

[1] *Rot. lit. claus.* p. 215a. He does not witness a charter at Windsor, 25 June, but witnesses charters at Winchester two days later.

[2] According to Wendover, William Marshal went to London to treat with the rebels.

[3] Langton was apparently with the king at Windsor on 9 June (*Mem. of St. Edmund's*, ii. 124, cf. *Histoire des ducs*, p. 149).

330

the 15th as a significant date. And if the Articles were sealed before that day, either the list of counsellors in the preamble to Magna Carta errs in including William, earl of Salisbury, or the *Histoire des ducs* is at fault in a detail where we should expect it to be accurate when it says that the earl was absent.[1] Moreover, it may be questioned whether a solemn charter of this sort would be finally drafted before the king took the homage of the barons who had defied him. He only took homages on 19 June, the day of the official, ceremonial peace-making. Finally, this hypothesis leaves a sort of vacuum between the events of Monday and the ceremonies of Friday : the king is unrecorded at Runnymede and the chancery issues from Windsor a bare dozen letters, of which only two or three concern pacification ; this is in strong contrast to the activity of the next few days (19–23 June).[2]

An alternative reading of the evidence seems to be preferable. It may be that the prolongation of the " truce " till 15 June, of which the king notified his captains on the 10th, meant that the rebels had not yet moved to Staines. (For had they arrived sooner, their stay at Runnymede would have ceased to concern the king's captains in other parts of the country.) Let us, then, suppose that the peace-terms, already debated between the king's representatives and the rebels during the preceding week, were brought to Runnymede on 15 June. A meeting with the king had been arranged on the understanding that he would agree to the Articles as we know them. The king rode to Runnymede on that day. A fair copy of the Articles was written, neatly enough in an official-looking clerkly hand, but perhaps hastily, for a few purely scribal omissions are corrected by interlineation. Also a few last-minute additions were made, and then the document received the royal seal, either at Windsor or at Runnymede.[3] Thus far, the accepted view seems plausible : that is, the Articles were sealed on 15 June.

---

[1] Though William might have urged agreement to the Articles when they were put to the king at an earlier stage.

[2] Fifty-four letters close and twenty-three letters patent. It might be argued that they were putting into effect at the earliest moment arrangements made before the ceremonial peace-making.

[3] See the original and cf. Blackstone, op. cit. p. xvii. The document itself is as silent about the place as about the time of its completion.

THE EVE OF MAGNA CARTA 331

But the Articles, apart from being only the first documentary step towards Magna Carta,[1] only represent one part of the work which the negotiators had to accomplish. To express in a generalized form the principles of sound government, as then commonly conceived, even if " politically inept ",[2] was no small achievement. But the appeasement of aggrieved individuals was fully as important a task, and the acceptance of the Articles by the king was not, of itself, sufficient to reconcile the extremists. Three more days, from Monday, 15 June to Thursday, the 18th were (on this hypothesis) consumed in debate and bargaining. The canons of St. David's found their opportunity in the king's embarrassment and got his assent to their election of a Welshman as bishop. The canons of York got permission to proceed to an election.[3] By Thursday the 18th the barons were ready to render their homage again and the scene was set for formal reconciliation with the king in person on Friday 19th. The peace-making took place, as recorded in several writs. The king received the barons with the kiss of peace. Since this was a bit of ceremonial to which all parties had agreed, the notice of it (like some modern newspaper reports or minutes of meetings) could be prepared before the event. That might account for the date, Thursday, 18 June, which appears in the Melrose annals and explain why one of the royal writs announcing that peace had been made on the 19 June is itself dated on the 18th.[4]

But the charter to be composed on the basis of the Articles was as yet unwritten. When it finally appeared, the Articles had undergone much re-drafting, which cannot have been

---

[1] Apart, that is, from the " Unknown charter of liberties ". This, interesting though it is, does not come into my account because I cannot fit it into the events of April-June 1215. Of the various suggestions for its dating which have been made (all of them highly conjectural), I think the earlier dates are the more probable. Professor Galbraith and Dr. Poole, on the other hand, would place it after 9–10 May 1215 (Galbraith, *Studies*, pp. 133–34; A. L. Poole, *From Domesday Book*, pp. 471–2). The problem would be much simpler if we had any evidence of the authorship or official character of the document.

[2] The phrase is Mr. Jolliffe's : *Angevin Kingship*, p. 303.

[3] *Rot. lit. pat.* p. 143ab.

[4] See above, p. 326.

332

carried out in a hurry.[1] The earliest date at which we hear of written copies of the Charter being in existence is Wednesday, 24 June; the king was apparently at Runnymede intermittently from Thursday, 18 to Tuesday, 23 June. The Annals of Southwark record the peace-making on the latter day. This was the day when tents were struck at Runnymede and it may well have been the day on which the terms of Magna Carta were finally agreed and it was ready to be engrossed and sealed.[2]

The peace (I have suggested) did not depend mainly on the production of this document. The things which made up the peace were, on the one hand, the king's acceptance of homage from those who had performed diffidation six weeks earlier; on the other hand, the choice of the committee of twenty-five (unrecorded in any official document which has survived),[3] and the restoration to the barons of lands, castles, hostages, and so on. Magna Carta consisted mainly of promises for the future: it did not give the individuals who sought it these immediate concessions; they were the subject of numerous letters issued after 19 June, that is, as soon as the barons had renewed their homage. In the patent roll we find them indicated by such marginalia as " Liberacio castri. Deliberacio obsidis. Custodia foreste liberate." The terms of the charter could be settled when these other measures were under way. It is noticeable that Ralph of Coggeshall, a contemporary Cistercian, without providing precise dates, gives a sequence of events which is consistent with this. He describes a meeting on the appointed day at Runnymede, the barons encamped on one side, the king and his followers in tents apart from them. Peace was sworn by both sides " and soon the peace-terms were brought together

[1] Cf. Art. ch. 25 (Magna Carta, ch. 52), 32 (M.C. 12–3), 37 (M.C. 55), 46 (M.C. 59).

[2] Mr. Richardson considered it " uncertain whether the first fair example, which seems to have been preserved in the treasury of the exchequer, was written and sealed on the 19th ", although he adopts the usual view that the Articles were sealed on the 15th and the Charter ratified on the 19th (" The morrow of the Great Charter: an addendum ", ante, xxix (1945), p. 183).

[3] It is for remark that the names of the 25 had apparently not been published when the charter was composed: " concedimus . . . quod barones eligant . . " (ch. 61); cf. Poole, op. cit. p. 472.

in a charter ".[1] The Cistercian annals of Waverley, we have seen, assign the making of this charter to 23 June. This seems to me a likely date.

It must be admitted that finality cannot be claimed for this hypothesis. It leaves certain questions unanswered. (1) Like the orthodox view, it assumes that the day on which the Articles were sealed (which we suppose to be 15 June) provided the chancery with a date to set upon the Charter. Yet the Articles were not a warrant, in the ordinary sense, and there must have been a later day when the draft charter was at last prepared, and approved, by the king, which would have served equally well for dating the document. (2) Then there is the dating clause : "Dat' per manum nostram in prato quod vocatur Ronimed." Whatever the significance of the appearance of the king in this formula,[2] it certainly implies that the king, when he authorized the charter, was at Runnymede. Either this element of the dating clause is to be taken as evidence of an otherwise unattested visit of the king to Runnymede on 15 June, when the great seal was set to the Articles, or it is incompatible with the time-date and refers to the period when the chancery is otherwise known to have been at Runnymede (19–23 June). But we know little of the diplomatic usages of John's chancery. Moreover, the Charter itself was an anomalous instrument and the circumstances—to put it mildly—unusual. These ambiguities of the dating-clause do not invalidate our conjecture, based on the concurrent witness of other records and literary sources. In short, it seems likely that the Articles were prepared in advance of the assembly at Runnymede on 15 June, and were sealed on that day. The work of drafting a charter on the basis of the Articles required further discussions and was only completed on 23 June.

So Magna Carta comes to be disengaged from the recorded ceremonial of 19 June. Had they been more closely bound together, contemporaries might have commented more often

---

[1] "Mox igitur forma pacis in charta est comprehensa" (*Chronicon anglic.* p. 172).

[2] It may simply indicate on this occasion that the datary could not be one of the king's subjects, since all were beneficiaries.

334

upon the Charter. In fact, only a few chroniclers, in describing the establishment of the short-lived peace, take account of the charter's existence; still fewer seem to know much about its contents. But this does not mean that the Charter was unimportant. It was not merely the record of an antecedent oral transaction; it was provided for as a necessary complement to the peace-making.[1] In some respects it was an enactment of law, not merely a re-statement of custom. Its concluding clause remained the justification for the activities of the Twenty-five in the following months. Then, too, the Pope's condemnation of Magna Carta stiffened the rebels in the civil war which broke out again in September, and probably drove many moderate men to their ranks. Finally, Magna Carta itself, shorn of its obnoxious sanctions and some dubious clauses, survived the papal thunders : after John's death, in its reissues, it became an instrument of genuine reconciliation and an earnest of good government.

NOTE ON THE EXECUTION OF MAGNA CARTA

In considering the order of events leading to the grant of Magna Carta I have avoided touching on the character of the Charter as a diplomatic instrument. But the tentative conclusion which has been reached above implicitly contradicts a view recently expressed by Mr. A. J. Collins. I must explain why this does not lead me to modify my opinion about the date.

Briefly, Mr. Collins argues that the Charter was inextricably tied up with the barons' resumption of homage, that as it embodied, so to speak, the peace-terms of a treaty, that peace could not be declared without a formal delivery of the Charter to the barons. This delivery to the barons of the Charter, " which was certainly the first exemplar to receive the Great Seal and which may actually have been sealed in their presence ", can only have taken place on the day when *firma pax*

[1] Cf. Articles ch. 1 (" exprimendum in carta "), 48 (" infra rationabile tempus determinandum in carta ").

was made, i.e. 19 June.[1] On this view, the question of chronology discussed above simply does not arise.

But there are various objections to this view of Magna Carta as a treaty. Diplomatically, it is a royal charter of grant, unlike any contemporary treaty in its form. The nearest approach to the terms of a treaty is in the final record that both king and barons have sworn to observe all the foregoing faithfully. Throughout the document there is no *quid pro quo* : the renewal of homage is not so much as mentioned. In the early thirteenth century a treaty implied an exchange of instruments between the parties. Recognizing this, Mr. Collins—in search for the counter-part of the "treaty" of Magna Carta—produces the Letters testimonial of the prelates.[2] But the prelates could not be regarded as a party to a treaty, or as representatives of the baron-ial opposition, and this document of theirs (which survives only in copy in the Red Book of the Exchequer) is a colourless, certified copy of Magna Carta. It is pure assumption that the first sealed exemplar of Magna Carta was handed to "the barons" (presumably in the person of Robert fitzWalter as Marshal of the Army of God) ; and an assumption of an extremely hazardous sort that the letters testimonial of the prelates were 'delivered to the Crown' as a complementary ceremony.

The significance of the prelates' letter has generally been ignored,[3] and deserves a few words. The barons in their Articles (*ad fin.*) had asked the king to guarantee by charters of the archbishops and bishops and Pandulf that he would not obtain revocation or diminution of his undertakings from the Pope.[4] But how could the representatives of the Church be ex-pected to comply and so seem to set limits on the Pope's power ? The demand was watered down to a very different consistency :

[1] Collins, loc. cit. pp. 244, 245, cf. 246 : "robed in the majesty of the deed publicly delivered into the hands of the barons of Runnymede." Professor Galbraith was not so explicit : "the completed Charter, which when duly sealed figured in the final ceremony of renewing homage" (op. cit. p. 135).

[2] Collins, loc. cit. p. 245 and pl. 13.

[3] Sir John Fox remarked upon it : *Eng. Hist. Rev.* xxxix (1924), 332.

[4] Cf. the security that the barons gave in May 1213 in support of the king's act of submission to Rome (*Foedera*, I. i. 112).

336

Magna Carta included the king's personal promise that he would
not obtain from anyone revocation or diminution of his grants.
Then, at the very end of the security clause, the king states that
he has caused to be made for the barons letters patent of the
archbishops of Canterbury and Dublin, the bishops named in
the preamble, and Master Pandulf, testifying to " this security
and the aforesaid grants ". Thus, in the drafting of the Charter,
the prelates' guarantee has become detached from the specific
question of application to the Pope. When this guarantee is
drawn up, there is further dilution. The document is a plain
vidimus, which does no more than certify that the copy of the
charter it rehearses is word-perfect. The prelates have avoided
acting as guarantors of the king and have avoided expressing
approval or disapproval of the transaction (except in so far as
approval is implied by including their names in the preamble).
Their letter simply prevents an untrustworthy king from tam-
pering with the text of his charter.[1]

The terms of the Charter suggest that, once the letter was
written (whether in the archbishop's chancery or the royal
chancery we cannot tell), it should be held by some representative of the baronial party. But in fact, the only copy with the
bishops' seals attached, of which we have record, resided in a
hamper of the Treasury of Receipt in or about the year 1323.
About then, it was copied into the Red Book of the Exchequer ;
and Mr. Collins offers reasons for supposing that it was already
in the Treasury in 1216.[2] How or why it came to be preserved
there has not been explained.

To return to the problem of the issue of Magna Carta. If
the Charter was not tied to the ceremonial of 19 June, what
procedure governed its issue ? Was there ever any ceremonial
delivery to a representative of the beneficiaries, who are described in the injunctive clause as " the men in our realm " ?
Such proceedings would seem to be unnecessary. Once the
Charter had been drafted, a copy might be engrossed and sealed

---

[1] The royal chancery was capable of issuing doctored documents ; see C.
Petit-Dutaillis, " Les copies du traité de paix du Goulet (22 Mai 1200). Vari-
antes et falsifications ", *Bibliothèque de l'Ecole des Chartes*, cii (1941), 35–50.

[2] Collins, loc. cit. pp. 251–2, and cf. Galbraith, op. cit. pp. 123–4, 139.

for preservation in the Treasury of the Exchequer, for there is some evidence that this had been a method of record in earlier times,[1] but there is no proof that this was done on this occasion. If a sealed copy of the prelates' *vidimus* was deposited, a copy of the Charter itself would be superfluous.

What happened next remains obscure. It is generally supposed that copies of Magna Carta were despatched by royal command to all the shires, there to be read publicly in county courts and afterwards placed for safe keeping in a cathedral or abbey. The grounds for this view are three, which may be considered in turn.

(1) *The inherent probability of such a course :* " there might have been doubt as to its validity ", says Mr. Collins, " had it not been proclaimed locally throughout the realm."[2] Expediency might suggest to the barons the need for giving wide publicity to the Charter ; but there is no evidence that its legal validity could have been impugned if it were not proclaimed in the shires.

(2) *The practice in 1215 followed well-established precedents :* In a classic essay,[3] R. L. Poole compared the circumstances of Magna Carta of 1215 with those of earlier and later " great charters ". The important factual contents of that essay have perhaps obscured the frequent recourse to conjecture where problems connected with promulgation crop up. Poole examined only two charters earlier than Magna Carta : the coronation charter of Henry I (1100) and the second charter of Stephen (1136). He did not notice the brief and comparatively unimportant charters of liberties given at coronation by Stephen (1135) and Henry II (1154). This is not surprising, for no clue to the method of their promulgation seems to exist ; but this very absence of evidence affects the general picture. Roger Wendover, speaking of Henry I's charter, declared that " as many charters were made as there are counties in England, and by the king's command they were deposited in the abbeys of

---

[1] Cf. J. H. Round, *The commune of London* (1899), p. 88.   [2] Loc. cit. p. 243.
[3] " The publication of great charters by the English kings ", *Eng. Hist. Rev.* xxviii (1913), reprinted in his *Studies in Chronology and History* (Oxford, 1934), pp. 308-18.

338

every county as a memorial ". Now Roger wrote more than a century later, and no contemporary of Henry I records this action. In support of the chronicler, however, Liebermann and Poole pointed to numerous copies addressed variously to bishops and sheriffs in different parts of the country.[1] This proves that many copies circulated but not that the king or his chancery took the initiative in sending out copies ; and the textual variants militate against a simultaneous promulgation in all directions. We have only Roger Wendover's word that the king ordered this distribution. Poole went on to discuss the second charter of Stephen, of which three survive from the cathedral muniments of Exeter, Hereford, and Salisbury.[2] On this he observed : " Though the charter *was certainly sent out* to three cathedral churches and *was no doubt published in every county*, its provisions did not become well known."[3] But there is no proof that the surviving copies were " sent out " rather than procured by the initiative of the bishops or other magnates of the localities concerned ; and there is no evidence whatsoever that the charter was ' published in every county '.

(3) *The contemporary evidence of 1215 points to a general distribution of Magna Carta.* By this time the chancery was highly organized and, as we may see from the Close Rolls, was accustomed to send administrative orders to all parts of the country simultaneously. It was not impossible for the king to send out copies of Magna Carta from chancery by his messengers, if this seemed to him necessary or desirable. But was this done ? Poole answered, yes. He quoted Ralph of Coggeshall, who says that the peace-terms were put into a charter " so that each county of all England should have its charter of the same tenor confirmed by the king's seal ". The Dunstable

---

[1] " The publication of great charters by the English kings ", *Eng. Hist. Rev.* xxviii (1913), reprinted in his *Studies in Chronology and History* (Oxford, 1934), p. 309.

[2] They have no address and all begin alike. They show minor variants in the text, witness-list, and dating. Besides these so-called " originals ", contemporary copies are found in *Historia novella* of William of Malmesbury and Richard of Hexham's *De gestis R. Stephani.*

[3] Ibid. p. 312 (italics are mine) ; cf. p. 311 : Poole says, " there are also signs of the charter having been accessible at Canterbury and Malmesbury ".

annalist says that " charters were made and deposited in a safe place in each bishopric " ; while " Walter of Coventry " suggests that " a copy was carried round towns and villages and everyone swore to observe it ". Now Coggeshall's words certainly imply, as Poole thinks, that the charter was officially despatched throughout the country, though they could be otherwise interpreted. The Dunstable annalist throws no light on the method of delivery. Walter of Coventry's account conforms to the terms of the draft writ to sheriffs of 19 June (and might indeed be derived from it) ; this speaks of " our charter which we have ordered to be publicly read throughout your bailiwick and firmly maintained ". The obvious implication is that royal officers bore the charter from place to place and exacted the oath for its maintenance. So Poole wrote : " The charter was not merely circulated ; it was proclaimed."[1]

But Poole's further discussion of the writ is curiously ambiguous. " The procedure with regard to preceding charters suggests [2] that what was sent to the sheriff was an original of the charter itself. But on no previous occasion was it commanded that the charter should be publicly proclaimed in the county court or in any other court.[3] We have difficulty in believing that so long and technical a document as Magna Carta could have been actually read aloud in Latin in the county courts ; and when we follow the text of the document which orders this reading, we may infer that its essential purpose was to enjoin obedience to the twenty-five guardians of the Charter and to provide for the election of persons to inquire into and to abolish the evil customs practised by the royal officers." Poole seems to suggest that the Charter was sent with the writ to each sheriff, but that formal proclamation did not involve a public reading of its text.

Regarding the evidence of the writ it must be noted that it is a draft, written upon the dorse of the patent roll, addressed

---

[1] " The publication of great charters by the English kings ", *Eng. Hist. Rev.* xxviii (1913), reprinted in his *Studies in Chronology and History* (Oxford, 1934), p. 314. [2] We have seen how valueless this argument is.

[3] The writ is only known from the patent roll, and in the twelfth century there were no enrolments.

340

" vicecomiti ",[1] etc., without specifying a shire. In other words, we rely on inference from the terms of the writ in supposing that writ and charter went out at royal command to all shires. This, however, is reckoning without the memorandum which follows the writ on the dorse of the patent roll,[2] a memorandum which Mr. Richardson analysed and discussed in a different context.[3] One interesting feature of this memorandum has been remarked above (p. 327) : that writs apparently went out in advance of any copy of the charter and that the charter is not mentioned before 24 June. But there is another point of interest. Most of these copies of the writ (each clearly earmarked to be the authorization for the particular sheriff and officials named in the copy) were not handed to royal messengers for delivery. One of John's soldier-sheriffs, Engelard de Cygoiny receives a copy, and Henry de Ver, a confidential clerk of the king, is provided with a writ or writs for twelve counties, ranging from Kent to Cornwall and Cumberland. But apart from these men and two bishops (of Worcester and Lincoln) the recipients of writs are persons associated with the baronial party. They include two of its leaders, the earl of Winchester and Eustace de Vescy, a lesser man, Philip fitzJohn, who later appears as a rebel, and (most conspicuously), Master Elias of Dereham, Archbishop Stephen Langton's famous steward. Not only did Master Elias receive the writs for the Cinque Ports and eleven counties : he also received ten of the thirteen copies of the charter which are mentioned in this memorandum. The remaining three were taken by the bishops.

The machinery of distribution is not made perfectly clear by this memorandum, but its main significance is unescapable. The chancery did not, of its own initiative, distribute writs and charters to all the shires of England. The Crown was in no hurry to see them delivered. Either the chancery did not accept any obligation to distribute these documents or

[1] The words " in eodem comitatu ", later in the address, forbid us to extend vic ' to vicecomitibus.

[2] Poole unaccountably failed to mention it. It is discussed by Collins, loc. cit. pp. 275–6, who gives a facsimile, pl. 14. Cf. above.

[3] " The morrow of the Great Charter ", ante, xxviii (1944), 426–8.

THE EVE OF MAGNA CARTA 341

else it proceeded so slowly with the task that the baronial party stepped in and organized a partial distribution itself. The writ was an administrative order and the responsibility for delivering it, once authorized, to the sheriffs should surely have rested with the chancery.[1] But Magna Carta itself may have been treated like any other grant to subjects of the king : if the beneficiaries wanted copies they must get them and pay for them. Likewise as regards enrolment : it has often been remarked that neither Magna Carta of 1215 nor any of its three reissues was enrolled by chancery. The reason would seem to be that nobody wanted to pay the fees.[2] This was not a document which chancery felt constrained either to copy or to enrol on its own initiative. Nothing in the evidence which has been reviewed seems to suggest the contrary.

[1] Cf. the writ of 27 June to the sheriff and twelve elected knights of Warwickshire. " Idem mandatum est omnibus vicecomitibus Anglie " (*Rot. lit. pat.* p. 145b).

[2] Cf. *Memorandum Roll I John* (Pipe Roll Soc., n. s. 21, 1943), p. xlvii, where Mr. H. G. Richardson, arguing along different lines, connects the absence of enrolment with the matter of fees.

ADDITIONAL NOTES

Pp.316-7,320 n.1: The triplex forma pacis has led to various conjectures, but the only acceptable explanation seems to be that of J.C. Holt, Magna carta (2nd ed., Cambridge,1969) pp.293-6.

P.326: The chronicle of the election of Hugh, abbot of St Edmunds (ed. R.M. Thomson (Oxford,1974) pp.168-71 and in Mem. of St Edmunds (Rolls series)ii.128) tells how the king visited Runnymede on 10 June. Cf. Holt, Magna carta pp.154-5.

P.331 n.1: The best discussion (and edition) of the 'Unknown charter' is by Holt (Magna carta,pp.151-2,296-9), who dates it between January and June 1215.

XIV

THE TWENTY-FIVE BARONS OF MAGNA CARTA[1]

DESPITE all the light that scholars have been able to throw upon Magna Carta and the circumstances of its issue in June 1215, much remains dark. Even the order of the most crucial events is hard to establish, with the principal document bearing a fictitious date, while other important secondary documents bear no dates at all. There is, of course, always some slight hope that new manuscript evidence will be discovered. But fresh material sometimes clouds rather than elucidates an historical problem. This may be true of the long-neglected manuscript which prompts this essay. It is an annotated list of the twenty-five barons who swore to enforce the Charter. Its text is printed at the end of this essay and raises new questions. To place it in its circumstances is not easy ; nor does it seem to fit into the usually accepted pattern of events. Discussion of it has inevitably involved a new look at the other evidence. This may be pleaded as extenuation for a somewhat discursive commentary and an oblique approach to the main text. It will also explain the tentative nature of the conclusion.

For various reasons historians have tended to look at the events connected with Magna Carta and its aftermath from the standpoint of the king's camp, even when they show little sympathy with the king's cause. This is encouraged by the natural tendency to treat the rebellion as an episode in the history of the Angevin monarchy, by the form of the Charter as a royal grant, and by the plain fact that royal records tell us more about the king than about the barons. We know where King John was on almost every day of that fateful month of June ; it is much harder to find out where the leaders of the baronial party were and what they were doing. Mr. H. G. Richardson, in two

[1] I am grateful to Professors V. H. Galbraith and J. C. Holt, who have both read a draft of this paper, for valuable criticism, from which I have always profited, even when I have ventured to disagree. They must not be held answerable for any of my opinions.

© *The John Rylands University, 1968*

281

important articles,[1] approached the conflict from the baronial standpoint and illuminated it with fresh records from the baronial side. But his study concerned the aftermath of Magna Carta, during the months of July—September 1215. There are still a good many unanswered questions about the activities of the baronial leaders during the months of May and June. Were they predominantly northerners, or northerners and East Anglians ? If so, to what extent did their demand for a charter attract support from other parts of England ? Who met at Brackley at the end of April and agreed in making formal diffidation ? Who rallied to the leaders in London after its fall on 17 May ? How were the twenty-five " executors " of the charter appointed ? And when ? Who composed their retinues and made up the bulk of the barons' fighting force ?

These are hard questions. Most of them are perhaps unanswerable. A few records provide names of men whom the king mistrusted at this time ; and the sending of an expedition to Exeter early in June shows that King John did not fear trouble only in the north and east of the country. If the recollections of camp-gossip by the " Anonyme de Bethune " and the more refined (but not necessarily more accurate) Latin narratives of Roger Wendover and " Walter of Coventry " could be treated as evidence, we might proceed a little further ; but much of this is dubious stuff. There is always a danger that the story is anachronistic, that the writer has confused events which happened before the Charter with those which belong to the time when civil war broke out again. In general, these writers support the opinion held by modern historians—and confirmed by evidence of other sorts, including the choice of the Twenty-five—that the north country and East Anglia were the original centres of disaffection. The most specific piece of relevant news is found in Wendover's chronicle. This gives forty-four names of barons assembled after Easter 1215, to which Matthew Paris adds the name of Conan son of Ellis.[2] The forty-four include nineteen of the

[1] " The Morrow of the Great Charter " and " The Morrow of the Great Charter: an Addendum", BULLETIN xxviii (1944), 422-43, xxix (1945-46), 184-200, and separately.

[2] Matthew Paris, *Chronica majora*, ed. H. R. Luard (Rolls Series, 1872-83), ii. 585.

TWENTY-FIVE BARONS OF MAGNA CARTA   282

Twenty-five who were chosen a few weeks later to control the king, although two important northerners among the Twenty-five —the count of Aumale and William de Mowbray—are missing.[1] Many of the others on Wendover's list are of northern or East Anglian origin, and most of them are recorded as rebels at some later stage of the civil war.

Wendover is of evil repute as a biased and inaccurate reporter. But critical work on his narrative for the reign of John has shown that he is not negligible. Many records came his way. He had papal bulls at his disposal, royal newsletters, administrative orders, and so on. Whether he knew it or not, some of these records were truncated or imperfect, or were mere drafts of instruments which had later been revised. Professor Holt has argued that he had a text of Magna Carta of 1215 which came between the Articles of the Barons and the final engrossment of the Charter.[2]   It appears, too, that his version of the Lateran decree for a crusade may be what was recited in the Fourth Lateran Council, though it does not correspond to the text officially published afterwards.[3]   So, when Wendover names the ringleaders of the rebellion in April, we must reckon with the possibility that behind his story lies some written document. He certainly did not compose his narrative of this year until ten years later ; it is unlikely that he recited all these names from memory.[4]   Perhaps he had before him the copy of some list

---

[1] Hugh Bigot, Geoffrey de Say, William de Albini, and the mayor of London— all of them members of the Twenty-five—are also missing.

[2] " The St. Albans Chroniclers and Magna Carta ", *Trans. Royal Hist. Soc.*, 5th series, xiv (1964), 67-88, at p. 85 and Holt, *The Northerners* (Oxford, 1961), 116-18, and see Luard in M. Paris, *Chronica majora*, II. xxxiv-vi.   On Paris's access to imperfect records see C. R. Cheney, " The Paper Constitution preserved by Matthew Paris ", *Eng. Hist. Rev.*, lxv (1950), 213-21.   On the accumulations of historical material at St. Albans in his day see Richard Vaughan, *Matthew Paris* (Cambridge, 1958), *passim* and " The Chronicle of John of Wallingford ", *Eng. Hist. Rev.*, lxxiii (1958), 66-77.

[3] S. Kuttner and A. García y García, " A new Eye-witness Account of the Fourth Lateran Council ", *Traditio*, xx (1964), 115-78, at pp. 134, 174-8.

[4] Though he may have embellished a written list with other names drawn from later sources or from hearsay or imagination, just as Paris added the name of Conan son of Ellis. Cf. Wendover's list of evil counsellors of King John *s.a.* 1211 (*Chronica majora*, ii. 533).

283

drawn up in the baronial camp or else an intelligence-report passed out of Brackley or Northampton to the king.[1]

II

The source of Wendover's list is likely to remain unknown, and historians are likely to debate for a long time to come the value of evidence of this sort.[2] But they have been very willing to accept another list, which Matthew Paris appended to Wendover's account of the Charter. It equally lacks any mark of origin, any note of authenticity. It is not known from any copy earlier than the one which Matthew Paris wrote, about the year 1250. This is the list of the Twenty-five barons chosen by the whole body of the baronage (so it was said) in accordance with the security clause of Magna Carta, to force the king to keep his engagements. When William Blackstone wrote his unsurpassed " Introductory Discourse " to the Charter in 1759 he reproduced Matthew Paris's list from the *Chronica Maiora*, where it is a marginal addition to Wendover's text, written in Matthew's hand.[3] It also occurs, in Matthew's hand, in the " Liber additamentorum " of St. Albans, and in another hand in a St. Albans historical collection of the same period.[4] Blackstone pointed to three mistakes in Matthew's text,[5] which he was able to correct by reference to another version of the list, entered in the margin of a text of the Charter in British Museum MS. Harl. 746, fol. 64r. not

[1] Cf. the sheriffs' reports in reply to a government circular of late March 1216 (*Rotuli litterarum clausarum*, ed. T. D. Hardy (Record Commission, 1833-4), i. 270a) in Rymer's *Foedera* (Record Commission, 1816-30), i. 144, R. W. Eyton, *Antiquities of Shropshire* (1854-60), x. 326-7, J. G. Edwards, *Calendar of Ancient Correspondence concerning Wales* (Board of Celtic Studies, 1935), p. 1. A fourth return, for Warwickshire, has lately come to light in the Public Record Office. See also the letter of an English magnate to a friend early in 1216, with news of Prince Louis's coming (*Chron. Rogeri de Hoveden*, ed. W. Stubbs (Rolls Series, 1868-71), iv. 189 n. 4.

[2] Holt, *The Northerners*, p. 107, n. 2, would reject it outright. Sidney Painter, *Reign of King John* (Baltimore, 1949), pp. 286-8, thought it of some use.

[3] Cambridge, Corpus Christi Coll. MS. 16, fol. 43ᵛ, formerly 39ᵛ.

[4] Brit. Mus. Cotton MS. Nero D.i, fol. 123ʳᵇ and Cotton MS. Vitell. A.xx, fol. 98ʳᵃ, on which see Vaughan, *Matthew Paris.*

[5] Actually there is only one variant of substance common to all three of the St. Albans group : the reading " Rogerus de Munbray " for Roger de Montbegon; see further below, pp. 291-2.

TWENTY-FIVE BARONS OF MAGNA CARTA 284

later than about the year 1300.[1] He did not comment upon the fact that after the first eleven names on the list, the order of appearance differs in the Harleian manuscript from the order of the St. Albans version.[2]

There is no direct evidence to show whence the St. Albans scribes got their list of the Twenty-five. We have to take it upon trust and hope for the best. In its emended form it is at least compatible with our other evidence. Indeed, it receives some slight official support from the undated treaty between the king and Robert fitzWalter and twelve named barons : for all these persons appear in the list of the Twenty-five.[3] Mr. Holt, looking for a channel through which Matthew Paris might have received information about the events of 1215 to amplify Wendover's account, suggests the name of Elias of Dereham, steward of Archbishop Stephen Langton, who was probably at Runnymede and was certainly concerned in distributing copies of Magna Carta in the following weeks. As Mr. Holt recognizes, " Elias is an interesting possibility, but no more ".[4] In any case, this list of the Twenty-five was probably in circulation at the royal court, for with it the St. Albans manuscripts preserve thirty-eight names of those magnates and civil servants who " swore that they would obey the mandate of the Twenty-five barons ".[5]

[1] W. Blackstone, *The Great Charter and the Charter of the Forest* (Oxford, 1759), p. xx, note u. Blackstone noted one error, " Boys " (actually " Roys ") for Ros. Cf. Holt, *The Northerners*, p. 109, n. 3 and *Magna Carta* (Cambridge, 1965), p. 338. Liebermann dated this manuscript for no clear reason " *c.* 1325 " (*Gesetze der Angelsachsen* (Halle, 1903-16), I. xxxix) but Blackstone was probably right (loc. cit.) in ascribing it to the reign of Edward I.

[2] Taking the St. Albans list as the norm, the sequence in Harl. MS. 746 is : 14, 13, 21-23, 16, 17, 25, 18, 20, 19, 15, 12, 24.

[3] Rymer, *Foedera*, i. 133, Holt, *Magna Carta*, p. 342, and cf. Richardson, " Morrow ", p. 424. The nine barons denounced by the papal delegates on 5 September 1215 are all of the Twenty-five, and all except Richard de Percy are among the thirteen in the Treaty (*Eng. Hist. Rev.*, xliv (1929), 92).

[4] *Trans. Royal Hist. Soc.*, 5th series, xiv. 86-87. It cannot, of course, be assumed that Paris obtained the text directly from an outside source: Cotton MS. Vitell. A.xx shows that it was known to someone else at St. Albans.

[5] This appears in Cotton MS. Vitell.A.xx, fol. 98ra preceding the list of the 25. In Paris's copies it follows the names of the 25 with the same title (reading " Hii iuraverunt " for " Isti iuraverunt ") and with a tailpiece which runs : " Omnes isti iuraverunt cogere si opus esset ipsos xxv barones ut rectificarent regem, et etiam cogere ipsum si mutato animo forte recalcitraret."

285

Mr. Richardson has argued cogently in favour of regarding these thirty-eight as simply " the first to swear " to the common oath to obey the Twenty-five ; they were available at court at the time.[1] If this interpretation is correct the St. Albans manuscripts preserve the copy of an eye-witness record. Moreover, if the list of thirty-eight represents the court before the king left Runnymede and Windsor about 25 June, then it provides a *terminus ante quem* for the appointment of the Twenty-five. This is important. For it must be remembered that the Charter set their appointment in the future. Its security clause, like the Articles of the Barons, provided for the later election of Twenty-five barons.[2]   At the time of drafting, it seems, they had yet to be chosen.

The delay may seem strange ; perhaps it is explicable by the charter-form adopted for the formal settlement. The physical appearance of the Articles of the Barons suggests that the drafts-men originally had other ideas. For here the concessions of the king—the written confirmation of liberties—are set out after the fashion of Henry I's coronation charter or the " Unknown Charter of Liberties ". Then the scribe left the space of three lines before setting down a fresh section : " Hec est forma securitatis . . .". This proposed two safeguards for the preceding confirmation of liberties. The Twenty-five were to be appointed to resist infringement,[3] and the prelates were to give assurances on the king's behalf that he would not get papal authority to repudiate his charter. It looks as though the draftsmen envisaged three documents to cover this unusual situation, which had a strong tincture of treaty-making in it : one document was to be a traditional charter of liberties, the second a treaty, the third a guarantee by the prelates. Had this division been carried out, the " treaty " might well have contained the names of those sworn to enforce it, just as international treaties and truces drawn

---

[1] " Morrow ", pp. 436-7. Cf. Holt, *Magna Carta*, p. 247.

[2] " Concedimus . . . quod barones eligant xxv barones de regno quos voluerint " ; and see c. 52, 55 : " xxv baronum de quibus fit mentio inferius in securitate pacis." The Articles read : " Barones eligent xxv barones de regno quos voluerint."

[3] The 25 are mentioned in Articles, c. 25 and c. 37, but without the " de quibus fit mentio inferius " inserted in the Charter at these points.

TWENTY-FIVE BARONS OF MAGNA CARTA 286

up in this reign bore the names of those who swore on behalf of each contracting party to maintain the terms of the settlement.[1] If the idea of three documents was adumbrated, it received a blow when the prelates refused their guarantee in the desired form, and presented other problems besides. It was abandoned during the week or more devoted to final drafting.[2] With the adoption of the charter-form there was less obvious need to state the names of the Twenty-five. Even if they were chosen and their names were known by the time the Charter was ready for final engross-ment, there was no compelling reason why the names should be inserted in it. Their election seems therefore to belong to the period between the sealing of the Articles (perhaps as early as 10 June) [3] and 25 June.

Blackstone found in Harl. MS. 746 a list of the Twenty-five independent of the St. Albans version. Does this teach us anything new about the appointment of the Twenty-five, apart from supplying the correction Roger de Montbegon for Roger de Mowbray ? It is worth looking for any signs of the origin of the list, even if certainty is not attainable. The Harleian manu-script contains a legal collection, neatly written in Edward I's reign, including the up-to-date Statute of Westminster I and Statute of the Jews (1275), and reaching back to the so-called Laws of Edward the Confessor, of Cnut, and of William I, and to Glanvill. This pre-thirteenth century material predominates. The manuscript is of interest because it stands on the fringe of a remarkable group of books connected with the city of London. It was used by Francis Palgrave [4] and was examined in detail by Felix Liebermann. The latter was particularly concerned with the pseudonymous legal treatises of the twelfth century which it contained and with its lists and genealogy of the Norman kings.

---

[1] E.g. Rymer, *Foedera*, i. 79 (1200), 95 (1206), 125 (1214).

[2] An observation of Mr. Holt on Wendover's version of the Charter suggests that the idea of a separate *forma securitatis* had not been immediately abandoned (*The Northerners*, p. 118). For the fate of the proposed assurance by the prelates see Cheney, " The Eve of Magna Carta ", BULLETIN, xxxviii (1955-56), 311-41, at pp. 335-6.

[3] See Holt, *Magna Carta*, pp. 156, 304-5, for arguments in favour of this as the date of sealing, and for other opinions.

[4] *The Rise and Progress of the English Commonwealth* (1832), ii, p. cxviii.

287

It is Liebermann's MS. S, and in describing it he observed that considerable parts shared a common source with his MS. Pl (MS. Phillipps 8078, now B.M. Add. MS. 35719), probably written late in Henry III's reign.[1] Further, it emerges from Liebermann's analysis that one text common to Harl. MS. 746 and Add. MS. 35719 is the " Libertas Londoniensis ", which only occurs elsewhere in the " London Municipal Collection ", represented by several manuscripts of the thirteenth and fourteenth centuries. The oldest known manuscript of the group is now divided between Manchester, Rylands Library Lat. MS. 155 and B.M. Add. MS. 14252. This was written early in the thirteenth century. Mary Bateson had opined that " the compiler of the Add. MS. was a Londoner, working most likely in the *camera* of the Gildhall ; his collection is not all of one date, but was gradually put together from 1206 to 1216 "[2]; but according to Liebermann's view of the matter Rylands Lat. MS. 155+B.M. Add. MS. 14252 was a contemporary copy, not the compiler's autograph.[3] If the original was in process of formation in 1215 it is easy to understand why some later copies of the London Municipal Collection contain the text of the " Charter of Runnymede ".

[1] *Gesetze*, i. p. xxxix.

[2] " A London Municipal Collection of the Reign of John ", *Eng. Hist. Rev.*, xvii (1902), 480-511, 707-30, at p. 482. By the " Add. ms." she referred to the section containing specifically municipal documents : the Rylands MS. was unknown to her.

[3] " A contemporary Manuscript of the ' Leges Anglorum Londoniis collectae ' " *Eng. Hist. Rev.*, xxviii (1913), 732-45, at p. 744, cf. p. 734. See also *Gesetze*, i. p. xviii regarding Add. MS. 14252 : " um 1210-20 in der Londoner Gildhalle geschrieben." This, " the earliest legal compilation of the commune ", says G. A. Williams (*Medieval London* (1963), p. 77, cf. p. 174), " probably emanated from the Cornhill family ". If the suggestion is acceptable—and it is supported by the fact that Add. MS. 14252, fol. 127^v contains a bogus genealogy of the Cornhills, printed by J. H. Round, *The Commune of London* (1899), p. 107—it is of interest to note the textual connections between some parts of the London collection and B.M. Cotton MS. Titus A.xvii (Liebermann's T : see his *Quadripartitus* (Halle, 1892), pp. 63-64 and *Gesetze*, i. p. xl). For the Cotton MS. comes from St. Augustine's, Canterbury, and appears to be the subject of references in late thirteenth-century notes in Rylands Lat. MS. 155 (see M. R. James's catalogue, pp. 269-70) and in Andrew Horn's collection, Cambridge, Corpus Christi Coll. MS. 70, fol. 172^v. The Cornhill family was connected in various ways with St. Augustine's : see W. Urry, *Canterbury under the Angevin Kings* (1967), pp. 56-58.

TWENTY-FIVE BARONS OF MAGNA CARTA 288

But the text in this London collection which has attracted most attention from historians is the version of the apocryphal Laws of Edward the Confessor which it contains ; for it has interpolations, over and above those of the version which Liebermann called ECf retr. Since Liebermann only found the interpolations of the Rylands manuscript in later texts of London origin, he inferred that they were added by the London collector of the time of King John. More recently Mr. Richardson has argued that this " third edition " of the Laws of Edward the Confessor was composed in the early years of Henry II and was not specifically a London product.[1] This is a tacit reversal of Mr. Richardson's earlier position.[2] The argument for the earlier date depends upon the assumption that the twelfth-century editor of the third recension was aware of the conditions of his own time and anxious to record them. But this is hardly convincing. He was embellishing a book which claimed to go back to Edward the Confessor, and can hardly have wished simultaneously to bring it up to date. On the other hand, Liebermann did not prove that the third recension was of the date of the London Municipal Collection, only that it had not been found in any other context. Whatever one thinks of Mr. Richardson's argument, the fact remains undisputed that a London collector with an interest in politics, in or soon after the reign of John, assembled texts of the ancient laws of England and the customs of London and some historical miscellanea. Were it not for this, we should not possess the text of the third recension of the Laws of Edward, and we have no evidence that this recension ever existed outside of London. Mr. Richardson refers to Bracton's knowledge of this recension as proof that it was not confined to the London group of manuscripts ; [3] but there is no reason why Bracton should not have had access to the existing Rylands+B.M. MS. or a copy of it.

[1] " The Coronation in Medieval England ", *Traditio*, xvi (1960), 111-202, at pp. 166-7 ; and Richardson and G. O. Sayles, *The Governance of Mediaeval England* (Edinburgh, 1963), p. 373 and *Law and Legislation from Aethelberht to Magna Carta* (Edinburgh, 1966), pp. 57-58.

[2] " Studies in Bracton ", *Traditio*, vi (1948), 61-104, at p. 75 and " The English Coronation Oath ", *Speculum*, xxiv (1949), 44-75, at p. 61.

[3] *Law and Legislation*, p. 58, n. 6.

289

Liebermann's manuscripts Pl and S seem to some slight degree related to the London Collection, for they contain one London document of the twelfth century, the " Libertas Londoniensis ",[1] and much of their contents agrees in a general way with the contents of that collection, including the Charter of Runnymede. One cannot fail to be impressed by the similarity of taste between the compiler of Harl. MS. 746 and the London compilers of Edward I's reign who copied and enlarged upon the original London collector's work. But the actual texts of the documents in the Harleian manuscript often belong to another tradition. Most conspicuously, Pl and S do not contain the interpolations in the Laws of Edward the Confessor which distinguish the third recension. In short, the evidence for connecting Harl. MS. 746 as a whole with London (apart from its inclusion of " Libertas Londoniensis ") remains very slight.

This is a pity. The presence of the Charter of Runnymede —a comparatively rare text—in this manuscript remind us that it occurs in the London collection and that London was the rebels' headquarters for the weeks when Magna Carta was incubating. Even if some leaders or representatives camped intermittently or permanently near Runnymede during the fortnight after 10 June, the main baronial force was based on London. And even if the choosing of the Twenty-five (by whatever means) did not take place in London, the news would reach baronial headquarters at once. London officials might be expected to know the details of these happenings, which concerned them nearly, and the mayor of London was chosen to be one of the Twenty-five. In MS. Harl. 746 the list of the Twenty-five is written in the margin of the Charter, on fol. 64^r. Although it is in a small neat charter-hand quite distinct from the main hand of the manuscript, both may be the work of one man and the list can be regarded as an integral part of the compilation.[2] But all this does not mean that we can ascribe the list in Harl. MS. 746 to a London source.

[1] On which see M. Weinbaum, *Verfassungsgeschichte Londons 1066-1268* (Vierteljahrschrift für Sozial- und Wirtschaftsgeschichte, Beiheft XV, 1929), pp. 26-27, and for the text see Liebermann, *Gesetze*, i. 673, iii. 351.

[2] With other marginalia in the same hand it was written before the rubrics were added, fols. 64^r and 66^r.

TWENTY-FIVE BARONS OF MAGNA CARTA   290

III

The point has now been reached when it may be profitable to look at yet another, hitherto neglected, version of the list. Lambeth MS. 371 is a small quarto volume from Reading Abbey, composed of many pieces, written in various good thirteenth-century hands. Most of the book consists of historical miscellanea, including extracts from William of Malmesbury (fols. 43 ff.) with additions to the beginning of Henry III's reign, including two brief accounts of King John's reign. This part was described by Stubbs in editing William's *Gesta Regum*, and he noted : " on fol. 56 is given the list of the executors of Magna Carta, and the *summa militum* or number of the knights bound to assist them, one thousand one hundred four score and three, M.C.IIII^{xx} et III ."[1]   On the page (fol. 57^v) next following the list is a text of Magna Carta of 1215, with a few mistakes and omissions. Then come (fol. 59^r) an extract from Ralph of Coggeshall on the reign of Richard I and (fol. 72^r) the chronicle of Martinus Polonus, abridged. Later in the book occur the *Expugnatio Hibernica* of Giraldus Cambrensis[2] and a French version of Cato's Distiches with the Latin text, by one Everard le Moine.[3]

The list of the executors of Magna Carta occupies the last eight ruled lines on fol. 56^v and lines 2-10 (line 1 being blank) on fol. 57^r (the rest blank). The hand is rather later than that of the brief chronicle which precedes it and of the text of Magna Carta which begins at the top of fol. 57^v. It appears to be not later than the last quarter of the thirteenth century. Neither the clear indications of two cataloguers—H. J. Todd in 1812 and M. R. James in 1932—nor Stubbs's intriguing notice have attracted the attention of connoisseurs of Magna Carta. The text is printed below for the first time.

The Lambeth list presents the Twenty-five in a new order,

---

[1] *Gesta Regum* (Rolls Series, 1887-9), i. pp. lxxxviii ff.

[2] See J. F. Dimock, *Giraldi Cambrensis Opera* (Rolls Series, 1867), v, pp. xxix ff.

[3] " Possibly to be identified with Everard de Gateley, monk of St. Edmunds ", M. D. Legge, *Anglo-Norman Literature and its Background* (Oxford, 1963), pp. 182, 267.

291

and introduces a mistake of its own in substituting Arundel for Aumale. The St. Albans, Harleian, and Lambeth lists all give more than half the names in differing order, and seem to represent three distinct traditions.[1] It is therefore of some interest to find that all three agree in the sequence (and in general in the description) of the first eleven. They include the seven earls, the sons of two earls (William Marshal junior and Gilbert de Clare), Robert fitzWalter, and Eustace de Vesci. These magnates were of such consequence that they practically had to be chosen. Perhaps they were named first, and the completion of the baronial committee came at a later stage. On this hypothesis, a list of those picked as the " first eleven " was given wide publicity in some official document or else in a news-letter, and this lay behind all three of the surviving versions. But the original compilers of these lists (or two of them) had to take the other fourteen names where they could find them ; and possibly relied on sources deriving from the spoken word ; there was no single official list and they had no common source for them.

Comparison of the St. Albans, Harleian, and Lambeth versions reveals another curious feature. The Lambeth text and the three St. Albans texts all read *Rogerus de Munbray* in place of the *Rogerus de Munbezon* of the Harleian text. The error, if it is an error, could be the work of a careless scribe, especially since the name *Willelmus de Munbray* had appeared earlier in each list. Moreover, a scribe writing about 1250 or after might more easily adopt the name of Mowbray since by then William de Mowbray's son Roger had made himself famous, whereas Roger de Montbegon died in 1245 without male heirs. But there is no other obvious reason for relating the Lambeth version of the list to the St. Albans versions. Did two scribes make the same mistake independently, or does this reading indicate that Roger de Mowbray was named before Roger de Montbegon became one of the Twenty-five ?[2] If the name of Mowbray is to be taken seriously it must refer, not to William's son, then a child, but to

---

[1] Compared with the St. Albans texts the order of the names in the Lambeth MS. is : 1-11, 25, 12, 13, 21-24, 20, 16, 15, 17-19, 14. For the sequence in Harl. MS. 746 see above, p. 284, n. 2.

[2] Montbegon was one of the 25 by the time of the Treaty made between the king and Robert fitzWalter, etc.

TWENTY-FIVE BARONS OF MAGNA CARTA 292

another obscurer member of the family, who appears repeatedly in records of John's reign.[1] But on balance it seems preferable to regard the appearance of *Rogerus de Munbray* as the result of scribal error.

The main interest of the Lambeth text was noted by Stubbs. Unlike the other versions it is not a bare list, but contains evidence (if only it could be rightly understood) of the circumstances of its origin. Briefly, it attaches to each baron's name a quota of knights : *cum cc militibus, cum xxx militibus,* and so on, without indication of how these figures were arrived at. It is primarily the record of some military muster. The list proper does not include the mayor of London as twenty-fifth baron ; but it is immediately followed by a note that the mayor of London will hand over the city of London to the barons if the king should want to contravene his charter. In that event all these earls with the knights enumerated and the community of all England must rise against (*insurgere in*) the king. The total of the knights is incorrectly given as 1183. If the first quota " septem viginti " should be emended (as seems probable) to " septies viginti ", the real total is 1187 ; as they stand the quotas amount to 1074, the twenty-four earls and barons excluded. The pattern of the record shows that it was composed not, like the other texts, merely to list the names of the Twenty-five, but to show how many knights each could bring into the field at the time.

Before the problem of these quotas is faced the reference to the mayor deserves attention for the light it throws upon the date of the record. It must be compared with the *conventio* or Treaty, in chirograph form, undated, between King John and Robert fitzWalter and other barons. Of this Treaty the part held by the king, with slits for thirteen baronial seals, is preserved in the Chancery Miscellanea (C. 47/34/1/1) and is on view in the Museum of the Public Record Office.[2] Comparison of what we

---

[1] *Rotuli litterarum clausarum,* i. 13b-481 ; *Pipe Roll 17 John and Praestita Roll* 14-18 *John* (Pipe Roll Soc., n.s. 37, 1964), p. 102.

[2] Printed by Holt, *Magna Carta,* pp. 342-3 with facsimiles, plates v and va. It was enrolled on the dorse of the Close Roll 17 John m. 27d, whence Rymer, *Foedera,* i. 133 and W. S. McKechnie, *Magna Carta* (2nd edn., Glasgow, 1914), pp. 495-6. Blackstone had printed it from one or the other source in *The Great Charter,* pp. 25-26.

293

may call the Lambeth Memorandum with the Treaty shows differing arrangements for the control of London.

According to the Memorandum the city, under its mayor (and in possession of a royal charter granted as recently as 9 May),[1] is free to control itself. By implication the baronial party, which had occupied London on 17 May and which certainly treated London as its headquarters throughout the summer, was not in *formal* control of the city. The Memorandum simply adds, as it were, to the security clause of Magna Carta a practical device for enforcing sanctions against the king: if the king opposes the barons the mayor of London will surrender (*tradet*) the capital to them. The Treaty reveals a different state of affairs from the Memorandum. It arranges that the barons " will hold the city of London by the grant (*de ballio*) of the lord king " until the feast of the Assumption (15 August), saving to the king in the meanwhile his farms, rents, and clear debts, and the archbishop of Canterbury similarly is to hold the Tower of London by the grant of the king until the same date, " saving to the city of London its liberties and its free customs and saving to anyone his right in the custody of the Tower ". City and Tower were to revert to the king at the feast of the Assumption if by then the oath to obey the Twenty-five had been taken throughout the country or if any failure to achieve this could not be blamed on the king. As regards the Tower, it should be remembered that it had not been under the citizens' control and at this juncture did not come into baronial hands. Its custody was claimed unsuccessfully by Geoffrey de Mandeville when baronial claims were being threshed out during the month after the making of peace. In June or July it was apparently transferred from royal custody to the custody of Archbishop Stephen.[2] We hear no more of it until it yielded to Prince Louis in November 1216. Whether it had been held for all the intervening period by the archbishop's men or had come again under direct royal control we do not know. As regards the city, it is well known that the king never

---

[1] *Rotuli chartarum*, ed. T. D. Hardy (Record Commission, 1837), p. 207; *Select Charters*, ed. W. Stubbs, 9th edition (Oxford, 1913), p. 311.

[2] *Memoriale fr. Walteri de Coventria*, ed. W. Stubbs (Rolls Series, 1872-3), ii. 221. Cf. Holt, *Magna Carta*, p. 173, n. 2.

TWENTY-FIVE BARONS OF MAGNA CARTA 294

regained possession of it. By the feast of the Assumption the manifold occasions of dispute and the near certainty that the Pope would denounce the Charter was causing the country to drift back to civil war. It results from this that the provision about London in the Memorandum—that the mayor will hand over the city to the barons if the king contravenes the Charter—must have preceded the Treaty, which puts the city into baronial hands until 15 August.[1] Until the Treaty was drawn up the mayor and citizens presumably could cling to the fiction that the city was theirs to hand over to the barons, even though the barons had been in military control ever since 15 May.

Both documents are undated, and the Treaty has been variously assigned to the third week in July by Mr. Richardson and to 19 June or thereabouts by Professor Holt.[2] Unfortunately the facts on which a conclusion must be reached are few and susceptible of more than one interpretation. But the discovery of the Memorandum introduces a new element. The capture of the city on 17 May had put London definitely in the power of the rebel barons. But the Memorandum suggests that the barons indirectly controlled the city's government rather than superseded it. Formal continuity of civic government may have been essential to any compromise over the holding of London which could contribute to the so-called *firma pax* of 19 June. Royal letters after 17 May show the alarm and despondency of the government at the loss of the capital[3] : it may have been the determining factor in persuading the king to negotiate with the rebels. And the king could best be brought to agreement if the barons claimed to respect the civic institutions. Two considerations might incline them to do so in the interests of peace. By

---

[1] Cf. A. J. Collins, " The Documents of the Great Charter of 1215 ", *Proc. Brit. Academy*, xxxiv (1948), 233-79, at p. 246, n. 3 : " The City might have been surrendered on any day after 19 June."

[2] Richardson, " Morrow ", pp. 424-5 ; Holt, *Magna Carta*, pp. 162, 171-4. Cf. Blackstone, *The Great Charter*, p. xxiv. Painter, *Reign of King John*, pp. 329, 338, by implication agrees with Richardson's dating.

[3] *Rotuli litterarum patentium*, ed. T. D. Hardy (Record Commission, 1835), p. 137b. Cf. the terms in which the Bishop of Winchester and his colleagues, writing on 5 September, speak of the perjury of the citizens in yielding London to the king's enemies : " Corone pariter et regni sui caput " (*Eng. Hist. Rev.*, xliv (1929), 92).

295

leaving the city formally in charge of the mayor they were leaving it with an ally : one who engaged with them in negotiating at Runnymede and who was chosen as one of the Twenty-five. Secondly (if the Memorandum may be interpreted as an unofficial note of some agreement between the barons and the citizens) the barons had a formal undertaking from the mayor—or a private understanding with him—that he would surrender the city to them if King John went back on his undertakings. As Mr. Holt has rightly observed : " It is scarcely likely that the king would agree to terms of peace without some arrangement being made on the fate of the capital ". " It was an essential part of the original settlement ".[1] The Memorandum appears to record this state of affairs. It cannot be earlier than mid-June, when the Charter was being drafted.

When, then, was the Treaty made ? Mr. Holt, having stated the case somewhat less definitely in the past, says categorically : " there is no real doubt that it belongs to 19 June or thereabouts." [2] His main argument rests on the fact that a royal writ of 23 July to the barons and others of Yorkshire orders them to restore castles, etc., which they have taken, saying that such restoration was part of the *reformacio pacis* and was to be concluded by 15 August. The only " reformacio pacis " in the records is that of 19 June ; the only document other than the writ which sets 15 August as a time-limit is the Treaty. Therefore, Mr. Holt contends, the Treaty must have been an integral part of the June " reformatio " : five weeks later the Yorkshiremen were told to see that a time-limit imposed in June was observed. The argument seems less than compelling.

The first question to be disposed of is : what grounds are there for supposing that the time-limit of 15 August was fixed at the time of the " reformacio pacis ", on or about 19 June ? The writ of 23 July orders the barons and others of Yorkshire " quod . . . terras . . . que abstulistis tempore guerre vel post . . . reddatis infra festum Assumpcionis Beate Marie proximo instans sicut in reformacione pacis continetur ". The action called for

---

[1] *Eng. Hist. Rev.*, lxxii (1957), 412, n. 1 and *The Northerners*, p. 126, n. 1. Cf.Holt, *Magna Carta*, p ·173.　　　　[2] *Magna Carta*, pp. 172-3, 339.

does not correspond precisely to any specific undertaking either in Magna Carta or in the Treaty, though it could be said to be involved in any honest implementation of the charter. Whether the " sicut " refers to the mode of restoration or to the date is not perfectly clear. The writ does not explicitly say that the time-limit of 15 August—or any time-limit—had been written into the " reformacio pacis ". This may seem to be the obvious, the natural, interpretation ; but it has to be studied in the light of other evidence.

If a time-limit *was* imposed on 19 June it is surely strange that instructions to people in the provinces immediately afterwards did not state it? There is no trace in any of the dozens of writs concerned with carrying out the terms of peace. In *The Northerners* Mr. Holt attached importance to the reference by " Walter of Coventry " to 16 August as a date fixed in June for the final settlement. But I think that the chronicler's words suggest that this date was not fixed until the situation had deteriorated after the granting of the charter.[1] Moreover, another chronicler, Roger Wendover, says that before the gathering at Runnymede dispersed the king appointed 16 July " ad hoc exequendum ".[2] The sixteenth of July came and the conditions of peace were not fulfilled. In the atmosphere of disappointment and distrust in which the parties met at Oxford in the third week of July, when the euphoria of Runnymede and dreams of immediate redress had faded, the fixing of a short term within which the settlement had got to be made is understandable. As Mr. Holt has said in a different context : " The optimism with which the Great Charter and the writs of 19 June referred to the newly agreed peace was soon put in question. By the middle of September the country was at war, and at war about the Charter. This was not a sudden or an accidental climax ; it was the result of a lengthy development which can be traced back through the summer months to Runnymede itself. The Charter was made possible by its imprecisions and inexactness ; these same qualities now meant that its application in practice was bound to become a

---

[1] *Memoriale fr. W. de Coventria*, ii. 223 ; *The Northerners*, p. 126, n. 1.
[2] M. Paris, *Chronica Majora*, ii. 606 ; cf. Richardson, " Morrow ", p. 422.

297

matter of increasingly bitter debate and, in the end, open dispute." [1]

There is, then, no *a priori* reason for supposing that the time-limit of 15 August had been fixed on or about 19 June. The supposition stands or falls on the dating we give to the undated Treaty. Since the only dated reference to the time-limit occurs on 23 July, the possibilities should not be too lightly rejected that this date had only just been fixed and that the undated Treaty belongs to the same day, 23 July, or thereabouts. The fact that its phraseology recalls the writs of late June does not prove that it was contemporary with them : the original terms for peace would have to be repeated at any later time when their enforcement was required. Even supposing the time-limit to have been fixed on or about 19 June it would remain to be proved that the decision was immediately enshrined in the un-dated Treaty. Mr. Richardson fitted the Treaty into the cir-cumstances of late July, when the king's advisers (and perhaps the king himself) met leaders of the baronial party. The royal chancery dated letters at Oxford from 17 to 23 July. The Treaty was copied on to the dorse of the chancery close roll, and the face of this membrane of the roll, as Mr. Richardson observed, bore letters " dated at Oxford on 18 and 19 July (i. 221), whence we may arrive at the approximate date of the agreement ".[2] But Mr. Holt interprets the evidence of the enrolments differently. We must therefore examine the arguments and try to decide between them. Two dates have been proposed for the Treaty : c. 17-23 July (Richardson) and c. 19 June (Holt).

In the first place, the face of the membrane contains the enrolment of earlier letters dated 11-15 July, besides those of 18-19 July noted by Mr. Richardson. (The next membrane has letters on its face dated 18-27 July and the dorse is blank.)[3] Secondly, as Mr. Holt observes, it is uncertain that documents were endorsed at the time of the dated enrolments on the face.

---

[1] *Magna Carta*, p. 242. The inclusion of the Security Clause meant that the pope was certain to condemn the Charter (cf. C. R. Cheney, " The Church and Magna Carta ", *Theology*, lxviii (1965), 266-72, at pp. 268-71).

[2] " Morrow ", p. 424, n. 3 ; cf. *Rot. lit. claus.*, i. 268b.

[3] *Rot. lit. claus.*, i. 220b-223a, 269a.

TWENTY-FIVE BARONS OF MAGNA CARTA 298

Thirdly, " the date of the composition of the treaty is quite another matter " from the date at which it was enrolled.[1] Theoretically, at least, these objections are valid. Mr. Richardson seems at first sight to weaken his case by his comment on the declaration of the bishops about the fealty of the barons : " although this declaration, which is undated, is entered on the dorse of m.21, which bears on the recto documents dated between 28 June and 2 [recte 3] July, there can be no real doubt that it comes from the Oxford council." [2] On the other hand, Mr. Holt weakens the force of his objection by adopting in the case of the declaration the reasoning which he rejects in the case of the Treaty. The bishops' declaration, he says, " in all probability " belongs to 28 June-3 July or thereabouts.[3] Each of these scholars seems to apply a rule of enrolment in one case and to ignore it in another case. But were there rules ? What were the habits of chancery clerks in 1215 ? When they wanted (for whatever reason) to copy a document on to the dorse of a roll, did they choose for the purpose that membrane of the roll which was in current use ? Full answers to these questions must await a fuller study of the rolls than they have yet received. On general grounds, and from a reading of the printed editions, a tentative surmise may be permitted. If enrolment was proceeding fairly punctually after the issue (or receipt) of letters, the tendency was for documents destined for the dorse of the roll to be written on the membrane of the corresponding date or on the preceding membrane. Often a scribe may have found it convenient to work on the dorse of the preceding membrane, of which the face was filled ; by this means he avoided interrupting current enrolment on the face. But unless the documents for endorsement came late to the chancery, as with " in-letters " from distant parts, they would not be enrolled on membranes which only bear letters of later date on the face ; for those membranes had not yet come into use. There is no obvious reason why enrolment of the dateless documents in question—the bishops' declaration and the Treaty—should have been delayed longer than other current

[1] Holt, *Eng. Hist. Rev.*, lxxii. 412, n. 1.
[2] " Morrow ", p. 425, n. 2. *Rot. lit. pat.*, p. 181 and Holt, *Magna Carta*, p. 348. [3] *Magna Carta*, p. 244, n. 1.

299

enrolments on the patent and close rolls. Even though neither was a normal chancery instrument, the declaration was doubtless inspired by the king and the Treaty must have received (on the other part) the great seal.

The bishops' declaration, though undated, contains within itself some significant evidence. It was issued by two arch-bishops, seven bishops, and " Master " Pandulf, the pope's nuncio.[1] The same persons, except for the bishop of Chichester and Pandulf, issued undated letters on the interpretation of Magna Carta, c.48, relating to forest customs ; these were enrolled with the Treaty on the dorse of the close roll.[2] Both the bishops' docu-ments were in the king's interest and must have been requested by the king. It is natural to suppose that they were drafted when these prelates were in attendance upon the king. Turning to the charter roll we find that Archbishop Henry of Dublin constantly attested royal charters between mid-June and mid-July, but none of the other prelates in question did. Bishop Peter of Winchester appears with the king at Corfe on 13 July after several weeks' absence[3] ; none of the other bishops is known to have been at court after 20 June until 18 July at Oxford. Langton does not figure in royal witness-lists until 23 July at Oxford.[4] He is recorded at Staines (21 June), Tarring (6 July), Slindon (9 July), and Pagham (12 July).[5] Bishop Hugh of Lincoln was in his diocese at Newark on 8 July.[6] It seems safest, therefore, to suppose that the bishops' declaration and interpretation were drawn up in the July council at Oxford.

Does this determine the date of the Treaty, which was en-rolled with the bishops' interpretation ? The evidence is not conclusive. Much more needs to be known about chancery practice ; and aberrations could doubtless occur in such abnormal

---

[1] The papal chancery did not style Pandulf *magister*, nor did Pandulf use the title in his own acts.

[2] I owe to the kindness of Mr. Holt the information that these two documents —the only items on memb. 27d—were probably both written at the same time by the same man.   [3] *Rotuli chartarum*, p. 213a.   [4] Ibid. pp. 214b-215a.

[5] *Acta Stephani Langton*, ed. Kathleen Major (Canterbury and York Soc., 1950), pp. 26-28, 165.

[6] *Reg. antiquissimum of the Cath. Church of Lincoln*, ed. C. W. Foster and K. Major (Lincoln Record Soc., 1931—), iii. no. 912.

TWENTY-FIVE BARONS OF MAGNA CARTA 300

times as these. But there is no obvious reason why the Treaty should not have been enrolled when it was composed, before the sealed original was sent to the treasury for permanent deposit. Moreover, now that we know that it had been preceded by a period, however short, when the mayor's formal surrender of the city to the barons could be expressed as a future contingency, there is no reason for tying the Treaty to the Charter. Mr. Richardson's view seems preferable : it was an outcome of the Oxford council.

Another pointer is provided by the parties to the Treaty. They are : " dominum Iohannem regem Anglie, ex una parte, et Robertum filium Walteri, marescallum exercitus Dei et sancte ecclesie in Anglia, et Ricardum comitem de Clara, Gaufridum comitem Essex', Glouc', Rogerum Bigot comitem Northfolc' et Suthfolc', Saherum comitem Wint', Robertum comitem Oxon', Henricum comitem Hereford', et barones subscriptos, scilicet Willelmum Marescallum iuniorem, Eustacium de Vescy, Willelmum de Mobray, Iohannem filium Roberti, Rogerum de Monte Begonis, Willelmum de Lanval', et alios comites et barones et liberos homines totius regni, ex altera parte." All of the thirteen named magnates belong to the Twenty-five. They include most, but not all, of the " first eleven". The fact that two of the eleven are missing, as also William de Albini, and that less distinguished persons are named (perhaps brought in, as Mr. Richardson has suggested, to make a quorum) suggests a date after some of the Twenty-five had left the baronial headquarters, and not the time of the Runnymede meetings when, if ever, the whole committee of Twenty-five probably assembled.

One document at first sight conflicts with this interpretation : the letter preserved by Roger Wendover, which Robert fitz-Walter wrote to William de Albini to announce that a tournament fixed for 6 July at Stamford would take place instead near London on 13 July. " You know well how very convenient it is for you and for all of us to safeguard (*servare*) the city of London, which is our headquarters (*receptaculum*), and what shame and damage we should incur if we lost it through our own fault." [1]

[1] Paris, *Chronica majora*, ii. 614-15. Cf. Holt, *Magna Carta*, p. 250.

301

This letter must have been written at latest in the first few days of July. It certainly implies that Robert fitzWalter and his associates considered that they virtually controlled London. No doubt they did. But the word *servare* need not mean formal control of the civic government, which was the situation created by the Treaty. Indeed, it might be said that Robert fitzWalter expresses apprehensions which are best understood if a royal garrison in the Tower of London was still a threat to the position of the baronial party in the city ; and under the terms of the Treaty the Tower was transferred to the custody of the archbishop. There is no reason to suppose that the Treaty was in existence when the letter was written.

A further possibility remains to be considered. At some time between the making of the Memorandum (in June) and the making of the Treaty (in July) the barons may have persuaded the mayor of London to " tradere civitatem " on the ground that the king had not performed the promises he had made in the Charter. If this happened, the Treaty simply recorded a *fait accompli*. This would indeed provide an attractive interpretation of the letter of Robert fitzWalter to William de Albini and would account for the bitter complaint against the Londoners by the bishop of Winchester and his colleagues on 5 September.[1] But it is not clear that the complaint implies any further overt act of treachery after the surrender of 17 May, although it implies that a city faction has continued to give comfort to the king's enemies. If London had been formally surrendered by the mayor to the barons after Magna Carta, the fact would hardly have escaped record and would surely have been part and parcel of a general insurgence which only occurred later, in August-September.

IV

The tone, as well as the contents, of the Lambeth Memorandum suggests that it was composed in the baronial headquarters at London. Its reference to the *communa totius Anglie* echoes the words of the Articles and the Charter, but the blunt *insurgere in regem* shows a realistic view of the security clause which is

[1] *Eng. Hist. Rev.*, xliv. 92.

TWENTY-FIVE BARONS OF MAGNA CARTA 302

masked in the legal instrument by talk of distraining and aggriev-
ing. Significantly, the mayor of London, who comes twelfth
in the Harleian list of the Twenty-five and fourteenth in the St.
Albans version, is only mentioned at the end of the Memorandum,
presumably because its accent is on military force. If, as seems
certain, the Memorandum records an arrangement preceding the
Treaty, it was drawn up between mid-June and mid-July.
That being so, what can these quotas of knights mean ?

One thing is clear. Although most if not all of the twenty-
four barons were tenants-in-chief of the king, the numbers of
knights here assigned to them bear no constant relation to the
numbers they held enfeoffed of the king. Only in the cases of the
earls of Hereford and Oxford is there any close correspondence
between their feudal quotas as indicated in the scutage accounts
of the Pipe Roll 16 John and the quotas in the Memorandum.
What is more, a comparison of the numbers assigned to the
various barons in the Memorandum does not point to a constant
relationship between the individual's quota and his total holding
of knights' fees, whether as tenant-in-chief or as mesne tenant.
The list is no general guide to the landed wealth or importance of
these men, as the examination of a few examples will show. If
the number *septem viginti* set against the name of the earl of
Clare is emended (as seems justifiable) to *septies viginti* (VII^{xx}),
then there are, in the whole list, only three quotas of more than
a hundred knights. Of these, two are assigned to Gloucester
and Clare, the two earls in the baronial camp who held the greatest
number of knights' fees ; but we are left with the quota of two
hundred knights assigned to William Marshal junior, whose
holdings were small in his loyal father's lifetime. If one descends
to the three quotas of eighty knights, eighty are assigned to the
earl of Norfolk (who was enfeoffed of more than double this
number of knights' fees), another eighty are assigned to another
magnate, William de Mowbray ; but the third quota of eighty is
assigned to the son of the earl of Clare, whose feudal holdings
were certainly far less than this. By contrast, the richly enfeoffed Robert fitzWalter, the " marshal of the army of God and
holy Church ", is only assigned fifty knights in the Memorandum.
This did not represent his feudal standing.

303

The late Sidney Painter paid attention to the composition of the barons' forces in 1215 and 1216. He analysed the evidence provided by the records of *reversi*, those who returned to the king's allegiance after being in rebellion in 1215 or 1216.

It would be extremely interesting [he wrote], to know how many of the minor rebels were vassals who had followed their lords. In theory an English mesne tenant was under no obligation to follow his lord in rebellion—in fact his first duty was fidelity to the crown. At the same time it seems clear that a vassal who followed his lord into revolt was considered to have committed a less serious offense than a man who rebelled without such a feudal connection. Unfortunately it is impossible to determine the feudal affiliations of the vast majority of the lesser rebels. The fact that the percentage of rebel barons from the various shires was roughly the same as that of the free-holders as a whole might indicate that vassals tended to follow their lords. But it may also mean simply that it was unwise to remain loyal to the crown in a region where the rebels were dominant.[1]

It is hardly surprising to find royal servants like Simon of Pattishall and Henry of Braybrooke were involved in the rebellion in May 1215, when the dissident barons swamped the counties of Northamptonshire and Bedfordshire where their properties lay. The position of the tenants of the honor of Trowbridge, in dispute between the loyal earl of Salisbury and the rebel earl of Hereford, cannot have been comfortable.[2]

The chronicler known as " Walter of Coventry " or " the canon of Barnwell " has a significant comment on the state of affairs when the barons took Northampton in May 1215 [3] :

They sent to those near at hand and far afield to throw in their lot with them. And many flocked to them, particularly the younger men, sons and nephews of the magnates, seeming anxious to make names for themselves in warfare. Hence it arose that many houses were divided against themselves : parents and elders stood by the king as their lord, while the juniors were in opposition. We have even known some who for love of their children went over to the other side. And there were some who, though at first they did not agree with the rebels, joined them later because they were friends of fortune or lovers of novelty.

Painter was disinclined to accept the chronicler's emphasis on the youth of the rebels and suggested that he " was clearly thinking of a few well-known cases. The presence of William Marshal the younger in the rebel ranks while his father was a staunch supporter

---

[1] *Reign of King John*, p. 299, cf. p. 290.   [2] *Rot. lit. claus.*, i. 194b, 200, 202.
[3] ii. 220.

TWENTY-FIVE BARONS OF MAGNA CARTA 304

of John must have attracted wide attention." [1] The emphasis is the more understandable when we see William Marshal's quota of two hundred, and Gilbert of Clare's quota of eighty knights. Between them these two young men apparently commanded nearly a quarter of the quotas of the twenty-four barons when the Memorandum was drawn up.

It is safe, then, to assume that the quotas of the Memorandum were neither recruited nor maintained according to any rules of feudal obligation. Whether or not the rules countenanced the mesne tenant who followed a tenant-in-chief into rebellion and copied his lord's diffidation, the legal aspect can have been of small importance. Some were in the baronial camp because they were tenants or friends or loyal servants of the rebel leaders. Some were intimidated by lords or neighbours. Others were there, as " Walter of Coventry " opined, because they were bellicose and wanted to cut a dash. There is no question of a royal army of mercenaries being confronted by a force composed of the combined feudal levies of those tenants-in-chief who had deserted the king. Whether the baronial forces at this stage included mercenaries is doubtful. Late in June the country contained many foreigners who had been recruited for the king and who were now faced with unemployment [2] ; but there seems to be no positive evidence.

The disparity between the presumed wealth of some of the twenty-four barons and the quotas assigned to them in the Memorandum suggests that the numbers of knights do not represent an estimate of the total potential force at their disposal. Their total potential resources, assuming that pressure could be consistently applied to tenants (which is unlikely), would include more than this. There were garrisons of castles up and down the country and knights enfeoffed on widely scattered estates. Eustace de Vesci and William de Albini, for instance, might well be concentrating most of the men they could muster on safeguarding their own castles of Alnwick in Northumberland and Belvoir in Leicestershire. The quotas of the Memorandum are

---

[1] *Reign of King John*, pp. 295-6.

[2] *Rot. lit. pat.*, p. 144 and *Histoire des Ducs de Normandie et des Rois d'Angleterre*, ed. F. Michel (Soc. de l'Hist. de France, 1840), p. 149.

305

much more likely to record the numbers (or at least rough estimates)[1] of knights actually under arms in the south east, probably
at London, at the immediate disposal of each of these twenty-four
magnates. " Walter of Coventry " says that about five hundred
knights left Northampton for London in mid-May.[2] If this is
approximately true the number in London a month later might
well be nearly twelve hundred, as the Memorandum suggests.
The purpose of the list can only be a matter for conjecture ; but
it is hard to see any useful purpose it could have served except as
an estimate of numbers of a fighting force : whenever and where-
ever it was composed there were no more knights at hand. It
implies that all available knights were grouped with a definite
object in view under the Twenty-five (or rather, the twenty-four
apart from the mayor of London). The command is vested in the
twenty-four. If there had been other commanders, each with his
posse of knights, they would surely have been mentioned and
their contributions to the *summa militum* set down.

Given the obscurity of the record, we cannot be certain that
all the quotas reflect the application of a single principle. They
may indicate partly the resources of individual barons, partly a
capacity for leadership and martial renown which had attracted
the unattached. Only the latter explanation seems to account for
William Marshal's large following. In any case, it would be
unwise to suppose that the quotas necessarily corresponded to
the command exercised by each of the twenty-four ; rather they
represent the disposition of a force notionally under unified
control, " the Army of God and holy Church ". This conjecture is supported by the evidence for William de Albini.
According to Roger Wendover (who, as prior of Belvoir, can for
once be taken to provide first-hand evidence), after Runnymede
William went home to occupy his castle of Belvoir, in Leicestershire. The other baronial leaders repeatedly summoned him to

[1] Only three or possibly four quotas are not of ten or multiples of ten. In a
copy made so late as Lambeth MS. 371 it is impossible to be sure that the exceptions are not due to copyists' errors, in the details as well as in the *summa*: William
of Huntingfield's quota of seven looks suspicious. But it is equally impossible to
put any faith in arbitrary emendation.

[2] ii. 220. It is generally agreed that this was followed by a landslide to the
baronial camp. Cf. *Chronica majora*, ii. 587-8.

TWENTY-FIVE BARONS OF MAGNA CARTA 306

come south and take charge of Rochester for them. He came to London after Michaelmas. The barons then picked a strong force and put William in command of it. He went to occupy Rochester with 140 knights and all their followers.[1] It will be noticed that William de Albini had only ten knights set against his name in the Memorandum. But this did not affect the command with which he was entrusted in October. Painter describes him as " perhaps the ablest and most experienced captain in the rebel army ".[2]

V

To conclude with a summary of tentative findings. No recognizably official list of the Twenty-five barons of Magna Carta is known, and the several existing versions were all written down long after the event. While one of them (the St. Albans version) seems to have a pedigree reaching back to the king's court, the Harleian manuscript may possibly be derived from a London municipal source, the Lambeth manuscript from a baronial source. A comparison of the Charter with the Articles of the Barons suggests that when the Articles were drawn up the draftsmen were planning an orthodox charter of liberties; separate documents were envisaged to safeguard its observance. But in the event the only safeguard was included in the Charter in the basically inconsistent sanctions of clause 61. What may seem to us a trivial matter of form had the effect of leading the pope, in condemning the barons' coercion of the king, to condemn the whole charter of liberties. When, seventeen months later, the liberties were divorced from the unconstitutional sanctions, the Church very naturally and properly approved them.[3] Our investigation has not discovered how or when the Twenty-five were chosen. But a comparison of the texts suggests that eleven of the chief magnates were designated as executors of the Charter before the remainder had been picked. As for the Lambeth text with its quotas of knights, so strangely neglected, the precise

---

[1] *Chronica majora*, ii. 621.   [2] *Reign of King John*, p. 362.
[3] Cf. C. R. Cheney, "The Church and Magna Carta", *Theology*, lxviii (1965), 266-72, at pp. 271-2.

307

occasion and purpose of the Memorandum is not evident. Yet it has its uses for historians. It helps to dispose of any illusion that the baronial party produced a quasi-feudal levy. Also it provides the first means available to scholars of estimating the numerical strength of the party in its London headquarters at some undiscovered time between mid-June and mid-July 1215.

Lambeth Palace Library, MS. 371, fol. 56ᵛ.

¶ Hec sunt nomina baronum qui electi sunt ad observandum omnia que continentur in carta regis secundum demandam baronum.

[column 1] ¶ Comes de Clara cum septemᵃ viginti militibus.
Comes de Arundell'ᵇ cum XL militibus.
Comes Gloucestrie cum CC militibus.
Comes Wintonie cum XL militibus.
Comes Herefordie cum XL militibus.
Comes Rogerus cum quaterviginti militibus.
[column 2] ¶ Comes Robertus cum XXX militibus.
¶ Willelmus Marescallus cum CC militibus.
¶ Robertus filius Walteri cum L militibus.
¶ Gilbertus de Clara cum IIIIˣˣ militibus.
¶ Eustachius de Vescy cum XXX militibus.
¶ Willelmus de Albeny cum X militibus.
¶ Hugo Bigot cum XX militibus.

[fo. 57r column 1] ¶ Willelmus de Munbray cum IIIIˣˣ militibus.
¶ Galfridus de Say cum XV militibus.
¶ Rogerus de Munbrayᶜ cum X militibus.
¶ Willelmus de Huntingfeld' cum VII militibus.
¶ Ricardus de Monte Fichetto cum XXX militibus.
¶ Willelmus Malet cum X militibus.
[column 2] ¶ Robertus de Ros cum XX militibus.
¶ Willelmus de Lanvallay cum XV militibus.
¶ Constabularius Cestrie cum XX militibus.
¶ Ricardus de Percy cum X militibus.
¶ Iohannes filius Roberti cum X militibus.
Maiorᵈ Londonie tradet civitatem Londonie baronibus si forte rex contra cartam suam venire voluerit. Omnes isti comites cum tot militibus et cum communa totius Anglie debent insurgere in regem si forte rex contra cartam suam venire voluerit. Summa militum M C IIIIˣˣ et III.

a septem *MS.*, ? *for* septies.
b Arundell' *MS.*, *for* Albermarlie.
c Munbray *MS.*, ? *for* Munbezon.
d *the remainder, following the entry for William Malet, written across the page to make full lines.*

XIV

ADDITIONAL NOTES

This note pretends to be no more than a warning, not an adequate re-
vision. To my arguments on pp.292-301 for dating the 'Treaty' between the king and Robert fitzWalter and other barons c.17-23 July,
J.C. Holt prefers a date c. 19 June. V.H. Galbraith 'had no hesita-
tion' in attributing the Treaty to 18 June ('A draft of Magna Carta
(1215)', Proc.Brit.Academy liii (1967)354 cf.356 n.2). While admitting the tentative nature of my suggestion, I still think it preferable to earlier datings.

Prof. Fred. Cazel, in a friendly letter, convinced me that my remarks on the feudal quotas were over-hasty and concealed in some
cases a correlation between the quota and the 'servitium debitum' of
a baron. In particular, he pointed out that the quota of William Marshal junior was explicable if William junior already controlled the
knights' fees of his mother. Taking the list as a whole, I still see in
these quotas simply a record of 'knights actually under arms in the
south-east, probably at London' (p.305) at some moment of time in
1215.

P.288 lines 8ff.: Richardson's arguments for an early dating were
already refuted by Ullmann in Speculum historiale (Festschrift J.
Spörl,1960) repr. in his The Church and the Law in the Earlier Middle Ages (Variorum Reprints, 1975) no.XV.

XV

THE CHURCH AND MAGNA CARTA

The studious tourist who enters the British Museum by its main south door has only to pass through the first open door on the right and walk a few yards through the Grenville Library to encounter, in the middle of the next room, a showcase which displays Magna Carta, in draft and in "original", as sealed by King John's orders at Runnymede in June 1215. In the same case he will find a document far more magnificent in format, and more carefully preserved: the solemn bull declaring Magna Carta to be null and void, uttered in August 1215 by Pope Innocent III, the lord of England (for John was then only a vassal-king).

Confronted with Magna Carta and its condemnation side by side, one naturally asks why the Church objected to the Charter. How can the high reputation of Magna Carta in later times be reconciled with this formal repudiation of it by the pope? How do we explain the presence of the bishops who attested the Charter? What did the baronial leader, Robert FitzWalter, mean when he assumed the title of "Marshal of the army of God and Holy Church"? These and other questions crowd upon us as we peer into the show-case. The best way of preparing to find the answers is to reconstruct the political situation in which Magna Carta was framed; and this has been made much easier by the work of historians in the last two generations. But at the very outset of the enquiry is a question of definition: what, in this connexion, do we mean by the Church?

The context is political and constitutional. While every Christian in the thirteenth century was encouraged to think of himself as a member of the *corpus mysticum*, the word *ecclesia* was most often used to mean ecclesiastical authority and the clerical order. In the present context the Church must be taken as the equivalent of the hierarchy: *sacerdotium* in contrast to *regnum*, the Church distinct from the State. It still remains to be determined how far the Church, in this sense, spoke with one voice, and adopted the view of its master, who held the plenitude of power. Did the *ecclesia Anglicana*, as represented by its prelates and dignified clergy, unite to condemn Magna Carta as wholeheartedly as did Pope Innocent III? Nineteenth-century commentators on the Charter were prone to treat it as the precocious act of a politically sentient nation, foreshadowing modern limited monarchy and democratic institutions. This was (as we shall see) bad enough; but Anglican writers of ecclesiastical history went on to erect the banner of the English Church in the "popular" camp. Dean Hook presented a clear division between the king "with the papal party" and "the patriotic forces". He assumed that Archbishop Stephen Langton was "the author of Magna Carta", and that most of the bishops who attested the Charter were "pledged to the same cause as the barons". A generation later came Hook's protégé and son-in-law, Dean W. R. W. Stephens, whose *History of the Church of England, 1066 to 1272* still provides the fullest account of this period. Stephens wrote in 1901: "The time was now come for all the powers in Church and State to unite in resisting the combined efforts of the king and the pope to overthrow the constitutional rights and liberties of the English people." Magna Carta "was the joint product of the three estates of the realm, clergy, baronage, and commons, associated to secure by one grand stroke the rights and liberties of every class in the community".

But the ideas have long since died that Magna Carta was won by a nation in arms against the king and that the freedom granted by the king to the Church was freedom from Rome. In 1215 the upper classes of English society were divided, the lower classes were inarticulate and, for all we know, unconcerned. If the king's character attracted little loyalty towards his person, as contemporaries make plain, there were certainly many experienced and influential men prepared to stand by him through thick and thin. They would not attack the Crown, and they disapproved of the rebels' programme of coercing the king.

For at least six months before Magna Carta was sealed attempts were being made to persuade John to repeat in writing, and enlarge upon, the promises of good government which were embodied in the English coronation oath. The less truculent of the opposition, at least, attached importance to a sworn undertaking of this sort. And during the early part of 1215 the pope was urging moderation. The Church could be trusted to be a force working for peace, so long as matters of faith and ecclesiastical authority were not in question. But likewise the Church would support established authority against innovation, on the same terms. In this case, though Innocent III received envoys of both king and discontented barons, his letters show that he accepted entirely the royal presentation of the case. John's envoys were probably the more skilled in diplomacy, and John had his pensioners in the Curia to work upon the pope. John was a papal vassal and a Crusader, with a double claim to Innocent's protection. So the pope was indulgent to him, threatened the barons with excommunication for disobedience, and rated the archbishop of Canterbury and his suffragans for failing to reconcile the barons with the king. It was a form of intervention which can have done no good; it exacerbated the opposition and prevented effective mediation by the local hierarchy.

The extremists went to war in May and won a quick success in capturing London. Thereafter negotiations with the king, in which the archbishop of Canterbury was the chief go-between, reduced the temperature and produced the semblance of a treaty in Magna Carta. It was a compromise accepted grudgingly by a king of autocratic temper and a group of embittered, belligerent barons. Between them more moderate counsellors had tried to act as peace-makers and to get some generalized guarantees of good government. The middle party included many of the more conservative barons, William Marshal, earl of Pembroke, prominently among them, and the bishops, headed by Langton. Langton's position was unenviable, and his action is so obscure to us today that it hardly deserves the total praise or ridicule that it has received from some modern historians. What is clear is his devotion to certain moral principles of political conduct: that lordship is office, that obedience is due to powers ordained by God. But he may not have been very adept at turning people to his point of view. According to a dictum reported from his days as a professor at Paris, he held that a man must obey any order of his king if it followed a judgment of the king's court. Even if it were unjust, it must be obeyed. But if an unjust order proceeded from the king's mere will, unsupported by the sanction of his court, it might be resisted. Now in the early part of 1215, when Langton indubitably was involved in negotiations between the dissident barons and the king, John on several occasions offered his opponents the judgment of his court. Was this the fruit of Langton's preaching? And if so, what was Langton's view of the matter when the rebels rejected the offers? With a realization that reforms were needed and with a strong sense of order in secular and ecclesiastical government, he must have been divided in his sympathies and he may well have vacillated. If he had to take a side, it had to be the king's side.

In the preamble to Magna Carta the king declares that he has granted the Charter on the advice of twenty-six named prelates, earls, and barons, and others of his subjects. It can be assumed that the names include none of those in open revolt. The first nine to be named are archbishops and bishops. Langton heads the list, as we should expect from his position as archbishop of Canterbury, traditionally the first counsellor of the king, and from his activities as intermediary in the preceding months. The eight other bishops who are named were without exception men who at some time or another had served the king in chamber, chancery, exchequer, or bench, and whose promotion to the episcopate had taken place with royal favour. There were, it is true, seven other English and Welsh bishops without close associations with the government, whose names are missing from this list; but of these only one can be definitely placed in the rebel camp: Giles de Braose, bishop of Hereford. With Braose stood a few dignified clerics connected with him or with Robert FitzWalter, and later events suggest that they were supported by various members of the chapter of St Paul's. Beyond this the evidence does not go. We conclude that the rebels had no very important following among the clergy, or we should have heard more about it.

If the moderates succeeded in coaxing King John and the rebel barons to come to Runnymede, they were less successful in controlling the extremists at the conference-table. Magna Carta, as it emerged from these deliberations, was not merely of mixed parentage: it was a document of anomalous form, with a sanction written into it which any moderate royalist must have condemned. The broad features of the Charter's contents can be briefly sketched. It settled a number of disputed points of law and feudal custom; it provided for new machinery of consultation and more frequent sessions of royal courts; it promised immediate redress of individuals' grievances respecting hostages and castles. It also contained two striking clauses, which in general terms promised (cl. 39) to every man legal trial, or judgment, by his peers or by the law of the land, and promised (cl. 40) that justice should not be sold or denied or delayed to anyone. Some have thought it unhistorical to attach much contemporary significance to these two clauses; but the more we realize that the makers of Magna Carta were a mixed bag of rebels, royalists, and the uncommitted, and that the ideas contained in clauses 39 and 40 had a precise relevance to common abuses of the time, the more their constitutional importance becomes evident. The sting of the Charter lay in its tail, the sanction or security provided by clause 61. This set up a standing committee of twenty-five barons (most, if not all, of the rebel party) to supervise the executive government and to coerce the king and his ministers if they acted in defiance of his undertakings. Clause 61 showed the strength of the baronial opposition. The extremists would not be satisfied with a bundle of miscellaneous promises of reform without the power to override a king they distrusted. But such a concession as this was a denial of royal authority as it was commonly conceived. On this rock the compromise foundered.

The influence of the Church upon the terms of Magna Carta must ultimately have resolved itself into the influence of individual prelates, bringing their arguments to bear on the deliberations of king and barons. What, if anything, did this amount to? It has been possible, without gross distortion, to describe the main features of the Charter without mentioning any clause which particularly benefited the Church. It is time to see what regard was paid to the Church's interests. The Church looms largest in the preamble and the first provision of the Charter. Interestingly enough, these had no counterpart in the "Articles of the Barons", which provided a draft for nearly all the rest of the Charter (nor in the "Unknown Charter of Liberties", which represents some earlier stage of drafting). It looks as though these brave words on behalf of the Church were something of an afterthought, which we may attribute to last-minute influence exercised by Langton and the bishops. Not that any of the parties concerned were likely to find these words exceptionable. They had only to be proposed and they would be adopted. All could approve of the exaltation of Mother Church, coupled with the honour due to God, as an object of the Charter, each interpreting the phrase as he chose. As for the promise of freedom to the English Church (cl. 1), this did not obviously commit the king to anything more than he had already conceded in the charter for free election of bishops and abbots. Apart from this concession the Charter safeguarded the ecclesiastical benefices of clerks fined for personal offences (cl. 22) and the clergy's customary control over the property of intestates (cl. 27). That is all. Had ecclesiastical influence weighed heavily upon the draftsmen of the Charter, surely some of the activities of the king's court distasteful to churchmen or contrary to canon law would have left their mark? In a more general way the Church stood behind the principle implicit in the Charter that the king was below the law, that peace and justice are the objects of civil government. The very wording of cl. 40 recalls words which Langton had used for the reform of ecclesiastical courts in his diocesan statutes of 1213–14; but this does not help very much. *Ius suum cuique* was a tag of Roman civil law; and complaints about the sale and delaying of justice are commonplaces in every age.

While it is probable that the bishops concerned with Magna Carta welcomed the idea of a virtual renewal of the king's coronation oath and of a clarification of certain points of law and custom, they must have seen the final draft with misgivings. The security clause, from their point of view, was a fatal flaw. Like the pope they believed in monarchical government in principle, and in practice many of them were committed to the government of King John. Four out of nine bishops named in the Charter had served the excommunicate king continuously during Langton's exile. But the security clause was a denial of normal kingly rights. This they could not be expected to approve. Moreover, approval or no approval, they could not expect the arrangement to lead to a lasting peace. The more clear-sighted of them must have attended the king at Runnymede with heavy hearts. This Charter would soon not be worth the parchment it was written on.

The predicament of the bishops is seen in a comparison of the concluding parts of the "Articles of the Barons" and of the Charter. The Articles proposed that the archbishops and bishops and the papal nuncio should give security that the king would not obtain revocation or diminution of his undertakings from the pope. This was virtually an admission that the proposals were unacceptable to the king **and** that he was only brought to accept them under duress. The final clause of the Charter shows that the prelates would not do what was asked of them. In other words, they would (and could) do nothing in derogation of the pope's right to entertain King John's complaint. The complaint was made and the pope condemned Magna Carta, condemned it on the grounds that it had been extorted from the king "by such violence and fear as might affect the most courageous of men, ... lessening unduly and impairing his rights and dignity".

In doing this Pope Innocent III acted according to recognized principles of justice and rules of law. In canon law a solemn oath such as John had sworn, to observe the terms of the Charter, was binding on condition that the oath had not been extorted by undue force. But the canonists, following in this the principles and the very words of Roman civil law, admitted the harsh facts of a violent age. There was no sanctity in an oath which was made under the pressure of extreme fear. The currency of oaths would be debased if the element of free will was removed. So the jurists devoted much time to estimating how much force and fear were necessary to invalidate an oath. In John's case, once he raised the question in Rome the issue can scarcely have been in doubt. The pope did not need to evaluate each clause of the Charter or consider whether John's vassalage to the Apostolic See was endangered by it. He could easily accept the king's account of how he had offered redress of grievances to his barons, how the English bishops had let him down, and how the barons had forced him to swear to submit to twenty-five over-kings of their own choice.

The pope's condemnation of Magna Carta, addressed to all Christ's faithful, can hardly have been published in England before the end of September. It only confirmed the nullity of a treaty which had already come to grief. The baronial committee had tried to impose its will on the king, civil war had been resumed. Langton, who (as Sidney Painter wrote) "could neither persuade John to accept the Charter sincerely and try to make it work nor induce the barons to be reasonable in their demands for personal benefits", was spared the heart-rending decision of taking sides at this stage. For in September he had been suspended from office by the pope's delegates, because he refused to excommunicate the rebels, and now, like most of his episcopal colleagues, he was on his way to Rome for the General Council, due to begin on 1st November. No one at that time can have doubted that Magna Carta was dead, without the benefit of priests to say its obsequies. No one could guess what lay ahead.

Within little more than a year King John himself was dead, and the civil war was intensified by the claim to the throne of Prince Louis of France. The regency government of John's nine-year-old son, Henry, was moved to attract support with a manifesto. It chose to do so by turning back to the rejected Magna Carta: not to the whole document, but to those parts which were compatible with traditional views of royal rights. The offensive security clause was now as unnecessary as it was distasteful to them. A new Magna Carta was made out of the old, one which the papal legate and the bishop of Winchester, as members of the regency council, could sanction on behalf of the Church. This was twice renewed, in 1217 and 1225, with minor alterations. What is more, the new Magna Carta received papal confirmation from Pope Honorius III. That marked no inconsistency in papal policy. The new charters were freely granted by the government and did not derogate from royal dignity. And so the Church could in the long run claim that it contributed to put Magna Carta on the statute book and to support those principles of government which later generations read into it.

This identification of the Church with what one may call lay demands for the rule of law (aided, no doubt, by the grant of freedom for the Church written into all versions of the Charter) was confirmed by Stephen Langton in 1225. Then, with the reissue of the Charter as the first solemn act of Henry III's coming of age, the prelates solemnly excommunicated all who infringed its terms. Throughout the thirteenth century this precedent was repeatedly followed. An elaborate ceremony in Westminster Hall on 13 May 1253 was particularly notable; the pope confirmed the sentence of the prelates, and it was copied into many manuscripts of English statutes in the later Middle Ages. Finally, in 1297, an understanding between the lay magnates and Archbishop Robert Winchelsey procured from Edward I a confirmation of Henry III's Magna Carta and his *Carta de Foresta*, together with some supplementary promises. This *Confirmatio Cartarum* was also fortified with sentences of excommunication against those who infringed the king's grant. As in John's day, so in the time of his grandson, a grant had been wrung from the king in a moment of political crisis. History repeated itself to the extent that eight years later Edward I prevailed upon a complaisant pope to release him from his sworn oath, on the grounds that he had granted the *Confirmatio* under duress, *plus coactus quam voluntarius*. But by then there was no question of reversing a constitutional trend now nearly a century old. Magna Carta had come to stay, and the English hierarchy was committed to safeguarding it.

XVI

ILLUMINATED COLLECTIVE INDULGENCES FROM AVIGNON

Much has been written in the last half-century about collective letters of indulgence, but the interest of this category of document is not exhausted. Père Hippolyte Delehaye indicated long ago what evidence they provide for obscure bishops *in partibus infidelium* and in minor Italian and Dalmatian sees in the fourteenth century.[1] While art-historians have been attracted by the subject,[2] the chief manuals of palaeography and diplomatic overlook it.[3] Already in 1925 Joseph Rest drew attention to this form of indulgence in relation to the Avignonese papacy and the kind of scribe and script employed there, and the persons engaged in procuring the documents;[4] but they find no place in Bernard Guillemain's work on *La cour pontificale d'Avignon* (1962). Hitherto the bulk of material for this study has been found in Germany and neighbouring regions. When in 1963 Enid Donkin brought to light a fragment of an illuminated col-

---

[1] H. Delehaye, "Les lettres d'indulgence collectives", *Analecta Bollandiana*, xliv-xlvi (1926-8).

[2] O. Homburger and C. Von Steiger, "Zwei illuminierte Avignoneser Ablassbriefe in Bern", *Zeitschr. für Schweizerische Archäologie und Kunstgeschichte,* xvii (1957), 134-58 and plates 39-50; D. Radocsay, "Ueber einige illuminierte Urkunden", *Acta Historiae Artium* (Budapest), xvii (1971), 31-61. Cf. W. Erben, "Bemalte Bittschriften und Ablassurkunden", *Archiv für Urkundenforschung,* viii (1923), 160-88.

[3] A laudable exception is Paulus Rabikauskas, *Diplomatica pontificia: praelectionum lineamenta* (3rd edn., Rome, Pont. Univ. Greg., 1970), Appendix II, pp. 146-7. A. de Boüard, *Manuel de Diplomatique,* i (1929), 349 only cites these indulgences as examples of multiple sealing. The usual form is analysed by Von Steiger, loc. cit., p. 136: hereafter *ZSAK*.

[4] J. Rest, "Illuminierte Ablassurkunden aus Rom und Avignon aus der Zeit von 1282-1364", *Festgabe... Heinrich Finke dargebracht* (Münster, 1925), pp. 147-68.

354

lective indulgence destined for English recipients, 1344-5, this appeared to be the only example in England.[5] The documents of 1328, 1345, and 1354 printed below comprise the only complete Avignonese indulgences in England known to me.[6] As documents produced on the margin of the Curia, they may merit the attention of the distinguished expert in whose honour this volume has been composed.

The institution of indulgences in the Catholic Church was already sufficiently developed by the time of the Fourth Lateran Council to produce decrees which laid down a standard formula and limited the benefits of episcopal indulgence (*Extra*, 5.38.14), and which forbade abbots to usurp this function of bishops (*Extra*, 5.31.12). After 1215, as before, it was not unusual for more than one bishop to grant an indulgence on the same occasion for the same purpose. Thus, at the English parliament assembled at Kenilworth in 1266 three bishops each remitted twenty days of penance, and one remitted fifteen days, for those who prayed for the soul of Bishop Henry of Lincoln or helped his cathedral church, and the same object attracted indulgences from five more bishops, amounting to 180 days' remission.[7] The extent of the benefit to penitents in such cases worried the theologians and canonists. The Lateran Council had laid down limits, and these were transgressed if a single penitent could benefit from a multiplicity of indulgences. Legally a bishop could only grant indulgences to persons within his own jurisdiction or must secure confirmation by the diocesan of an indulgence attached to a particular place. Late in the thirteenth century Hostiensis favoured a rigorous application of the Lateran decree, but he admitted that this was customarily transgressed every day.[8]

---

[5] Enid M. Donkin, "A collective letter of indulgence for an English beneficiary", *Scriptorium*, xvii (1963), 316-323.

[6] Two badly damaged indulgences for chapels in Diss and Yarmouth (Norfolk) respectively, both dated 1300, are in London, P.R.O., E 135/6/39 and E 135/18/21.

[7] *Registrum antiquissimum of the cathedral church of Lincoln*, ii (Lincoln Record Soc., xxviii, 1933, ed. C. W. Foster), 123-9. Other indulgences given on the same occasion are illegible (ibid., pp. 129-30).

[8] *Summa aurea*, lib. v de remissionibus §§ 5, 6 (ed. Lyon, 1531, fo. 288[r.v]). Cf. Delehaye, *An. Boll.*, xlv. 323-4, xlvi. 339-41 on complaints of laxity.

Out of this custom grew the practice of framing a single letter in which a group of bishops collectively granted their indulgences. Whatever the strict doctrine, it was not to be expected, as Delehaye points out,[9] that bishops would get together simply to grant a favour which anyone of them could have bestowed alone. So the formula of the collective letters, which had not originally put the matter beyond doubt, came to be "*singuli nostrum* quadraginta dies indulgentiarum ... relaxamus*". And we may be sure that limitation to the subjects of the grantors was disregarded, if not in the early days of the practice, at least in the fourteenth century, when indulgences were granted by groups of bishops who exercised no effective jurisdiction. As early as 16 February 1287 a collective letter was given by twelve bishops at St Peter's, Rome,[10] and Leon Kern discovered no less than twenty-five issued by the German bishops in council at Würzburg in 1287.[11] To judge by the list which Delehaye compiled, the practice increased enormously during the next fifty years, and the majority of such indulgences were issued in or near the papal court. A fine example was produced at Rome in 1288 for the church of Veroli in which pride of place went to a visitor from the Orient, Rabban Sauma, here described as "Barbazoma Thartarus orientalis [episcopus]".[12] The height of popularity of these grants was reached in the pontificate of Clement VI, the period of the Hopton document printed here.

The system of indulgences was always notoriously open to abuse, and collective indulgences were exposed to one particular abuse which we can infer from the names of the grantors. In the Avignonese period, the groups of bishops whose seals are set to these documents are almost all the occupants or titular occupants (one cannot say "would-be" occupants) of sees in which they did

---

[9] *An. Boll.*, xlv. 104.

[10] Ibid., xliv. 351-2.

[11] L. Kern, "A propos des lettres d'indulgence collectives concedées au concile de Wurzbourg de 1287", *Schweiz. Beiträge zur allgem. Geschichte*, xiii (1955), 111-29. Cf. C. J. Hefele-H. Leclercq, *Histoire des Conciles*, VI.i (1914), 307-14.

[12] M. H. Laurent, "Rabban Sauma, ambassadeur de l'Il-Khan Argoun, et la cathédrale de Veroli (1288)", *Mélanges d'Archéologie et de l'Histoire*, lxx (1958), 331-65.

not reside. They are all found together at Avignon over long periods of time. We can hardly doubt that fees were charged for the favours of these "displaced persons" which made welcome additions to their precarious revenues. We may also suspect frauds in which they were not personally concerned.[13] The bishops who flocked to the neighbourhood of the Curia at all times provided a counter-attraction for those who had come to petition for papal indulgences. Groups of bishops would grant an indulgence for a total of days far in excess of what could be hoped for from the Holy Father. Nor did the bishops often insert the restrictive clause found in many papal indulgences: "presentibus post decennium minime valituris". Probably, too, their indulgence cost less than the papal chancery instrument. It is observable that the indulgences printed below are not matched by any enregistered petitions or indulgences from the pope; and this would seem to be true of many other collective letters. There is a suggestion of "cut-price" practice in the endorsement on a collective indulgence of 1342: "Due marce de consuetudine deberentur, sed quidquid vestre paternitati placuerit, ad ea paratus sum stare contentus."[14] Presumably some jobber in the Curia undertook to get an indulgence for his client, made arrangements with a scribe and an illuminator, and paid bishops or their secretaries for the authentication by seal. This may explain the presence of names of bishops with titles of bishoprics which they had lost through resignation or deprivation. If so, although the bishop lost his see, his seal was not always destroyed in conformity with the approved custom.[15] On an indulgence for Königsfelden of 6 September 1329 there figure simultaneously two bishops of Sulcis, in Sardinia, one of whom, Boniface, had been replaced by the other, Angelus, in 1325. Boniface remained about the Curia after 1325, continuing to share in the granting of indulgences under the title of Sulcis (as in the Wombridge specimen below), until in 1332 he received the see of Krbava

[13] Delehaye, An. Boll., xlvi. 305-7.
[14] Quoted, J. Rest, loc. cit., p. 153. Even though the note does not make clear whose fee was in question, the inference holds that there was a standard rate and that there was room for bargaining.
[15] W. Ewald, Siegelkunde (1914), pp. 107-11; C. R. Cheney, English Bishops' Chanceries 1100-1250 (Manchester, 1950), p. 50.

in Dalmatia.[16]   What is more, in several indulgences of 1332-3 Boniface figures twice, as bishop both of Sulcis and Krbava.[17] These collective indulgences generally add a proviso: "dummodo diocesani voluntas ad id accesserit et consensus", so as to avoid the appearance of usurping the rights of the ordinary. Whether this clause normally led to formal confirmation by the diocesan is doubtful. A collective indulgence granted by twelve bishops at Rome in 1300 in favour of the chapel of the Blessed Virgin Mary in the parish of Yarmouth has a note written in a small English charter-hand in the top margin: "Nos pater I. permissione divina Norwycensis episcopus has indulgencias infrascriptas... quantum in nobis est ratificamus... roboramus.   Dat' apud Mildenhall iii id. Maii a.d. m° ccc^{mo} primo et consecracionis nostre secundo."[18]   On an indulgence for a hospital at Bern, dated at Avignon 22 October 1335, the bishop of Lausanne used his seal to attach a separate certificate of approval more than four years later.[19]   None of the three indulgences printed below show any sign of endorsement or appendage for this purpose.

Although these indulgences were not official products of the papal chancery or of any other curial office, their features suggest a fairly high degree of organization. The papacy provided enough business for draftsmen, scribes, and illuminators to ensure the presence at Avignon of many professionals, who were in the Curia but not of it.[20]   Draftsmen of papal petitions would easily turn

---

[16] *ZSAK*, p. 138 n. 36 and pl. 39. Cf. *An. Boll.*, xlvi. 295 and C. Eubel, *Hierarchia Catholica*, i (2nd edn., Münster, 1913), 468 n. 5. As bishop of Krbava he visited England, where he acted for the busy Richard de Bury, bishop of Durham, in 1338 and 1341 (*Registrum palatinum dunelmense*, ed. T. D. Hardy (Rolls series, 1873-5), iii. 106, 194, 203, 216).

[17] *ZSAK*, pl. 44-6 and *An. Boll.*, xliv. 368, xlvi. 295.

[18] London, P.R.O., E 135/18/21. The document is too much damaged and faded to show whether the bishop's seal was attached. Dr David M. Smith kindly calls my attention to the confirmation by the archbishop of York on 25 Aug. 1301 of two indulgences for the chapel of St Helen, Driffield, granted (i) by Peter archbishop of Arborea and other bishops, Orvieto, 1291 and (ii) by John archbishop of Lund, primate of Sweden, and other bishops, Rome, St Peter's, 1297. York, Borthwick Institute, Reg. T. Corbridge fo. 6^v (formerly fo. iv^v), incompletely summarized in the printed register.

[19] *ZSAK*, pl. 40. Other cases of delay are noted by Rest, loc. cit., note 20.

[20] Such a one was the married clerk from the diocese of Coutances, with a wife and marriageable daughter on his hands, who on 25 Feb. 1345 petitioned Clement VI. He declares that, with little profit and much labour, he has written

their hands to collective indulgences, notarial licences from imperial delegates,[21] and other private business. So the indulgences become as thoroughly standardized as the *litterae gratiosae* prepared in the chancery. "Universis sancte matris ecclesie filiis ad quos presentes littere pervenerint" becomes the invariable address.[22] One of the arengas (*inc.* "Pia mater ecclesia") occurs in sixteen collective letters for Germany between 1326 and 1337,[23] while two other arengas often used by groups of bishops come straight out of chancery formularies.[24] The formulas of the text recur, over the years, with astonishing regularity. The physical features of originals likewise point to shop-work and commercial production. In a wide-ranging essay Otto Homburger studied the illuminations which adorn many of these documents, and showed affinities, both in style and motif, in indulgences granted at Avignon by different groups of bishops for different recipients.[25] Joseph Rest noted that (as with papal indulgences and Mendicants' letters of fraternity in the fifteenth century) collective indulgences were sometimes prepared with blank spaces, so that names could be inserted as required.[26]

and still writes "in curia sanctitatis vestre prope vestrum sacrum palacium apostolicum Avinione", and out of reverence and respect for his holiness, he always decorates the petitions he writes with roses and lilies. He asks the pope to license him as a notary public (P. M. Baumgarten, *Von der apostolischen Kanzlei* (Köln, 1908), p. 22). The rose was the badge of Clement's family, the lily the badge of France.

[21] C. R. Cheney, *Notaries public in England in the Thirteenth and Fourteenth Centuries* (Oxford, 1972), pp. 83, 87, 158.

[22] Papal letters patent generally began, after the pope's title, with "Universis Christi fidelibus presentes litteras (*or* hanc paginam) inspecturis".

[23] *ZSAK*, pl. 42-7.

[24] "Quoniam ut ait apostolus" (ibid., pl. 49, 20 Aug. 1333) as in IV Lateran Council c. 62. "Splendor paterne glorie" (ibid., pl. 40, 22 Oct. 1335; *Scriptorium*, xvii. 318*a*, 1344-5; below, p. 368, 18 Dec. 1345; *Registres de Benoit XII*, ed. J. M. Vidal (Paris, 1903-11), no. 2200, 9 Feb. 1335), is in the fourteenth-century chancery formulary in M. Tangl, *Die päpstlichen Kanzleiordnungen* (Innsbruck, 1894), p. 330. It had been used in the papal chancery as early as 1256 (P.R.O., S.C. 7/2/9). Cf. *An. Boll.*, xlvi. 313.

[25] Above. note 2.

[26] Loc. cit., pp. 147, 156, and see *ZSAK*, pp. 135, 154 n. 49. For the blank-form letters of fraternity see W. G. Clark-Maxwell, "Some letters of confraternity", *Archaeologia*, lxxv (1925), 19-60, lxxix (1929), 179-216, *passim*. In *Journal of Eccles. History*, xviii (1967), 177-8 I raised the question whether

XVI

The three documents printed below, of 1328, 1345, and 1354, provide good examples of episcopal lists, introducing about two dozen of those bishops who were habitually involved in the business. This business, as Delehaye points out, attracted men unknown except as grantors of indulgences, and their dioceses are among those which have little or no history, even when they can be identified. Their identification is made harder by the ignorance and indifference of scribes to whom the place-names were totally unfamiliar [27] For convenience, the names in these three documents are assembled and, so far as possible, identified in the Appendix below. A few names which present special interest are noted here. The earliest list, from Wombridge, includes Boniface, bishop of Sulcis, who is using this title long after he had been deprived of the see. [28] In the Hopton indulgence of 1345 we meet with Anancius, whose see of Xanthia figures in the Roman *provinciale* as the sole suffragan under *archiepiscopatus Messinopolitanus.* [29] But neither the province nor the diocese seems to be identifiable, and they may have been no more than names in the void when Anancius became bishop. Wherever his see lay, Avignon was his home for many years. He added his seal in indulgences granted there between 1342 and 1354 [30]. Manfred of Ajaccio is, by contrast, bishop of a recognizable see. But if Eubel is correct, the death of Manfred left Ajaccio vacant by 20 June 1345, six months before the date of this letter. So we must reckon with the possibility that his name and seal were being used by some unauthorized person after he died. Like Manfred, Gregory of Oppido appeared as signatory of an indulgence after the date of his presumed death. [31] Peter of Cagli was deprived of his see as early as 1319; but he retired to Avignon and continued to use his title for thirty

some *privilegia communia* of Innocent III for the Cistercians might have been originally written with space for inserting the name of a particular house. In the collective indulgence, unlike other types of grant, the names of the grantors are sometimes later insertions.

[27] See *An. Boll.*, xlv. 291 and the following list of bishops, pp. 300-5.

[28] Above, p. 356.

[29] *Al.* Messipolitanus: Tangl, *Kanzleiordnungen*, p. 29.

[30] *An. Boll.*, xliv. 372, 374, xlvi. 296; H. Wartmann, *Urkundenbuch der Abtei Sanct Gallen*, iii (1882), 594 no. 1469, 25 Jan. 1350.

[31] Wartmann, loc. cit. Eubel records his death before 18 May 1349.

360

years.[32] Thomas of Knin was another bishop who used his title after resignation.[33]

The twelve signatories of the Smithfield indulgence present their share of problems. The name of Dyrlaus Clatensis is recorded much later in the century as a suffragan of Bratislava, but where his titular see was located is a mystery. Probably the scribe of this indulgence wrote *Clat'* in error for *Elat'*, as he wrote *Carminen'* for *Caminen'*. For the title of Galterus Nicopolensis we have the choice of three episcopal sees, all named Nicopolis.

For the rest, nearly every one of these prelates is recorded at Avignon over a period of years. It is unlikely that those who nominally ruled the dioceses in the Mediterranean islands, southern Italy, Dalmatia, Armenia, and Turkestan ever visited their sees. They were probably appointed at Avignon and at Avignon they died. None of them seems to hold an official post in the Curia or share in business conducted by curial officials, as recorded in the papal registers. Those who commonly lent their names to the traffic in indulgences were not men of weight or high repute. Henry Lubicensis and John Imelacensis were prelates of a rather different sort; but both of them belonged to the floating population of Avignon for some years. Henry of Bocholte had been canonically elected to Lübeck and conse-crated in the absence of the archbishop of Bremen from the metropolitan see. His archbishop contested his appointment and started a lawsuit which took the bishop-elect Henry to the Curia in 1320 and detained him there for more than seven years. Eventually he secured confirmation from John XXII on 21 August 1327. We are told that he had spent 7000 florins in the process, and that his cameral dues amounted to 1400 florins. It may be that he could not return home until he had settled his debts: this would explain his presence at the Curia as late as 25 January 1328, when his name appeared on the Wombridge indulgence. He had already put his name to an indulgence before his confir-mation.[34] The Irishman John Esmond had been elected and

[32] Eubel, i. 158 n. 5.

[33] *An. Boll.*, xlvi. 296, 304. His name figures on an indulgence of 1350 (Wartmann, loc. cit.). He had granted an indulgence at Avignon as early as 1335 (*ZSAK*, p. 141 n. 53). According to Eubel (pp. 485-6) he resigned before 1344.

[34] On 25 April 1326 (Mon. Germ. Hist. *Scriptores*, xxv (1880), 493; Eubel, i. 311 n. 2).

consecrated bishop of Emly in 1349. But this election was quashed. When Bishop John put his name on the Smithfield indulgence in 1354 he had no right to the title. He was probably hanging about the Curia in hope of the provision to Emly which eventually issued on 28 February 1356. [35]

The uncertainty about the production of these documents is matched by the obscurity which surrounds their discontinuance. One is tempted to believe that this was a curial reform of Urban V, for the flow of collective indulgences from the papal city diminished and almost dried up in the 1360 s. [36] The degree of responsibility of the earlier Avignonese popes for the efflorescence of these documents was stated in delicately balanced terms by Hippolyte Delehaye, and one cannot do better than quote him. These collective indulgences, he says, " ne sortent pas, il est vrai, de la chancellerie pontificale, et on n'a aucune raison d'affirmer que les papes aient expressément approuvé ou positivement encouragé le système des lettres collectives.   On peut même dire qu'ils n'ont guère surveillé de bien près cette pratique. Mais il est difficile de penser qu'elle ait pu s'établir et durer à l'ombre du trône pontifical sans une tolérance qui ressemble beaucoup à l'approbation tacite.   C'est ainsi qu'un usage introduit subrepticement peut se dépouiller, par le silence de l'autorité, de son vice d'origine. " [37]

It is now time to describe the three documents in turn.

I. *Indulgence for Wombridge Priory, 12 January 1328.*

London, Brit. Mus. ms. Egerton 3712 fo. 89v (formerly 92v). [38] In a late fifteenth-century cartulary of the small Augustinian house of Wombridge, co. Salop.   The scribe copied this after a series

---

[35] He was still at Avignon and granted an indulgence on 17 Oct. 1356 (Eubel, i. 283 n. 4).

[36] *An. Boll.,* xlv. 325-6. Towards the middle of the fifteenth century groups of cardinals resident in the Curia revived the practice (ibid., and D. Radocsay, loc. cit., pp. 43, 58-9).   I have noted two examples in England of these later collective indulgences by cardinals: Maidstone, Kent Archives Office, P R C 49, 17 June 1496, and London, P.R.O., Court of Wards 2/178/1, 1503 (fragment only).

[37] *An. Boll.,* xlvi. 311-2.

[38] A badly garbled abstract of the document is printed in a calendar of the cartulary, *Trans. of the Shropshire Archaeological Soc.,* 2nd series vii (1900), 218-9.

of papal bulls for his house, of which the privileges are given *copies figurées.* In copying the indulgence he was at pains to imitate the miniature in the initial *U* and to indicate the ornate character of the first line. Crude though his drawing is, the scribe is clearly reproducing the head of Christ, with three pointed strands of a beard and side-locks, as it is to be seen on certain original indulgences from Avignon in 1326-1327. They are connected by Otto Homburger with celebrated legendary portraits of Christ. Like them, the Wombridge copy shows hair, eyes, nose, and mouth, within a nimbus, and nothing else.[39]

The text has a few misreadings of which one – the faulty date – may be explained by a damaged original. The scribe read the initial of Guillelmus Tergestinensis as a *B*, perhaps because, as an Englishman, he did not recognize *Guill'* to be the equivalent of *Will'*. His list of bishops is so short as to arouse the suspicion that he curtailed it.

The formulas of the indulgence do not depart significantly from those of other collective indulgences of the fourteenth century for visitors to churches and chapels. Following a common practice when a church was dedicated to St. Mary, the preamble invokes the Virgin. Prayers are solicited for a prior and canon of Wombridge and specified layfolk, who presumably include the founder of the new chapel.[40] The list of saints' days to which the indulgence applies is, by fourteenth-century standards, short. Longer lists will be found in documents II and III.

Universis sancte[a] matris ecclesie filiis ad quos presentes littere pervenerint, nos miseracione divina Madius Demitensis episcopus, Iohannes Ameliensis episcopus, Guillelmus[b] Tergestinensis episcopus, Rodulphus Sinquensis episcopus, Bonifacius Sulcitanus episcopus, et Heynricus Lubicensis episcopus salutem in domino sempiternam. Serena virgo, mater plena deliciis, dulcis dei genetrix salvatoris, humanarum laudum preconiis digne meruit venerari,[c] que solem iusticie dominum nostrum Iesum Christum mundo edidit salvatorem, de cuius uberum dulcedine egris medicina languentibus solamen reis culpe remissio cunctis

---

[a] *ms.* sante [b] *ms.* Buill' [c] *ms.* venerati

---

[39] *ZSAK*, pp. 145-6, 149-50, and pl. 47 nos. 19-21. The general pattern of the Wombridge copy resembles no. 21.

[40] Philip ceased to be prior in 1321. Canon Richard de Kembricton (Kemberton) may be the son of Richard and Alice Gregory who were buried at Kemberton.

ipsius implorantibus patrocinium misericordie rivulus noscitur emanare. Cupientes igitur ut ecclesia et nova capella monasterii sancte Marie et sancti Leonardi de Wombrugg' ordinis sancti Augustini Coventrensis et Lichefeldensis diocesis congruis honoribus frequententur et a Christi fidelibus iugiter venerentur, omnibus vere penitentibus et confessis qui ad dictam ecclesiam sive ad dictam capellam [fo. 90ʳ] in omnibus et singulis festivitatibus gloriosissime virginis Marie antedicte et in festis Natalis et Translacionis sancti Leonardi antedicti et in dedicacione ipsius ecclesie ac in festo Corporis Christi, et per octavas dictarum festivitatum causa devocionis, oracionis, aut peregrinacionis accesserint seu qui missis, predicacionibus, matutinis, vesperis, aut aliis quibuscumque divinis officiis ibidem interfuerint, seu qui Corpus Christi aut oleum sacrum dum infirmis portentur secuti fuerint, vel in serotina ᵈ pulsacione⁴⁰ᴬ secundum modum curie Romane flexis genibus ter Ave Maria dixerint, aut qui cimiterium eiusdem ecclesie pro animabus corporum inibi iacencium exorando circuerint, necnon qui ad fabricam, luminaria, ornamenta, aut quevis alia dicte ecclesie sive dicte capelle necessaria manus porrexerint adiutrices vel qui in eorum testamentis aut extra aurum, argentum, vestimentum, pallium, vel aliquod aliud ornamentum ecclesiasticum, aut aliqua alia caritativa subsidia dicte ecclesie sive dicte capelle donaverint, legaverint, aut donari vel legari procuraverint, et qui animabus Philippi quondam prioris dicti monasterii, Ricardi de Kembricton' canonici eiusdem monasterii, Ricardi Gregori et Alicie uxoris sue liberorumque suorum, quorum corpora in cimiterio de Kembricton' requiescunt humata, et omnium fidelium defunctorum, oracionem dominicam cum salutacione angelica pia mente dixerint, quocienscumque premissa vel aliquid premissorum devote fecerint, de omnipotentis dei misericordia et beatorum Petri et Pauli apostolorum eius auctoritate confisi, singuli nostrum quadraginta dies indulgentiarum de iniunctis eis penitenciis misericorditer in domino relaxamus, dummodo diocesani voluntas ad id accesserit et consensus. In cuius rei testimonium presentes litteras sigillorum nostrorum iussimus appensione muniri. Dat' Avinion' xxv die mensis Ianuarii anno domini mᵒ cccᵐᵒ xxviii et pontificatus domini Iohannis pape xxiiᵉ anno duodecimo ᶠ.

II. *Indulgence for the chapel of Hopton Cangeford, 18 December 1345.*

Chelmsford, Essex Record Office, D/DW T I/21.⁴¹

A parchment sheet 662 mm. broad × 470 mm. high + 50 mm. fold. Space occupied by text, 492 × 320 mm.

ᵈ *ms.* seroturea   ᵉ *ms.* xii   ᶠ *ms.* duodecimo *follows* Avinion'.

⁴⁰ᴬ "serotina pulsacione": for this phrase see *An. Boll.,* xlvi. 323-4.

⁴¹ Deposited in E.R.O. in 1949 as part of the Wythes family archives. The manor and advowson of Hopton Cangeford, otherwise Hopton-in-the-Hole, co.

Space occupied by initial *U*, with Christ blessing, 156 × 162 mm. Ruling in drypoint, to limit top as well as bottom of each line of lettering. Space between lines of text, 11 mm.

Under fold, centred: "Anno creatoris caeli ac terrae 1355" in a sixteenth-century hand. The same hand may have re-touched the words "Beate Margarete" in line 7, to convert the final *e* into *æ*, and made short illegible notes in the righthand margin. Endorsement: "19 Ed. 3 anno domni 1345... 17 Dec. 1631 inst. 28 (?) ? dies post (?) ", in a seventeenth-century hand.

On the fold holes for nine seal-cords; six hemp cords remain, two natural-coloured, four green; small fragments of red wax remain on three.

The four corners of the document are pierced, and the parchment around the upper holes appears to have been stretched, as if suspended from these points.

Script and decoration call for more expert analysis than the present writer can give. I confine myself to a description in general terms, and refer the reader to the facsimile plate. The script is markedly different from the chancery script of papal privileges of the period with which, on account of its origin, as well as of its size and pompous format, the indulgence invites comparison. It is a spacious bookhand, showing marked Italian features, as do some of the Avignon books of this age.[42] It resembles the writing of the somewhat earlier Bern indulgences illustrated by Homburger and the contemporary Gatwick fragment,[43] but the letters are less condensed and more suitable for public display, bold and clear, but no masterpiece of calligraphy. This indulgence, though large, is not as large as some. The Bern indulgence of 6 September 1329 measures no less that 835 × 605 mm.; only the very largest products of the papal chancery approach

Salop, apparently belonged to the Hopton family until the mid seventeenth century. By 1709 it was in the hands of the Conyers family. The property was sold in 1727; but this document must have remained with the Conyers family who later acquired the Copped Hall and Epping estates. These passed in 1870 to the Wythes family. I am obliged for this information to Miss N. Briggs of the E.R.O., and acknowledge with thanks the Archivist's permission to reproduce a photograph of the indulgence here.

[42] See P. Pansier, *Histoire du Livre et de l'Imprimerie à Avignon*, t. I (Avignon, 1922).

[43] *ZSAK*, p. 157 and *Scriptorium*, xvii pl. 31.

that in size.[44]   These documents were written in a big script so that they might be hung in church upon a board or a door where they could be seen by all; and the simple (not to say crude) illuminated initial conveyed the idea of benediction to those who could not read the terms of the indulgence.   This is probably one of the many indulgences to be used as posters.[45]

As for ornament, one notices first the spacious lay-out of the first line.   The initial *U* of "Universis" occupies ten lines in depth.   Its roughly square frame, extending above the top line of decorated letters and into the left margin, is enclosed by thick pen-strokes of brown ink.   At three corners the bounding line of the frame is extended with a pen-flourish to a curling end.   The *U* encloses the nimbed head of Christ, with a slender neck and two raised hands, the left open and the right, emerging from a sleeve, giving benediction in the Greek fashion.   The thin fringe of hair, coloured bluish grey, continues in an equally thin fringe of beard.   The eyes, eyebrows, elongated nostrils, and mouth are penned in the most simple stylized form.   Parts of the nimbus are coloured vermilion, also narrow fringes on the left of the *U* and triangular patterns of the garment.   The frame on the left and the triangles are dark red, and dark red covers part of the vermilion on the left of the nimbus.   The rest of the nimbus is mainly yellow in colour, corresponding to the body of the letter *U*.   The background to the head is buff; the rest is uncoloured. The yellow sides of the *U* have none of the floral decoration found on other Avignonese indulgences.   The rest of line 1 is occupied with "Niversis Sancte Matris Ecclesie", the initial letters being large and coloured in dark red, vermilion, and yellow, but not further decorated; the other letters are in elongated script which recalls the opening line of a papal privilege, with the final *s* composed of four or five circles arranged vertically.   In the

---

[44] e.g. Battelli, *Acta pontificum* (ed. 2, 1965), pl. 18, 19, 22.

[45] Pierre F. Fournier, "Affiches d'indulgences manuscrites et imprimées des xive, xve, et xvie siècles", *Bibl. École des. Chartes*, lxxxiv (1923), 116-60.   Cf. *Scriptorium*, xvii. 319.   The treasury of the Teutonic order in Vienna preserves a fourteenth-century wooden triptych with copies of indulgences by popes from Celestine III to John XXII, followed by a record of indulgences given by twenty-two archbishops and bishops (not named), the whole in latin and german.   The preamble and the popes' names are in red.

text of the indulgence are five conspicuous but uncoloured capitals, at Splendor, Cupientes, Seu qui missis, Necnon qui, and Quocienscumque. Despite the decoration, the effect it gives now is drab. All the colours lack lustre, and seem to have faded badly. This is understandable if, as the holes at top and bottom suggest, the document was mounted and exposed to light over a long period. The whole decoration invites comparison with the indulgences (of a rather earlier time, 1326-1337) illustrated and discussed by Otto Homburger, particularly with the Bern indulgence of 22 October 1335.[46] This also frames the ornamental U; it uses the same form of final s in the first line; and the capitals in the first line are of the same form. But the Bern indulgence has much more elaborate ornament: a full-length figure of Christ, and a miniature of St. John the Baptist which fills the right margin.

As regards internal features, this indulgence for Hopton Cangeford (a manorial chapel in Shropshire) follows the usual pattern and formulas. Like most of those collective indulgences concerned with a chapel under lay patronage, it solicits prayers for the patron and his family and alms for the poor, besides gifts for the fabric and ornaments of the church. The preamble is a common one, inc. "Splendor paterne glorie", a form used in the papal chancery in the thirteenth and fourteenth centuries and found in the formulary printed by Tangl under the rubric: "Indulgentia omnibus ecclesiam... visitantibus."[47] Lists of feast-days on which indulgences were operative naturally vary from region to region and place to place.[48] The Hopton list is a long one, but it has few surprises and nothing peculiar to English calendars. Among the saints St. Benedict, St. Cecilia, and St. Martha are names sometimes absent from Avignonese indulgences. The common exhortation to venerate relics in the church is absent; probably the little chapel had none worth advertising.[49]

The manor of Hopton Cangeford was held in 1317 of Theobald de Verdon by John de Hopton, and John was still the tenant on

---

[46] ZSAK, pl. 40, 41 b.

[47] Above, p. 358, n. 24.

[48] An. Boll., xlvi. 316-8.

[49] For a closely similar document see an indulgence from Avignon, 12 Aug. 1342, tor a chapel in the church of Merchtem (Brussels), printed in An. Boll, xliv. 372-4.

1 March 1344.[50] It must have been his death soon afterwards which led his son William to obtain this indulgence which solicits prayers for the soul of John de Hopton, once lord of Hopton. The free chapel of St. Margaret, to which the indulgence attaches, leaves no trace before 1322 when, on the resignation of the incumbent, the bishop of Hereford instituted a priest to serve the chantry of the chapel on the presentation of John de Hopton.[51] It is described in the indulgence as a free chapel because it was extraparochial, independent of the parish church of Stanton Lacy. Discussing this sort of free chapel, J. H. Denton observes: " the freedom was from the parish, not freedom from the bishop. A free chapel of this sort had no parochial responsibilities, and all the rights of the local parish church were themselves safeguarded.[52] It can be regarded as a sign of the Hopton family's affluence and status that they maintained a chapel. Since the indulgence asks for prayers for the soul of John and no other named departed member of the family, it may be inferred that he was founder of the chapel, in the early years of the fourteenth century. The dedication was to St. Margaret, and Margaret was the name of John's wife. While the indulgence shows that William had succeeded John by December 1345, the next recorded presentation to the chapel was made by John's widow, on 15 February 1349.[53]

[50] The name of Cangeford or Cangefot is found c. 1200 in association with this estate. Later in the thirteenth century the place is recorded as Hopton Candenot, Candinant, Candyvant, Cangefot, Cangynont, etc. See further a Shropshire essoin of 1203: "Herbert de Gangeford [recte Cangeford] per Rogerum de Hupton, Pleas before the King or his Justices 1198-1212, iii (Selden Soc. vol. 83, 1967), 67 no. 667; R. W. Eyton, Antiquities of Shropshire, v (1857), 12-4; Calendar of Inquisitions post mortem (H. M. Stationery Office), vi. 39 no. 54; Calendar of Close Rolls 1343-6 (HMSO), pp. 277-345.

[51] Registrum Ade de Orleton episcopi Herefordensis 1317-27, ed. A. T. Bannister (Canterbury & York Soc., 1908), p. 387; another presentation occurred in 1325 (ibid., p. 332). The foundation is not recorded in the episcopal registers, which begin in 1275.

[52] English Royal Free Chapels 1100-1300: a constitutional study (Manchester, 1970), p. 9. Cf. D. M. Owen, Church and Society in medieval Lincolnshire (Lincoln, 1971), pp. 5-6, 16, 22, 93.

[53] Reg. Ade de Orleton, p. 332. She appears also as patron in 1358 and 1365. The Black Death may account for William's disappearance. Figures for the beneficed clergy of the diocese give a notion of the rate of mortality. Six churches were vacated by death Dec. 1348-Feb. 1349, compared with two in the

368

UNIVERSIS SANCTE MATRIS ECCLESIE filiis ad quos presentes littere pervenerint nos miseracione divina Anancius Xanchiensis episcopus, Manfredus Aiacensis episcopus, Benedictus Simisiensis episcopus, Gregorius Oppidensis episcopus, Iohannes Tribuniensis episcopus, Petrus Calliensis episcopus, Thomas Tyniensis episcopus, Franciscus Vrehensis episcopus, et Petrus Lexinensis episcopus salutem sinceram in domino nostro eternam. Splendor paterne glorie qui sua mundum ineffabili claritate illuminat pia vota fidelium de clementissima eius maiestate in se sperancium tunc benigno precipue favore prosequitur cum devota ipsorum humilitas sanctorum meritis et precibus adiuvatur. Cupientes igitur ut libera capella beate Margarete de Hoptone Candenot Herefordensis diocesis congruis honoribus frequentetur et a Christi fidelibus iugiter veneretur, omnibus vere penitentibus et confessis qui ad dictam capellam in omnibus festis suorum patronorum et in dedicacione eiusdem ac in aliis festis infrascriptis, videlicet Nathalis domini, circumcisionis, epiphanie, parascheves, pasche, ascensionis, pentecostes, trinitatis, corporis Christi, invencionis et exaltacionis sancte crucis, in omnibus festis beate Marie virginis, sanctorum Iohannis baptiste, et evangeliste, beatorum Petri et Pauli, ac omnium apostolorum et evangelistarum, sanctorumque Stephani, Laurencii, Martini, Nicholai, Gregorii, Augustini, Ambrosii, Ieronimi, et Benedicti, sanctarum Marie magdalene, Katarine, Margarete, Cecilie, Lucie, Agathe, Agnetis, et Marthe, in commemoracione omnium sanctorum et animarum, et per octavas dictarum festivitatum octavas habencium, singulisque diebus dominicis et sabbatis, causa devocionis, oracionis, aut peregrinacionis accesserint, seu qui missis, predicacionibus, matutinis, vesperis, aut aliis divinis officiis ibidem interfuerint, aut corpus Christi vel oleum sacrum cum infirmis portentur secuti fuerint, seu qui in serotina pulsacione[54] campane secundum modum curie Romane genibus flexis ter Ave Maria dixerint, necnon qui ad fabricam, luminaria, ornamenta, aut quevis alia dicte capelle necessaria manus porrexerint adiutrices, vel qui in eorum testamentis aut extra aurum, argentum, vestimentum, librum, calicem, aut aliquod aliud caritativum subsidium dicte capelle donaverint, legaverint, aut[a] procuraverint, aut qui pro anima Iohannis domini quondam de Hopton' et pro salubri statu Willelmi de Hoptone et Katarine eius uxoris dum vixerint et eorum animabus cum ab hac luce migraverint et animabus omnium eorum parentum, amicorum, benefactorum, et omnium fidelium defunctorum pie deum exoraverint vel exorari, vel Christi pauperibus cibum, potum, hospitalitatem, vel aliud

[a] *Other indulgences add* legari.

preceding twelve months; thereafter the rate increased (*Registrum Iohannis de Trillek episcopi Herefordensis, 1344-61*, ed. J. H. Parry (Canterbury & York Soc., 1912), ii. 374-7).

[54] Above, n. 40 A.

caritativum subsidium donaverint vel procuraverint, quocienscumque, quandocumque, et ubicumque premissa vel aliquid premissorum devote fecerint, de omnipotentis dei misericordia et beatorum Petri et Pauli apostolorum eius auctoritate confisi singuli nostrum quadraginta dies indulgenciarum de iniunctis eis penitenciis misericorditer in domino relaxamus, dummodo diocesani voluntas ad id accesserit et consensus. In cuius rei testimonium presentes litteras sigillorum nostrorum iussimus appensione muniri. Dat' Avinion' die xviii mensis Decembris anno domini millesimo CCC⁰ xlv et pontificatus domini Clementis pape vi anno quarto.

III. *Indulgence for the hermitage in Smithfield, London, 1354.* [55]

London, P. R. O., Exchequer, King's Remembrancer, Eccles. Docts., E 135/15/1.

A parchment sheet (probably trimmed, top and sides), 635 mm. broad × 475 mm. high + 49 mm. fold.

Space occupied by text, 560 × 320 mm.

Space occupied by initial *U,* with Virgin and Child, 120 × 130 mm.

Ruling in pencil; space between lines of text, 16 mm.

No endorsements are visible, since the sheet has been backed with parchment in recent times.

On fold, holes for seven seal-cords.

A small hole at each top corner of the sheet.

The script is in a somewhat freer hand than that of the Hopton indulgence. It is also rather larger, with high ascenders, and the *d* projects far to the left. But the general effect is still more of a formal bookhand than of chancery products of this period. After the first line (of very tall and broad letters) there are no conspicuous capitals.

The illumination has artistic merit. The main ornament is a miniature within the initial *U.* This occupies seven lines in depth. The top of the frame of the *U* is decorated with a leafy pattern which forms a border along the top margin and down the left margin. Within the framework of the *U* is the Virgin, seated on a bench or an altar, holding a Child standing on her

---

[55] Briefly noted by E. Margaret Thompson, *The Carthusian order in England* (1930), p. 169. The photograph is reproduced here by courtesy of the Keeper of the Public Records.

370

left knee, with an elaborate gothic canopy above. The background of the figures and the Virgin's head are gold, and there is gold in the foliated border. The other colouring of the miniature and border is mainly pale blue and red. The Virgin wears a blue cloak over a white dress and has a blue nimbus behind a red crown. The Child is dressed in red with a red cross on a white nimbus. Although the colours of the illumination are faded and the text is rendered illegible in a few places by holes and stains, the general effect is sumptuous. it must have cost more than the Hopton indulgence, and reflects the superior status of the foundation.

The text of the indulgence allows for it to be operative on a great many days. It invites prayers for the founder of the hermitage, Sir Walter Mauny, and his wife, and for the two hermits, Thomas Stapelow and Walter of Dorset, and for the bishop of London, who has confirmed the establishment. This is of some interest for the pre-history of the London Charterhouse.[56] Sir Walter Mauny, a soldier and courtier, had bought property adjacent to Smithfield to accommodate a cemetery, at the time of the Black Death. On 14 March 1351 he got from Pope Clement VI the authority to found there a college of twelve priests with a warden. But no foundation of the sort took root. There was, however, a chapel in the cemetery, and on 12 August 1352 Sir Walter applied for and obtained a papal indulgence for visitors who should give alms for the maintenance of the chapel.[57] Within about two years, as the present collective indulgence shows, two hermits had been attached to the chapel, perhaps because the intended college was too ambitious a project. The bishop of London – either Ralph Stafford († 17 April 1354) or Michael Northburgh († September 1361) – confirmed the foundation of the hermitage. It was only in 1361 that a broader scheme took shape, to build a Carthusian monastery on the site; and only in 1371 did the building of the house begin. The hermi-

---

[56] E. M. Thompson, *op. cit.*, pp. 167-8; W. H. St. John Hope, *The History of the London Charterhouse* (1925); David Knowles and W. F. Grimes, *Charterhouse: the medieval Foundation in the light of recent Discoveries* (1954); D. Knowles in *Victoria County History, Middlesex*, i (1969), 159.

[57] *Calendar of Papal Letters*, iii (HMSO, 1897), 468; cf. *Calendar of Papal Petitions*, i (HMSO, 1896), 234.

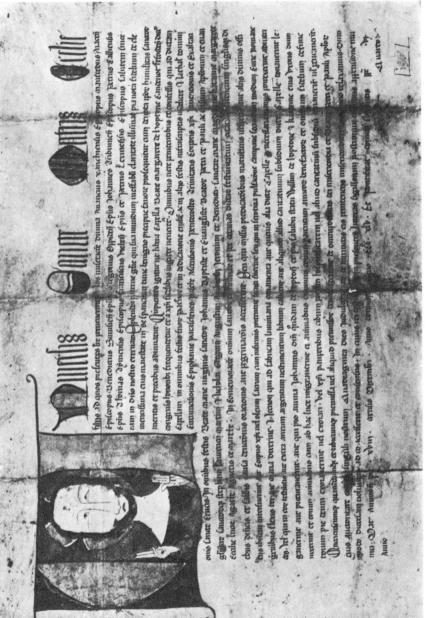

Fig. 1 – Chelmsford, *Essex Record Office*, D/DW, T 1/21.

Fig. 2 – London, P.R.O., *Exchequer, King's Remembrancer, Eccles. Docts.*, E 135/15/1.

tage is not mentioned again.   A change of dedication, or at least of title, took place during these years.   When Mauny first bought the land for the cemetery, the ground was consecrated by the bishop of London on the feast of the Annunciation, 1349, and on the same day the foundations were laid for the chapel, on the site of the later Carthusian church.   In a later record this first chapel is described as the church of the Annunciation.   But in 1354 Sir Walter Mauny is expressly said to have founded and dedicated a hermitage in honour of the Assumption.[58]   Finally, when in 1371 Sir Walter gave his charter to the Carthusians, he desired the new house to be called the house of the Salutation of the Mother of God.   This is the title under which London Charterhouse was known throughout the later Middle Ages.

UNIVERSIS SANCTE MATRIS ECCLESIE FILIIS ad quos presentes litere pervenerint, nos miseratione divina Kyriacus Galatensis archiepiscopus, Petrus Valonensis, Bernardus Milcoviensis, Bonifacius Sibenicensis, Petrus Botentonensis, Theodorus Cephalonensis, Galterus Nicopolensis, Iohannes Carminensis, Iohannes Imelacensis, Dominicus Gallipolitanus, Nicholaus Primisliensis, et Dyrlaus Clatensis episcopi salutem in domino sempiternam.   Vere credimus deum habere propicium si sanctos eius qui in celestibus habitant devote honorari procuramus in terris et fideles invitamus[a] ad pietatis subsidia pauperibus et religiosis deo servientibus conferenda.   Cupientes igitur ut heremitagium in cimiterio novo iuxta Smithefeld per nobilem virum dominum Walterum de Mauny in honore Assumptionis beate Marie semper virginis fundatum et dedicatum congruis honoribus frequentetur et religiosis ibidem existentibus misericorditer provideatur, omnibus vere penitentibus et confessis qui ad dictum heremitagium sive ad capellam in singulis sui patroni festivitatibus, videlicet Assumptionis beate Marie virginis ut predicitur et in omnibus festis eiusdem, ac in omnibus aliis festis infrascriptis, scilicet Natalis domini, Circumcisionis, Epiphanie, Cene, Parasceves, Pasche, Ascentionis, Pentecostes, Trinitatis, Corporis Christi, in utroque festo sancte Crucis, sancti Michaelis archangeli, Nativitatis et Decollationis sancti Iohannis baptiste, beatorum petri et Pauli apostolorum, ac omnium aliorum apostolorum et evangelistarum, quatuor doctorum, Omnium Sanctorum, et in commemoratione Animarum, et in dictorum heremitagii sive capelle dedicatione, omnium sanctorum martirum,

---

[a] *ms.* mutamus

---

[58] The date was probably before November: the bishop of Cephalonia of the indulgence, Theodore, became bishop of Motula 27 october 1354.

confessorum, atque omnium sanctarum virginum, et per octavas omnium festivitatum octavas habentium, singulisque dominicis diebus et sabbatis tocius anni, causa devotionis, orationis, aut peregrinationis accesserint, seu qui missis, predicationibus, matutinis, vesperis, aut aliis divinis ibidem interfuerint, necnon qui ad fabricam, luminaria, ornamenta dicti heremitagii manus porrexerint adiutrices aut qui dicto heremitagio seu quibuscumque heremitis ibidem existentibus aurum, argentum, vestimenta, libros, calices, panem, vinum, cervisiam, carnes, pisces, aut quevis alia eis necessaria donaverint, legaverint, transmiserint, donari, legari, vel transmitti procuraverint, aut qui pro salubri statu dicti domini Walteri de Mauny baronis, patroni[b] heremitagii et capelle de quibus super fit mencio fundatoris, domine Margarete eius uxoris, ac fratrum Thome Stapelowe et Walteri de Dorsete heremitarum, presentium indulgentiarum impetratorum, necnon pro salubri statu reverendi domini patris episcopi Londoniensis...[c] confirmatoris, dum vixerint et animabus eorumdem cum ab hac luce migraverint, ac pro animabus patrum, matrum, fratrum, sororum, parentum, benefactorum predictorum tam vivorum quam defunctorum, et omnium fidelium defunctorum, preces deo...[d] direxerint quocienscumque, quandocumque, et ubicumque premissa vel aliquid premissorum devote fecerint, de omnipotentis dei misericordia et beatorum Petri et Pauli apostolorum eius auctoritate confisi, singuli nostrum .xl. dies indulgentiarum de iniunctis eis penitentiis[e] misericorditer in domino relaxamus, dummodo diocesani voluntas ad id accesserit et consensus. In cuius rei[f] testimonium sigilla nostra presentibus sunt appensa. Dat' Avinion' .xvii. die mensis...[g] anno domini millesimo .ccc[mo]. liiij°. pontificatus domini Innocentii pape anno secundo.

[b] ms. putunn   [c] word oblit   [d] hole in ms.   [e] -arum... penitentiis
missing, hole in ms.   [f] ms. omits rei   [g] -ensis... missing, hole in ms.

L. B. H. & F.

PUBLIC   LIBRARIES

APPENDIX

Grantors of the indulgences for Wombridge, 1328 (= W), Hopton, 1345 (= H), and Smithfield, 1354 (= S). "E" indicates references to Eubel's *Hierarchia catholica*, vol. i.

H   Aiacensis = Ajaccio (prov. Pisa). *Manfredus* de Calcinaria, O.F.M.
     † before 20 June 1345 (E)
W   Ameliensis = Amelia (central Italy). *Iohannes* Grocei (E)
S   Botrentonensis (*al.* Botrotensis) = Butrinto (prov. Corfu).
     Petrus (E p. 143 n. 3)
H   Calliensis = Cagli (central Italy). *Petrus* depr. 1319 (E p. 158 n. 5)

S   Carminensis (*recte* Caminensis) = Kamien (prov. Gniezno). *Iohannes*

S   Cephalonensis = Cephalonia (prov. Patras). *Theodorus* ejected, bp. of Motula 27 Oct. 1354 (E pp. 181 n. 2, 353 n. 3)

S   Clatensis (*al.* Elatensis)? = Elath (Palestine) or Elateia (Greece). *Dyrlaus*, O. Pred. occurs as Dirslaus Klaten. al. Elat. 1370-98 (E p. 182 (Cereten., n. 1) and p. 555 *ad fin.*)

W   Demitensis (*al.* Delmitensis, Dumnensis) = Duvno (prov. Split). *Madius* (E)

S   Galatensis (? suff. of Alexandria). *Kyriacus* archiep. O.S. Bas. (E)

S   Gallipolitanus = Gallipoli (prov. Otranto). *Dominicus* (E)

S   Imelacensis = Emly (prov. Cashel). *Iohannes* Esmond (E)

H   Lexinensis = Lesina (prov. Benevento) or Hvar (prov. Durazzo). *Petrus* (not in E)

W   Lubicensis = Lübeck (prov. Bremen). *Heynricus* de Bocholte (E)

S   Milcoviensis = Milkow (prov. Esztergom). *Bernardus* O. Pred. (E)

S   Nicopolensis = Nicopolis (? Armenia, Bulgaria, or Palestine). *Galterus* O.S.B. (E p. 364 n. 2)

H   Oppidensis = Oppido (prov. Reggio). *Gregorius* (E)

S   Primisliensis (*al.* Premisliensis) = Przemisl (prov. Halicz). *Nicholaus* O. Pred. (E)

S   Sibenicensis = Sebenico (prov. Split). *Bonifacius* (E)

H   Simisiensis (*al.* Semiscantensis) = Mesched (Turkestan). *Benedictus* (E)

W   Sinquensis (*al.* Signensis, Singnensis) = Senj (prov. Split).[1] *Rodulphus* (not in E)

W   Sulcitanensis = Sulcis (prov. Cagliari). *Bonifacius* O.F.M., depr. 1325 (E p. 468 n. 5)

W   Tergestinensis = Trieste (prov. Aquileia). *Guillelmus* Franchi, O.F.M. (E)

H   Tribuniensis = Trbinje-Mrkanji (prov. Dubrovnik). *Iohannes* (E)

H   Tyniensis = Knin (prov. Split). *Thomas*, res. 1344 (E pp. 485-6)

S   Valonensis = Avlona (prov. Durazzo). *Petrus* (E)

H   Vrehensis ? = Vregensis, Vrellensis (prov. Durazzo). *Franciscus*[2] (not in E)

H   Xanchiensis (prov. Messinopol.)[3]. *Anancius* (not in E)

---

[1] Rodulphus *Siriquensis* occurs in an original indulgence for Königsfelden, 6 Sept. 1329 (Homburger and Von Steiger, loc. cit., pl. 39). Delehaye gives the same form from an indulgence of 7 June 1328 (*An. Bol.*, xlv. 363, cf. 367, xlvi. 294, 304). In the *Provinciale* the form is Signensis (ed. Tangl, p. 11 *b*). Eubel has no bishop of Senj between 1308 and 1333.

[2] Franciscus appears on a collective indulgence of 25 Jan. 1350 (Wartmann, *op. cit.*, iii. 594 no. 1469).

[3] Possibly = Santoriensis, Santorin, but Eubel records no bishop Anancius here.

XVI

P.354 ,line 4 :   A collective indulgence issued by twelve prelates,
mostly Italians or in partibus infidelium, dated at Avignon on 25 May
1364, well-preserved with fragments of eleven seals, is in the Berkeley family archives and was printed by I.H. Jeayes, Descriptive
catalogue of the charters and muniments...at Berkeley Castle (1892)
pp.170-2 no.538. It concerns the chapel of the B.V.M. and St John
evangelist in the castle, and asks for prayers for the souls of,in particular Sir Maurice de Berkeley, his wife Elizabeth, his father Thomas and his mother. The document is plain, but its broad margins
and an initial U of inordinate height (occupying seven lines) suggest
that illumination was intended. The arenga is that of no.II (p.368
above). For a photograph of this I am indebted to my colleague, Dr.
P.N.R. Zutshi.

INDEX

Abbreviations used are bp for bishop, card. for cardinal, ch. for church, dn for deacon. Names of religious Orders appear as Aug(ustinian), Ben(edictine), Cart(husian), Cist(ercian), Clun(iac). Places are located by county in England and Wales, by department in France. An asterisk indicates an additional note.

INDEX OF MANUSCRIPTS